MEDIA
LITERACY in the
INFORMATION
AGE

Current Perspectives

INFORMATION AND BEHAVIOR, VOLUME SIX

Robert Kubey
EDITOR

MEDIA LITERACY in the INFORMATION AGE

Current Perspectives

INFORMATION AND BEHAVIOR, VOLUME SIX

TRANSACTION PUBLISHERS
New Brunswick (U.S.A.) and London (U.K.)

Copyright © 1997 by Transaction Publishers, New Brunswick, New Jersey 08903.

All rights reserved under International and Pan-American Copyright Conventions. No part of this book may be reproduced or transmitted in any form or by any means, electronic or mechanical, including photocopy, recording, or any information storage and retrieval system, without prior permission in writing from the publisher. All inquiries should be addressed to Transaction Publishers, Rutgers—The State University, New Brunswick, New Jersey 08903.

This book is printed on acid-free paper that meets the American National Standard for Permanence of Paper for Printed Library Materials.

ISSN: 0740-5502
ISBN: 1-56000-238-7
Printed in the United States of America

Contents

Acknowledgments

No book is a solo effort, especially an edited volume with over twenty-five contributing authors. My thanks go to each of the authors who worked often at great distance, under less than ideal conditions, and with considerable patience.

I wish also to express my deep appreciation to the Annenberg Scholars Program at the Annenberg School for Communication at the University of Pennsylvania. The program, in its first year when I was a fellow, afforded five scholars a half-year to focus on individual research problems in media education.

Some of the work that appears in this volume, the chapters by Máire Messenger Davies, Roger Desmond, Tamar Liebes, and Dafna Lemish, was completed while we were Annenberg Scholars. Without the support of the Annenberg School I would not have been able to travel as widely as I did and meet with as many of the authors who have contributed chapters. While we were at Annenberg, Dean Kathleen Hall Jamieson, Professor Elihu Katz, who directs the Scholars Program, and the faculty, students, and staff of the school made for an incomparable period of study for each of us.

Thank you also to Bill White, the book's assistant editor, who helped me go over manuscripts in the early phase of the book's development.

At Transaction, Laurence Mintz helped shepherd this work, and Lynn Guarente did a quick and thorough job of copyediting once the manuscript was placed in her capable hands.

I am also grateful to Dean Richard Budd and Professor Linda Lederman, who have supported my work and have helped carry out the commitment of Rutgers' School of Communication, Information, and Library Studies to the *Information and Behavior* series. Thanks also to Richard McGuire for an expert job of indexing the book, and to the faculty and staff of the Department of Communication at Stanford University, who made me feel at home as I completed the editing while on sabbatical as a Visiting Professor.

Most importantly, I wish to acknowledge the constant support of Professor Brent Ruben, series editor of *Information and Behavior.*

This book would not exist were it not for Brent Ruben. Brent had the original idea for a book on the broad topic of literacy in the information age, and we originally planned to edit it together. But as Brent took on the important and formidable assignment to found and direct Rutgers' new university-wide program in Quality and Communication Improvement, the work on the book became mine and more focused on media education. Still, Brent contributed in supporting my efforts and in taking care of procedural problems that always come up in an undertaking such as this.

I wish to thank my wife, Barbara, as usual, for her constant support, patience, and wise counsel. And thanks to Benjamin for letting me work on this book when he wanted me to help him build a model and watch his favorite TV program, "Rescue 911."

Finally, a special thank-you to Daniel for accurately distinguishing between the papers on Daddy's desk and all other papers, books, periodicals, rugs, drapes, tables, and windows that he is accustomed to so creatively marking up with his crayons. Both of these young colleagues help me appreciate on an hourly basis the media education proviso that we must all learn to "decode, evaluate, analyze, and produce both print and electronic media."

Preface

Brent D. Ruben

The Information and Behavior series was born in 1983 at a time when one could be only partially aware of the importance that the information-behavior relationship would come to have in the years ahead. At that time, the expressions, "the information age" and "the information society" were beginning to find popular acceptance, and were typically used as catch-phrases to refer to the contemporary, post-modern, high-technology period. It was the view of the series editor and the editorial board that beyond the newly-found words and phrases there were important issues of substance that would increasingly occupy the attention of scholars from a wide range of fields.

The significance of the concept of information and its relationship to human behavior was clearly not a novel idea in 1983. As was noted in the introduction to *Information and Behavior: Volume 1* the processing of information had been described as one of two primary means through which living organisms interact with their physical and social environments. Moreover, information and information processes were seen as basic to higher-level cognitive processes in humans. It was indicated also that information and information processes were understood to be fundamental at the interpersonal, social, and cultural level of analysis, and basic to the establishment and maintenance of relationships, groups, organizations and societies, and to the cultures, and normative realities, rules, and roles of each. Finally, it was observed that information is a fundamental concept in generic theories in system theory, cybernetics, information theory, and in disciplines such as communication, media studies, information science, computer science and cognitive psychology pointed in the direction of heightening interdisciplinary interest and significance for the information concept.

But it was difficult to envision then precisely how popular the information concept would become. We also did not fully recognize the potential value of information to link and further scholarship across disciplines, and in many ways we have still only begun to appreciate this later potential.

In the years since its inception the Information and Behavior Series has been devoted to exploring tissues pertinent to this challenge. Early issues focused on a range of topics pertinent to the information, communication, media and human behavior. More recent volumes have examined topic issues including mediation, the communication-information relationship and identity.

Volume 5: Media Literacy

One of these challenges is literacy.

Reading, writing, and speaking have long been regarded as the cornerstones of the concept of literacy. However, the traditional conceptualization is of increasingly of limited usefulness for dealing with the realities of the so-called "information age." Among the most obvious characteristics of contemporary society is the dramatic increase in the sources, channels and forms of news, entertainment, and information of all kinds that are available to us.

Ironically, for all the richness of information in our environment, we have not experienced a comparable increase in our human capacity to understand, manage, share, and productive use this voluminous wealth of information. Thus, in a pragmatic sense, the communication/information explosion is a mixed-blessing, giving us many more choices, but at the same time requiring us to develop new concepts and competencies in order to understand and respond appropriately to these opportunities.

It would seem that at the very least, we need better skills for selecting, processing, and using information, and even more fundamentally, we need new and broadened ways of thinking about the nature of literacy. It is to this goal that provides direction for the current volume of Information and Behavior, edited by Robert Kubey.

Introduction

Media Education:
Portraits of an Evolving Field

Robert Kubey

As is the case with media studies and media education, topics and ideas in this volume are necessarily interwoven and interdependent. It is impossible to make clean breaks among topic areas when one studies or teaches about the media—one cannot completely separate industry and audience practices and processes from one another or either of them from text. Likewise, conceptual approaches to media education differ from locale to locale, as do curricula, so that in this book, chapters about locale are also simultaneously about educational philosophy, curricula, and pedagogy.

Part I, "Where We've Been and Where We're Going," presents three chapters that will help readers gain their bearings. First, Len Masterman, long the single most influential media educator in the English-speaking world, sets out in this essay, also written for the Council of Europe, to describe how media education developed in the 1980s. In this essay, one sees one of the reasons for Masterman's prominence—he writes engagingly and with great knowledge. And he rejects the protectionist, or inoculation, approach to media education and the propensity among U.S. popular writers such as Postman and Winn to see television only as a threat.

Masterman understood before many that successful media education requires an *appreciation* of media products—that the quickest way to turn off a group of students is to walk into a classroom and immediately savage their favorite television shows, movies, and video games. But appropriately, Masterman also sees problems with the media and is more than prepared to point them out.

Masterman also discusses how media education reconstitutes the relationship between teacher and student by taking the students' responses and interpretations seriously. Indeed, the importance of students developing their own critical autonomy is paramount for most media educators worldwide today as it is for the authors of the chapters in this book.

Next up is Cary Bazalgette, a long-time practitioner and advocate of media education in Britain, and now the Principal Education Officer of the British Film Institute. Bazalgette has watched media education grow and flourish, and of late, be threatened in England. Her contribution to this volume follows Len Masterman's because, just as he draws on the course of media education during the 1980s and 1990s, Bazalgette forces us to consider what obstacles media educators are likely to encounter for the rest of the 1990s and for the foreseeable future in what she calls the "second phase of media literacy development."

Bazalgette points to five current and future problems, among them that media education remains in the province of enthusiasts, weak evidence on how media learning progresses—or even if it progresses, and a lack of research. There is no question but that solid research on the effectiveness of media education is scanty at best. In fairness, it should be noted that there is often very weak evidence for the efficacy of most traditional and innovative educational approaches. One wonders if traditional English teachers would fair any better in defending or explaining their efforts than the contemporary media educator. Last year, an article in *The Atlantic Monthly* documented the high level of enthusiasm for "Whole Language" approaches in primary education, but the general lack of research supporting the approach.

Last, but certainly not least in this first section, is Patricia Aufderheide's contribution. As some readers may know, in December of 1992, the Aspen Institute's Communications and Society Program convened twenty-five media scholars, educators, and activists for a national leadership conference designed to help catalyze the development of media education programs in the United States. In three days of intense meetings, the group worked on many issues and arrived at a consensual definition for media literacy: "*the ability to access, analyze, evaluate, and communicate messages in a variety of forms.*"

The group also developed a plan for the further development of media education in the United States and established task forces toward this end. Patricia Aufderheide was assigned the difficult task of bringing together this group's far-reaching discussions, and did so marvelously in the report that we are pleased to reprint here.

The first contribution in part II, "Theoretical and Conceptual Perspectives," is a true tour de force by Jacques Piette and Luc Giroux. The editor first heard Jacques Piette present his taxonomy of the theoretical underpinnings of media education programs at a media literacy conference sponsored by the Bertelsmann Foundation in Germany. By the estimation of many, his was the most thoughtful presentation of the conference.

With great care, Piette—in that venue, and again here with Luc Giroux—examines the wide variety of media education programs around the world, focusing on three U.S. programs and three from Europe. The authors show how educational and theoretic assumptions underlie each pedagogy as well as its view of the role of the media, and the nature of the audience.

As with Bazalgette, they wisely point to the need for more empirical work on media education. Few treatments of media education have been more carefully considered or are more likely to bear fruit than this contribution which forces us to think about the theoretical foundations of educational practice.

The next chapter, by Paul Messaris, presents a very developed and detailed approach to visual literacy, one that raises basic questions about the nature of visual literacy, how it is formed and develops, and indeed, whether it is innate, questions that must be considered in our future understanding of how to conduct media and visual education.

Messaris also points to intercultural communication problems in media education, problems that are likely to be with us for the foreseeable future. In this provocative essay, Messaris considers how the meaning of visual images is constructed among people who are unfamiliar with the formal features being used or the relevant cultural references. Messaris concludes, not surprisingly, that there are many such interpretation problems. But what is of most interest is the way he comes to his conclusion and how he gets us to think about aspects of our own visual literacy that we take for granted.

Picking up where Patricia Aufderheide left off (I told you this book could have been organized in a different manner), Renee Hobbs, one of the participants in the Aspen Institute's leadership conference, works to expand the concept of media literacy to include the four critical intellectual processes laid out by the Aspen group: *to access, analyze, evaluate, and communicate media messages.* Hobbs argues for extending education beyond the symbol systems of words to texts of all sorts, and for a full-fledged assessment of how meaning is conveyed.

Hobbs considers how messages construct social reality and how certain forms and genres of communication exhibit unique characteristics. The chapter explores the relevance of media literacy programs to educational reform, authentic learning, and assessment. In so doing, she advocates the development of close links among the classroom, the home, and the community, especially as we think about how to achieve multicultural educational goals.

Now we turn our attention more closely to some of the ways that media education has developed in different parts of the world, from England and Australia, to South Africa and Israel. In part III, "International Perspectives," Peter Greenaway starts off by touching on the development of media education in different countries and a consideration of why it has been slow to develop in the United States. He believes that the improvement of the Australian media industries has helped fuel a simultaneous consideration of the impact of foreign cultural products in Australia and the development of media education. Greenaway also considers parallels between media and arts education as well as the importance of hands-on production experience, another theme that cross-cuts numerous chapters. We'll reexamine the Australian situation in the next section, in chapter 14, by Robyn Quin and Barrie McMahon.

Andrew Hart's chapter looks at the current controversy in England over the new National Curriculum, which has called for media education, and the even newer propensity by members of the Tory government, to call for a back-to-basics approach to English education. As have other media educators, Hart tells us that hard-to-motivate students often excel in their media classes, not an unimportant concern at a time when educators are struggling to find successful strategies to engage all students.

For some educational traditionalists, language, syntax, and grammar only refer to words. But for media educators, there is also a language, syntax, and grammar to images and sound. The value of traditional approaches to literacy remains but does not go nearly far enough.

The traditional pantheon of great literary works is also undergoing reexamination as the preferred approach of media educators involves close examination of very popular texts that provide pleasure, controversy, and meaning to teachers *and* students. Contemporary media education is controversial, in part, precisely because it challenges both the traditional pantheon of what constitutes great literary and communicative work just as it challenges the traditional knowledge base and authority of the teacher (not to mention the culture at large).

We move next to Israel and the chapter by Dafna Lemish and Peter Lemish, which analyzes how Israel established a national curriculum in media literacy and how it developed out of public pressures, and from the input of teachers, scholars, and politicians.

What is particularly striking in the Israeli context is that political operatives with highly divergent political and ideological perspectives came to agree on the need for a national curriculum and did not substantially interfere with its development, something that is hard to imagine happening in the U.S. and many other countries. Of course the Israeli curriculum is still largely voluntary, it is not required, and so, in time, greater conflict over media education in Israel may develop.

Developing the curriculum has required that the Israelis define both media literacy and the role for teachers in the new curriculum. But Lemish and Lemish report that what has developed in Israel does not conform well to what was intended—not an infrequent outcome in many educational reforms. The chapter raises issues that face each nation as it develops education policy and national curricular goals. The authors also point to the importance of media professionals and media teachers working together to develop media studies programs, another limitation in most parts of the world.

Last, we have Costas Criticos's contribution, which examines the role of media education in the struggle to end Apartheid in South Africa. At the center of his chapter is the ideal of critical pedagogy, that learners be creators rather than receivers of knowledge.

Here, the students' *metathinking,* their constructions and understandings of their own experience, and the world they inhabit is at the forefront of education. As with others, Criticos's chapter could readily have been included elsewhere, either in part IV, "Curricular and Research Perspectives," or in part II, "Theoretical and Conceptual Perspectives." For example, a particularly ingenious application of critical pedagogy and media literacy goals is offered in Criticos's intriguing description of what happens when students create a huge newspaper thirty-five feet wide. Discussion of a proposal to help empower students by permitting them to vote at age fourteen is worthy of consideration by adults and educators in every society.

Now we move from different countries to part IV and different "Curricular and Research Perspectives." David M. Considine, originally from Australia, has worked intensely on media education in the U.S. and draws on years of experience to provide wisdom about the impediments to media education in the U.S. and the directions change needs to take. His chapter focuses, as does Criticos's and Hobbs's, on how media education must become an integral part of school restructuring and reform.

In this view, media education is one of the best ways to facilitate critical thinking and student centered education, but as Considine points out, to do so will require substantial changes in teacher education and in the educational establishment itself.

Considine points to the ways in which the U.S. educational system stymies meaningful educational reform. He alerts us to the natural allies of media educators, those concerned with critical thinking, democracy, health education, and, in particular, library media specialists. Considine provides the long view, taking us back to 1923 and showing us how, in some instances, little has changed in U.S. education in more than seventy years.

The next contribution comes from Máire Messenger Davies, who considers the steps necessary to educate future media workers, and in so doing illuminates important challenges facing faculty who teach undergraduate production and media courses.

A media educator with experience in both the U.S. and Britain, Davies offers revealing observations about the two cultures, their media systems, and the educational process. Undergraduates must understand different kinds of texts and in that process come to better understand their own experiences and the experiences of others. Students must also learn to produce their own texts.

Davies clearly comes down on the side of liberal arts education as opposed to pure production skills training. And she is opposed to the notion that one media text is as good as the next. Instead, Davies argues that there are some media texts worth teaching about and preserving and others that do not deserve attention. She strongly supports the need for students and faculty to be able to articulate what differentiates one from the other. To be sure, the relativism of many contemporary approaches to cultural studies is problematic, and Davies is adamant about improving the ability of students to write and talk intelligently about their media experiences.

David Buckingham and Julian Sefton-Green's contribution exemplifies the British cultural studies approach to media analysis and media education in which the audience is seen as actively negotiating texts and constructing their social worlds and identities through active engagement with media. The authors focus their discussion on how they work with students in the creation and analysis of media texts and, in particular, how children and adolescents use and receive pleasure from video and computer games. Future media texts will become increasingly based in multimedia (and therefore increasingly polysemic) and multimedia poses new challenges for media education.

Next we have Robyn Quin and Barrie McMahon, who together, more than any other two individuals, have seen to it that Australia is, to the best of my knowledge, the first country in the world to mandate that media education be part of every student's schooling from kindergarten through the twelfth grade. Though still not reaching 100 percent of Australian students by 1995, their efforts have gone further than anyone else's in the world.

In this essay, Quin and McMahon consider the importance of media education in an age of increased exposure to information and media products. They seek to expand the scope of media education from text-based analyses to examination of the audience and the broader technological environment. A theoretical curriculum model encompassing text, audience, and context is offered.

Roger Desmond's chapter is a model for some of the kind of work that needs to be done in future media literacy research studies—it is theoretical, conceptual, and empirical. Drawing on his review of the research literature, Desmond considers the possibility that there may be a critical period between ages three and six when heavy television viewing may be particularly influential, especially on subsequent reading ability. Though he draws inferences from relatively little data, his proposition may be plausible, especially for particular at-risk populations of children. If nothing else, the idea needs to be explored by researchers.

But Desmond's contribution doesn't stop there. He goes on to weigh the impact of two different approaches to children's learning and to their use of media, the *deficit* versus the *acquisition* model, and considers both the political advantages to the development of media education and the pedagogic value of each.

Tamar Liebes's chapter reports on an innovative, experimental media literacy curriculum developed in Israel and used with high school students to enhance their understanding of news production processes and their ability to interpret news. Liebes shows that students are far more able to critique news of a familiar nature than news that is more distant and in line with the interests of the state. For her, and in keeping with the goal of broader integration of media analysis across the curriculum, the study of democratic processes has been improperly segregated to the fields of political science and history and must also consider communication principles and processes. Liebes also makes a strong case for the legitimacy of the journalistic enterprise, its role as the guardian of the public interest, and why news must necessarily focus on the unusual and deviant.

In part V, "Perspectives on Computer, Information, and 'Museum' Literacy," we offer five chapters that are in the same vein as those that have come before, but which also extend our thinking beyond the issues and topics raised thus far.

First, W. Lambert (Scot) Gardiner's chapter takes the reader on an odyssey through his theoretical approach to contemporary education and what he believes needs to be done to make it more appropriately student centered. This chapter might be read together with those of Hobbs, Considine, and others who champion school reform and restructuring.

Critical to Gardiner's view is a reconsideration of the concept of literacy with a primary focus on the potential role of the computer as a critical enhancement to cognitive function. His ideas about teaching as an inside-out versus an outside-in process are worth every educator's consideration.

Next, Micheline Frenette raises novel questions about *technological literacy* and makes a case for the need for traditional literacy classes to include training that will help fledgling readers become more adept at negotiating the increasingly complex, computer-mediated, everyday world that we all now encounter.

In groundbreaking, exploratory research, Frenette has been looking at how contemporary literacy training with illiterate adults might best be designed. Frenette gets us to think about a kind of literacy education that few educators consider.

Charles R. McClure's chapter is next. It focuses on *information literacy* and raises a whole new set of concerns by carefully considering the profound changes in our telecommunications infrastructure and pointing out how educators are falling behind these rapid developments. McClure argues that how these issues are addressed is critical to our future and whether equitable access will be achieved.

He focuses in particular on the important role that librarians must play in this changing communication and information environment, proposing a strategy for "reconnecting" various societal segments, ensuring social equity, and enhancing the roles of educational institutions and libraries in reaching these goals.

Next, Carol Kuhlthau focuses on the role of information literacy training in preparing students for work, for citizenship, and for human interaction—what she believes are the three basic charges of education in a democratic society. Technological change and the need for lifelong learning as well as critical, creative, and abstract thinking on the part of citizens and workers are placing new demands on the educational establishment and ultimately result in the need for school restructuring. Kuhlthau draws on her program of research studies to lay out six stages in the information seeking and meaning construction process.

In the final chapter, and in keeping with the spirit of media education shaking up one's complacencies as to how and what things are—including the scope of this book—we present a chapter by Tamar Katriel that asks a question very familiar to media educators but one very rarely, if ever, applied to the phenomenon of museumgoing. To the point, how do museums serve to legitimize particular perspectives and ideologies?

Katriel studies Israeli museums through narrative and discourse analysis, how museums communicate, and how museumgoers become literate. Just as we *read* cultural objects beyond texts, so too do we read museums, institutions rarely analyzed in terms of their communicative role. How is a particular kind of literacy assumed in the practices of museum curators, or for that matter, in the practices of producers of most any cultural object or media creation?

As Katriel points out, one interesting aspect to museum narrative and storytelling that frequently separates it from other kinds of stories is that museums often tell the story of how they chose to tell the story that they tell. This *metanarrative* is not unlike the kind of *metathinking* encouraged by many media educators who advocate the importance of media education including the study of differential audience responses and interpretations.

Readers new to the field might ask themselves why audience studies should have any relevance to basic education. The answer coming from media educators is that it is critical, and increasingly so as we develop multicultural approaches to education, because students must come to learn, early on, that different people and different groups often understand and interpret the same texts and communication acts differently.

One way to advance and teach tolerance, then, is to encourage students from very early on to understand that the person next to them in school, or on the street, or in the living room, may be having an altogether different response to the same picture, story, or television program.

I have seen this approach to media education being developed quite effectively in a number of countries. In Israel, a curriculum developed by Dafna Lemish has children as young as five and six first pick out favorite pictures from magazines at home and bring them into school. Students then talk, or *write* at older ages (I watched nine-year-olds, for example) about what they see in these pictures, and they are asked to tell a story. What they see and tell varies. So here, at the youngest ages of formal schooling, children begin to learn how their schoolmates from different ethnic, national, and racial backgrounds see, interpret, and create differently.

Another clever exercise has the teacher only expose a small portion of a set of magazine pictures chosen in advance. The students examine the exposed portions and try to guess what's going on in the hidden part of the picture. Kids (and adults) have great fun with this and see different things. Here again, we have a way to get people at very young ages to appreciate the effects of selective editing as well as how people think and respond differently.

On a site visit to a school outside of London, I had the opportunity to see a media production exercise being piloted under the auspices of the British Film Institute and under the direction of Cary Bazalgette. Here, kindergartners were given inexpensive still cameras to take on a walk about their school and to a nearby park. They took photos of the school and its immediate environs (see Greenaway's chapter).

Later, working with their teachers, the students make decisions on how to tell a story with the developed pictures, and then they choose and set music behind the pictures for a multimedia show about their school, where it is, and what goes on about it.

In this extraordinarily well-devised exercise, five-year-olds learn how to use a camera and that the camera only sees so much, that editing decisions about what audience members will see are being made from the very beginning of media production. Students experience the editing process again later as they storyboard their photos and see how some pictures help tell the story better than others, how some pictures end up on the kindergarten room (cutting room) floor, and then how different musical choices enhance and set different moods. At project's end, the children have learned quite a lot about media production through hands-on experience. And most experienced media teachers believe that students of all ages become much more adept at interpretation and criticism when they have themselves produced and edited their own media products. Readers interested in similar innovations might look at how Criticos employs enormous newspapers in South Africa, or how Desmond created personalized readers in Philadelphia.

We began discussing Katriel's chapter with consideration of how the communicational situation of the museum is often one of a meta-or self-referential narrative. Following from that we have presented examples of curricular exercises that help very young students engage in metathinking and meta-analysis. These are among the many goals of contemporary media education and what makes it an extraordinarily exciting and dynamic field in which to work and do research. Contributors to this volume, along with thousands of media educators around the world, are helping show us the way toward educational innovation and reform. If it can be done so effectively with children as young as five, one should think it can be done with the rest of us as well.

Part I

Where We've Been and Where We're Going

1

A Rationale for Media Education

Len Masterman

Introduction

The aim of this chapter is to provide teachers with a guide to the field of media education appropriate for the 1990s. Its starting point is the Council of Europe (1989) Resolution on Education in Media and the New Technologies (paragraph 5) adopted by European Ministers of Education at their Standing Conference in Istanbul in October, 1989. It is a statement that admirably summarizes the major developments in the field during the 1980s and sets an outline agenda for the 1990s:

> Education in the new technologies and the media should play an empowering and liberating role, helping to prepare pupils for democratic citizenship and political awareness. Thus pupils should be given an understanding of the structures, mechanisms and messages of the mass media. In particular, pupils should develop the independent capacity to apply critical judgement to media content. One means to this end, and an objective in its own right, should be to encourage creative expression the construction of pupils' own media messages, so that they are equipped to take advantage of opportunities for the expression of particular interests in the context of participation at local level.
>
> Given the major role that media such as television, cinema, radio and the press play in children's cultural experience, media education should begin as early as possible and continue throughout compulsory schooling. Nor should the role of parents in media education be overlooked. Further research is necessary to establish what media knowledge children bring to school, and the ways in which their media understanding, knowledge and skills may be developed by media education.
>
> However, to ensure the value of this education, reflection on the ethics of communication and information is required. Educators must play a role in this questioning. For it is not only a question of adapting school to the world of the New

Information and Communication Technologies but also of getting the world of the media to listen to the questions posed by educators about respect of men, women and young people in the broadcasting of information. (Council of Europe 1989)

This chapter is an elaboration of that statement, which itself represents a settlement of some of the major debates and developments which have taken place in Europe over the past forty years. Our objective has been to provide a guide through those debates as a way of understanding where we stand at the beginning of the 1990s and as a prelude to suggesting some possible agendas and ways forward for the future.

For if the 1980s was a decade of spectacular development for media education, the 1990s promises to be every bit as exciting. The motor which has driven the developments of the eighties—a period, let us not forget, generally characterized by educational retrenchment and conservatism—has been the determination of media teachers to ensure that an era of unprecedented expansion and technological development in the media has been matched by a commensurate expansion in the critical consciousness of students and pupils. It was that task which generated the motivation, the commitment and the creativity of many hundreds of European media teachers and their students during the past decade.

And simply keeping abreast of media developments in the nineties, and ensuring the relevance of what we teach to the life experiences of our students, will continue to provide a serious challenge to dominant notions of what constitutes effective teaching and learning in most European educational systems. The task of media teachers—making sense of the activities of one of society's key set of institutions, industries, and cultural practices (the media) through the routines and practices of another (the educational system)—will remain exhilarating and important enough.

But whereas in the eighties the complex relationship between the media and educational systems developed in the context of a stable, knowable, and unproblematic "Europe," in the nineties transformations in "Europe" itself are already running faster than our ability to comprehend, let alone respond adequately to, them. What is certain is that the major political, economic, social, and cultural changes currently taking place in Europe, whatever their final outcomes, are going to reverberate throughout the continent's media and educational systems well beyond the next decade. Moreover, the commanding role played by the media themselves in the changes taking place in eastern Europe tangles even further the already complex web of cross influences and determinations of media/education/ Europe relations.

When lives have been lost, and blood shed for a television station, then the democratic control of the mass media becomes both a matter of the widest public interest and debate, and a key marker in determining how democratic both established governments are and the "new" governments have become.

There is already evidence, as eastern European teachers begin the long process of educational reconstruction, of a great deal of interest in media education as it has developed in Western Europe. Key works are being translated and disseminated, teacher organizations in film and media education are being formed, and a host of personal contacts are being forged. It would be a mistake to regard this as a one-way traffic of ideas, the east catching up with the west's more developed and sophisticated practice.

For in respect to the mass media the democratic aspirations of our eastern European colleagues are more far reaching than our own. "Democratic" is not the word which most readily springs to mind when one considers Western media; "plutocratic" certainly, "paternalistic" of course, and at best, in a handful of Western European countries, "pluralistic," perhaps. But democratic power in Western European media remains almost exclusively concentrated at the point of consumption. The supreme sign of our democracies is *choice*—of media, as of toothpastes, hamburgers, or jeans. We exercise our power through what we do or do not choose to buy.

So, too, the most potent symbols of the failure of eastern European regimes to meet the needs of their citizens have always been the empty shop windows, and long queues, images ceaselessly purveyed to us down the decades by Western media. Those very media are now, of course, assuring us that, with the collapse of many of the old eastern European regimes, "our system has won."

But the situation is marginally more complicated than this with consumption becoming a substitute for democracy. Emphasis upon choice at the point of consumption effectively masks the lack of choice, which too often exists at the point of production, the workplace, and the 1980s have seen in Western Europe significant erosions in the rights of employees in the face of increasingly authoritarian employers no less in the media industries than elsewhere. Events in eastern Europe have placed the question of the democratic control and accountability of their media somewhere close to the top of their political agendas.

It is a question which in the West we have scarcely begun to contemplate. When we do—as I hope we will in the 1990s—it is possible that we may have much to learn from our colleagues in eastern Europe. Our primary objective in this chapter has been to provide for teachers, educators, and policymakers in member countries of the Council of Europe a guide to the ways in which media education might develop in the 1990s. In undertaking this task we have risked a number of predictions and recommendations for future practice. But in order to try and make sense of the future we have found it necessary to clarify the nature of media education in Europe now, and to trace the major historical shifts and developments that continue to influence current developments.

The chapter, then, is divided into three main sections. In the *first section* we look at the major paradigms within which the media have been studied over the past fifty years. In the *second,* we describe some of the major principles informing the best European media education practice today. The *third section* looks to the future and presents our projections and recommendations for the 1990s.

We have not attempted in this chapter to provide a detailed nation-by-nation account of specific developments in member countries of the Council of Europe. These are available in *The Information Society—A Challenge for Educational Policies?* (National Reports, 1989). Len Masterman's pamphlet, *The Development of Media Education in Europe in the 1980s* (Masterman, 1988) outlined some of the principal shifts and developments taking place in the theory and practice of media education during the 1980s. Narrower in scope than the present study, it contained an earlier elaboration of some of the themes and issues considered in more detail here.

Why Study Media? An Historical Review

Clarifying Objectives in Media Education

In this section we will be examining explanations as to why we should study or teach about the media. Different rationales for media education have produced very different kinds of practice, and it is evident that, before any effective teaching program can be devised, a great deal of consideration will need to be given to its ultimate purposes and objectives. This section, then, aims to present a historical review of the changing objectives of media education in order to help educators answer for themselves the question, "Why study or teach about the media?"

Nothing will affect the quality of the teaching and learning which takes place in the media studies class more than the clarity and precision of the teacher's own objectives, and his/her ability to communicate these to the students. If there is a single difference between a successful and an unsuccessful media class, it lies in this fact: that in a successful class, teacher and students alike understand the connections which exist between this particular discussion or activity or exercise, and larger, shared objectives to which they are all committed. This is essentially what gives a "good" class its sense of purpose, motivation, and drive. In a poor class the kids are simply doing the exercises. The teacher has failed to deliver an answer to the question hanging silently over every student group, "Why should we do this?" and all of the potentiality of media education is lost. The subject becomes as pointless, depressing, and de-motivating for students and teachers alike, as any other.

So, the *sine qua non* of successful media teaching are:

• clear thinking about objectives by the teacher;
• careful discussion of these with students, with appropriate amendments in the light of their own comments, priorities, and enthusiasms;
• a *regular* check, review, and (if necessary) revision of objectives, however informally carried out, together with a more *formal* evaluation of both teacher and student objectives at the end of the course.

The necessary starting point for all media teachers, then, is to clarify for themselves their own purposes in teaching the subject. We come clean about our own objectives later on, but in order to help teachers clarify their own objectives we present a brief historical review of some of the major reasons for studying the media which have had currency in the past. If our account does nothing else it should certainly demonstrate how every aspect of one's teaching—the selection of appropriate content, teaching styles, and methods of evaluation—is determined by one's ultimate objectives. We should stress here that we are not advocating a narrow, mechanistic view of teaching: the setting of, and testing for a narrow range of attainable targets. Far from it. We believe that the objectives of media education should be ambitious, challenging, open ended, and liberating. But they must be precise. For we wish, above all, to promote rigorous teaching and learning about the media.

In the next section, we set out the precise principles which we believe should underpin an effective media education practice but, before that, it is necessary to demonstrate how these principles have evolved from nearly half a century of debate about the role and functions of the media, education, and media education.

Historically, it is possible to discuss three major approaches to teaching about the mass media, each making its own characteristic assumptions about the nature of the media, and each having a clear set of teaching objectives and attendant practices.

Inoculative Approaches: The Media as Agents of Cultural Decline

The dominant view of the mass media adopted by most educationalists has been one of deep-rooted mistrust. It is a tradition with a long history. A report on English education in 1938, for example, spoke of media corrupting a whole generation (The Spens Report, 1938, 222–23). This view of the media (even before the advent of television) as corrupting influences, or virulent diseases—rather like diphtheria or polio—which threatened the cultural and moral health of us all, particularly children, is perhaps best understood as part of an even longer tradition of respectable middle-class fears of the cheap and debased amusements of working people.

This view produced one of two responses from teachers. On the one hand, the media could be legitimately *ignored* as irrelevant, indeed antithetical to the proper processes and legitimate functions of schooling in inculcating and protecting cultural standards. And that is precisely the stance which most educationalists continue to adopt today. On the other hand, the increasing popularity and persuasiveness of the media led to a call for schools to adopt a more active role of cultural *resistance* to the shallow emotional responses which they were believed to encourage.

Herein lay the unpromising origins of media education, and of the attitudes which were to be characteristic of the first and longest phase in the subject's development, lasting from the early 1930s to the early 1960s. It was from the outset, a defensive and paternalistic movement whose function was to introduce popular forms into the classroom only in order to dismiss them as commercial, manipulative, and derivative—the culture of the machine—in comparison with more traditional "high" cultural forms. Media education was, thus, in its earliest manifestation, education *against* the media; its function to encourage pupils to develop discrimination, fine judgement, and taste by grasping the basic differences between the timeless values of authentic "high" culture (in which teachers were themselves initiated) and the debased, anti-cultural values of largely commercial mass media (Leavis and Thompson, 1948).

This view of the media as agents of cultural decline produced its own classroom priorities for teachers, in terms of the media topics they considered. The study of advertising, for example, assumed particular importance because it typified all that was most dangerous about the media their manipulation of their audiences, their materialistic values, and their corrupting influence upon language. "Popular" literary forms such as pulp fiction, women's magazine stories, and children's comics also came under scrutiny since their use of predictable plots, stereotyped characters, and tired cliched language could be compared, to their detriment, with the creativity and vitality of literature.

It would be as foolish to underestimate the importance and significance of this tradition as to assume that it is now completely exhausted. For what was at stake in early media education was, for its practitioners, a matter of cultural life and death. The very future of society was deemed to hang upon, for example, the simple task of analyzing an advertisement. For what was involved in such an analysis was the capacity of children to stand back from the text, to reflect upon the motivations of those who produced it, to understand the ways in which it was working upon them and, crucially, to discriminate between authentic and unauthentic uses of languages.

This particular tradition, then, cast the teacher in a role of the greatest cultural significance. That, almost certainly, explains the commitment of its practitioners and its longevity as a movement. It is still far from exhausted. Though it would be very unusual at a meeting of media teachers anywhere in Europe today to find adherents of the view that the media are agents of cultural decline, it is an opinion which remains common enough amongst educators generally. Media teachers, indeed, could be said to constitute an important lobby *against* advertising, and stands as a reminder that "inoculative" media education has not yet had its day.

The Media as Popular Arts

It was not until the early 1960s that there was any significant movement away from "inoculative" media education. By then, however, a new generation of teachers was entering schools, teachers who actually liked popular cultural forms—particularly films—could see value in them, and were unwilling to discuss them as *inevitably* corrupting influences. It was this new generation of teachers which was to provide the impetus behind the second great phase of media education, the Popular Arts movement (Hall & Whannel, 1964). It was a movement which involved not so much an abandonment of "protectionist" approaches to media study as a modification and extension of them. Discrimination—the ability to make fine critical judgements—was still a primary objective. But discrimination now became something to be exercised not *against* the media, but *within* them.

The distinct step forward was primarily made possible by developments in film theory in the late 1950s. Whereas "inoculative" media education had been underpinned by the pessimistic "mass-culture" theories of the Frankfurt School in continental Europe and the influential work of Leavis in Britain, the emergence in France of a corpus of serious critical writing around the journal *Cahiers du cinéma* established the legitimacy of film theory in a way that impinged directly upon educational practice throughout Europe and North America. The auteur approach, first expounded by François Truffaut in the pages of *Cahiers du Cinéma* in 1954, was an explicit attempt to establish the work of some directors as being of more interest and importance than others. In spite of the collaborative and industrial nature of film production, some film directors could be seen as being the genuine authors of their work in the sense that their personal vision and style could transcend the often unpromising material they were handling. Film could be understood, that is, as the work of "great," or at least "interesting" directors, in a way which directly paralleled the study of literature as the work of great writers.

The effect of these theoretical developments upon media education in the 1960s was profound. Film was singled out as a privileged area of study and the 1960s became an era in which film studies courses were established in many educational institutions throughout Europe and North America. It is worth observing that this development was taking place at a time when the mass audience for cinema was beginning to decline, and film had fewer claims to being considered a genuinely popular medium than at any previous time in its history. The primary cause of this was the increasing influence and popularity of television, a medium about which the new criticism had little to say. Where it was considered at all, television tended to be evaluated as an inferior form of cinema.

Educational practice was very much following in the wake of exciting developments in both film-making and film theory. In seeking academic respectability, however, both film theory and educational practice frequently confused conceptual rigueur with a predilection for often obscurantist theory. Even film journals intended primarily for teachers dabbled in the kind of high theory which signalled "keep out" for the *majority* of teachers and their students. It is a legacy—of inaccessibility, obscurity, and irrelevance to the needs of classroom practitioners from which media education, and its attendant theory, continues to suffer.

Whilst the Popular Arts movement, then, did constitute a distinct step forward from inoculative media education, it did not break entirely with older attitudes. The "value" question remained central. Discrimination (*within,* not *against* the media) remained a primary objective. Media education continued to be "protectionist." In encouraging pupils to distinguish between "good" and "bad" films (and, by extension, good and bad television programs and newspapers), the assumption still held that students' media tastes needed to be improved. Media education continued to be an essentially defensive and somewhat negative enterprise. Little surprise, then, that it ultimately failed to mobilize the energies and enthusiasms of large numbers of teachers and students. The 1970s were to reveal more fully, precisely what the difficulties of teaching "discriminatory" forms of media education were.

First of all, very little theoretical work had been done to establish criteria for evaluating the media. It was, therefore, difficult for anyone—critics, teachers, or students—to make evaluative judgements abut the media in a way which carried authority, or could be argued back to generally agreed principles or assumptions. Even more seriously, there were doubts about the very *appropriateness* of applying aesthetic criteria, derived from the arts, to the vast majority of media output (e.g. news, photojournalism, advertising, etc.). As we have seen, some work had been done on film. But "authorship" scarcely seemed a concept applicable to critical work on television or even most journalism. As a result, the Popular Arts movement had relatively little to say about arguably the two most powerful mass media, television and the press, and their study remained scandalously neglected throughout the 1960s and much of the 1970s.

In addition, discriminatory approaches to media study raised two further problems.

First, in focusing so sharply upon value questions, discriminatory approaches tended to pay particularly close attention to *textual analysis*. This was at once a strength of the movement and a source of weakness. For what the movement neglected were the *contexts* within which media texts were produced, distributed, and consumed. What were held at bay were crucial questions of ownership and control, production determinants, marketing, sale and distribution, and audience.

Second, held at bay were questions of interpretation and readership. Though the "value question" was of central concern to the Popular Arts movement, the crucial question was always, "Precisely how good is this particular text?" This approach was actually based on an extremely naive notion of "value." Value was held to be transcendental, a timeless quality of the text itself, awaiting discovery by the careful and sensitive reader. What remained unquestioned were the acts of reading and interpretation themselves, and the ideological and social bases of particular judgements. Always left hanging, largely unanswered by discriminatory approaches were the questions: Value for whom? Value for what? And value according to what criteria of judgement?

We have spent some time in looking at the problems raised by attempts to encourage students to discriminate between "good" and "bad" media products, and in explaining why this particular form of media education failed to produce a viable classroom practice. This has been necessary since discriminatory approaches, though no longer as dominant as they were in the 1960s and 1970s, continue to have currency amongst some educators as a common-sensed objective for media study. Here, for example, is part of the Danish National Report on the reading of mass media published by the Council of Europe (National Reports, 1989):

> In many circles, including teachers and parents, there are reservations about instruction in mass media on the ground that pupils should not deal with trash. This point of view is untenable for at least two reasons:
> *a*. In between the very trashy subject-matter, there is also subject-matter of high quality.
> *b*. Individual pupils must be made capable of distinguishing between what is good and what is bad. This requires them to be capable of analyzing, interpreting and assessing the different concrete forms of mass communication as they meet them in their day-to-day lives. (34)

At this point, we must acknowledge some possible protests from many teachers and parents at our attempt to consign this view of media education to the history books. Are teachers to be denied the right to help their students distinguish between the creative and the third-rate, the worthwhile and the worthless in the media? Are commercial media to be allowed to set cultural agendas, free from all criticism? Are educators to be deprived of the opportunity of demonstrating precisely why this newspaper is so contemptible or that television program so valuable? To deny these as self-evidently worthwhile objectives will seem to many teachers to be a fundamental abdication of their responsibilities to their students, and, indeed, to their culture as a whole.

We need to stress, therefore, that we are not advocating that value questions should have no place in media education. But we are arguing that questions of value should be moved from center stage in order to facilitate our chief objective: increasing our students' understanding of the media—of how and in whose interests they work, how they are organized, how they produce meaning, how they go about the business of representing "reality," and of how those representations are read by those who receive them. And that word "understanding," with its emphasis upon the development of a critical intelligence in relation to the media, needs to be given a centrality previously accorded to the concept of discrimination. Much of what passes for media "criticism" by educators and academics is of little worth because it is so ill-informed. "Cheap shots make bad weapons," as the saying goes. Our primary duty as media teachers is to make sure that we and our students have as full an understanding of the complexity of media issues as possible before we begin the process of evaluation. Media education for teachers and students alike is primarily an investigative process—a process of finding out—rather than primarily an evaluative one.

What we are arguing against are approaches to media education which constitute thinly veiled attacks upon the media tastes of pupils and students, and which use the teacher's own media tastes as the touchstones of value. And we are opposed to media education approaches which rush too quickly to judgement. Judgement, in our view, should be suspended for as long as possible, and mass media material examined—simply seen as closely as possible so that more complex meanings and issues can become apparent. One of the keys to unlocking student responses is to move them toward making statements which seem to them to have some validity irrespective of their own personal feelings and tastes. For the objective of arriving at value judgements closes up rather than opens out discussion and dialogue. It is indeed all to easy too obtain immediate evaluative responses from students, and, thereafter, too difficult to move beyond them, for the process of making evaluative responses can force students to make individual stands and take personal positions, a more threatening procedure, and one less productive of dialogue than a systematic group exploration.

Once the process of investigation is complete, questions of value will inevitably be raised. The question, "Precisely how good or bad is this newspaper or television program?" is still a question worth asking. Indeed, such questions as, "What, precisely, are the characteristics of news reporting which we would wish to encourage and defend?" or "What ethical questions faced this documentary film-maker in relation to both the subject of, and the audience for the documentary, and how were they answered?" take us to the heart of some of the most important media issues of our day. And they are issues about which media professionals themselves have principled differences of opinion.

Finally, students and teachers will need to understand and discuss the value question as a transitive one (Value for whom? Value according to what criteria? Value for what purposes?). Statements like, "This is a good film," or "This is an unsuccessful TV program" tend to be personal evaluations masquerading as normative judgements, and without further elaboration are relatively meaningless. They tend to posit a transcendental, transcultural, transhistoric notion of value which suggests that value is a textual quality rather than a function of its usefulness, relevance, and interest for particular sets of readers. It is axiomatic in media education that texts are likely to be valued in different ways by different audiences.

The fact that different audiences are likely to produce different readings and evaluations of the same text has important implications for the media education classroom. For students are active meaning-makers too. The objective of textual analysis should not be to produce consensual evaluations and interpretations, but to encourage and respect diversity. Pupils' own responses need to be nurtured and taken seriously, and not simply subordinated to the teacher's tastes, the text's immanent meanings, or the dominant views of the majority. In a class with a heterogeneous gender, class, or ethnic mix, diversity of response should be expected and, indeed, encouraged by the teacher, who may nevertheless wish to challenge the assumed "naturalness" of these responses. What problems have been raised by these different and even incompatible responses? And how, precisely, have they been produced?

So far, we have looked at two historically important answers to our opening question, "Why study and teach about the media?" As we have shown, they are answers which still have currency amongst teachers and parents today. However, the first answer ("To provide a counter-balance to the conformity and passivity induced by the media, to the shallowness of media values, and to the manipulative nature of media texts by exposing children to the timeless values and moral qualities of 'high' or established culture") had largely run its course, for teachers seriously interested in the media, by the early 1960s. The second answer ("To enable pupils to discriminate between the 'good' and 'bad,' the authentic and the unauthentic within the media") had, for reasons we have discussed in detail, run into major problems by the mid-1970s.

We have demonstrated, too, how each of these rationales produced its own priority areas for study within the media. The first privileged the study of advertising, the second the study of film, but these priorities had little to do with the relative importance of these media within society. In particular, film studies courses may have been proliferating in schools and colleges in the early 1970s, but it was becoming clear everywhere else that television was both the dominant medium in the lives of almost all pupils, and a medium of the greatest ideological significance across European cultures generally. Historically, media education came of age in the 1970s when it turned away from narrowly aesthetic questions toward more broadly based "culturalist" concerns, and when it turned its full, though not exclusive, attention toward television.

The Media as Representational or Symbolic Systems

It became clear throughout the 1970s that the priorities of film studies could not be transferred to the study of other media. The study of television and newspapers raised quite different, and, in many ways, much more urgent problems. This led to a fragmentation of the subject in which very different questions were raised of different media, and a typical media studies course might consist of a term's work on film, a term on television, a little time on popular music, some work on advertising, and so on, with students bringing to bear questions and critical approaches to different media which had little in common with one another. Slowly, however, by the early 1980s media teachers had begun to integrate and synthesize within their practice a number of intellectual concerns of the 1970s which led to a more conceptually coherent understanding of the role and function of the media as a whole, and of how to teach about them. Particularly important were developments in the fields of semiotics, theories of ideology, and the social contexts of media production and consumption.

Semiotics. First of all, there was a revival of interest in semiotics, the study of signs, and sign systems, proposed in the early years of this century by the Swiss linguist, Ferdinand de Saussure, in his *Cours de Linguistique Générale* (de Saussure, 1974). It was the French critic, Roland Barthes (1973), however, who was principally responsible for applying a semiotic approach to the analysis of media texts. His key work, *Mythologies,* first published in 1957, mainly consisted of short essays on different aspects of popular culture (wrestling, toys, striptease, plastic, etc.).

Semiotics, then, helped establish the first principle of media education: the principle of nontransparency. It was a principle which particularly illuminated the nature of television, but also had a surprising degree of potency across all media and for that reason came to gain from media teachers an almost universal acceptance. It drew attention, precisely, to questions of representation and gave to media studies the world over a characteristic discourse in which media teachers and their students spoke not of (say) "women," "poverty," "prisons," "Africa," or "class," as revealed or described by the media, but of representations of these things. Indeed, in English that central unifying concept of representation has become a kind of professional pun: the media do not present reality, they represent it.

Another way of expressing this is to say that the media are symbolic systems; not simply reflections of a reality which must be accepted, but languages which need to be actively read, and interrogated. It is not surprising, then, that some of the most interesting early work in media studies concentrated on "media language" and incorporated media study within the wider concerns of communications courses. Unsurprisingly, too, given the provenance of the revival of semiotics, much of this work originated in France. This approach had a good deal of influence in France and Spain, whilst Jean-Pierre Golay's work on the language of image and sound toward the end of the 1960s provided many concrete examples of the ways in which visual literacy might be taught with primary and lower-secondary pupils.

The English translation of Golay's (1974) *The Language of Image and Sound* and its distribution by the British Film Institute was an important moment for English-speaking media teachers who were just beginning to move away from film studies and were feeling their way toward more broadly based media work.

Semiotics' second great contribution to media education was scarcely less momentous than its first. As we have seen, the history of media education up until this point had generally devalued popular cultural forms. Its primary objective, to encourage discrimination, had originally assumed the superiority of high culture and later led to the evaluation of popular art forms by aesthetic criteria having their bases in the traditional arts. The value question, "How good is this work?" remained central to the whole media education project.

Barthes overturned all of this. His very choice of subjects—striptease, wrestling, toys, tourist guides, a plate of steak and chips—involved the sharpest possible rejection of established tastes. For if a plate of steak and chips or a margarine advertisement were as worthy of serious attention as a poem, then a significant step had been taken toward a truly scandalous *equation* of these objects. There did not seem to be any process of discriminatory filtering either in Barthes's selection of some subjects for analysis, rather than others, or in his treatment of them. Indeed, subjects were chosen at random as they were suggested by topical events. Implicit in Barthes's very methodology was an undermining of the bedrock distinctions between cultural objects and between the qualities and values supposedly inherent within them upon both media studies and literary studies before it had been constituted.

Yet, some important continuities between Barthes's project and traditional approaches to literary and media studies remained. Barthes was interested in "culture," albeit newly defined as "a way of life" rather than as "the best that has been thought and written in the world." And any and every aspect of culture could be treated as a "text" and subjected to rigorous scrutiny and analysis. What *Mythologies* guaranteed was the future of a much more broadly based and nonevaluative form of textual analysis within any study of the media. And perhaps most importantly of all, in its generosity of spirit, its openness to all aspects of culture, and its confident, unapologetic tone, *Mythologies* highlighted the timorousness, narrowness, and besetting exclusivity of previous writing about and study of popular culture. After *Mythologies,* for the media educator at least, things could never be the same again.

Ideology. Developments in semiology dovetailed interestingly with an increasing interest in the 1970s in theories and ideology. Ideological questions had been conspicuous by their absence from media education programs up until the 1970s, a curious lacuna given the original interest in the manipulative role of the mass media (the "culture industry") in advanced capitalist societies shown by the Frankfurt School in the 1930s. Instead, following the lead of literary culture, media education, as we have seen, had at its center a theory of value (aesthetic, and moral) which existed above and beyond politics. Louis Althusser's (1971) influential *Ideology and Ideological State Apparatuses* reasserted and developed traditional Marxist arguments on the role of the media and educational systems as essentially Ideological State Apparatuses' (ISAs) and reasserted, too, the notion of ideology as a body of dominant and more-or-less coherent ideas and practices which are imposed (via the media and educational systems) upon subordinate groups, and which result in "false consciousness" (a failure by subordinate groups to recognize their own objective class interests, and a willingness to interpret their circumstances according to categories supplied by dominant groups).

Althusser's formulation was a doubly pessimistic one for media teachers. It offered a bleakly negative and deterministic view of both the system within which teachers worked, and the system about which they taught. Caught between two of the major ISAs, teachers were offered little scope for action and progressive struggle.

A resurgence of interest in the writings (from the 1920s and 1930s) of the Italian Marxist, Antonio Gramsci (1971), however, offered media teachers, as well as other cultural workers, a much more energizing vision of their role. In particular, Gramsci had developed the concept of hegemony to explain how a dominant class's leadership can come to be accepted by consent, as well as by force, by subordinate groups. The concept of hegemony is an important one for media teachers since it defines both the media and educational systems not as irresistible steamrollers of the state, but as important sites for struggle between hegemonic and counter-hegemonic ideas. For hegemony is never won or lost for all time, but has to be constantly fought for in order to be secured and maintained. If we had to choose the most influential model of the mass media which underpinned most of the important developments within media education during the 1970s and 1980s, it would be this one: the media as a "site for struggle," a struggle within which both media teachers and their students could play their due part.

In addition, the concept of hegemony provided a sophisticated conceptual tool for understanding and analyzing the workings of dominant ideologies. Hegemony, in Raymond Williams's words, "is not limited to matters of direct political control but seeks to describe a more general predominance which includes, as one of its key features, a particular way of seeing the world and human nature and relationships" (Williams, 1976, 118). That "way of seeing the world" is not simply— as Althusser would have it—the dominant class's, imposed on subordinate groups from above. It has to speak, to be effective, to the interests of subordinate groups, making whatever concessions are necessary in order to establish equilibrium and win legitimacy, without compromising the existing fundamental structures.

One way of achieving this is for dominant groups to find discourses in which their own objective interests can be articulated as the interests of all. When this is achieved, class interests can be articulated as the common interest (e.g. the national interest, the public interest), or as simply "common-sensed" and "natural." Thus, politics evacuates the field of social relations. This is one of the reasons why "ideology" had become such a slippery concept. It can refer, in one definition, to any explicitly political (and generally doctrinaire and inflexible) set of beliefs (e.g. as in fascist or Marxist ideologies), in another, to its opposite, the realm of common sense, as manifested in our taken-for-granted beliefs and everyday language.

It would of course be foolish to suggest that classroom teachers were following these theoretical debates on ideology with bated breath. Yet, the ways in which these arguments were moving did connect with the down-to-earth concerns and practices of media teachers. They, too, were encouraging their students to hold up to question the media's "decorative display of what-goes-without-saying." And they, too, were attempting to challenge the media's common-sensed representations by asking whose interests they served, how they were constructed, and what alternative representations were being repressed. What the debates on ideology did was to bring a sharper political focus to these concerns. They established the importance of a politics of representation. They demonstrated how questions of choice, of values, of attitudes were woven into communication processes at every level. They affected attitudes to the often mundane task of teaching: it was an important site for struggle over meaning. And they provided a demystifying strategy for dealing with topical media material in the classroom.

Since the mystification of media's images was tied up with their "naturalization," their "evaporation" of politics and history, the task of the teacher was precisely to provide some sense of the wider political and historical contexts within which these images were produced and could be understood. Most fundamentally, however, the "ideology debates" placed questions of politics, rather than aesthetic value, at the heart of what were now thought to be the key functions of contemporary media. And they did so, not by resurrecting the "mass society" theories of the 1930s, but by connecting to our common-sensed ways of watching television and consuming media's images. And that had an obvious relevance to media teachers everywhere.

The social contexts of media production and consumption. The 1970s also saw an increasing interest in the sociology of the mass media. Developments in both semiology and theories of ideology had obvious implications for textual analysis. But as we have seen they also raised questions about the contexts within which media texts were both produced and consumed. To make the fullest sense of a media text it was necessary to go outside of the text itself, and explore a range of rather complicated issues which went far beyond the confines of traditional literary criticism and models of communication based on a simple sender → message → receiver paradigm. The 1970s and 1980s, then, saw an explosion of illuminating studies on different aspects of the sociology of the mass media. At the production/encoding end of the communication process there were studies of broadcasting institutions, and of the routine assumptions and working practices of media professionals, particularly journalists. There was a great deal of interest in questions of media ownership and control, and in the influence of news sources, advertisers, governments, the state, the legal system, and even audiences upon the production of meaning by the media (Masterman, 1985).

As we have suggested, it is important to see the interest in these kinds of questions as interlocking with, and logically connected to developments in semiology and ideology. For if the media, far from reflecting reality, produced representational constructs characterized (through their "naturalized" quality) by their ideological potency, then the question, "Who produces?" or "Who constructs—and in whose interests?" becomes the logical one to ask. And, as with earlier media paradigms, these developments produced their own characteristic "skew" in terms of which aspects of the media were deemed to be the most worthy of serious study and investigation. Television, for the first time, came into its own, out-running, in ideological importance, all other media in weaving its seamless flow of "naturalized" images into the fabric of everyone's day-to-day existence. And within television it was the study of "factual" programs such as news and documentary—those areas in which the medium's ideological masking, its naturalism, was at its most potent—that became of consuming interest.

In turning to the question, "Who constructs/produces?" media sociologists were compelled to face up to the nature of the media as consciousness industries. There were, it is true, attempts to apply the auteur theory to television, but these faded into insignificance in comparison with the proliferation of ethnographic studies of media institutions and audiences taking place in the 1970s and early 1980s. What these studies increasingly revealed were the complexities of both the industrial processes of production/encoding, and the processes of audience reading/decoding.

The industrial processes of production/encoding. The logical question "Who constructs?" invites a personalized answer and early investigators were concerned to reveal patterns of ownership and control within and across the media, concentrating particularly upon the activities of high-profile media entrepreneurs as well as the power and influence of a number of family media dynasties. Important, too, were the activities of multinational conglomerates with media interests, which demonstrated an increasing concentration of ownership, and a concomitant lack of genuine diversity within the media, as well as the fact that the media were connected with a vast range of consumer and service industries. The media, it could be easily demonstrated, were not isolated cultural phenomena, but very significant links in a vast capitalist chain.

These early developments in media sociology produced some dilemmas for media teachers: how to relate questions of ownership and control to the interests and experience of pupils; how to handle information overload; how to avoid a mechanical reading off of texts from the interests of their producers.

Indeed, the whole question of the relationship between media ownership and media products proved, upon investigation, to be much more complex than had at first appeared. It wasn't simply that the influence of owners and controllers frequently seemed to be indirect, covert, diffuse, long term, and devilishly difficult to pin down with any precision. It was also that there were clearly other sources of media power and influence which might actively contest those of owners. This was not to suggest a simple pluralistic model of media influence; the media was equally open to a whole range of diverse forces. Clearly, owners and proprietors could and did wield tremendous power, often firing their editors and journalists at will, and, in the case of Rupert Murdoch, taking a surprisingly detailed interest in the output of his vast world-wide media empire.

Yet, there were clearly constraints upon owner power. Any newspaper, for example, has its own characteristics, style, and form which has evolved over many years. It will be one which commands the loyalty and support of its readers, and through them its advertisers upon which the profits of the newspaper will largely depend. An individual proprietor meddles with such established networks, particularly if profitable, at his peril. In addition, the newspaper will have to operate within the constraints of the law, and may be subject to self-regulatory mechanisms set up either by the newspaper industry or by the individual newspaper itself. If it values good industrial relations, and competent writing and production skills, it will treat its workers as professionals and accord them a good deal of power and respect, and it will wish to maintain good working relationships with its chief sources of news and information. Of course proprietors can, and indeed have, ridden roughshod over such "constraints," but in general terms it remains true that there is a rather complex network of influences at play within any media organization, and that the teacher's task is to encourage students and pupils to weigh a number of different factors in the balance in assessing the determinants of, and influences upon, any media text.

Our understanding of the precise determinants at play has been illuminated by major studies by media sociologists of such influences as advertising, the institutional socialization and control of media workers, the media as primarily economic or commercial systems, the influence of news sources, the influence of the government and the state, and the power of audiences. As a result, it is much less easy to make sweeping generalizations about the ability of individuals, governments, or institutions to impose their will, in a relatively unhampered way, via the media. Clearly many powerful voices and interests do have privileged access to the media, but the precise strengths and limitations of their influence do need to be unpacked with some care. Without being pluralistic, Western European media, nevertheless, are—we use the phrase again—sites for struggle between contending influences. There has, therefore, been a distinct and important movement in the past decade away from a model of the media as ideological institutions whose strings are pulled and manipulated by individual and corporate owners. Today the media are generally understood as secondary definers of social events, which are heavily dependent upon authoritative and accredited sources. The media, for the most part, reproduce definitions which have their origins elsewhere.

Attention then, has moved away from media institutions to those major institutions and sources who have (often privileged) access to the media: in particular national governments, the various arms of the state, and the PR industry. Attention, too, is now focused upon journalists not so much as unwitting tools of a "dominant ideology," nor as victims of their own unreflective practices, but much more as professionals whose integrity in discriminating between the corporate hand out and the genuine facts of the case is one of the threads upon which media freedom hangs today.

The processes of reading/decoding. Major changes have also taken place in our understanding of how media texts are decoded and consumed. Indeed, there has been a major reconceptualization of the significance of media audiences since the early 1980s. At the beginning of the 1990s it seems clear that the future of media education will be as "audience-centered" as it was "text-centered" in the past. Indeed, we need to understand audiences not simply as the more-or-less passive receivers of meanings determined elsewhere, but, in more senses than one, as the chief product of the mass media. How has this transformation occurred?

Up until the early 1980s audiences remained, throughout the history of media education, a relatively neglected phenomenon. This is curious given that media audiences had been, from the outset, the dominant focus of attention for media researchers. There were two main reasons for media education's general neglect of this important area. First of all, it could be seen as part of media education's literary legacy, an inheritance of literary criticism's subordination of readers to the twin authorities of authorship (justified by the transcendence of "genius" or "creativity"), and the text itself (the transcendence of immanent "meaning"). As we have seen, media education, like literary criticism, had predominantly been based upon the beliefs that textual meanings were produced by authors (writers/directors/producers), were inherent within texts, and gave themselves up only to experienced and sensitive readers. Interpretation in this view was an ideologically innocent activity, taking place in a social and historical vacuum, rather than a construction reflecting or refracting the ideological positions of readers.

The second reason that media education had tended to neglect audiences as an area of concern was that though, in more widely based communications research, audiences had been of great importance, the position allotted to them had scarcely been more dynamic than it had in literary-based models. In communication models, audiences have been generally conceived of as receivers of messages, and a great deal of well-funded research had been undertaken to discover the effects of different kinds of communication upon their audiences. As is well known, this research generated few positive results, largely because of the difficulties of separating the influence of communications from the influence of other social phenomena, such as the family, the peer group, opinion leaders, and so on.

For all its interest in audiences, most empiricist communications research has had little of interest to say about them. It has been concerned not without significance but with quantification in its approach to the analysis of both communication content and audiences. What has generally been held to be of most importance is the number of viewers watching a particular program, or the number of interviews given to trade unionists or employers in a week's media coverage, rather than the ways in which the treatment of content might structure audience responses in predictable ways, or the significance which these experiences might have for audiences.

The development of communications research has been largely a development toward more complex understandings of media content and audience responses. So-called uses-and-gratifications research, for example, was a distinct advance on earlier communication models since it posited a more sympathetic and active view of audiences. Audiences were seen as actively using the media and making positive choices, based on their assessment of the likelihood of the media gratifying particular needs.

There were, however, problems with this view of media audiences. Uses and gratifications research still generally tended to be psychologically, rather than sociologically based, with an emphasis upon choices which were held to be freely made by individuals, rather than uses which were structured by considerations of race, class, or gender. Further, uses and gratifications research had little to say on the ways in which wants or needs are themselves produced, and the active role played by the media in this process. It had little to say about the ways in which media content might structure audience responses in quite predictable ways, and still less about the possibilities that questions of audiences might be important determinants of media content and forms. Nor did it open up many of the complex ways in which audiences work upon texts, accepting, negotiating, or rejecting the rich diversity of positions offered to them by texts.

Since 1980 a good deal of important research has been published on these questions. Since it has significant implications for the development of media education a brief résumé of some of its important strands is necessary.

Recent research on audiences. One very important strand of audience research has attempted to investigate different interpretations of media texts by audiences in terms not of individual psychologies, but of the shared "cultural codes" which members of different groups might bring to them. Are different sections of the audience, researchers asked, likely to read media texts in ways which are systematically related to their socioeconomic and subcultural positions? Crudely, in any culture is a working-class male likely to "read" television in a way which connects with readings made by other working-class males and differs from readings made, for example, by middle-class women, or members of a particular ethnic minority group? Even in its most basic form it is clear that this idea makes a break with the notion that different interpretations and evaluations of the same text necessarily involve "inaccurate" or "incorrect" readings, or simply result from differences in personal taste.

Yet, these had been the presumptions of media education up until this point. Different textual decodings within a group of students tended to be treated as "problems" to be overcome and resolved through discussion and consensus. But now, such differences could be understood, by both students and teachers alike, as refractions of perhaps important gender or subcultural differences within the group. Students' readings and judgements, in other words, were not to be praised or damned by virtue of their degree of conformity to the authoritative judgement of the teacher. Rather, they were to be understood by both students and teacher alike as being systematically related to more widely available cultural codes. Student views could be both liberated from conformity to a consensual view, and denaturalized through a tracing of their major determinants.

Research on audiences has developed a great deal from this basic position over the past decade. Indeed this area has been, arguably, the most heavily researched of all in the recent history of media studies. It is impossible to do justice to the volume and complexity of this body of work here, but a brief indication can be given of some of its most important aspects.

Encoding. Sensitivity to the liberating possibilities of differential decoding did not blind early researchers to the importance of discovering the dominant meanings encoded within the text. And it remained an important purpose of media education to provide students with the media competencies which would enable them to explicate the encoded text as fully as possible. What was "open" was the audience's (the student's) interpretation and acceptance of that text.

Audience responses: a basic model. A basic model adopted by a number of researchers offered three broad positions for readers of media texts:

a. *Dominant:* when audience decoding is aligned with the dominant encodings of the text;

b. *Negotiated:* when decoders take the meaning broadly as encoded, but modify or inflect it in the light of their own values and contexts; and

c. *Oppositional:* when decoders recognize the dominant encoding but interpret it in an oppositional way.

Sub-cultural readings. Some researchers hypothesized that these positions might form the basis of different class-orientated meaning systems, but others argued that real audience responses were much more complex than this (see *Subjectivity,* below) and could not be "read off from class/gender/ethnic/age/subcultural positions." Studies of the mass media from specific subcultural positions, however, flourished in the 1980s. Particularly important were feminist readings of film and television which asserted the significance of such forms as melodrama and soap-opera, previously somewhat despised because of their predominantly female audiences. Similarly, studies appeared which looked at the media from the perspectives of the elderly, ethnic minorities, gays, and even parents. The significance of such studies was that they tended to turn conventional media values and interpretations on their heads, establishing the validity and coherence of a whole range of alternative viewing positions. They also tackled head-on questions of representation and stereotyping.

Criticism became a counter-weapon in the hands of those mis- or underrepresented in the media who drew specific attention to the politics of representation, and to the power relations always inscribed within stereotyping. What was at stake was the power which some groups possessed to define others; "outsider" groups were outsiders precisely because they were rarely allowed to name their world, or to control their own definitions of themselves. Beneath the stereotypes lay the institutionalization, both within the media and outside of it, of sexism, racism, homophobia, and class politics.

These developments made their due impact upon media educators. "Representation," as we shall see, become a centrally important concept within media education and a number of educators argued that media education should be an explicitly anti-racist and anti-sexist activity. Others suggested that it might be more effective, as well as more consistent with the desire to encourage critical autonomy, to adopt a less propagandist approach. But all agreed that questioning and challenging dominant media representations, and the power relations inscribed within them, should be a centrally important activity within media education.

Subjectivity. Subcultural studies have certainly made an invaluable contribution to our understanding of media audiences. Yet, how accurate is it to speak of a "female," "black," or "gay" audience? Are such audiences made up of coherent, unified subjects who produce identifiably similar responses?

Whilst these are timely reminders of the complexity, diversity, and frequently contradictory nature of audience responses, they do not necessarily undermine the importance of subcultural studies. Clearly, for any individual subject some "positions" (trade-unionist/black/female) may be more powerful in generating and stimulating responses than others. An acknowledgement of heterogeneity ought not to produce a slippage into the incoherence of the subject. It may well be, however, that the literal impossibility of "speaking for" a subculture may deter future writers from speaking from a subcultural position. And this would be a great pity—an example of how seemingly legitimate calls for more objectively verifiable and "scientific" evidence can produce a profound conservatism and may actually silence the voices of minorities.

Some conclusions on audience research. The major implications of developments in audience research for media education may be briefly summarized:

a. The research encouraged a movement away from an almost-exclusive attention on textual meanings to an exploration of the sense made of texts by different audiences. In the classroom this movement helped liberate pupils and students from the text, and encouraged their teachers to see them as meaning makers. Slowly, many media teachers began to pay attention to the competencies and attitudes which pupils were bringing to the text, and to encourage diversity of response rather than consensus.

b. The study of subcultural responses to the media, and the articulation of specific responses to the media by a range of "outsider" groups, established subcultural studies as an important part of media studies. This took the form of an interest in "images of . . ." particular groups, as well as in subcultural readings of mainstream media.

c. Questions of audience and their contexts for viewing became important considerations within textual analysis. Audience and contexts, indeed, came to be seen as important determinants of media texts and forms in a radical reversal of traditional communication models.

d. As we shall see, audiences can now be argued to the chief product of contemporary media. Academic research and marketing philosophy have reached a common conclusion: that the major function of contemporary (and certainly commercial) media is the identification, segmentation, production, packaging, and selling, not so much of programs, but of audiences.

Media Education Now: Some Basic Principles

We have charted some of the principal influences upon media education practice in Europe between 1970 and 1990. In particular, we have looked at the influences of semiology, of theories of ideology, and of developments in the sociology of the mass media, especially those relating to questions of media production and reception. In this chapter, we begin with a summary of some of the basic principles of media education as it is currently practiced in Europe today. We then consider some of the major issues and controversies within media education, and attempt to formulate some further principles which represent, we believe, the current "settlement" of these issues. We include here the issue of appropriate teaching methodologies for media education; the media studies/media education debate; media education across the curriculum; and the role of parents and media professionals within media education. We begin by summarizing some of the major principles of media education today.

Some Principles of Media Education

The central and unifying concept of media education is that of representation. The media do not reflect reality, but represent it. The media, that is, are symbolic or *sign* systems. Without this first principle no media education is possible. If the media were "windows on the world," or simply reflected reality, to study them would be as purposeless as studying a pane of glass. We could not properly study media on such a basis, but only the subject matter conveyed by the media (i.e. news, sport, drama, etc.). Media study is based on an assumption of media nontransparency, on an assumption that the media shape the subjects they present in characteristic forms. From the assumption that the media represent, rather than reflect reality, all else flows.

A central purpose of media education is to "denaturalize" the media. Media education challenges the "naturalness" of media images. It reveals them as constructs, by:

a. engaging with questions of production;

b. examining the techniques used to create the "reality-effect";

c. raising questions about the ideological impact of the media's construction of "common sense"; and

d. considering how audiences "read" and respond to media content.

Media education is primarily investigative. It does not seek to impose specific cultural values. It aims to increase students' understanding of how the media represent reality. Its objective is to produce well-informed citizens who can make their own judgements on the basis of the available evidence. In so far as media education deals with value judgements, it does so in ways which encourage students to explore the range of value judgements made about a given media text and to examine the sources of such judgements (including their own) and their effects. It does not seek to impose ideas on what constitutes "good" or "bad" television, newspapers, or films.

Media education is organized around key concepts, which are analytical tools rather than an alternative content. The earliest forms of media education *were* content-based. This tended to produce a fragmented view of both the subject and the media themselves. The problem here was that different principles, concepts, and modes of enquiry were employed in studying different media. Media education only came of age as a disciplined field of study when its concepts had relevance across a range of media. There is now widespread agreement across Europe on what these key concepts are. They are concepts which are intended to make the textual investigation of any medium more systematic and rigorous. They include: denotation and connotation, genre, selection, nonverbal communication, media language, naturalism and realism, audience, institution, construction, mediation, representation, code/encoding/decoding, audience, segmentation, narrative structure, sources, ideology, anchorage, rhetoric, discourse, and subjectivity.

Such concepts as these do, of course, vary enormously in complexity. Some (selection, construction) can be taught to everyone from the youngest children to adults. Others are more complex. The art of media teaching lies in breaking down their complexity to simpler, yet intellectually respectable forms, and using them via a spiral curriculum.

These key concepts should not be regarded as an alternative content. It would probably be unwise to teach directly about media institutions or ideology, for example. These are concepts which have to be used in making sense of the media, and their importance and complexity should become evident through their use in illuminating the nature of specific media texts, rather than being taught as abstract concepts. The key concepts are analytical tools and not an alternative content.

Media education is a lifelong process. Interest in and attachment to the media begins, for most children, well before they attend school and continues throughout their adult lives. A media education which fails to recognize the implications of this will fall short of its fullest potentiality. High student motivation, for example, must now become rather more than a desirable spin-off from effective teaching. It must become a primary objective. If media education is not an enjoyable and fulfilling, as well as instructive experience, then pupils will have no encouragement to continue learning about the media after they have passed beyond the gates of school.

Media education aims to foster not simply critical understanding, but critical autonomy. Seeing media education as being, inevitably, a lifelong process has other important effects. It changes classroom objectives in fundamental ways. Media education becomes an education for the future as well as the present. The whole point about media education is that it should develop in children enough self-confidence and critical judgement for them to be able and willing to apply critical judgements to television programs and newspaper articles which they will encounter in the future. The acid test of the success of any media education program lies in the extent to which pupils are critical in their own use and understanding of the media when the teacher is not there. The primary objective of lifelong media education is not simply critical awareness and understanding, but critical autonomy.

The importance of this objective has profound implications for course content, teaching methodology, and methods of evaluation. It is no longer good enough for pupils to process or reproduce ideas or information supplied to them by their teacher (as they do in most other lessons). Nor is it adequate for teachers to encourage pupils to develop their own critical insights in the classroom (though this is certainly important). The really important and challenging task for the media teacher is to produce in pupils both the ability and the willingness to want to go on doing this for the rest of their lives.

In the classroom, this means—as I have already suggested—that high pupil motivation becomes an important priority. It also means that it is essential to teach for transfer. That is, it is always going to be necessary for teachers to move their pupils beyond an understanding of this or that particular issue or text toward an understanding of those general principles which will have relevance to the analysis of similar issues or texts. Pupils should not evaluate on what they know but on how they respond in situations where they do not know the answer. So, it is possible to say, as a further general principle, that:

The effectiveness of media education may be evaluated by two principal criteria,

a. the ability of students to apply what they know (their critical ideas and principles) to new situations; and

b. the amount of commitment, interest, and motivation displayed by students.

Media education is topical and opportunistic. It seeks to illuminate the life-situations of the learners by harnessing the interest and enthusiasm generated by the media's coverage of topical events. It uses the wealth of material and resources produced by the media for educational purposes. This is the excitement of teaching and learning about the media. But it does constitute a challenge to the teacher, who must work quickly and creatively in collecting and organizing material for class use. It is, however, frequently possible to predict media coverage of some events (e.g. elections or major sporting events), and topical material can yield an interest, motivation, and level of cognitive understanding which textbooks and more conventional materials will be unable to match. Further, work on topical issues and texts will be reinforced by students' experiences out of school. This is what make topical issues such powerful stimuli to learning: understandings gained in the classroom will have a direct relevance to, and can genuinely illuminate the world outside of school. As we have already suggested, however, media education is not limited to the topical. Rather, it uses the topical to explore those wider historical and political perspectives generally ignored by the media.

Teaching Methodologies

Traditionally, teaching methodology within media education has taken the form of what may be called disguised narrative in which the real agenda of the teacher has been hidden from the pupils. This manipulative form of teaching was the logical outcome of the paternalistic objectives of early media education, which sought the subtle improvement and development of pupils' media tastes. Central to this methodology was the discussion, a liberal form in which pupils were offered the illusion of discursive freedom within a situation tightly controlled by the teacher.

As media education matured and developed, so did teaching styles appropriate to it. Simulations, practical audio and video work, sequencing exercises, prediction exercises, code-breaking games, and a whole battery of techniques for encouraging effective group learning became, by the mid-1980s, part of the armory of most media teachers. They were techniques which encouraged pupils to take on much more responsibility for their own learning. They were appropriate to the objective of encouraging the critical autonomy of the pupil, since this could only be accomplished by gradually loosening pupils' dependency upon teachers and nurturing confidence in their own ideas and judgements.

But it was not simply the changing objectives of media education which encouraged an evolution away from discussion (in which teacher-pupil hierarchies were perpetuated in disguised form) toward dialogue, which offered the promise of resolution of some of the contradictions between teachers and learners. This movement was encouraged by the nature of the media themselves. For the media equalized teacher and pupils. Both were equally and equal objects of the media's address. Furthermore, the media tended to communicate laterally, rather than hierarchically. They spoke across, rather than down to their audiences addressing them, for the most part, in familiar and homely terms. Contrary to popular belief, the media did not encourage passivity. Teaching, because of its predominantly hierarchical mode, did that far more effectively.

What the media encouraged, given the right circumstances, were reflection and dialogue. Why was this? Simply, the introduction of media images into the classroom offered, to both teachers and pupils alike, objects for critical reflection. The simple act of projecting an image on to a screen possessed, almost magically, the potential to transform the teacher-pupil relationship because it introduced a third element into the classroom one which was just as familiar to pupils as to teachers and one which could be investigated on equal terms, and from different perspectives by them both. It opened up the potential for genuine dialogue. Earlier media education had not taken advantage of this situation. The teacher tended to be the sole arbiter of what was taught and of the "appropriate" conclusion which could be drawn from a discussion. This greatly discouraged genuinely critical questioning since this could pose a threat both to the personal authority of the teacher and to the knowledge with which his/her status was associated.

Ultimately, then, media education was as much about new ways of working in the classroom as it was about the introduction of a new curriculum subject. During the 1970s and early 1980s, one of the major leaps forward in the thinking of many teachers lay in their understanding of the hidden curriculum, and the ways in which the most important educational messages were being transmitted by teaching methodologies. Critical autonomy could not be achieved by methods which actually encouraged student passivity. So it was that media teachers began to encourage students to take more responsibility for and control over their own learning, to engage in joint planning of their courses, and to develop new dialogic ways of working in which both teachers and students could learn from one another as co-investigators.

Finally, what this involved for media education was the development of a distinctive epistemology. Knowledge was not something possessed by teachers and transmitted to students. It was not something "out there" which students had to accommodate to. Ideas and information existed "out there" in the world, it is true. But they were not the end of education, but its beginning. They had to be subjected to critical investigation. And out of this investigation and dialogue new knowledge—their own knowledge—could be actively created by students and teachers. These, then, are the two major principles of media pedagogy:

- Media education offers the possibility, not simply of new curriculum content, but of new ways of working. Teaching effectively about the media demands teaching methods which are lively, open, participatory, democratic, and active as possible, if the aim of critical autonomy is to be achieved.

- Media education has a distinctive epistemology in which knowledge is not so much deposited upon students as actively created by them through a process of investigation and dialogue.

Practical Work

As we have suggested, media education is essentially active and participatory. It is about doing things. And most media programs have allowed students as many opportunities as possible to communicate their own ideas through the production of their own newspapers, radio and television programs, films, photographs and photomontages, and advertising posters and campaigns.

Practical activity does not, in itself, constitute media education, however. In the early 1980s, many media educators fell into what we will call the technicist trap: the belief that media education could be reduced to a series of purely technical operations, and that through their involvement in practical projects, students would automatically acquire critical abilities. Much of this early work was in fact a form of cultural reproduction, as students attempted to emulate professional media practices rather than subject them to critical scrutiny. Far from demystifying the media, this kind of work all too often increased media mystification when students compared their own tentative efforts with the polished products of media professionals. This was a practice which naturalized, rather than deconstructed media codes and conventions.

By the late 1980s, it had become much clearer that:

a. the link between practical work and analytical activities needed to be consciously forged by media teachers. It had to be worked for. It could not be assumed;

b. practical work was not an end in itself, but a necessary means to developing a critical understanding of the media. If students were to understand the nature of media texts as constructions, it was of great importance for them to have first-hand experience of the construction process from the inside;

c. reaffirming the primacy of cultural criticism over cultural reproduction led to a fundamental reassessment of priorities for practical work. Many media teachers now argued that the most significant forms of practical activity were not necessarily those highly publicized (and often time-consuming) projects which called for the use of elaborate and sophisticated equipment. They were very often rather simple activities, doggedly low-tech, and within the reach of every teacher in every classroom: manipulating still images, writing commentaries, editing news stories, experimenting with interview techniques, and the like. Some practical work might call for the use of more sophisticated equipment, but even here most media teachers were concerned to encourage students to experiment with alternatives, and to break or play with, rather than simply reproduce, dominant media forms.

Cultural reproduction, then, is a poor aim for media education. It is uncritical. It enslaves rather than liberates. It freezes the impulses toward action and change. It naturalizes current conventions, and thus encourages conformity and deference. Media education, on the other hand, in raising questions about how media texts are constructed (and might be constructed differently) and in its insistence upon the nature of media texts as the products of specific human choices, aims to encourage in the words of Scottish media educator, Eddie Dick, both "practical criticism and critical practice."

The major principle of practical work within media education at the present time may, then, be briefly summarized.

Technical competence in the media does not in itself constitute media education. Whilst every encouragement should be given to students to express themselves through the media, practical work should be primarily a critical rather than a reproductive activity.

Media Studies and Media Education

Four basic curricular models for media education can be identified within European educational systems:

a. Media studies as a specialist discipline in its own right;

b. Media education as a coherent element taught within an already established curriculum subject (generally as an aspect of mother-tongue teaching, though it may also be studied as a coherent part of art, drama, social studies, etc.);

c. Media education across the curriculum. Here media material may be thoroughly integrated into the teaching of language, literature, history, geography, and the like. At its best, this work may be encouraged and developed by a coordinator, and can even reach into such unlikely curricular areas as science and math;

d. Aspects of media studies as a topic within an integrated (nonsubject-based) curriculum and generally taught by an interdisciplinary team. This form of media education is most frequently found within primary school curricula.

Which is the most effective way of teaching about the media? Should teachers and policymakers be arguing for media studies (a) or media education (b, c, or d)?

The first thing to say about any attempt to set up an opposition between media studies and media education is that the dichotomy is a false one. In order to promote media study, it is important to push ahead with and support developments on as many fronts as possible. For specialist media studies, teaching will have little effect if its approaches do not permeate and influence the ways in which media materials are used and discussed in every other curriculum area. Similarly, the success of media work within or across established subjects seems to be highly dependent upon the existence of a member of staff with a specific and specialized interest in the media.

Secondly, for the vast majority of European teachers, the curriculum slot into which media work is inserted is less a matter of choice than of opportunism. Media teachers tend to take advantage of any curriculum spaces which are available to them. In the vast majority of European countries, for example, media studies as a specialist subject is simply not an option for most teachers, nor is it in primary schools anywhere in Europe. It is possible, however, to suggest some of the general strengths and weaknesses of different curriculum models, and to indicate ways in which teachers might maximize the strengths and minimize the problems of the curricular models they adopt.

The advantages of establishing media studies as a subject specialty are considerable. Virtually all of the approaches to media education advocated in this chapter will be easier to achieve within a specialist media studies department which has its own identity, its own funding, its own rooms and equipment, its own resources and library facilities, and an established status and permanent presence within the school. This ensures continuity of teaching, makes the subject less dependent upon the presence of within the school. This ensures continuity of teaching, makes the subject less dependent upon the presence of individual teachers, and makes possible the serious, long-term development of the subject, as media studies teachers begin to establish contact with one another and inaugurate newsletters, journals, associations, and their own in-service courses and conferences. The outstanding progress in establishing the coherence of media education in the last decade can largely be ascribed to this: the continuing process of dialogue at local, national, and international levels, between practitioners who are wholly or principally committed to the field. And it has undoubtedly been the very success and coherence of specialized media studies courses, and their ability to attract widespread student support, which has stimulated developments across the curriculum.

The "media studies" label is a powerful one. It makes an important statement. It says that the mass media are important contemporary phenomena, well deserving serious study in their own right. This uncontentious statement, however, has far-reaching consequences for the school curriculum. For it suggests that the curriculum should be organized around important issues, topics, and questions, and that the traditional academic disciplines should be thought of as "tools of investigation" rather than primarily in terms of their content. In order to make sense of contemporary media we need to make use of the findings and techniques of sociology, literary studies, semiology, history, politics, philosophy, economics, linguistics, and cultural and communication studies. The "media studies" label sanctions the exploration of those very connections between the political the historical, the economic and the cultural which the traditional disciplines have kept firmly apart.

This is precisely why, for all its short history, the achievements of the media studies movement have been considerable. It has developed genuinely new ways of working with students which have integrated the practical and the critical, the imaginative and the investigative. It has been taught on the basis of a widely accepted conceptual map which is light years ahead of the content-bound syllabuses of most traditional subjects. And it has encouraged teacher-student dialogue by acknowledging the expertise of students and encouraging teachers to adopt the role of coinvestigators rather than accredited authorities (something difficult to achieve in traditional subjects where teachers are accredited experts and do genuinely know more than their students).

These advances are much more difficult to achieve, and may even be put at risk, when media education is studied as an aspect (or subdivision) of another subject. The priorities of media study are then likely to become subordinate to, and shaped by, the priorities of the parent discipline. And, as we have seen, the history of media education provides plentiful examples of such distortions. Past attempts to treat media study as an extension of literary studies, for example, ultimately proved to be a major obstacle to the development of the subject and put the cause of an effective media education practice back for almost a generation.

There have been compelling reasons, then, for regarding the establishment of specialist media studies courses in secondary and tertiary education as the most effective way of spearheading and encouraging developments in media education elsewhere: at primary level, within other specialist subjects, across the curriculum. Yet recently, even in those countries where "media studies" has a distinctive presence, some have argued that there are certain advantages in opting for the second and third curricular models: media education taught within already established curriculum subjects, either as a coherent element in its own right, or as an integrated part of the subject as a whole.

Most importantly it has been argued this is the most effective way of ensuring that every child and student learns about the media. If media education is an entitlement, part of an education for responsible citizenship to which every child has a right, then its incorporation within an established subject is the most effective means of achieving this end. Educational systems which tend to have some degree of centralized control of the curriculum are those in which it is often difficult to introduce new subjects like media studies. The integration of media education into an established subject is, therefore, a strategy born of necessity. But it is a strategy which has a compensating advantage. For if the arguments in favor of a media education entitlement for all children can be won, if politicians, civil servants, and policymakers can be convinced of its value, then the place of media education within the system can be secured.

For some, then, media education has the potentiality to be a "Trojan horse," a progressive influence which can both exist within, and challenge some of the most sacred assumptions of subject-based teaching. The dangers of this strategy are all too evident, however. For a media education which is recuperated to, and serves the priorities of a "parent" discipline would be a major step backwards. It would reduce the status of media specialists, fragment their subject, and consign the movement to a future in which it will be chiefly concerned to hold the line and rerun the arguments of the past rather than to develop confidently into the future.

Media Education across the Curriculum

So far we have discussed alternative curriculum models for the intensive study of the mass media. However, media materials—films, videos, newspapers, photographs, and images—are increasingly used in the teaching of all subjects. And they are frequently used as "innocent" visual illustrations of the topic being taught, rather than as constructs to be analyzed. It is evident, then, that media teachers will need to be aware of the importance of developing media education awareness across the curriculum if only because their own teaching is unlikely to be effective if it is being actively counteracted elsewhere in the school. One aspect of this issue is particularly relevant at the present time.

Hit by severe financial cutbacks, many schools are finding it difficult to provide as wide a range of educational materials as they did in the past, and are beginning to rely, increasingly, upon glossily packaged and presented film, video, and other materials produced by multinational corporations, government departments, and other well-financed institutions and agencies. It is a matter of some importance that such material should not be consumed innocently, but read critically. In particular, the basic media literacy technique of relating media messages to the political, social, and economic interests of those who are producing them, needs to be encouraged as a matter of course by teachers of all subjects.

Some simple ways in which media education may be integrated into other curriculum subjects can be briefly suggested:

History

—The assessment of historical evidence available through the media of contemporary photography, film, newspapers, and broadcasting;
—the sequencing of historical visual evidence in its correct chronological order;
—the accuracy and use of representations of the past in the popular media (e.g., in TV and film costume dramas, nostalgic advertisements, etc.);
—the representation of history itself (e.g. as a unitary, one-dimensional "truth") in, for example, educational programs, quiz shows, etc.;
—the compilation of oral histories via the audiovisual media.
These kind of activities should sharpen awareness of the close parallels which exist between the dominant practices of the media producer and of

the historian; both attempt to represent reality through the judicious selection and filtering of a wide range of evidence. And the danger of both practices is that their representations may be read by their audiences, not as constructions, but as unmediated "reality." Both practices, therefore, have the potentiality for either ideological enslavement or liberation.

The media may also be used by students as modes of presentation within history lessons through the imaginative use of newspaper, radio and TV forms in the reporting of historical events and the assessment of historical evidence.

Science

—The image, function, and status of science and scientists in the media (e.g., the use of scientists as experts in documentaries and advertisements); the scientist as hero (in soap operas) or as madman (as in much science fiction);

—the validity of scientific tests and principles used in advertisements (e.g., via the replication of scientific tests or experiments);

—the integration of popular programs about science into the formal school curriculum. Drawing connections between scientific issues raised by the media and the scientific principles underlying them;

—the exploration of the different philosophies of sciences implicit in, say, advertisements (science as verifiable fact) and documentaries (science as a fertile area of disagreement);

—the creative use of video and audio media by students to present ideas and areas of controversy within science.

Social studies/Political education

—Comparison of media representations and images with information obtainable from other sources (e.g., images of race, gender, the elderly, crime, etc.);

—images of foreigners or the "enemy: in the popular media;

—basic media literacy for all students as part of personal/ social education programs;

—the media and propaganda;

—the part played by the media during elections (importance of photo-opportunities; pseudo-events; the packaging of politicians; presidential-style campaigning; techniques of media population by politicians);

—presentation by different media of specific social or political issues and events.

Language and literature

—The language of the media (the study of generic conventions; rhetorical devices; narrative forms, etc. in the popular media);
—writing material appropriate for media presentation (e.g., radio news stories; TV soap operas; TV documentary commentary, etc.);
—communicating via the audiovisual media;
—similarities and differences between critical approaches to literature and the media;
—techniques of persuasion in the media (e.g., in advertisements or politics);
—popular media adaptations of literary texts.

Geography

—Images in geography textbooks analyzed in terms of their construction of different nationalities and cultures. Analysis of the Eurocentric, sexist or racist assumptions of such images;
—media stereotypes of urban and rural landscapes, and comparison with geographical/cultural/economic realities;
—analysis of geographical films in terms of their construction of a point of view and narrative, and an examination of their rhetorical techniques and ideological positions. Whose interests are served by such constructions? What values are encapsulated within them?;
—popular media representations of the culture, country, or nationality being studied. Television appears to be the most important source of information about other countries available to children. This opens out exciting possibilities for the study of image-regions, those popular images which we immediately conjure up at the mention of a particular region, country or even continent.

Media education across the curriculum: some conclusions. There are, then, three distinct ways in which media education may be developed across the curriculum:

1. Because so much educationally relevant material appears in the mass media, teachers are increasingly responding to the argument that

they should use such material in order to make their teaching more interesting, relevant, and up-to-date. There is, for example, a European-wide Newspapers in the Classroom movement which encourages teachers of all subjects to use the press as a source of lively and topical material. The media, it is argued, are like well-resourced and glossy encyclopedias. Why not make the fullest use of them?

These arguments make a great deal of sense and there is much to be said for a more thorough integration of media materials with more traditional text-book approaches in the teaching of all subjects. Proponents of this view are careful to point out that they are not advocating the use of media materials as a substitute for text books, but as an addition to them. But what this argument leaves out of the account is the vital question of the status of the knowledge which is transmitted to, and received by pupils through the media. Because the media encyclopedia may not be an especially reliable source of information there is a distinct danger in using it, as the majority of teachers appear to, as a transparent carrier of knowledge. In this respect, it is important for every teacher to be a teacher of media education, and to raise basic questions of how this TV program/newspaper/film is constructing the world, in whose interests using what techniques for what audiences, and what the underlying values are.

2. It is evident too, in the teaching of every subject, that much more could be done to encourage even the youngest pupils to present their ideas through a variety of communicative media. There is still too much reliance on producing exclusively print-based responses, yet in the world outside of school print rarely appears without the accompaniment of images. Indeed, print is itself a visual medium, and much more could be done to encourage pupils and students to think about, use, present, and package different print formats and different combinations of print and images, in presenting their work. In addition, of course, photographs, collected images, drawings, slide displays, tapeslide presentations, audiotape and radio presentations, and simple video and film work all have exciting possibilities for the presentation of student ideas in every subject. Even a little encouragement by teachers for students to choose an appropriate media form in presenting their work would allow students to demonstrate any abilities they might possess in communicating via nonprint forms and to develop new skills. Certainly student use of the media across the curriculum is an important and much neglected aspect of media education.

3. Finally, and more controversially, teachers of every subject should think of ways of moving beyond even critical explorations of educationally orientated media material. They need to take the impact of popular media representations of their subject very seriously indeed. For the media are not encyclopedias. Children and students do not use them as they might use reference books. They use the media, as we all do, much more casually for relaxation and enjoyment. What they pick up are, along with many interesting and stimulating ideas, all kinds of misconceptions, prejudices, stereotypes, and assumptions about all kinds of subjects. The media are less encyclopedias than a kind of bizarre alternative curriculum, the impact of which all teachers will need to take into account if they are to teach effectively.

So, when a teacher of any subject begins to teach a class, she should be aware that her students will not have blank minds on her subject. They will be bringing into the room with them all kinds of representations, insights, ideas, and misconceptions, many of them fragmented, but some of them remarkably coherent, which have been picked up from advertisements, soap-operas, and popular entertainment programs, as well as from news media, films, and magazines. Only when all teachers take seriously the ideas, assumptions, and representations of the topics they are teaching which already exist in students' heads will they be making the fullest use of the media for their subjects.

The Role of Parents in Media Education

Parental understanding and support is vital to the successful development of media education, and many media teachers regard the forging and strengthening of links with parents as one of their most important priorities. It is important for media teachers to open up lines of communication with parents as early as possible, preferably even before any teaching has begun, in order to explain precisely what they hope to achieve, to describe the kinds of activity that students will engage in, and to explore the active role that parents themselves might play in the media education of their children. This is not a counsel of perfection. Without parental understanding and support, media education is likely to run into major difficulties. This is because:

1. Media education will not simply be a new subject area for most parents, but one which will be especially open to misinterpretation and

misunderstanding. For example, without some form of teacher explanation, the introduction of popular television programs into the classroom is likely to be regarded by many parents with suspicion and even hostility. On the other hand, when parents are kept informed of the teacher's intentions, our experience has been that they are strongly supportive, and complaints and misunderstandings rarely arise.

2. In fact, media teachers have to make some contact with parents. This is because media education is likely to impinge upon domestic habits of media consumption. Without some form of teacher intervention, conflict is likely to be provoked by pupils going home and insisting that they must watch a particular program, "because the teacher has told us to." It is vital, therefore, for the media teacher to assure all parents, before the course begins, that, though it might occasionally be useful for pupils to watch particular TV programs, this will never be essential.

Parents can do more than simply support from the sidelines, however. For the most part children watch TV with their parents, and parents should be encouraged to make that experience as stimulating and communal an activity as possible. It is not that parents should be encouraged to "tell" their children things. They might, rather, think of using television as a way of encouraging dialogue with their children about the representations on the screen, perhaps playing prediction games with them (What's going to happen next? How's it going to end?), and generally sharing their perceptions, pleasures, and understandings.

Our own experience has been that some parents start to become very interested in the subject themselves, and begin to consider the media in a new way. They have even asked for the titles of books they might read. Many media teachers have organized evening workshops specifically for parents in order to encourage this kind of interest, whilst others have taken exhibitions and displays of children's media work into local community bases such as libraries and community centers. Media teachers have also been successful in persuading local and national media to take an interest in their work. If some topical "peg" can be found on which to hang the item, the media have been very willing to cover stories in which children are involved in media production or analysis, and many media teachers have taken advantage of this kind of coverage to inform a wider parental and public audience about their work.

So there are plenty of opportunities for media teachers to engage the interest and active support of parents. Since, as we have suggested, some contact with parents is an inevitable part of media education, it will be in the interests of teachers to think carefully about how they should go about this. The adoption of a strategic plan for involving parents will almost certainly prove rewarding for all parties—teachers, students, and parents—and considerably enhance the quality of the media education which the school offers.

The Role of Media Professionals in Media Education

Collaboration between media teachers and media professionals (journalists, broadcasters, advertisers, photographers, etc.) can also have a major impact upon the success and quality of media education. Indeed, to be effective, any media teacher will need to develop a wide range of contacts within the media industries in order to keep abreast of current developments. In general, media teachers do not think of themselves as media experts. They know that they do not and can not possess the experience and knowledge of many professionals working in the media, and they seek to use the day-to-day understanding of their work which professionals possess by inviting them to work with and talk to their pupils and students.

Before considering some simple steps which media teachers can take in order to develop collaborative relationships with media professionals, one should consider some of the major obstacles which exist to this kind of cooperation. For, in spite of the possible benefits, contacts between teachers and media professionals are frequently characterized by a high degree of mutual hostility and distrust. When teachers and media people do get together, they need to be aware that they are entering a minefield of possible confusions and misunderstandings.

Conclusions

In attempting to clarify the obstacles to effective collaboration between media teachers and practitioners, it has been necessary to draw what may seem an overly pessimistic picture. However, there are a number of simple steps which teachers can take to encourage such collaboration:

1. First of all, an active attempt should be made to counteract the misconceptions and obstacles analyzed above. Media teachers can assure professionals that they are not concerned to grind any particular

moral or political axe, but to increase their students' understanding of the mass media. In order to achieve this, they need as much professional help as they can get.

2. In general, media educators make few claims to expertise in the media. They can claim some expertise in pedagogics, and they do attempt to keep themselves as well-informed on current developments in, and academic studies of the media. They make no claims to match the on-the-job expertise of media professionals. Indeed, they need access to that expertise in order to teach effectively. And because they are interested and well-informed outsiders, they do sometimes possess a critical distance on media practices which it is difficult for media professionals to achieve.

3. Media teachers should, however, leave practitioners in no doubt that their contribution to media education should not be a form of public relations. To this end they should seek out those professionals who are prepared to talk about their own work and the problems and difficulties they face since it is invaluable for students to have an insight into those areas where professionals disagree. Media education is a critical (though not a negatively critical) activity in which students will need to reach their own conclusions on the basis of the best—albeit often conflicting—evidence which is available.

4. Once the ground has been cleared of basic misconceptions, an important question still needs to be asked by media teachers: "Why should media practitioners get involved in media education? What is in it for them?" Media teachers wishing to involve practitioners will need to come up with some convincing answers. There are some, we believe. Responsible journalists and broadcasters are generally very interested in public responses to the media, especially given the fact that most of them often receive surprisingly little feedback on their work. The very existence of responsible journalism depends upon the prior existence of a responsible and well-informed audience. Journalists have a vested interest in the creation and sustenance of such an audience. Without it, press and broadcasting freedom would quickly atrophy. We accept that many media professionals will have neither the time nor the inclination to involve themselves with media education. Our own experience, however, has been that large numbers of journalists are concerned about issues of press and broadcasting freedom, and are willing to participate in activities which support and defend it. And many, too, are very attracted by the possibility of attaining direct access to an important segment of their present and future audiences.

5. Finally, we should mention here our own view that a major reconstruction and reconceptualization of teacher-practitioner relationships is an urgent priority for the future. It is a matter of the greatest importance that these two groups should not see themselves, defensively, as being on opposite sides of the media fence: the producers versus the critics. Rather, they need to understand their commonality of purpose in relation to the long struggle to safeguard and extend democratic values. This is an issue which we will address in some detail in our next section on the future of media education, and it is to a consideration of future policies and priorities that we will now turn.

Media Education in the 1990s

Aims and Objectives

In considering some of the ways in which media education might develop in the 1990s, it is necessary, as always, to reassess fundamental objectives. During the 1980s, media education attempted to respond to a number of quite specific contemporary developments:

— the saturation of all contemporary societies by the media, and the high rate of media consumption by individuals. Media education constituted an attempt to ground learning in the experiences of the learners, and to illuminate an important aspect of their experience;

— the influence of the media as consciousness industries; their construction of social knowledge, their setting of public agendas, their relaying of dominant definitions, their control of representations;

— the growth in the management and manufacture of information (particularly by national governments and states) and its dissemination by the media;

— the fast-growing national and international pressures to privatize information and to treat information as a commodity. Applying the "disciplines" of the market place to public information systems and institutions (public service media, educational institutions, museums and libraries, subsidized theaters, etc.) has resulted in a withering away of the philosophy that information and ideas have an inherently social and public function. Ultimately, as Herbert Schiller has pointed out, this affects the kind of information which gets produced; information and ideas which are profitable, or which serve the interests of those which wealth and power, rather than ideas which are socially useful;

— the increasing penetration of media into our central democratic processes. Even in the most limited sense of "democracy"—of exercising, on a rational basis, one's right to vote, or of assessing the policies of political parties—media education clearly has a vital role, given that national elections are now essentially media events, and political leaders are packaged and marketed like products. On a wider definition of "democracy," media literacy is even more essential. The democratization of institutions, and the long march toward a truly participatory democracy, will be highly dependent upon the ability of majorities of citizens to take control, become effective change agents, make rational decisions, (often on the basis of media evidence), and to communicate effectively perhaps through an active involvement with the media. It is in this much wider sense of "education for democracy" that media education has seen itself as having an important role.

Many of these trends will continue to be relevant into the 1990s. The 1990s will also be an era of deregulated, multichannelled broadcasting and narrowcasting, of interactive cable systems, of television data systems, of the everyday use by majorities of people of video-cassette and disc materials, and of a general convergence of advanced media and computer technologies.

But it will also be an era in which the media themselves will be central to debates about the future orientation of European culture. Though these debates take place, at the moment, within the parameters of concern about national cultures, it will become clear, through the 1990s, that these issues and concerns cross national boundaries just as surely as do the media themselves. It is proper to speak here of "European culture" since, throughout Europe, the media have traditionally played a role of cultural as well as commercial significance. Here, we are not simply thinking of the support which national broadcasting organizations have given to the traditional arts such as music or drama.

Rather, we are pointing to the undoubted fact that, whereas in the United States broadcasting has been seen primarily as an instrument for selling, a way of delivering customers to advertisers, in Europe it has played a pivotal role in the development of culture as a whole. Whereas in the U.S. most of the output of radio and television is regarded as culturally and socially impoverishing, even by those who work in them, in Europe, broadcasting has been arguably an instrument of some cultural and social enrichment. What is certain is that the issue of whether

European broadcasting systems can retain a strong commitment to public service—a commitment, that is, to the production not simply of audiences, but of high-quality programs—will be a question upon which the future of popular European culture as a whole will turn. Media education can play an important part in this debate by helping to create the informed and articulate public opinion on which an effective expression of the public interest and the future of a public service are dependent.

The future of European media is not only central to the future of European culture generally. It will also continue to be central to the future democratic health of European societies. All of the signs are that, across Europe, the 1990s will see a continued exponential growth in the public relations industries, in the management and manufacture of news and information, and in the engineering of public consent. In this situation, it is fast becoming difficult to see European media as healthy bastions of free speech, essential to the preservation of our democratic freedoms. They appear, rather, to provide a readier platform to societies' established interests. One of the greatest areas of inequality across Europe lies in the gap which exists between those who have access to the media and those who do not, between those who have the power to define and those who are always defined, between those who are allowed to speak about the world as they know and understand it and those whose experiences are inevitably framed for them by others. The development of a widespread critical consciousness in relation to media issues must, we believe, be one of the starting points for challenging these inequalities and raising questions about the democratic structures and responsibilities of broadcasting, and questions of human rights in relation to communication issues.

We believe that this is a task worthy of the dedication of media educators, but not of them alone. Both the cultural and wider political questions raised by the future of media developments in Europe are, of course, also of the greatest concern to journalists and broadcasters themselves, as well as to a very wide public constituency. Media teachers should see themselves in the 1990s as one constituency amongst many who are concerned to preserve, and where possible extend, democratic values within European media.

The general but important objectives for media education—to articulate the public interest, and to extend democratic values within and through European media—suggest some immediate strategies and priorities for media education in the 1990s.

The Defense and Transformation of Public Information Systems

All teachers working within public educational systems have a *de facto* commitment to the principles of open and universal access to information, such access providing for their pupils the basis for their future participation in a democracy. This commitment to universal access is also necessarily a commitment to preserving the independence of at least some information producers and centers (public service broadcasting systems, educational institutions and research centers, public libraries, galleries and museums, etc.) from undue commercial or governmental interference. For without such independence, access is of little value. Indeed, it may be as positively dangerous as drinking from a contaminated well.

These commitments cannot and should not be expressed as a narrow and uncritical partisanship, but rather as an open and generous allegiance to democratic values, an allegiance which is in harmony with the impulses of progressive movements everywhere, north and south, east and west. For their part, pupils and students will need to consider the issues and make up their own minds. Where public service media remain, as they frequently do, under the control of narrowly based bureaucracies or social elites, it will be necessary not simply to defend, but to transform them. This is now distinctly possible. Paternalistic forms of public service media are being shaken to their foundations, either by the onset of deregulation or by the forward march of democratic political movements. The sole justification of such media—that they do indeed serve the public interest—is being subjected to an unprecedented degree of critical scrutiny.

Under this pressure, there has been a discernible movement toward greater public accountability and democratic control of public service broadcasting. At the end of the 1980s, choices for public service media systems could scarcely be starker. If they do not strengthen their democratic and representative bases, they are unlikely to survive into the twenty-first century.

But, as always, the expression of democratic interests is dependent upon the existence of an educated and informed public. It is the role of the media teachers to beckon that public into existence on media issues. Hence, the priority which media education programs will need to give to a consideration of public policy issues, and hence the case for media teachers to reverse over a decade's nonjudgemental teaching, and actively to present the case for the defence and transformation of public information systems. We are not suggesting here that teachers necessarily teach directly about the issues of public service versus commercial media, but that is a theme which will need to be consistently addressed via the detailed study of specific media texts.

Closer Collaboration with Media Professionals

The 1990s will have to see a reversal of the mutual misunderstandings and antipathies which characterized relationships between media teachers and media professionals for much of the 1980s and which we have described in the second section. There, we noted the extent to which the values of the school and the media (the teacher and the journalist) have traditionally stood in opposition to one another. In the 1990s, we will have to pay much more attention to what the two professions have in common. Once recognized, the parallels are remarkable.

Teachers and journalists are both concerned with one of contemporary societies' most important functions: the production, circulation, distribution, and (crucially) the legitimation of information and ideas. Both are powerful creators and mediators of public consciousness, of social knowledge. Both have an important ideological role in the societies they serve, hence, the interest taken in the sphere of education and media by political and social elites. Workers in each of these spheres are faced with often quite stark choices. Their work may have either a liberating or an enslaving function. They may carry out either a responsible or a debased version of their craft. The stark choice lies in their relationship to the information and ideas they handle. It may be reproductive: a passing on of approved or official representations of reality which have their origins elsewhere (in the text book; in the press release; in the government edict). Or, it may be critical, and informed judgement of the validity of "official" accounts in the light of the available evidence. Teachers and journalists alike may have a sense of themselves as functionaries whose independence is severely constrained by the hierarchies of the institutions within which they work. Or they may think and act as professionals exercising their autonomous judgement on the basis of their own experience and knowledge. Good teachers and journalists share a sense of idealism, a sense of the wider values at stake in their work.

The parallels which exist between the roles and functions of journalists/broadcasters and teachers should encourage a revaluation of the ways in which each profession thinks and relates to the other. Of course, in teaching about news, for example, media teachers will still want to stress the inevitably selective, constructed, and value-laden nature of news production. They will still wish to interrogate the professional routines and practices of working journalists and to question the myth of news's ideological neutrality. But this important and necessary work has frequently been accompanied by a certain slippage into a position in which all journalists and broadcasters are cast as unwitting and unreflective dupes of ideologies embedded and naturalized in their own professional practices. For some Marxists this position is a necessary extension of the belief that the media are either ideological state apparatuses or the tools of dominant capitalist institutions. It is the hoariest and most vulgar Marxist position of all. Yet, every decade or so it is represented as the latest intellectual revelation (for the most recent version see Noam Chomsky and Edward Herman's "propaganda model" of the mass media).

The problem with that position is that it is crudely deterministic. It discourages reflection upon real journalistic practice because its conclusions are already assured. They are entailed by the argument's premises. It is a visionary position, claiming for itself the high ideological ground, whilst placing working journalists in a situation in which they can never win. It matters little, on this analysis, whether the journalist is well informed, responsible and critical, or a passive conduit for approved information and ideas. In that sense, the argument is profoundly un-Marxist because it is undialectical.

In failing to see journalism as a site for struggle between contending values and ideas, in failing to analyze and work with the contradictions of journalistic practice, it absolves itself from any commitment to that struggle. It misses out on the real problems facing real journalists. And it represents a signal failure to support and defend one of the slender threads upon which media freedom and independence actually hang today: the willingness and ability of at least some journalists to insist upon making their own independent and informed judgements in spite of the political, commercial, and institutional pressures to do otherwise.

As media teachers, we need to be explicit in the 1990s about what we would define as acceptable journalistic practice, and be prepared to defend that practice, wherever we encounter it. We have, of course, a further role to play. If journalistic integrity is vital to media freedom, so too is the existence of an informed and skeptical public audience. The two are interdependent. Without the existence of one, the other dies. That is why good journalists and media teachers have to be mutually supportive. Not only do they share common objectives; each is responsible for creating the conditions in which the other can thrive. Effective lines of communication between media teachers and media workers need to be established as a matter of some priority for the 1990s.

Building National and International Media Education Networks

In spite of the progress made by media education over the past decade, it is worth reminding ourselves that many European countries are still undergoing a period of profound educational conservatism and retrenchment in which even "established" creative arts subjects as drama, art, and music are under threat, and are given low status and decreasing resources in the face of the increasing dominance of utilitarian and instrumental philosophies of education.

In this situation, the ability of media educators to organize themselves and to participate in and influence public debate by putting their case as forcibly as possible becomes of paramount importance. The case for the future of media education is a formidable, even an overwhelming one. But without the practice of a lively and energetic educational politics, it is a case which is likely to go by default. What this means in practical terms is that:

a. At school level, as we have suggested, media teachers have to do more than simply teach their subject. They must become advocates for it, advancing its cause wherever they can within their own institutions, and amongst students, colleagues, parents, and policymakers;

b. At local and national levels, media teachers and policymakers need to build up support networks to share ideas and resources. The most successful national media associations currently existing—in Scotland and Australia—have in common the fact that they are national networks of strongly autonomous regional and local groups. They have a federal rather than a centralized structure, and this allows a sharing of responsibilities for organizing conferences and producing journals, and ensures that the organization maintains close contact with the grass-roots constituency from which it has developed;

c. At the international level, the exchange of resources, ideas, and personnel between English-speaking cultures is already highly efficient.

Books and materials produced in the UK, Australia, and Canada have an immediate international market, and English-speaking media teachers can now benefit from a wealth of ideas and resources that have been generated across three continents. European cooperation has faced greater difficulties, but has received much encouragement from a whole range of conferences for teachers organized by the Council of Europe, whilst the opening up of the European Economic Community in 1992 presents even greater opportunities for cooperation between media educators throughout the continent. Even in the most difficult, yet most important field of all—collaboration between media education agencies and teachers in developed and developing countries—important progress has been made in a series of international conferences (and associated publications) organized by Unesco. This kind of international collaboration may appear remote from the specific concerns of individual media teachers working within their own classrooms. But it isn't.

For it has produced genuinely better and more mature ideas which have affected media education philosophy and practice across the world; it has validated, disseminated, and given all teachers access to the best ideas wherever they have been produced; it has built confidence and cemented a growing realization that media education is now a great international movement; and it has produced a number of formal international declarations and statements on media education which have given invaluable support to teachers working on media education policy documents in their own schools. There are, in short, many good reasons why media teachers should both know about international developments in their subject, and seek to participate in them in the future.

Worldwide Foundation Courses in Media Literacy
as an Entitlement for all Pupils and Students

The next decade should be one of consolidation as well as development. The publication of the *Ontario Media Literacy Resource Guide* in 1989 demonstrated that the media education movement could now identify with some confidence the constituents of an effective media literacy program. Although in its detail any media literacy program would have to be culturally specific, using local and topical examples wherever possible, there is, nevertheless, now widespread cross-cultural agreement both on the basic components of media literacy, and on the most effective ways of teaching it. It should now be possible to design a basic media-literacy foundation course together with appropriate resources and teaching ideas for adaptation and use in all European countries and, indeed, throughout the world. Such a project, which would have as its aim an entitlement to media literacy for every school pupil, would, we believe, be an imaginative way of harnessing the expertise of media teachers in all countries and provide a specific focus for long-term international cooperation in the field.

A New Paradigm for Media Education: Teaching Critical Marketing

With the proliferation of commercial media in the 1990s it is clear that the study of advertising, as the preeminent influence on those media which survive and flourish, will become central to a media education which is relevant to the 1990s. This will involve a fundamental shift in and expansion of our concept of advertising to include not simply "paid-for" ads, but a whole range of marketing techniques, whose practitioners include not only commercial organizations, but, crucially, national governments, special interest groups, and institutions of every size and shade of opinion. What we wish to suggest is that the time has come for another paradigmatic shift in our understanding of the role and function of the media as a whole, a shift which will be every bit as important as those of the past which we have described in the first section of this chapter. It is a shift which will recognize what must now be regarded as the primary function of commercial media in Europe: the segmentation, packaging, and selling of audiences to advertisers.

Gearing up for Topicality: A Commitment to
the Principle of Continuous Change

The future remains, as it must, clouded in uncertainty. What is certain, however, is that in whatever direction media and information systems develop, we, as media educators, must develop with them. We have tried, in this section, to indicate some priorities for media educators in the next decade. Our overriding commitment, however, should be less to this or that paradigm, topic, or course or action than to the principle of continuous change itself in our attempts to keep alive a widespread critical media consciousness in a period of unprecedented media expansion and development.

References

Althusser, L. (1971). Ideology and ideological state apparatuses. *Lenin and philosophy and other essays.* London: New Left Books.

Barthes, R. (1957/1973). *Mythologies.* London: Paladin.

Council of Europe. (1989). *Resolution on education and media and the new technologies,* paragraph 5. Standing Conference of European Ministers of Education. Sixteenth Session, Istanbul, 11 and 12 October 1989. Strasbourg: Council of Europe.

de Saussure, F. (1974). *Course in general linguistics* (English translation). London: Fontana.

Golay, J. P. (1974). *The introduction to the language of image and sound.* London: British Film Institute.

Gramsci, A. (1971). *Selections from the prison notebooks.* New York: International Publishers.

Hall, S., & Whannel, P. (1964). *The popular arts.* London: Hutchinson.

Leavis, F. R., & Thompson, D. (1948). *Culture and environment.* London: Chatto and Windus.

Masterman, L. (1985). *Teaching the media.* London: Routledge.

———. (1988). *The development of media education in Europe in the 1980s.* Strasbourg: Council of Europe.

National Reports. (1989). *The information society—A challenge for educational policies?* Strasbourg: Council of Europe.

The Spens Report. (1938). *Report on secondary education.* London: HMSO.

Williams, R. (1976). *Keywords.* London: Fontana.

2

An Agenda for the Second Phase of Media Literacy Development

Cary Bazalgette

Campaigns to establish education for media literacy generally pass through an initial phase of fighting for recognition, when high-flown rhetoric and extravagant claims are to be expected. This first phase comes to an end when a level of official approval, usually marked by the insertion of media education requirements in regional or national curricula, signals the acceptance of media literacy as a desirable educational goal. At such a point, now reached in many countries, it is appropriate to examine critically the achievements of the first phase. Five limitations that may hamper further development can be identified: media education remains the province of enthusiasts; there is little evidence about progression in learning; notions of what media literacy actually is remain diverse; there is a gap of suspicion and misunderstanding between media teachers and media practitioners; and there is a lack of research and informed debate. Research should be the first priority in overcoming these limitations. It must be informed by an imaginative grasp of how new technologies may transform media literacy: the increasing availability of digital post-production techniques to educational and domestic markets, and the proliferation of new broadcast and narrowcast channels, will mean that the media-literate person should be as much a producer as a consumer.

One of the most tiresome burdens teachers have to carry is that everyone expects us to know what we are doing. But, however dutifully we go about making our lists of assessment criteria and clarifying our pedagogic goals, and however devoutly we believe in the need for shared conceptual frameworks and common terms of reference, there is always an anarchic little voice whispering in our ears, "Who are you trying to kid?" We need to admit, if only to ourselves, that we never really know what learners are going to remember, what they will forget, and what they will transform into new and subversive ideas. Their capacity to surprise us, to come up with perceptions and insights that we have never thought of, is what makes the job worthwhile.

This is not to say that we should not have working hypotheses about what we are doing, or that debate, planning, and indeed books like this, are a waste of time. But such projects must be undertaken with a proper degree of humble speculation. When the subject under discussion is something as slippery as media literacy, the importance of this principle is even more paramount. Of the many differences that can be noted between education and the media, perhaps the most salient is that the media change fast, and education does not.

Nevertheless, humility and uncertainty are hardly characteristic features of what I am going to call the "first phase" of media literacy development. In some countries, such as Britain, this phase has lasted some twenty years; in others it has been shorter. Whatever the length of the first phase, extravagant assertions and impassioned rhetoric are the order of the day. This is to be expected, however, in a period when a marginal subject is fighting for recognition within school systems which are almost always already in crisis. Throughout the "developed world," the arrangements that were made for mass education earlier this century or late in the last have been well overdue for reform. In many countries such reforms are well under way: some wholesale, some piecemeal, some informed by respectable research, some crippled by shortsighted political interference. In the midst of all this, calls for "respecting our cultural heritage" slug it out with calls for "preparing citizens for the twenty-first century." Within these debates, media literacy is gaining ground. It has generally been supported by the "twenty-first century" faction, although there is no reason why it should not be supported by the "heritage" faction as well, given that cinema is now an older cultural form than the mass-circulation novel was when it received academic respectability in the 1920s.

There are momentary aberrations in this process, such as the British government's attempts in 1992 and 1993 to delete media literacy requirements from the national curriculum for England and Wales, only two years after inserting it.[1] But overall, it is reasonable to expect that school curricula in most "developed countries" will include some kind of requirement to pay attention to audio-visual as well as print media. Such requirements tend to be minimal, since few governments are yet prepared to take the political risk of abandoning traditional subject-based curricula, even though these are bursting at the seams. Education for media literacy—a process which I shall, on the British model, term *media education*—may thus get linked to mother-tongue teaching, or to creative arts, or information technology; or it may simply remain a cross-curricular theme or option. Its name may also be hotly debated: it is worth noting, for example, that the term *literacy,* in its present English usage, simply does not translate into other languages such as French or Spanish. Each name carries different connotations in its own language: "media education," "medienpädagogik," "l'éducation aux médias," "educación para los medios," and so on.

Even so, despite all these variations, the principle of media literacy has been widely established, if only in a cautious and limited way. Curriculum documents tend to make rather generalized and inoffensive statements such as, "Pupils should be introduced to a range of media texts" (Department of Education and Science, 1990). Such caution nevertheless marks the end of the first phase of development. Once it has been acknowledged at the official level, however minimally, that television programs or cinema films could be recognized objects of study like Pythagoras's Theorem or *Romeo and Juliet,* a significant moment has come. It becomes possible to imagine media literacy as a universal right. Such a possibility has huge implications, not the least of which is how to arrive at a universal agreement of what media literacy is, anyway!

The caution of official documents nevertheless comes as a big disappointment to many of the first phase's doughty campaigners. The rhetoric of these campaigns saw media education as essentially radical and subversive. For example, Masterman (1985) was among many who argued that "teaching effectively about the media *demands* non-hierarchical teaching modes" (27).

But what has been the reality behind such claims? Where media teaching has a relatively well-established theoretical base—as it does in the examination syllabuses taught to some 25,000 students annually in Britain at GCSE (for sixteen-year-olds) and at A Level (for eighteen-year-olds)—it draws upon critical theories that are as entrenched and dictatorial as only a new discipline searching for academic respectability could make them.

Where media teaching has no such base—where teachers have little or no formal training—it draws upon the folklore of the twentieth century that we all know so well: "The Child Who Couldn't Tell Fantasy from Reality," "Violent Videos Turned Ordinary Kids Into Monsters," and "When Advertisers Ruled the World." Like all good folklore, these tales have some recognizable relationship with external reality, but their real concerns are with our inner fears and fantasies: loss of identity, moral uncertainty, inscrutable malignant powers. Their healing formulae emerge as plausible pedagogic goals: if children can be taught to deconstruct media texts, the magic mantra goes, then they won't be taken in by the fantasy, seduced by the violence, or manipulated by commercial ploys. Media education, in this scenario, is the pedagogic equivalent of a tetanus shot.

It will be apparent from the jaundiced tone of the foregoing that I regard some of the rhetorical claims of the early media education campaigners (including myself!) as well overdue for some tough interrogation. In my view it would be disastrous for national curricula to import uncritically the efforts made in the first phase of development to define the goals and conceptual frameworks of media literacy. These efforts have been laudable, and crucial to the establishment of an agenda for debate; it is also inevitable that they took the forms that they did. But we must acknowledge that they belong to the initial phase. With the wider recognition of media literacy as an acceptable goal at institutional and national policy levels, we should see ourselves as ready to plan for the second phase. Despite its modest beginnings, this will be a phase in which media literacy comes to be regarded as a universal right, not merely a privilege or a randomly available opportunity for a few.

This will be a profound change, and it will take time. To prepare for it, we should not be wasting time bewailing the shortcomings of the initial institutional provision—which is bound to be minimal at first. We should, rather, be evaluating the achievements of the first phase; a process that is useless unless it includes recognizing its limitations. At present I can identify five factors that are severely limiting the development of media education on a large scale.

Media Education is the Province of Enthusiasts

Of course, this is an advantage as well as a limitation. Nothing develops without enthusiasm, and in education as in any other endeavor there will always be an "avant garde" at the cutting edge of new ideas. But if, for want of investment and high-level commitment, media education were to remain the exclusive province of enthusiasts, it would remain an optional specialty open only to a few. In addition, there is no guarantee that the enthusiast *will* be at the cutting edge, or is capable of remaining there. I have met many an "enthusiast" who is still fired up on twenty-year-old ideas. If media literacy is to become part of basic literacy, then we have to address the enormous question of how to incorporate it into all teachers' initial training, and into their continuing professional development.

Little Evidence about Learning Progression

While it has been confined to the interstices and margins of the traditional curriculum, most classroom practice in media education has taken the form of single topics and projects, visited by a class just once in a year. Monitoring what pupils learn through a systematic and continuing program of media education has thus been impossible. Without such evidence, it is premature to specify curricular goals and assessment criteria. Nor do we have adequate evidence about pupils' starting points. Arguments for media literacy regularly cite the "passivity" and "gullibility" of children's media consumption as though these were scientifically established. Accounts of media teaching frequently exclaim at how readily children take to the work and how easy they find it. Does this tell us that large numbers of pupils are unusually talented, or that much teaching is not challenging enough? The proliferating portmanteau-style textbooks on media education feed a "quick-fix" approach and constantly recycle the same old projects, irrespective of age level: devise your own advertising campaign; do a class survey of favorite programs on TV. What is being learned here? And how could you tell?

Diverse Notions of Media Literacy

One or more of the following may constitute "media literacy," depending on what country you are in and what level of education you are addressing: mastery of a repertoire of semiotics-based techniques for the analysis of visual images; the ability to plan and record/shoot (and maybe even edit) a film, video, audio tape, or photo sequence; the acquisition of a range of critical theories from sociology, or cultural studies, or art history, and the ability to redeploy them in relation to media; knowledge of the history of one or more media forms; knowledge and appreciation of certain key texts (usually films) and the ability to speak or write about their aesthetic, dramatic, or moral values; knowledge of the industrial and economic structures of media industries; a general awareness of the economic and ideological functions of media texts and the ability to identify stereotypes and bias. Confronted with a list like this, teachers tend to acknowledge the value of most items, but in practice, and for want of training or resources or both, few attempt more than one or two, and the last one tends to predominate.[2]

Gap between Media Teachers and Media Practitioners

Although much media teaching thus focuses on negative aspects of the media, such as commercialization, stereotyping, and bias, young people who have the option are flocking to media courses in the hope of getting jobs. Media teachers tend to be ambivalent or uncertain about the relationship between what they are teaching and the professional practices of the media. They range from the explicitly oppositional ("I help them see what's *really* going on") to the enthusiastically partisan ("They feel as though they're making a *real* news story!"). Either way, it is hard for teachers to maintain up-to-date knowledge of rapidly changing industries. It is therefore understandable that media teaching tends to concentrate on what is teachable—and assessable—rather than on the actual practices of production. Thus, storyboarding—rarely used in film and television production except to plan complex action sequences and commercials—has become a standard source of "evidence" about whether a pupil can plan a visual sequence, even if the pupil has never handled a camera. The analysis of visual composition and image sequences takes precedence over the analysis of dialogue, music, and sound effects, although these often carry more meaning. Planning and shooting are more important than editing, whereas the reverse is often the case in professional production. Information about the decision-making processes in media production is sketchy, out-of-date, and often reduced to crude economic determinism. Clearly, teachers cannot expect to reproduce or even communicate the conditions of professional production in the classroom. But everyone needs to be a lot clearer about what an appropriate relationship between media education and professional practice would look like. Media producers and teachers alike have a responsibility here to drop their mystificatory or suspicious stance towards each other and to investigate more fruitful partnerships.

Lack of Research and Informed Debate

Conferences and seminars on media literacy tend to exhibit an excessive respect for the diversity of classroom practice analogous to Samuel

Johnson's famous dictum on women's sermons being like a dog walking on its hind legs: remarkable for being done at all, rather than for any particular skill. Until now it has seemed churlish if not downright dangerous to draw attention to the shortcomings of some media teaching, or even to establish criteria for the assessment of good practice. There has always been some politician lurking in the wings, waiting to denounce all media education as a soft option and a "Mickey Mouse" subject. But we cannot go on like this. If claims for the effectivity of media education are not backed up with some reasonably rigorous evidence, then we have no basis for breaking through the other limitations I have cited.

I hope it is already evident that these five limiting factors do not each require a separate solution. The key to some will open up others as well. In fact I would identify the fifth as the essential stumbling block to progress. The development of systematic and continuing research into teaching and learning about the media will help to clarify goals, define policy, provide evidence about progression in learning, identify good practice, and lay the foundations for effective teacher training.

In order to achieve this, it will be essential to recognize a broad enough definition of "research." Teachers themselves are as well, if not better, placed than academics to study some aspects of the learning process. Longitudinal and qualitative studies of small groups of learners should have equal status with large-scale quantitative surveys. The recording, transcription, and analysis of children's talk, and classroom observation, would be crucial components in almost any study. It will also be essential to investigate the perceptions of learners themselves about what they think they are learning, and why. One can envisage these kinds of research being carried out through partnerships between research institutions and groups of schools.[3]

Larger-scale studies will also be important. It will be as useful to investigate and evaluate the factors that motivate policy and define pedagogic goals, as to find out whether or not these policies and goals have been achieved. The commitment of national institutions to commissioning research, disseminating findings, and fostering debate is necessary if the aim really is to make media literacy a general educational entitlement.

However, none of this will be adequate unless it takes account of current and future changes in the media themselves. The buzz word here for the past year or so has been "convergence." Although media producers themselves seem increasingly unsure about what this may mean, some changes can be predicted now. Whether through narrowcasting on cable or through telephone/computer links, the numbers of channels through which combinations of still and moving images, voice, text, graphics, and music can be circulated are going to increase. In addition, the digital software that enables these textual forms to be "grabbed" from different sources and edited into new texts will become more widely available, in desktop systems, to educational and domestic markets. One of the many implications of these changes seems to be that, for students and teachers who have access to the right hardware, the status of the exclusively written text will inexorably diminish. Writing will take its place alongside other communication systems in new kinds of text; the distinction between public and private circulation will become blurred; "copyright" will be an anachronism and "authorship" a word with many possible meanings. On the other hand, once sound tracks can be manipulated as easily as visual tracks, video, television, and film will no longer be called *visual media*—the term was always a misnomer anyway—and be recognized for what they are: *audio*-visual media. Other media forms are also bound to emerge: video diaries (already the success story of British television in the 1990s), video letters and postcards, outrageous comedy, deeply esoteric satire, home-generated interactive games and, yes of course, innumerable new forms of piracy, libel, propaganda, and pornography. In one scenario, these developments will be virtually unpoliceable; alternatively one can envisage, at least in the short term, a giant leap in the skills and agility (and incomes) of copyright lawyers.

The implications of these changes for media literacy pale into insignificance beside the implications for the very concepts of schooling, democracy, even knowledge itself. Public debate so far has concentrated on apocalyptic visions of the new consumer, doped to the eyeballs by trash on 500 channels. But there are much more interesting questions to be asked about the new producers. A far higher proportion of people in the future will have access to the means of circulating their own audio-visual products to unknown audiences as well as their own immediate circle.

It is about as hard for us to imagine the implications of this for media education as it would have been for the Venerable Bede to imagine the implications of the ball-point pen. But it must inevitably mean that production and critical analysis will become much more closely linked. A critique of, say, a news item or a drama sequence will be able to incorporate a re-edited version, replaying key moments with voice-over commentary, or demonstrating how a different sequence or different pacing could create different meaning. Editing is likely to become the central creative act of authorship, when words (written, spoken, and sung), musical phrases, image sequences (still and moving), drawn and painted shapes (still and animated), sound effects, and atmospheres are all capable of being combined in a single text.

What should today's primary school children be learning in preparation for this kind of authorship? We must be open to the possibilities of experiments in which very young children have access to digital editing and computer networking. I have a video recording of six-year-olds in a London school operating a hefty Panasonic camcorder by themselves with confidence and panache, as part of a project that enabled their teacher to set up the camera, tripod, and monitor permanently in the classroom as an informal resource for children to use as they wished.[4] These children were clearly able to manage the relationship between viewfinder, zoom, camera angle, the orientation of the tripod and the image appearing in the monitor, adjusting these until they obtained the images they wanted. I would hypothesize that they would also have been able to explore editing techniques with equal rigor. The processes that can be observed, as children discover the potential of audio-visual language through play, are complex and extended. Much more work of this kind is necessary if we are to devise even something as basic as a working hypothesis about how children of different ages learn, first, that there *is* an audio-visual language, and then, that it can be used. In order to observe this, teacher-researchers themselves will have to have experience of production processes and must abandon the sense of obligation to come up with a "proper" end product every time children get their hands on a camera.

The longer-term implications for today's media producers are even harder to predict. Will concepts such as "rights" and "ownership" adapt to the new environment? If they do not, then "investment" and "profit" will be redundant too. Reflecting upon such questions revives the radical aspirations of earlier media education campaigners in a new guise: will it be the agile button punching of network-surfing kids that finally brings the Murdoch and Berlusconi empires to their knees? And if it does, what will the kids be doing for a living? As usual, we don't really know what we are doing—but then, neither does anyone else.

Notes

1. For an account of recent curricular developments in Britain see Bazalgette (1994).

2. In a survey carried out by the National Foundation for Educational Research, the aspects identified by the largest number of teachers as "key features of media education: were advertising, marketing, representation, and stereotyping" (Dickson, 42).

3. An example of such a project already under way is the Utah Media Education Project at the University of Utah, Salt Lake City under the direction of Dr. James Anderson and Karen Webster.

4. Naomi Rich's account of this project at Brecknock School, London, will be published by the BFI.

References

Bazalgette, C. (Ed.). (1994). *Report of the Commission of Inquiry into English in the National Curriculum*. London: British Film Institute.

Department of Education and Science. (1990). *English in the National Curriculum*. London: Her Majesty's Stationery Office.

Dickson, P. (1994). *Survey of media education in schools and colleges*. London: British Film Institute.

Masterman, L. (1985). *Teaching the media*. London: Comedia.

3

Media Literacy:
From a Report of the National Leadership
Conference on Media Literacy

Patricia Aufderheide

The Aspen Institute Communications and Society Program, directed by Charles M. Firestone, convened twenty-five educators and activists for a National Leadership Conference on Media Literacy in December, 1992. At this meeting, the group established a definition, vision, and framework for developing media literacy programs in U.S. education, and set up task forces to further its goals.*

Media literacy, the movement to expand notions of literacy to include the powerful post-print media that dominate our informational landscape, helps people understand, produce, and negotiate meanings in a culture made up of powerful images, words, and sounds.

Definition

A media literate person—and everyone should have the opportunity to become one—can decode, evaluate, analyze, and produce both print and electronic media. The fundamental objective of media literacy is critical autonomy in relationship to all media. Emphases in media literacy training range widely, including informed citizenship, aesthetic appreciation and expression, social advocacy, self-esteem, and consumer competence. The range of emphases will expand with the growth of media literacy.

---

* Reprinted with permission from The Aspen Institute, Queenstown, Maryland.

Just as there are a variety of emphases within the media literacy movement, there are different strategies and processes to achieve them. Some educators may focus their energies on analysis—perhaps studying the creation and reception of a television program like *The Cosby Show,* and thus its significance for a multicultural but racially divided society. Others may emphasize acquiring production skills—for instance, the ability to produce a radio or television documentary or an interactive display on one's own neighborhood. Some may use media literacy as a vehicle to understand the economic infrastructure of mass media, as a key element in the social construction of public knowledge. Others may use it primarily as a method to study and express the unique aesthetic properties of a particular medium.

There have been and will be a broad array of constituencies for media literacy: young people, parents, teachers, librarians, administrators, citizens. And there are a variety of sites to teach and practice media literacy: public and private schools, churches, synagogues, universities, civic and voluntary organizations serving youth and families, mass media from newspapers to television.

But no matter what the project, constituency, or site, media educators share some beliefs. Media educators know that understanding how reality is constructed through media means understanding three interacting elements: the *production process* (including technological, economic, bureaucratic, and legal constraints), the *text,* and the *audience/receiver/ end-user.* In a slightly different formulation of the same understanding, they understand some basic precepts in common:

- media are constructed, and construct reality
- media have commercial implications
- media have ideological and political implications
- form and content are related in each medium, each of which has a unique aesthetic, codes, and conventions
- receivers negotiate meaning in media

Finally, media literacy educators in principle agree on a pedagogical approach. No matter what the setting or project, but particularly for formal learning, media educators insist that the process of learning embody the concepts being taught. Thus, media literacy learning is hands on and experiential, democratic (the teacher is researcher and facilitator), and process driven. Stressing as it does critical thinking, it is inquiry based. Touching as it does on the welter of issues and experiences of daily life, it is interdisciplinary and cross-curricular.

Building on Experience

It is ironic and also understandable that the United States is the premier producer of international mass media, but that media literacy education is only beginning in this country. The United States has a culture fascinated with individualism and with the potential of technology to solve social problems. Its culture is also pervaded with commercialism such that, as one participant argued, it simultaneously produces a "culture of denial" about the cultural implications of commercialism. Media literacy is thus an especially difficult challenge in the United States.

The U.S. experience until recently has been that of a blizzard of idiosyncratic projects, typically driven by the passion of individual teachers and organizers. These include the regional media arts center Appalshop's efforts to rescue regional self-images: the Foxfire teaching experiment; the network building of the National Telemedia Council; individual media literacy courses in schools and universities; programs with teenagers; people in housing projects and prisons; civic initiatives in support of the First Amendment; public forums on media influence in conjunction with industry organizations; the adoption of a Girl Scouts' merit badge for media literacy; citizen activism around children's television legislation; cable access programs and practices; youth ministry programs in churches and synagogues; teacher education at the school and district level; and public television programs and outreach activities. Corporate projects and materials, in search of markets for new technologies, have also explored media literacy. This diversity reflects, among other things, the decentralized nature of U.S. education.

In the last several years, leaders in various media literacy arenas have coalesced around basic definitions, approaches, and goals for media literacy. This emerging process has been reflected, inter alia, in the creation of the National Association for Media Education, and indeed in the conference itself.

The experience of other nations, as well as the history of individual efforts within the United States, may be important to the growth of media literacy here.

The Canadian Experience

In Ontario, Canada, teachers built on English and Australian media literacy programs and practices, as well as on academic work in cultural studies. Recently media literacy became a mandated and funded element for grades 7–12, within language arts programs. Integrating it into formal schooling gave it unparalleled legitimacy. Currently Canadian media education organizations are lobbying in other provinces to repeat the Ontario initiative.

Elements of the Ontario success story include:

- a grassroots base with teachers, who first experimented with media literacy and then pressured provincial educational authorities to mandate it in the schools, specifying a percentage of time to spend on the subject in different grades;
- active support from boards of education;
- in-service training;
- consultative staff for teachers;
- publishing of textbooks and teacher-support materials;
- professional organizations;
- using evaluation methods that do justice to the processes implicit in media literacy activities;
- collaboration between teachers, parents, researchers, and media professionals.

The German Experience

In Germany, media literacy or *media competency,* as it is termed, is a voluntary program in the schools, mostly for grades 5–10. It has a broad mandate, with the following specific goals:

- to compensate for negative media effects;
- to lead students to reflective reception;
- to educate students to authoritative use of all media;
- to encourage students to create media themselves.

Germany's media education is beset with the usual limitations of a voluntary program, including poor teacher preparedness (at most a third of teachers get university training in media). Textbooks and ample support materials do exist, although they are not typically tailored to particular age groups or subjects. Media competency classes are now extending beyond an initial focus on electronic media to all information technologies, from books to computers.

Also relevant is a mandatory curriculum in computer-information technology, exemplary in its integrative approach joining technological with sociopolitical concerns.

Initiatives in the United States

Within the United States, both in-service and pre-service programs for teachers have attempted to put media literacy on the curricular agenda. In-service efforts are decentralized and diverse, offered variously by such groups as Educational Video Center in New York, Strategies for Media Literacy in San Francisco, Center for Media and Values in Los Angeles, Southwest Alternate Media Project, the National Council of Teachers of English, and others. The 1993 Institute on Media Education, supported by Harvard Graduate School of Education and drawing on the expertise of leading U.S. media literacy activists, is an example of training that also deepens institutional commitment to the approach.

As well, an adaptable and successful model for teacher training is the experience of the National Writing Project for English teachers, a project of the National Council of Teachers of English. The Project is an in-service, intensive teacher training summer program that is community based and stresses learning by doing. This voluntary program reaches veteran teachers who want to learn better both how to write and teach, and both builds on and creates a community of reference for them.

Perhaps the most sustained institutional effort at preservice training within formal schooling has been at Appalachian State University, where North Carolina's largest teacher training institution requires competence in media literacy and offers courses to that end. The success of that program reflects some useful strategies:

- searching for ways that media literacy fulfills existing mandates;
- finding links to other areas (e.g. health education and social studies), so that media literacy is not isolated within one course;
- paying attention to institutional context, particularly principals and library media specialists;
- training not only for subject matter but also in how to be change agents;
- defining and operationalizing productivity, effectiveness, and evaluation.

The Current Landscape

Challenges

For those who want the heterogeneous experiences of local U.S. individuals and groups to grow into a movement, there are dramatic challenges in the current landscape, not least of which are the rapidly evolving technological possibilities.

Several key things have until now been lacking:

- a *central mission or mandate,* which could unite different expressions with differing goals. Thus, the constant need to differentiate oneself from a rival when appealing to funders has tended to divide potential allies;
- *infrastructure*—an operating foundation, a professional association, a central database and network;
- *legitimacy* of the kind granted by requiring such material in the schools;
- *basic information* on such areas as:
  — What are media literacy success stories, and their lessons for repeating them?
  — What curricula have been developed by individual teachers and schools?
  — What are current educational objectives that might be met by media literacy?
  — What kinds of teacher training for media literacy have been effective?
  — What teacher training objectives could be met by media literacy?
  — What don't people know now that demonstrates a need for media literacy ("pre-testing")?
- *evaluation* for media literacy. Outcome assessment, the measure of a media literate person and the programs that brought him or her to that state, is still in a primitive state; the best extant evaluation models are extremely labor intensive, and come from England and Australia.

Those who see formal schooling as a major target perceive the unyielding bureaucracy of both public schools and teacher training as a major stumbling block. They note that media literacy's natural link with critical pedagogy and the implicit reform agenda in its empowerment goals makes it suspect with traditional teachers and bureaucrats.

Furthermore:

- the school day is presently broken up into approximately forty-five-minute segments, too short for much media experimentation;
- expensive, labor-intensive teacher training is needed, both at pre-service and in-service levels;
- budgets are being cut, while subsidies and release time for teachers would be necessary to encourage media literacy;
- textbooks and curricular materials are lacking;
- corporate media, most boldly Whittle's Channel One, have entered the schools with a commercial rather than educational agenda.

Opportunities

Some of these very problems might also provide opportunities. For instance:

- Channel One offers a chance to enter into public dialogue and education on media, whether as part of the controversy over its acceptance or as an object of critical analysis and media literacy instruction.
- Some commercially funded enterprises, for instance the outreach efforts of the cable industry's Cable in the Classroom, may prove beneficial to teachers who understand how to use them.
- Although public schools may be hidebound by bureaucracy, alternative, private, and religious schools (particularly Catholic) may be open to media literacy projects and programs. The 1992 Catholic Connections to Media Literacy Project will likely have a spillover effect for both public and private education.
- The need for educational reform is patent, and may be the subject of presidential concern in the new administration; media literacy might become part of a reform agenda. Pending legislation such as the re-authorization of the "Elementary and Secondary Education Act" and the "Ready-to-Learn Act" could be sources for federal funding of media literacy pilot projects at test sites around the country.
- The ever-more contentious battle between cable and telephone companies for entering into each other's businesses may provide opportunities to influence policy in support of media literacy. Citizen activism that uses this policymaking juncture to insist on a portion of the resources being devoted to educational and nonprofit purposes could highlight media literacy objectives.
- The frustrations of trying to introduce new material and different pedagogical approaches to entrenched teacher training programs might militate toward creating an entirely new degree instead—an M.A. in media education, offered perhaps to mid-career teachers.
- Teachers bucking the forty-five-minute classroom might be able to join forces with other teachers and thus pool class time.

Toward a Media Literacy Movement

If media literacy is to become a nationwide movement with a coherent image and clear mandate, permitting widely flexible goals, it must take steps to meet some basic needs.

Needs

The growing movement for media literacy in the United States has several kinds of clear and urgent needs:

- *Data.* Researchers need to get some basic information on the kinds of questions listed in "Challenges."
- *Publicity.* Media literacy needs a coherent image and definition, so that individual programs are correctly perceived to participate in a larger movement.
- *Infrastructure.* The movement needs a home in several senses: an agenda-setting institution such as an operating foundation, a network, or an association.
- *Productive relationships.* The movement needs to build bridges with policymakers, with educational reformers, with creative people working within mass media and new technologies, and with activists and officials in voluntary organizations and public television.

Approaches

Participants in the leadership conference took several steps toward building a media literacy movement in the United States.

In terms of *data:* Nodes of task forces, which would involve people not present at the conference, were created to address fact finding in the areas of teacher training, networking, and the creation of an operating foundation for media literacy.

In terms of *publicity:* Two major actions were taken. First, participants endorsed in principle and set in motion the creation of a mission statement, which could become a common platform for diverse projects in media literacy. As well, a prize for model curricula in media literacy was proposed, through the National Council of Teachers of English.

In terms of *infrastructure:* The National Telemedia Council and the National Association of Media Education were encouraged in their respective networking efforts. It was recognized that the movement's diversity was part of its strength, and that networking among efforts was a highly constructive step. It was also recognized that task force efforts, including the creation of a common mission statement, would lead to establishing other institutions, such as an operating foundation.

In terms of *productive relationships:* the conference participants endorsed in principle a test site for media literacy in the schools, in New Mexico. New Mexico now has a media literacy requirement on the books. Thus, this project can become a place to garner publicity, establish relationships, and build networks.

Part II

Theoretical and Conceptual Perspectives

4

The Theoretical Foundations of
Media Education Programs

Jacques Piette and Luc Giroux

During the last twenty years, interest in media education programs has risen dramatically, judging from the number of such programs that have sprung up in countries all over the world. But on examination these programs are seen to vary enormously from the standpoint of content as well as pedagogical approach. Our objective in this paper is to demonstrate that manifest differences among the programs conceal differences of a more fundamental character. They are differences ascribable to unobtrusive links these programs have established with the major theoretical trends in media study. We accordingly propose to systematically describe six typical media education programs—three American and three European—focusing on the role these programs regard the media as playing as well as on the characteristics of the audience addressed by the media. Our analysis will show that the pretheoretical assumptions of these six programs correspond in all essentials with six major trends in media research. This compels the conclusion that, if media education is to establish itself as an autonomous research field or even as a well-grounded pedagogical field, it will have to render explicit its theoretical foundations.

This paper will also attempt to demonstrate that, although most media education programs do not present themselves as enterprises indebted to theory, they in fact do depend heavily on media theory. An overview of the status of media education around the world will first be presented, followed by a brief description of the major media research paradigms. An illustrative sample of six programs will then be analyzed and compared to the theories they are assumed to be affiliated with.

An International Overview of Media Education

During the last thirty years or so, a constantly growing number of countries throughout the world have been actively promoting the inclusion of media education programs in school curricula. Thanks to these programs, more and more students have obtained insight into how major mass media like television, the cinema, newspapers, and the radio impact on their lives. These programs, of course, vary in accordance with the student clientele they target. But they do have one objective in common, and that is to foster the right critical stance toward the media.

In Europe, credit for launching media education belongs to Finland. This took place in the early seventies within the framework of a Finnish program regulating instruction in the mother tongue (Committee Report on the Curriculum Planning for Comprehensive Schools in Finland, 1970; Minkkinen, 1974; Minkkinen & Nordenstreng, 1983). Norway was another Scandinavian country that chose to experiment with media education during this period (Dahl, 1981, 1983, 1985; Ministry of Cultural and Scientific Affairs of Norway, 1983). Denmark eventually followed suit: it created a Center of Mass Communication Research and Media Education which, during the last few years, has been experimenting with ways of teaching a critical approach to the media (Tufte, 1988, 1991).

It was during the eighties, however, that Europe as a whole began to grasp the importance of media education. Swiss educators in the German (Amt für Unterichtsforschung und Plannung der Erziehungsdirektion des Kantons Bern, 1981; Doelker, 1979, 1992; Grosmann & Mayer, 1983; Saxer, 1992; Saxer, Bondafelli, & Härtenschwiller, 1980; Sturm et al., 1979) and the French and Italian cantons (Berger, 1983; Centre d'Initiation aux Mass-Media, 1983, 1984; Golay, 1988; Groupe de travail romand et tessinois de l'audiovisuel à l'école, 1988) devised teacher-training strategies intended to help students cope with the intrusive presence of the mass media in their lives. An identical concern prompted the French government, in the early eighties, to take concrete measures for encouraging the development of a series of media education activities, collectively labelled *Jeune Téléspectateur Actif*. Many government ministries helped implement it. It aimed at fostering throughout the different regions of the country original ways of helping young learners cope with television (Centre national de la documentation pédagogique, 1981; Pierre, 1983). This governmental initiative did not result, however, in the formal implementation of a national curriculum program, though this remains an objective of organizations like the Institut du Langage Total (Faurie-Roudier & Vallet, 1983) and the Centre de Liaison de l'Enseignement et des Moyens d'Information (CLEMI).

European leadership in the promotion of media education has rapidly been assumed by Great Britain. Within that country, organizations like the Society for Education in Film and Television, the British Film Institute, and the Scottish National Council (Cowle & Dick, 1984) have been militantly backing the development of media education. These organizations produce and distribute pedagogical materials of the kind teachers need to help students make sense of the media. They also periodically hold conferences and training seminars that allow teachers to share information concerning their classroom experiences in media education. Teachers in Great Britain have also created associations strongly committed to the promotion and implantation of media education programs. And to help coordinate their activities, they have launched an assortment of learned journals, like *Initiatives* and the *Journal of the Association for Media Education in Scotland.* Moreover, media education and its place within the British school system have been subjected to stringent theoretical analysis by thinkers like Masterman (1980, 1983a, 1983b, 1985, 1986, 1991, 1994), Lusted (1985), and Alvarado (1977, 1992). It has accordingly become impossible to ignore the centrality of media education in the debate today over the future of education in Great Britain.

The importance assumed by media education is reflected in the policies adopted by other European countries and the Council of Europe. Belgium is a case in point: it has created a teacher-training program designed to induce teachers to make an effective use of television in their classrooms (Mediacteurs, 1993; Fondation Roi Baudoin, 1993). Belgian media specialists also publish (in French and in English) the journal called *Educommunication,* a major source of information about experiments in media education throughout the world. Germany is also upgrading its educational programs, and educators there are clearly very aware of the growing importance of media education. Certain administrative regions (Länder) have in effect already made media education part of their school curriculum (Bayerischen Staatsministerium für Unterricht und Kultus, 1988; Eschenauer, 1989, 1992; Schermer, 1992; Six, 1992; Tulodziecki, 1992a, 1992b; Tulodziecki & Schöpf, 1992; Wilke & Eschenauer, 1981). Countries outside Europe are also showing a keen interest in promoting the advance of media education. Foremost among these is Australia, a country that, for more than twenty years now, has been working to develop media education programs for both primary and secondary school levels within the framework of objectives and priorities adopted by the educational authorities of the different States (Benson, Hollosy & Turbull,

1989; British Film Institute, 1990; Canavan, 1972, 1975; McMahon & Quin, 1986; Pungente, 1985). The South Australia Education Department, for instance, laid down general guidelines for the integration of media courses within all levels from kindergarten to high school, then made sure its project would not lack the pedagogical resources necessary for its implementation (South Australia Education Department, 1983a, 1983b, 1983c). The New South Wales Department of Education made a similar decision to furnish media courses at every stage of its educational program (New South Wales Department of Education, 1984). Media specialists are grouped in an association called the Australia Teachers of Media (A.T.O.M.), and they publish accounts of their experiences in media education in a journal called *Metro* (Media and Education Magazine). Only just recently, some of the most forward-looking media scholars in Australia have launched one of the very small number of research projects actually devoted to ascertaining student response to media education programs (McMahon & Quin, 1992).

Canadian involvement in the promotion and development of media education has also been quite conspicuous during the last few years (Association for Media Literacy, 1991, 1992; Carpenter, William & Worsnop, 1988; Duncan, 1988, 1992; Emery, 1993; Lively, 1987; Lively, McMahon, Pungente & Quin, 1990; National Film Board of Canada, 1989). It was in 1989, for example, that the Province of Ontario implemented its decision to include media courses in the curriculum by publishing a resource guide for its teachers (Ontario Ministry of Education, 1989). Ontario's francophone teachers were also provided with a French version of this document (Ministère de l'Éducation de l'Ontario, 1989). Ontario also has the distinction of putting out *Clipboard,* a newsletter read internationally whose objective is to provide information concerning the latest developments in the field of media education in Canada as well as in other regions of the world. Furthermore, a Canada-wide body was created, the Canadian Association of Media Education Organizations (CAMEO). It provides a forum for the various provincial organizations that are striving to implant media education. Awareness of the importance of media education has also grown in the Province of Québec, where community organizations have been laboring now for many years to promote it (Association des Cinémas Parallèles du Québec, 1991; Institut québécois du cinéma, 1992, 1993a, 1993b; Ministère de l'Éducation du Québec, 1995; Piette, 1985, 1991, 1992, 1993; Trudel, 1992).

In the United States, interest in media education dates back to the early seventies. The first program in visual communication was created at that time (Fransecky & Ferguson, 1973), together with programs designed to promote television literacy (Anderson & Ploghoft, 1975a, 1975b). But the movement in favor of media literacy really came into its own when the Federal Department of Education created a funding scheme for the launching of a variety of pilot projects (Boston University School of Public Communications, 1981a, 1981b; Corder-Bolz, 1979, 1980, 1982; Farwest Laboratory of Educational Projects, 1989; Southwest Educational Development Laboratory, 1979; WNET/Thirteen 1980a, 1980b, 1980c; Withrow, 1980). Other university scholars (Anderson, 1980, 1983, 1988; Dorr, Browne-Graves & Phelps, 1980; Ploghoft & Anderson, 1979, 1982; Singer, Zuckerman & Singer, 1980; Singer, Singer & Zuckerman, 1981a, b), in concert with teachers (Kahn, 1979, 1982; Lehman, 1980; Potter, Faith & Ganek, 1979; Potter, Haneman & Faith, 1980, 1981) and community organizations (Media Action and Research Center, 1979) also set about developing teaching aids for use in programs designed to foster television literacy.

But the last decade was also the decade that gave prominence to the "back-to-basics" movement in the domain of education, thereby shifting interest to the teaching of the traditional subjects. Not surprisingly, then, the campaign in favor of media literacy lost something of its impetus. At the start of the nineties, however, it is clear that media literacy evokes strong interest again throughout the United States, though it must be admitted that levels of media education development fluctuate considerably from one region to the next (Dorr & Brannon, 1992). Associations of different kinds have been publicizing the merits of media education, among them the Strategies for Media Literacy (Lloyd-Kohlin & Tyner, 1991), the Center for Media and Values, and the National Telemedia Council, all of which publish informative journals (*Strategies, Connect, Telemedium*).

In certain countries, media education owes its growing vogue to the fact that more and more people consider it to be one of the most effective ways of eradicating the social inequalities generated by unequal access to the means of information. Certain Latin American countries are a case in point (Dominguez, 1990; Reyes Tores, 1988; Reyes Tores & Mendez, 1988); the Philippines is another. In the Philippines can be found organizations closely linked with the religious establishment—Manilla's Office of Social Communications, for example—organizations that are teaching media literacy to the underprivileged. Moreover, countries like South Africa have also committed themselves to developing media education within the framework of programs set up to aid the Third World (Pinsloo & Criticos, 1991).

It should also be pointed out that Unesco has been actively promoting media education since the early sixties. It has done this by periodically organizing international conferences and using some of its publications to describe experiments in media education development conducted by a variety of countries (Geretschleager, 1987; Unesco, 1977, 1982, 1984). In 1978, moreover, Unesco commissioned the media specialist Sirkka Minkkinen to create a prototype media education program whose features would recommend it to users all over the world (we will be examining it later) (Minkkinen, 1978). Unesco's interest in media education stems from its conviction that this type of education provides an innovative solution to the problems generated by the tight control, international in scope, that the industrialized nations maintain over the principal means of communication. Media education accordingly becomes a feasible way of creating the new world system of information advocated by the MacBride Report.

Current Developments in Media Education Research

Media education is in the process of attracting the attention of increasing numbers of leading scholars throughout the world. More and more of them are closely identifying themselves with media education, declaring it to be their chief research field. Every year these media education specialists flock to international conferences in order to disseminate the results of their research. They also publish these results in a growing number of learned journals devoted to media education. It would accordingly not be rash to say that media education is progressively acquiring the status of a new autonomous field that stands somewhere between the sharply discriminated spheres of education and communication. The partisans of media education are urging its recognition as a specific field of research with links to the broader field of mass communication. Some are even inclined to regard it as an autonomous discipline, as is apparent from a decision reached by the International Association of Mass Communication Research (IAMCR) at its Congress in Brazil in August, 1992. This decision affirms media education's right to be considered an autonomous section of IAMCR deliberations, and not merely a topic to be raised in one of its many workshops, as had been the case before. Now IAMCR, as is well-known, has many European scholars on its roster with enviable reputations in the field of mass communication. The fact that such people regard media education as yet another important facet of the sphere of mass communication lends weight to the claims put forward by the partisans of media education.

Until recently, it was certainly the case that developments in the field of media education were not being as efficiently reported as they could have been. For this reason, schools found it difficult to ascertain how well studies in media education were progressing at an international level. The outlook seems to be much brighter now. Carefully crafted investigations into how media education is developing worldwide are now becoming available (Brown, 1991; Geretschlaeger, 1987; Unesco, 1977,1982, 1984; Piette, 1993).

A cursory examination of media education literature does, however, reveal that relatively few studies focus on the theoretical foundations of media education. This is true even in the case of the studies commissioned by Unesco; it is pointless trying to find in these studies comparative analyses bearing upon the theoretical foundations of media education. Their authors are primarily concerned with describing the features of existing programs: their objectives, the circumstances surrounding their implantation, and their prospects of development. Basically the same criticism might be levelled at the journals concerned with mapping international developments in media education; more often than not, such journals confine themselves to giving factual descriptions of existing programs.

When the theoretical foundations of media education do come under scrutiny, it is always with reference to the broader educational process. The British scholar Masterman, for example, has for many years been laying down theoretical guidelines for the proper implantation of media education programs. His approach has generated considerable controversy within education circles. For him, as for numbers of other British theoreticians, media education has to be viewed as a radical departure from traditional practices in education. In their view, media education affords educators a unique opportunity to enrich the curriculum with courses specifically devoted to mass culture, a topic consistently spurned by the educational establishment. Masterman argues that media education is capable of radically altering the elitist character of a system of education mired in tradition. It is possible, he claims, to set up an educational system that is hospitable to culture in its myriad forms—a system whose philosophical underpinnings can be found in the thought of Paolo Frere, and which motivates the student to leaven his or her mind with the culture of the mass media. Masterman's innovative views can be studied with reference to a variety of contexts, but it is quite clear that he had the British education system in mind when he elaborated them. And we particularly have to deplore the fact that he has shaped his proposals for educational reform while virtually ignoring what is being done along those lines in other regions of the world. Masterman's colleagues in Great Britain suffer from the same narrow limitation of outlook. They discuss media education solely with reference to the future of the British educational system.

Toward a Communication-Oriented Approach

There is yet another way of coming to grips with the theoretical aspects of media education. Instead of dealing with them from an exclusively educational standpoint, it is possible to view them as they bear upon mass communication. One such theoretical aspect worth exploring concerns the nature of the link between media education programs and the theoretical approaches in mass communication. Since media education is increasingly perceived as the connecting link between the domains of education and communication, attention must also be paid to the nature of the links that exist between media education and the theories of mass communication.

But it is all too obvious that, up to now, these links have undergone very little critical scrutiny. In fact, only one researcher has tried to unearth the theoretical connection between media education on the one hand and theories of mass communication on the other. This scholar is James A. Anderson, one of the first American media specialists who, during the years 1960 to 1980, strove to create programs designed to foster television literacy. Anderson hypothesized that there is in effect a very close link between media education programs and theories of mass communication. His analysis has one major drawback, however: it is based only on the television education programs created in the United States during the seventies and early eighties. But media education today has achieved international prominence, and this in turn has spawned a broad range of theoretical approaches that must be taken into account if a true view of the development of this field of research is to be obtained. Nor should we lose sight of the fact that the influences shaping the theoretical approaches are significantly different in the United States from what they are in Europe, which will be demonstrated later.

In this paper, we will make further use of Anderson's hypothesis regarding the connection between the media education programs and the theories of mass communication. It must be admitted, however, that Anderson outlined rather than demonstrated this connection. Our objective must accordingly be to anchor his hypothesis to fact, thanks to the use of a formal grid analysis.

Overview of the Major Theoretical Approaches in Mass Communication

It goes without saying that current theories in mass communication display a considerable number of differences. They propose very different ways of approaching and understanding the processes of mass communication, of ascertaining the influence mass communication exercises on other spheres of social activity, together with the impact it has on the individual. On taking stock of the differences between these theories, we have tried to single out the differences likely to prove the most useful in linking the theories to the media education programs. Two approaches have seemed to us particularly fruitful: (1) the way in which the theories appraise the *influence* of the media (e.g., limited, potent, direct, indirect, short-term, cumulative), and (2) the way in which the theories assess the *nature of the audience* (an aggregate of atomized individuals, or of passive victims, or of shrewd and active consumers, etc.).

Restrictions in space do not permit a detailed and exhaustive description of how theories of mass communication have evolved down through the years. But plenty of scholarly papers have dealt with this question, each of them advocating either different or complementary points of view (for additional readings see Bennet, 1982; Breton & Proulx, 1989; DeFleur & Ball-Rokeach, 1989; Kubey & Csikszentmihalyi, 1990; Lowery & DeFleur, 1988; McLeod, Kosicki & Pan, 1991; McQuail, 1987; Morley, 1980). For our purposes, however, it would be useful to point out in a summary fashion the differences between the principal theories, envisaging these from the standpoint of the two approaches indicated above, namely, their perception of the influence of the media and their mode of appraising the audience. The fact that the American and European approaches have developed along relatively independent lines constitutes a principal characteristic of scholarly research in mass communication. Only recently have research trends in one region started to influence those in the other. For this reason, we intend to provide separate examinations of mass communication theories as elaborated first in the United States, then in Europe.

American Approaches

The S-R model (the "hypodermic needle" approach or the "magic bullet" theory). This communication model dates back to the very beginnings of inquiry into the role and influence of mass communication, that is to say, the period from 1920 through 1940. At that time, the prevailing research approach emphasized the need to study the effects of the media. It was supposed that the audience was essentially a passive aggregate of atomized individuals, while a more extreme approach cast this audience in the role of victims shorn of all capacity to resist the all-powerful influence of the media. The behaviorist model (stimulus-response) colored all speculation during this era. Media messages were accordingly viewed as stimuli impinging directly and homogeneously on all persons receiving them:

> The image of the mass communication process entertained by researchers had been firstly, one of an "atomic mass" of millions of readers, listeners and movie-goers, prepared to receive the messages; and secondly . . . every message [was conceived of] as a direct and powerful stimulus to action which would elicit immediate response. (Katz & Lazarsfeld, 1955, cited by Morley, 1980, 1)

While arousing prominent scholarly opposition (e.g. Chaffee & Hochheimer, 1985), this mass communication model nevertheless came to be known under the familiar names of *hypodermic needle approach* and *magic bullet theory*. Schramm (1971) has pointed out that, at that time,

> communication was seen as a magic bullet that transferred ideas or feelings or knowledge or motivations almost automatically from one mind to another relatively passive and defenseless, and communication could shoot something into them just as an electric circuit could deliver electrons to a light bulb. (6)

The uses and gratifications approach. Research in mass communication conducted in the United States during the period from 1940 through

1950 undermined the victimization view advocated by the partisans of the magic bullet theory. Katz and Lazarsfeld (1955), for example, demonstrated that interpersonal relationships play an important role in shaping the way people interact with the media. They put forward a two-step flow of communication hypothesis according to which the messages transmitted by the media undergo transmission in turn within the network of interpersonal relationships that people establish (primary groups and leaders of opinion). The result is a paradigmatic shift in the way media research is conceived: "a shift from a view of the audience as *passive* to the realization that its members are *active* in their selection of preferred content and messages from the media" (DeFleur & Ball-Rokeach, 1989, 187, italics in original).

This is tantamount to discarding the behaviorist model emphasizing effects and adopting instead the functionalist perspective of mass communication, which has nothing to do with a mass communication model emphasizing effects: "Traditionally, uses and gratifications has been seen as an *alternative* to media effects research rather than as a complement to it, replacing message-driven effects ('what media do to people') with an audience-driven perspective ('what people do with the media')" (McLeod et. al., 1991, 250, italic in original). Thus the notion of a passive audience reacting in a homogeneous way to the messages emanating from the media is displaced by the notion of an active audience whose members rationally and selectively decide to receive these messages in accordance with the gratifications they hope to draw from them. Media message is no more perceived as a single stimulus that can elicit an immediate response; it is instead "a disparate sign which can be read any way, according to the need-gratification structure of the decoder" (Morley, 1980, 10). Capitalizing on the theories of selective perception and exposition, proponents of the uses and gratifications approach contend that the media have only a limited impact that translates, as a rule, into a strengthening of the opinions, beliefs, and behavior patterns of people. Accordingly, the extent to which the media impinge on people's lives would depend as much on individual psychological differences as on the particular social strata they belong to and their affiliation with certain networks of interpersonal relationships.

The cultivation theory. During the seventies, media research came strongly to the fore again in the United States. It reemphasized the notion that the media have powerful effects. Not surprisingly, the hypothesis of a minimal effect, which goes hand in hand with the uses and gratification approach, was subjected to an increasing amount of criticism, and this led in turn to the theoretical reformulation of the effects paradigm. The S-R model, we recall, posited a direct, homogeneous, and short-term effect; but what was now envisaged was an indirect and cumulative media effect, at once middle and long term. The cultivation theory was developed by George Gerbner and his associates in the course of their researches on the influence wielded by television. This theory played a pivotal role in the United States, buttressing the scholarly attempts to reformulate the effects paradigm (Gerbner & Ross, 1976).

The cultivation theory rests primarily on the contention that the media exercise a very powerful influence on all the people exposed to them. The reason for this is that the media have become the principal means of forging the new symbolical conventions that help people shape their conceptions of social reality: "Television, among modern media, has acquired such a central place in daily life that it dominated our 'symbolic environment,' substituting its message about reality for personal experience and other means of knowing about the world" (McQuail, 1987, 283). The studies on the impact of violence in television demonstrate that the ways in which television depicts reality "influence behaviour by shaping people's beliefs" (DeFleur & Ball-Rokeach, 1989, 263). By exerting influence on the members of society, the media may be said to shape the attitudes of society as a whole. Gerbner in effect contends that television's principal function could be the promotion of social conformity and the preservation of the existing social order. This is, at any rate, McQuail's reading of Gerbner's position: "Television is a cultural arm of the established industrial order and as such serves primarily to maintain, stabilize and reinforce rather than to alter, threaten or weaken conventional beliefs and behaviours" (McQuail, 1987, 284).

Such an assessment of the influence exerted by the media totally ignores the factors that mediate between the individual and the media. The individual is in effect perceived as undergoing mental conditioning by media adept at the social construction of reality. Central to this explanation of how the media influence people is precisely this concept of a social construction of reality by the media. The media audience is implicitly viewed as being composed of a heterogeneous mass of passive individuals, shorn of all links with each other, and who come to share an identical vision of the world under the prompting of the media. Gerbner

and Gross have described this audience as "the most far-flung and heterogeneous mass publics in history" (Gerbner & Gross 1976, 176).

The agenda-setting theory. Gerbner and his associates studied the
impact that leisure-oriented media programs have on the creation of new
behavioral patterns. Other researchers, however, were at that time more
concerned with studying the extent to which the more informative type of
media productions shape public attitudes. In 1972, McCombs and Shaw
devised a theoretical framework within which studies of this kind could
be profitably pursued. They argued that the media mold public opinion
through their choice of topics and their mode of handling them. If this be
the case, the media must be said to wield enormous influence, since they
would be determining the relative importance of social events. This is
what is meant by the agenda-setting function of the media. Furthermore,
to accept the hypothesis of the media's agenda-setting function is to believe in the existence of "a correspondence between the order of importance given in the media to 'issues' and the order of significance attached
to the same issues by the public and politicians" (McQuail, 1987, 275).
This is as much as to say that the media exercise an indirect influence:
they do not tell us *what* to think, but what we should be thinking *about*.

The studies that take this view of media action do not deal in any
specific way with the nature of the media audience. They implicitly
consider the audience to be what Gerbner and his associates described
as a mass of heterogeneous individuals. But the agenda-setting perspective does bring into sharp relief the extent to which media consumers behave submissively toward the media, particularly when they are
confronted with topics remote from their daily concerns. Issues that
are national rather than local in scope accentuate the dependence of
media consumers. The conclusion, then, must be that the media do in
effect wield a most potent influence, the more so as their influence is
exerted systematically over a long period of time and in a cumulative
manner (Lowery & DeFleur, 1988.) Studies emphasizing the media's
agenda-setting function may seem, on a first view, to have a meager
theoretical basis, but to criticize them for this involves losing sight of
the broader role they play in helping redefine the effects paradigm according to which the media are the chief agents in the construction of
social reality. DeFleur and Lowery have correctly observed that the
agenda-setting function of the media "can also be seen as one part of
the social construction of reality, or, more specifically, the social con-

struction of shared meanings that takes place as a result of both interpersonal and mass communication in modern society" (341).

European Approaches

The critical perspective: The Marxist approach. The philosophers
associated with the Frankfurt School exerted a dominant influence on the
direction taken by studies on mass communication in Europe. They gave
prominence to the most alarmist views of mass society entertained by the
social scientists of that day, and adopted an equally alarmist stance toward the phenomena of mass communication—a stance colored by a
Marxist bias. Later, and more orthodox, Marxist approaches reoriented
media studies along lines different from those followed by the members
of the Frankfurt School. Nevertheless, a certain number of assumptions
characteristic of this school have found their way into most of the studies
that take a critical view of recent developments in mass communication.

Regardless of the variant forms it has taken, the critical approach
views the influence exerted by the mass media in much the same light as
does the behavioristic model S-R. This means that it assimilates media
messages to stimuli impinging directly on the consciousness of individuals. We recall that the American model dating back to the opening years
of the century regarded media messages as reflecting a complex of values linked to modes of behavior that, socially, were either acceptable or
unacceptable (violence, stereotypes, delinquency). The critical approach,
on the other hand, evaluates media influence from an essentially ideological standpoint. It propounds the view that the media can be compared to a hypodermic needle, because they have the power "to 'inject' a
repressive ideology directly into the consciousness of the masses" (Morley,
1980, 1).

Proponents of the critical approach also agree with the advocates of the
"bullet theory" in thinking that media consumers are passive victims of the
irresistible power of the media. This is to regard the media audience as
made up of isolated, atomized individuals, left to cope alone with the ideological manipulation of the media. What becomes clear, at this point, is the
ideological gulf separating the critical approach from the American model.
The critical approach rests on that foremost bastion of Marxist thinking,
the conviction that the classes constituting human society are locked in
mortal conflict. The media consumer accordingly belongs to a social class

that determines the extent to which he is likely to be influenced by the media. This is of course tantamount to saying that the media are part of the apparatus created by the capitalist system to ensure both its survival and its growth. They are in the hands of a ruling class who uses them as instruments for keeping the working classes in line:

> Media work ideologically by disseminating the ideas and world views of the ruling class, denying alternative ideas which might lead to change or to a growing consciousness by the working class of its interests and by preventing the mobilization of such consciousness into active and organized political opposition. (McQuail, 1987, 63)

The "classical" semiotic approach. Recent developments in semiotics have prompted a variety of novel approaches to media study in Europe, theoretically as diversified one from the other as are the approaches indebted to Marxism. Today there exist many different ways of interpreting conceptual meaning (Tomasseli & Shepperson, 1991).

Semiotics as the study of the relations between signs and things achieved prominence with Barthes (1957, 1964a, 1964b, 1966), Metz (1964, 1966), and Eco (1966); but as a distinct tradition of inquiry into human communications, it was founded by the Swiss linguist Ferdinand de Saussure. Semiotics posits the existence of two levels of meaning: denotation and connotation. Denotation is the function communication performs when it uses the referential language of factual information; the sign it uses means primarily some thing, process, or state of affairs in the world outside language. Connotation, on the other hand, adds to this purely minimal meaning the overtones and suggestions that are not explicit in it. Connotation accordingly acquires a subjective quality that allows us to interpret a message in terms of the cultural and ideological codes regulating social organization. A sign, therefore, cannot of itself connote: its full meaning is a function of the cultural context in which it is used and the ideological overtones it conveys.

Practitioners of "classical" semiotics contend that the media exert a very potent influence because they have become the matrix of the new myths flourishing in Western society. Myth may be said to achieve the status of fact when denotation becomes one with connotation, their oneness seeming so natural that nobody would think of questioning it. In the mythical universe as elaborated by the media, messages progressively lose their polysemous quality, and an image arises of a world devoid of contradictions, a world that, in Barthes's view, "goes-without-saying."

As a rule, the messages emanating from the media can be seen as depoliticized utterances that Barthes likens to "miraculous evaporations from history." These "evaporations" hinder whoever is subjected to them from grasping what they really are, that is to say, "fragments of ideology" (Barthes, 1957). Myth, as Barthes maintains,

> demolishes all dialectic, hinders all attempts at seeing beyond what is immediately apprehensible. It sets up a world that lacks contradictions because it lacks profundity, a world that is concrete because it is evident. A welcome clarity characterizes the world of myth; things in such a world have a meaning independently of anything else. (231, the translation is ours)

"Classical" semiotics does not comprise a theory of the receptor. Experts in this field are totally unconcerned about media consumers. All of their attention is focused on textual analysis. The semiotician may even take the view that for him to take media consumers into account might somehow interfere with his semiotic appraisal of the message. For this reason,

> he excludes himself from the ranks of all consumers of myth; which is no mean feat. The obligation to do so is not so great if the public is restricted in size. But when the myth colors the thinking of an entire society, disengaging it requires the semiotician's isolation from that society. (245)

Decoding media messages amounts, in short, to "isolating oneself from those who find such messages entertaining as well as those who find them morally bracing. The mythologist is forcibly cast into the role of a theoretical member of society" (245, the translation is ours).

The cultural studies approach. Starting in the mid-seventies, the volume of research devoted to mass communication increased enormously in Europe, as was also the case in the United States. Under the aegis of the University of Birmingham's Centre for Contemporary Cultural Studies, Great Britain took the lead in renewing interest in this line of research, emphasizing its kinship with the new trend in cultural studies (Stretter, 1984).

This trend may be viewed as congruent with the critical approach. In line with this approach, it rejects the view that the media are nothing more than mirrors reflecting a reality that is external to them. It maintains, on the contrary, that they are actively engaged in the process of creating meaning. For meaning to be produced, a process of encodement must be used, because media messages are complex signs constructed in such a way as to convey a particular meaning:

Message is treated as a complex sign, in which a preferred reading has been inscribed. . . . The message is thus a structured polysemy. It is central to the argument that all meanings do not exist "equally" in the message: it has been structured in dominance. (Morley, 1980, 10)

The cultural studies approach also harmonizes with the critical one in contending that real insight into the structure of media messages can be obtained through study of the theories concerning the ideological and hegemonic role of the media. Nevertheless, it remains critical of the Marxist view according to which the media are merely the transmitters of the opinions and values of a ruling class. Partisans of the cultural studies approach take the very opposite view that the media afford a kind of arena for conflict between divergent conceptions of society.

In short, partisans of the cultural studies approach reject the mechanical Marxist conception of the media as tools used for ideological purposes. The relation, as they conceive it, between the public and the media requires that public to be active. The media may, in effect, bias to some extent the content of the messages they convey in response to some ideological imperative, but that does not rule out the possibility of many meanings being read in those messages: "The activity of 'getting meaning' from the message is also a problematic practice, however transparent and 'natural' it may seem. Messages encoded one way can always be read in a different way" (Morley, 1980, 10). Media audiences, accordingly, cannot be regarded as passive; they are not made up of individuals victimized by the media. What we have, instead, is

a model of the audience, not as an atomised mass of individuals, but as a number of sub-cultural formations or groupings of "members" who will, as members of those groups, share a cultural orientation, towards decoding messages in particular ways. (Morley, 1980, 15)

But the cultural studies approach, though it does rest on the premise of an active receptor, diverges nonetheless drastically from the idiosyncratic model of an active audience, which underlies the American approach of uses and gratifications. Its partisans contend that media consumers, when they decode media messages, are not prompted solely by their individual psychological characteristics. In other words, their responses to the media are not conditioned only by the needs they might have or the satisfactions the media might afford them: "In this approach, the message is treated neither as a unilateral sign, without ideological 'flux', nor, as in 'uses and gratifications' as a disparate sign which can be read any way, according to the need-gratification structure of the decoder" (Morley, 1980, 10). Hall (1980) has identified four broad message decoding strategies that media consumers apply: dominant, professional, negotiated, and oppositional. Which of these strategies media consumers use depends on which of the different subgroups they belong to, each of the subgroups being understood as having a commonly shared view of how media messages are to be understood and interpreted.

American and European media researchers are increasingly becoming conscious of each other's contributions to media theory. One result is that the new theoretical orientations bear the impress of research trends from abroad. One such trend has achieved prominence during the last few years; the studies it has spawned all concur in emphasizing the centrality of the concept of an active audience. Barriers, moreover, are breaking down between the various theoretical orientations of media research; the tendency nowadays is to regard them more as complementary than as contradictory.

Table 4.1 schematically lists the divergences between the principal theories of mass communication in terms of the way in which they envisage the influence of the media and the nature of the audience.

The Theoretical Foundations of Media Education Programs

In this section, we intend to show that it is possible to uncover the links that theory has forged between the different media education programs. We will do this by laying bare the notion program makers entertain of the influence wielded by the media and the nature of their audience.

In order to verify the hypothesis of an underlying connection between the assorted media education programs and the theories of mass communication, we have drawn up a list of programs, American and European, some of which may no longer be in use today. If they come under scrutiny here, it is because they illustrate how media education has developed as a field of research over the last twenty years or so. Our list, of course, is not exhaustive, but it does have the merit of comprising the main theoretical approaches adopted up to now. We are confident that it will shed abundant light on how the adoption of one approach instead of another results, at the practical level, in some significant modification of the media education program.

TABLE 4.1

Mass Communication Theories

Theories	How media influence is perceived	How the audience is perceived
The S-R model: the "hypo-dermic needle approach," the "magic bullet" theory	Very powerful direct effect. Communication is seen as "a magic bullet." The media "do things to people." Every message is a direct and powerful stimulus which elicits immediate response.	Audience is essentially a passive aggregate of atomized individuals. Individuals are victims shorn of all capacity to resist all-powerful influence of the media.
The uses and gratifications approach	Limited influence. The media do not do things to people, people do things "with" the media. The message trans-mitted by the media undergo transmission in turn within the network of interpersonal relationships.	Members of the audience are active, they select rationally messages in accordance with the gratifications they hope to draw from the media.
The cultivation theory	Powerful indirect and cumulative effect. Television dominates our symbolic environment; it influences behaviors by shaping people's beliefs. The media shape the attitude of society as a whole; they maintain a social conformity and the status quo.	Audience is implicitly viewed as being composed of a heterogeneous mass of passive individuals shorn of links with each other. Individuals share an identical vision of the reality constructed by the media.
The agenda-setting theory	Very powerful indirect and cumulative influence. The media are successful in telling us "what" and "whom" to think about; they impose their priorities.	Audience is implicitly viewed as being composed of heterogeneous mass of individuals.
The critical perspective: the marxist approaches	Very powerful effect. The media "inject" a repressive ideology directly into the consciousness of the masses. The media disseminate the ideas and worldviews of the ruling class.	Individuals belong to a social class that determines the extent to which there are to be influenced. Audience, mainly the working class, is made up of passive victims.
The "classical" semiotic approach	Very powerful. The media have become the matrix of the new "myths" in society; they transform ideological representations into myths accepted as "natural"; they reduce the polysemious character of messages.	It does not comprise a theory of the receptor, but implicitly individuals are viewed as passive recipients of already structured meanings imposed by the "myths."
The cultural studies approach	Very powerful influence. Getting meaning is problematic: message is a complex sign structured in dominance; a "pre-ferred meaning" is inscribed although never fixed; messages encoded in one way can be read in a different way. The media are sites for struggle between conceptions of society.	Media audiences are not made up of individuals victimized, but a number of sub-cultural formations or groupings of "members" who share a cultural orientation toward decoding messages in particular ways.

The three American programs we have chosen provide satisfactory insight into the different theoretical approaches from which were developed the television education programs of the early eighties. They are: *Getting the most out of tv* (Singer, Singer & Zuckerman,1981a, 1981b), *Critical television viewing* (WNET/Thirteen, New York, 1980a, 1980b, 1980c); and *Television literacy* (Boston University School of Public Communication, 1981a, 1981b). We have chosen the following European programs: *A general curricular model for mass media education* (Minkkinen, 1978); *Initiation aux Mass-Media* (Centre d'Initiation aux Mass-Media, 1983, 1984); and *Selling pictures: A teaching pack about representation and stereotyping* (Bazalgette, Cook & Simpson, 1983).

Since we intend to demonstrate the underlying connection between the media programs and the theories of mass communication, we have had at the outset to explain how these programs evaluate the influence of the media and the nature of the audience. We have then gone on to determine whether the alleged theoretical connection impinges in some palpable way on the programs' contents, by which we mean the statement of their objectives, the actual organization of the contents, and the pedagogical strategies they adopt. In this way, our two initial variables, namely, the influence of the media and the nature of the audience, are coupled with three other variables: the overall objective, the organization of the contents, and the pedagogical strategies.

The American Programs

Getting the Most out of TV: The S-R Model

This program mainly targets pupils who will soon be completing primary school. It involves the use of a teacher's manual containing a set of lessons that the teacher is expected to read to the pupils. Along with these lessons, the manual provides lists of questions for the pupils to answer and spaces where they may write their own observations once the teacher has given them all the information they require concerning the many roles television has to play. The program, suitably adjusted, also targets the parents of the pupils: *Teaching Television: How to Use TV to Your Child's Advantage* (Singer et al., 1981b). This adaptation of the original program figures in our analysis, because it provides a more elaborate description of the program's orientation than can be found in the manual designed for the pupils.

How media influence is perceived. The authors of this program quite clearly take the view that television exerts a very powerful influence on viewers. They believe this with such conviction that they do not hesitate to suggest that children should not be allowed to look at television before having reached school age:

> There are some parents who feel it is best for children not to see TV at all until they are in elementary school and already reading. We are inclined to agree, yet most families are not prepared to implement such a drastic policy. (Singer et al., 1981b, x)[1]

They contend that television has an unmistakably negative impact on young minds, particularly when TV shows are violent. When the child repeatedly sees violence on television, he almost automatically becomes more aggressive:

> When we asked elementary school children about television violence, many of the children were aware that TV violence influences them in negative ways. They described how they sometimes imitated TV violence by chasing their friends on bicycles, and frequently described angry interactions with family members. Many children said they were angry "right after watching a program that had a lot of violence." (Singer et al., 1981a, 71)

It is additionally claimed that television also negatively affects the child's personality development: "Viewers of 'action' shows [have] special difficulty in language development and in imaginative play" (Singer et al., 1981b, 11). Worse still, the child, thanks to television, finds himself at a loss to distinguish between reality and fiction. But what worries the authors most is the possibility that children, as well as people of all ages, might mimic the socially unacceptable modes of behavior presented in certain TV shows: "When people see TV characters solving their problems with violence, they will get the idea that violence is a good way to solve problems" (Singer et al., 1981a 76).

How the audience is perceived. This program views the children as being an essentially passive audience. It contends that television's hold upon children results from a "passive-TV viewing syndrome" (Singer et al., 1981b, ix). Children must accordingly learn to respond less passively to televised messages: "The emphasis is on teaching children about television so that they can better understand the medium and what it offers, and so that they can learn to be less passive viewers and more discriminating consumers" (Singer et al., 1981a, ix). One peculiarity of television is that the speed with which it disseminates its messages induces in viewers a "mindless watching, so that by the end of the program there is little comprehension of what has been watched and often scarcely any memory" (Singer et al., 1981b, 7). Another peculiarity is its capacity to elicit a uniform response from the audience: "Certainly it is true that television creates a uniformity of experience across grossly different cultural groups within the country and, indeed, internationally" (Singer et al., 1981b, 9).

General objective. The program's general objective is to reduce the child's direct dependence upon television, thereby attenuating some of the negative effects of excessive televiewing: "This age-group could benefit from intervention strategies designed to enhance learning skills and to reduce negative effects of excessive TV viewing or dependence" (Singer et al., 1981b, xi).

Organization of contents. The program's contents have principally been devised to promote the acquisition of information calculated to help pupils distinguish between reality and fiction in televised messages. It is obviously in line with the theory according to which mass communication victimizes its users; media messages are regarded as acting like stimuli, directly eliciting from a passive public a uniform response. The first two chapters focus on the purely technical aspects of television; however, subsequent chapters are intended to help pupils avoid the confusion that television engenders between reality and fiction. One such chapter is called "The Magic of TV": "The purpose of this lesson is to help children understand the kind of techniques the TV uses to distort reality" (Singer et al., 1981a, 24). Chapter 4, "Characters We See on TV," warns children against the danger of making real people out of the characters they see in their favorite telecasts. Chapter 5, "Action and Violence," explains how violence on television differs from the physical and verbal violence in the real world; it also makes clear that television fails to explore the consequences of violence for the victims. Chapter 6, "The Real World of TV," analyzes the televised newscast. Children are told that television, as a purveyor of news, gives a true picture of the real world; but they do not get such a picture from fictionalized television fare. The last chapter, "You and TV: Who's in Charge?" instructs the children on ways in which they can resist television's propensity to dictate their very thoughts: "In this lesson you will learn how television tells us what to think, and how you can decide for yourself whether you agree or disagree" (Singer et al., 1981a, 105).

Pedagogical strategies. Classroom activities are devised with reference to two types of logs, which the children have to fill out once the teacher has finished explaining what each of the program's lessons is all about. The first type of log helps them to better grasp certain fundamental features of television viewing (reckoning of the number of viewing hours, identification of the different kinds of TV shows, tally of the instances of physical and verbal violence as well as of the number of commercial breaks). The second type of log teaches them how not to mistake fiction for reality. It does this by showing them how special effects distort reality and by explaining why the characters in TV shows are not to be confused with the actors who play them; it also details the ways in which stereotypes create misleading impressions of certain social groups. The pedagogical strategies, in short, are basic to an approach designed to help children uncover the potentially negative features of television viewing.

Critical Television Viewing: The Uses and Gratifications Approach

This program targets middle high school students. It includes a teacher's manual, *Critical Television Viewing: Teacher's Annotated Edition* (WNET/Thirteen, 1980a); a workbook for the students, *Critical Television Viewing: A Language Skill Work-A-Text* (WNET/Thirteen, 1980b); and a training manual for the organization of workshops designed to explain program features to teachers, *A Training Manual for Teacher Trainers* (WNET/Thirteen, 1980c).

How media influence is perceived. This program is not concerned with studying the student-television relationship from the standpoint of the impact television has on students. Its concern is, rather, with the uses that students put television to. What it tries to do, basically, is bring out whatever positive features television can lay claim to. The question as to what kind of influence television exerts is addressed from the twofold standpoint of the use that the young learner makes of television (his or her televiewing habits) and his or her reasons for looking at it (the "satisfaction" he or she hopes to derive from it). The program, in short, aims at helping him or her become a more discriminating televiewer; he or she must learn how to compel the medium to minister to his or her personal needs and expectations. If, for example, he or she is taught how television commercials are put together, he or she gains real insight into the techniques of mass persuasion; this insight in turn helps him or her to shield his or her mind against any excessive media influence:

> If children learn to recognize persuasion techniques in television commercials, they can become more aware of why certain commercials influence them more than other . . . so students become more familiar with the ways of persuasion, they will be able to better evaluate and respond to it. (WNET/Thirteen, 1980a, 70)

The thrust of the program is thus in the direction of helping students to better grasp the nature of their rapport with television. They manage to do this "by charting their TV viewing habits, analyzing the reasons that motivate their viewing and comparing their viewing habits with those of other people" (WNET/Thirteen, 1980a, 16).

How the audience is perceived. The creators of this program reject the view that the media public is a mere aggregate of atomized individuals who take in media messages in a passive and uniform way. The position they adopt is completely different. In the very first pages of their student manual, they affirm that media consumers "use the media for different purposes; for example—for entertainment, for information or for companionship" (WNET/Thirteen, 1980b, 2). And to help young learners become more conscious of the different uses people put the media to, they are required, at the very outset of the program, to conduct a survey on habits of media consumption in their immediate environment. The theory is that, once better apprised of certain features of television viewing they where previously unaware of, the young learners will display a greater readiness to respond more autonomously to messages emanating from the television and evaluate them in terms of their own needs and expectations. Basic to this whole program is a philosophy of media education whose chief premise is the need to help students translate their television viewing into an enriching experience: "It [the program] will encourage children to analyze and make judgements about the [television] program they see and in doing so, they begin to tailor their viewing to meet their newly developed criteria" (WNET/Thirteen, 1980c, 46).

General objective. The program aims at helping students acquire a greater awareness of their needs as televiewers. They must acquire habits of mind that make for a more discriminating attitude toward television, an attitude that reflects their own needs and expectations: "This *Critical Television Viewing Work-A-Text* is designed to help students develop the critical thinking skills and inner resources they need to wisely choose and to evaluate the programs they watch" (WNET/Thirteen, 1980a, 8).

Organization of contents. The authors of the program contend that, if students are to acquire the proper critical stance toward television, they must first possess a clear idea of the uses they intend to put it to. Obtaining this clear idea is an essential first step; students cannot avoid making it without jeopardizing the process whereby they become in the end judicious televiewers. The importance of this first lesson cannot be overestimated: it goads students into circumscribing the precise role that television plays in their lives. The final lesson, on the other hand, teaches them how to modify their viewing habits so as to meet the criteria they have set for themselves. The program's eight other lessons focus on little-known features of the television industry, such as the production of TV shows, the financial returns of game shows, the composition of news items, and the tricks of the advertising trade. The program, however, avoids all mention of industry features that are likely to arouse controversy. Nothing is said, for example, about violence on television or about the values it transmits:

> The purpose of teaching critical viewing is not to initiate classroom debates over values presented on television, but to teach students how to analyze any television program. Highly controversial programs should, in fact, be avoided as students will become distracted from the analytical task at hand. (WNET/Thirteen, 1980c, 49)

Pedagogical strategies. The authors of the program take the view that, where young learners are concerned, acquiring knowledge of the makeup of television programs is a very important step toward developing the right critical stance toward the medium: "An important step towards analyzing a TV program is to analyze and evaluate its individual elements" (WNET/Thirteen, 1980c, 115). Once capable of making this evaluation, young learners are now in a position to comprehensively assess the worth of TV programs: "Once familiar with these elements and how to evaluate them, children can relate them to the programs they watch. They will develop criteria which can determine the merit of the program's content and its production elements" (WNET/Thirteen, 1980c, 115). What this program does, in the final analysis, is induce young learners to adopt a personal stance toward television. Addressing them directly, the program states: "There are no right or wrong answers. In fact, as a critical television viewer, *your opinion* is as 'good' as the opinion of a professional TV critic—as long as you *support* your opinion" [WNET/Thirteen, 1980a, 103 (italics in original)].

Television Literacy: The Cultivation Theory
and the Agenda-Setting Theory

This program is intended for college-level students as well as for students enrolled in adult education programs. It requires the use of three manuals: one for the students, *Television Literacy: Critical Television Viewing Skills* (Boston University School of Public Communication, 1981a); one for the teacher, *Television Literacy: Instructor's Guide* (Boston University School of Public Communication, 1981b); and a student workbook, *Television Literacy: Workbook* (Boston University School of Public Communication, 1981c).

How media influence is perceived. To the question whether television exerts a potent influence, the authors of the program respond with an emphatic "Yes": "Does it affect our opinions, our outlook, even our lifestyle? The answer is yes. Although no one can prove absolutely that TV has altered and continues to alter the American mentality, the evidence is provocative" (Boston University School of Public Communication, 1981a, 3). They also take the view that television exerts its influence in an indirect, largely elusive and insidious way, pervading every facet of the cultural scene: "The fact, however, that television is saturating our culture inclines us to question, to consider the 'hidden' or at least more subtle effects of the TV fare" (Boston University School of Public Communication, 1981a, 3).

Thanks to its capacity to frame new definitions of social reality and to impose new rules and new social norms, television becomes the prime originator of the symbolical conventions that shape social organization: "The medium reinforces and often creates 'rules' for behavior in many social situations" (Boston University School of Public Communication, 1981a, 96). It is even the case that "broadly, television has the power to 'certify,' to 'OK' certain behaviors and values" (Boston University School of Public Communication, 1981a, 100). Television may also be said to fashion the way in which individuals perceive the world around them. In its news-dispensing role, for example, television participates in the construction of social reality by imposing its agenda on the nation at large. Broadcasters in organizing the TV news "look for a way to tie together the day's events in a thematic whole: good/bad, helpful/discouraging, exciting/tragic. Thus, TV newscasts sometimes tend to make the viewer believe that there exists a single, coherent national agenda for the day" (Boston University School of Public Communication, 1981a, 138). Television therefore significantly influences an individual's perception of reality. As the authors point out: "It seems reasonable to assume that who's on and what's on contributes to shaping the viewer's impression of what the world is like" (Boston University School of Public Communication, 1981a, 147).

How the audience is perceived. The program sheds little light on how its creators evaluate audience attitudes. The dominant impression is that the television audience is made up of an heterogeneous mass of individuals who respond in a uniform way to media messages. All of the individuals watch "the same program simultaneously, receiving the same information at once. The factor of simultaneity instantly creates an intense effect on social perceptions" (Boston University School of Public Communication, 1981a, ii). This emphasis on uniformity of response leads the program's creators to talk of the audience in general terms; they take no cognizance of its members as individuals capable of recognizably individual responses. For this reason, when they analyze audience response to commercial messages, they present a rather stereotyped image of the televiewer. The emergence of this stereotypical televiewer is very clearly imminent, according to the program's creators:

> In general, the constant adult and vid-kid commercial onslaught may be turning America's population into a neurotically compulsive consumer society. Basic desires for friendship and love may be translated rapidly into a new car, a doll that sings or purple lipstick. Thus, the population, young and old, may be persuaded that acquisition of "things" will solve problems that have to do with people and their relationships with one another. (Boston University School of Public Communication, 1981a, 56)

The authors also deplore the fact that the very speed with which television diffuses its messages hinders the audience's capacity to grasp their full import:

> Everything is reduced to the same electronic images parading across the same screen with the same sound. The cues that distinguish one type of programming from another are subtle and fleeting. If a viewer fails to spot these cues, he/she may confuse fact with fantasy, news with wizardry. (Boston University School of Public Communication, 1981a, 42)

General objective. The program's general objective is to help tele-viewers develop a more critical stance toward television by learning how to spot the "behind-the-scenes realities." The information they acquire in the process will help shield them against the highly developed manipulative powers of television. Addressing the televiewers directly, the program's creators alert them to the fact that "if you are aware of the medium's behind-the-scenes realities, you will not be stunned or manipulated by its messages. You also will be better able to understand its potential benefits in your home, community and society" (Boston University School of Public Communication, 1981a, 4).

Organization of contents. The program enables students to reap greater benefits from the culturally enriching experiences television is able to provide. It also compels them to take a critical look at the influence television exerts in every sphere of social activity, whether this be politics, the economy, cultural and artistic activities, or consumer habits, interpersonal relations, even moral values. Its different sections have been organized in such a way as to generate in students an awareness of the symbolical conventions that television strives to impose. Its introductory section, for example, deals with the techniques used in the production of television programs. Student are required to determine how important a role the technical aspects of audiovisual language play in creating the global impression we derive from the television images. Here are some of the questions that the student is induced to ask: "Is there substance to the idea behind the show or is the goal merely to provide a certain look? . . . Are props, sets, and costumes integral to the drama or are they simply window-dressing, a gloss designed to hook the audience? Is the show overloaded with stars and gimmicks?" (Boston University School of Public Communication, 1981a, 26). The section dealing with advertising is intended to show that the symbolical reality inherent in television advertising more often than not conveys an irrational, stereotypical, and simplistic view of social realities: "Although much television advertising provides useful information for the consumer, it is obvious that some advertising fosters an aura of social misconceptions through its narrow definitions of normalcy, beauty, and success" (Boston University School of Public Communication, 1981a, 50). Each of the program's four sections focuses on some dominant aspect of the influence wielded by television.

Pedagogical strategies. The program's pedagogical approach comprises two types of strategy: (1) locating and defining (identification of television's specific features), and (2) analyzing (evaluation of the impact televised messages have on the individual and society at large). The program also contains exercises that help students perfect their writing and composition skills. They are required to produce short written evaluations of televised messages along with alternative ways in which these messages might be expressed.

The European Programs

A General Curricular Model for Mass Media Education: The Critical Perspective

In 1978, Unesco entrusted the Finnish media specialist, Sirkka Minkkinen, with the task of devising a program of media education that could be used internationally (Minkkinen, 1978). This program is essentially a more elaborate version of the Finnish model she had helped develop during the seventies (Committee Report on the Curriculum Planning for Comprehensive Schools in Finland, 1970; Minkkinen, 1974). We have chosen to examine the Unesco program rather than the original Finnish version, because the Unesco program contains much more information concerning the pedagogical strategies commonly used in a program of this sort.

How media influence is perceived. The media, as this program envisages them, exert a very potent influence both on the individual viewer and on society at large: "They provide an essential linkage between the individual and society. They are of vital importance since they socialize children and adolescents and inculcate values, norms and philosophies of life" (Minkkinen, 1978, 25). This influence, however, can be either positive or negative:

> According to its uses mass media can be an enhancing factor in the individual's life, and a means of national identity and development, international understanding and peace, by giving more real and adequate information on each other's lives. It can, however, turn out to be a new opium for the masses or it may deteriorate the norms and become a means of cultural supremacy. (Minkkinen, 1978, 12)

In capitalist societies, according to Minkkinen, the media's impact is decidedly more negative than positive, because their primary role in such societies is the manipulation of public opinion:

> Concern about the manipulative influence of the media on social concepts is particularly discernible in countries where the ownership and control of the means of production and distribution of the media is not correlated with the distribution of political opinion in the countries concerned. (Minkkinen, 1978, 28)

Minkkinen also contends that the media's manipulative skills can actually be used to breed fanaticism in media consumers: "The mass media will then have conditioned them to react passively and this can, in turn, generate pessimism about the future and a mystical fanaticism" (Minkkinen, 1978, 27). Minkkinen is even fearful "that these media may manipulate social concepts, especially those of children and adolescents, and impede the spontaneous and unbiased formation of opinion" (Minkkinen, 1978, 28).

How the audience is perceived. The program is predicated on the vulnerability of media consumers. They even come to seem like victims capable merely of a passive reaction to the onslaught of the media messages. Children are particularly at risk, because they

> have become the most vulnerable targets for the mass media. Despite the increasing use and the ample supply of pictures, children's ability to understand them has by no means improved. It seems probable that only the most salient features are understood and the semantic nuances remain undetected. Emotional receptivity remains undeveloped or even regressive. (Minkkinen, 1978, 26)

Children have no very firm grasp of social realties, which is why the program regards them as incapable of reacting in an autonomous manner to media messages: "At first, [children] may even be merely perplexed by what confronts them. Their knowledge of reality generally needs to be deepened and rendered more many-sided and to make this possible is a basic objective of media education" (Minkkinen, 1978, 63).

General objective. Helping the young learner come to terms with the world of the media is certainly a primary aim of media education programs, but such programs have nonetheless broader social purposes than that. The Unesco program strives, in effect, to bring about a radical transformation in the young learner. On becoming an adult, he or she must help ensure that the media genuinely promote democratic ideals. Media education "should enable pupils to act, as private individuals or as members of citizen organizations, towards the development of mass communications of high quality as information, art and ethics in a democratic spirit" (Minkkinen, 1978, 50).

Organization of contents. The program does not focus solely on the influence wielded by a single medium; its survey encompasses all the mass media. It probes analytically into their political, social, and economic aspects. It surveys, for example, the consequences for the free circulation of information in the world of the control that the great press agencies in the West exercise over the diffusion of information. It also studies major media topics of concern like the lack of uniform access to information due to social inequalities, ownership of the media concentrated in such few hands as to threaten freedom of information, and the role the media play in maintaining the cold war mentality.

Pedagogical strategies. The young learner is systematically made aware of the many contradictions that plague the mass media network: "It is vitally important that pupils be shown methods for identifying and resolving such contradictions, and taught how the logical examination of content can reveal the origins of contradictions and the way out" (Minkkinen, 1978, 106).

Initiation aux Mass-Media: The "Classical" Semiotic Approach

This program targets students who are about to leave the primary school and enter secondary school. Originally developed by the Centre d'Initiation aux Mass-Media, it was officially adopted by the educational authorities of the Swiss Canton of Fribourg in 1979 (Centre d'Initiation aux Mass-Media, 1983, 1984).

How media influence is perceived. The Swiss creators of this program take the view that the media exercise a very potent influence, since they manage to induce consumers to accept their vision of reality:

> Whether we like it or not, we are all of us influenced by the mass media. . . . Within our homes, newspapers and magazines convey their view of world events. . . . The mass media wield such power over our minds that we often find it difficult to arrive at a genuinely personal opinion concerning events either close to or remote from us. (Centre d'Initiation aux Mass-Media, 1984, 19).[2]

The media's power to shape public opinion stems from their capacity to weaken the polysemic character of messages. This adversely affects the media consumer's ability to frame personal interpretations of media messages. The media, in other words, exercise a monopoly of sorts over the meanings that media messages are perceived as bearing. Since they severely curtail the liberty of the individual media consumer, from the public's standpoint they pose a distinct threat: "The great systems of mass communication try, as a rule, to blur the polysemous character of their messages in order to give their meaning greater weight. And this poses a threat to the freedom of the media consumer" (CIMM, 1984, 1).

How the audience is perceived. Little in the way of concrete information appears in the program concerning its mode of perceiving the audience. Indeed, all that is said along those lines is that students, on being taught how to "read" the media messages, undergo a distinct change in attitude. They become, in effect, capable of a more highly intellectual and emotional response to these messages. Left to their own devices, students fail to grasp the more hidden meaning of media messages. However, "on mastering the processes of mass communication, students will become actors, so to speak, within these processes. They will conscientiously sift the messages emanating from the media" (Centre d'Initiation aux Mass-Media, 1984, 1).

General objective. The program basically aims at arousing in young learners an esthetic response to media messages by teaching them how to read the text of these messages competently. Clearly, competence in this area helps counter the tendency routinely observed in the media to blur the polysemous character of their messages. The program, in sum, "aims at creating an awareness in students of the characteristics of artistic expression. In other words, it prepares them to *read* media messages on their own" (Centre d'Initiation aux Mass-Media, 1984, 1).

Organization of contents. The program developed by the Centre d'Initiation aux Mass-Media differs from other media education programs in this respect: it does not confine its investigation to one medium in particular. What it does, essentially, is analyze the language of the media, putting particular emphasis on its iconographic variety. The young learner must be made to understand the grammar of visual language; the course contents must accordingly provide him or her with the means to do so. The program's central activity involves study of the mass media text which, when subjected to semiotic analysis, lays bare its full meaning. The program's first part, "The Mass Media," introduces the young learner to certain theoretical aspects of mass media communication. The second part, "Reading an Image," constitutes an introduction to semiological analysis. Its third part, "Codes of Connotation," enables him or her to decipher the grammatical subtleties of images. It will therefore be seen that this program ignores all matters relative to the production and diffusion of images, its sole focus being the reading of the text of those images.

Pedagogical strategies. The program revolves entirely around the attempt to have the young learner master the concepts, borrowed from "classical" semiotics, of denotation and connotation:

> The young learner must from the very start be taught how to elaborate denotations and connotations that are precise and rich from a semantic point of view. The ability to do this constitutes the course's only stringent requirement—a requirement that may appear somewhat exacting at times. The idea is never to allow the young learner to feel satisfied with vague, imprecise denotations/connotations. (Centre d'Initiation aux Mass-Media, 1984, 25)

The program provides exercises designed to help the young learner assimilate the technique of decoding the grammar of images. These exercises involve the use of advertisements in magazines and cartoon strips, as well as photographic representations of objects that qualify as art as traditionally understood.

Selling pictures. A teaching pack about representation and stereotyping: The cultural studies approach. British media education specialists have put together a great many media education programs since the early eighties. Among the programs found most useful by teachers are those created by the British Film Institute, such as *Reading pictures* (British Film Institute, 1982) and *Selling Pictures* (Bazalgette et al., 1983). We will look at *Selling pictures* here—a program that targets young learners in the fourth and fifth years of high school.

Selling pictures makes no claim to completeness as a media education program. It limits the scope of its analysis to the stereotypes purveyed by the pictures in popular magazines. It contains three sections: "The Picture and the Audience," "The Makers of Pictures," and "The Picture and the Stereotypes." The first and third sections address the needs of the teachers; they are the ones we will be looking at here.

How media influence is perceived. The authors of the program are thoroughly convinced that the opinions of individuals and groups bear the very strong impress of stereotypes put out by the media. They even take the view that these stereotypes determine to a considerable extent the nature of the relationships that exist between the different social groupings. They view stereotyping as "a process that constructs a relationship between two groups in which one categorizes and evaluates the other" (Bazalgette et al., 1983, 18). Certain groups have discovered stereotypes to be an effective means of ensuring their domination over other groups. And this domination, in turn, both legitimates and guarantees the preservation of the status quo. When media stereotyping becomes really efficient, it "makes the possibility of other self-definitions difficult to imagine, let alone bring about; most stereotyping preserves the *status quo*" (Bazalgette et al., 1983, 20).

But the question as to how the media exercise their influence is a very complex one, according to the authors; it is futile to look at it merely from the standpoint of cause and effect. The media cannot be said to instill their vision of the world into the minds of their audience in any direct and uniform fashion. They suggest rather than impose a certain way of interpreting the messages they put out. And they do this by inserting a preferred meaning that ordains how messages are to be decoded. Media stereotyping, in short, amounts to "a process of evaluation. Stereotyping does not just offer categories for describing people; it suggests an attitude to be taken towards the group of people categorized" (Bazalgette et al., 1983, 18).

To understand how the media go about instilling their stereotypes into the minds of media consumers, it is necessary to view the phenomenon of the media in all its complexity, according to the authors of this program. This means that attention must be paid to the processes whereby the symbolical representations that media messages essentially are, are produced, circulated, and consumed. It is accordingly inadvisable to take a rigid view of how the media function, of the role they play, and of the influence they exert. The more correct view of the media is that they are places where conflict erupts, where tensions reign, where different visions of the world strive for mastery; hence the patent contradictions so often discernible between the messages they convey. It comes, therefore, as no surprise that "representation and stereotyping are contested and contradictory areas" (Bazalgette et al., 1983, 1).

How the audience is perceived. The authors of this program do not regard the audience as a collection of individuals who passively respond to media messages. Audience and media enter into a process of negotiation, according to them. The negotiation centers on the meaning that the audience ascribes to the message, and it takes place because the audience is not merely, as was said above, a collection of isolated individuals: the audience is a separate hence definable entity. The authors of the program acknowledge the importance of social class by devising exercises that incorporate questions intended to uncover "the ways in which the images and words on magazine covers perform this process of negotiation in relation to class, sex, and ideas or romance" (Bazalgette et al., 1983, 5). The decoding performed by the audience cannot be known simply by computing the sum of the individual exercises in decoding—which is the procedure advocated by the partisans of the uses and gratifications approach. The authors of this program are rather of the opinion that decoding outcomes are conditioned by variables that govern the individual's status within the social organization.

General objective. The program enables the young learner to understand certain key features of the media industry by basing its approach on the production, circulation, and consumption of media messages. The exercises it contains are intended to "broaden students' understanding of the dominant system of circulation through which images reach audiences: the entertainment, leisure and advertising industries" (Bazalgette et al., 1983, 1). The program's general aim, moreover, is "to open up issues and enable students to discover that representation and stereotyping are contested and contradictory areas" (Bazalgette et al., 1983, 1). In the final analysis, therefore, studying the media helps unearth the contradictions vitiating social organization.

Organization of contents. The sections of the program devised for the teachers each contain two principal exercises. The first teaches students to record the kind of observations that will help them answer the central question: "What do these images offer?" The second enables them to grasp the role that the stereotypes play in shaping society's class-based power structure. The questions with which they are plied are the following: What is stereotyping? How does this process work? Who creates stereotypes? Who gets stereotyped? Why stereotype? What's the effect of stereotyping?

Pedagogical strategies. Selling pictures anchors its pedagogical approach to discussions and exchanges between the students. They are prodded into evaluating and criticizing each other's interpretations of the media images under study. The exercises are not intended to help them identify the stereotypes lurking in media messages so that they may, once they have found them, condemn them. Students are expected, rather, to understand the processes whereby stereotyped images are produced and circulated and thus to grasp the role such images play in shaping the social power structure. Stereotypes, we are reminded, are:

> Concepts, held by groups, which are constructed and maintained through many different discourses; which is why a single advertisement, or one character in a

TABLE 4.2
The Theoretical Foundations of Media Education Programs

a) Media education program: Singer et al. *Getting the Most Out of TV.*

1) *How media influence is perceived*
—Very powerful influence.
—TV has a direct and negative impact.
—Children imitate TV violence.

2) *How audience is perceived*
—A "passive-TV syndrome."
—There is little comprehension of what has been watched.

3) *General objective*
—Attenuate some of the negative effects of excessive viewing.

4) *Organization of contents*
—Principally devised to help children distinguish between reality and fiction.

5) *Pedagogical strategies*
—Designed to help children uncover negative features of TV.

6) *Theoretical foundation*
—The S-R model: hypodermic needle approach.

b) Media education program: WNET/Thirteen. *Critical Television Viewing.*

1) *How media influence is perceived*
—Limited influence, students watch wisely choose and evaluate what they watch.

2) *How audience is perceived*
—Students respond autonomously to messages in terms of their needs.

3) *General objective*
—Help students to television for the satisfactions they hope to derive from it.

4) *Organization of contents*
—It goads students into determining the role television plays in their lives.

5) *Pedagogical strategies*
—Analyze and evaluate the individual elements of a program.

6) *Theoretical foundation*
—The uses and gratifications approach.

c) Media education program: Boston School of Public Communication. *Television Literacy.*

1) *How media influence is perceived*
—TV has the power to certify behaviors and values, it tends to make believe that there is a single national agenda.

2) *How audience is perceived*
—TV audience is made up of an heterogeneous mass of individuals.

3) *General objective*
—Help shield students against developed manipulative power of TV.

4) *Organization of contents*
—Influence exerted by TV through its symbolical conventions.

5) *Pedagogical strategies*
—Analyzing the impact of messages on the individual & society.

6) *Theoretical foundation*
—The cultivation and agenda-setting theories.

TABLE 4.2 (continued)
The Theoretical Foundations of Media Education Programs

d) Media education program: Minkkinen. *A General Curricular Model for Mass Media Education.*

1) *How media influence is perceived*
—Very powerful in the manipulation of public opinion, media impede the unbiased formation of opinion.

2) *How audience is perceived*
—Children have become the most vulnerable targets for the mass media.

3) *General objective*
—To implant the desire to change the mass communication system.

4) *Organization of contents*
—Analysis of political, social and economic aspects of mass communication.

5) *Pedagogical strategies*
—Analyses of the many contradictions that plague the media.

6) *Theoretical foundation*
—The critical perspective.

e) Media education program: Centre d'Initiation aux Mass-Media. *Initiation aux Mass-Media.*

1) *How media influence is perceived*
—Mass media blur the polysemous character of their messages; this poses a threat to the freedom of the media consumers.

2) *How audience is perceived*
—Children are often too passive in their "readings" of media messages.

3) *General objective*
—Helps children to "read" media messages correctly.

4) *Organization of contents*
—The codes and grammar of images.

5) *Pedagogical strategies*
—Rules for mastering the concepts of denotation/connotation.

6) *Theoretical foundation*
—The "classical" semiotic approach.

f) Media education program: Bazalgette et al. *Selling pictures.*

1) *How media influence is perceived*
—Media insert a "preferred" meaning that ordains how messages are to be decoded; they suggest rather than impose interpretations.

2) *How audience is perceived*
—Audiences are always in a process of negotiating the meanings with the media.

3) *General objective*
—Help students understand how images reach audiences.

4) *Organization of contents*
—The roles that stereotypes play in shaping society's class-based power structure.

5) *Pedagogical strategies*
—Evaluating and criticizing interpretations of media images.

6) *Theoretical foundation*
—The cultural studies approach.

TV program, cannot easily be discussed as 'a stereotype.' It may be an instance of the ongoing process of stereotyping, but it is also fixed in its particular form and context. (Bazalgette et al., 1983, 18)

Table 4.2 presents in outline form the results of our analysis of the theoretical links between the media education programs we have chosen to focus on in this study.

Content-Oriented and Process-Oriented Perspectives

On completing our analysis of these media education programs, we feel justified in concluding that there exists a very clear link between the methods used to develop these programs and the prevalent theories of mass communication. We would even contend that the way in which program implementation is envisaged displays equally strong links with the theories of mass communication. For this reason, we are led to doubt whether media education can actually be viewed as an autonomous field furnished with its own distinctive theoretical framework. Our view is rather that media education fits as a field within the broader framework of theoretical advances in mass communication. As we see it, media education has not succeeded in developing an autonomous theoretical framework from which practice can develop in a coherent way. And since curriculum development cannot take place apart from the mass communication theories, is media education research always fated to trail behind mass communication research? If it were, a theoretical dependency might arise—which is something not altogether desirable.

Beyond their theoretical lineage, there is another way to differentiate the programs from each other, a way that could be more useful for identifying directions for the development of media education. Programs can be classified into two categories: those that are content oriented, and those that are process oriented.

In the programs that are content oriented, practice is oriented toward the acquisition of information concerning the specificity of the media. These programs postulate that a better factual knowledge about the media will better guarantee the acquisition of critical skills. What is important for these programs is that students be able to understand what is distinctive about each medium—for example, how television is different from cinema or radio—and to understand how the media influence us.

The American programs aimed at promoting television literacy are for the most part content oriented in their approach.

In programs that are process oriented, the goal is to acquire information concerning the role that the mass media play in the social system. They postulate that a better comprehension of the dynamics of mass communication will guarantee the acquisition of critical skills. For these programs, it does not matter so much what differentiates one medium from another. Media education is regarded as a process whereby widely differing modes of mass communication come under critical scrutiny, modes as various as magazines, comic books, films, television programs, etc. This is why we may say that the European programs are more process oriented in their approach.

Another important point our analysis has brought into sharp focus is that research on media education has essentially concentrated on the development of didactic materials. Evaluating this material has not been a major concern. For this reason, questions like the following are not being asked: What is the impact of those programs? Do they succeed in developing critical skills? How do we measure this? In the present state of research, not enough attention is paid to the question of evaluation. It is as though, for the researchers in media education, programs automatically succeed in developing critical skills. One may wonder if there is not a kind of wishful thinking here on the part of those programs' creators. We think that research in media education should concentrate more on the notion of critical thinking, which is a central concept of media education. In fact, the objective of promoting critical thinking is what all the programs have in common. So curriculum development should be based on the operationalization of the concept of critical thinking, which is the core concept of the discipline.

This analysis has demonstrated the need to pay greater attention to the theoretical dimensions of media education. It is thus important that further research be oriented toward the elaboration of a more autonomous theoretical framework in order to guide a more efficient practice.

Notes

1. To make our demonstration as graphic and convincing as possible, we have purposely chosen not to eliminate the redundancy that will unavoidably occur when the citation largely repeats the terms of our analysis.
2. We have translated the citations from French.

References

Alvarado, M. (1977). L'initiation aux médias en Europe occidentale: le Royaume-Uni. In Unesco (Ed.), *Études des médias en enseignement*. Études et documents d'information, No 80 (42–53). Paris: Unesco.

———. (1992). *Media Education in Great Britain in the 1990*. Paper presented at the International Association for Mass Communication Research (IAMCR), Sao Paulo, Brazil.

Amt für Unterichtsforschung und Plannung der Erziehungsdirektion des Kantons Bern. (1981). *Medien-Erziehung: Projekstudie*. Bern: Mediendidaktische Arbeits und Informationstelle (M.A.I.) der Berner Schulwarte.

Anderson, J. A. (l980). The theoretical lineage of critical viewing curricula. *Journal of Communication, 30* (3), 64–71.

———. (1983). Television and the critical viewer. In J. Bryant & D. R. Anderson (Eds.), *Children's understanding of television: research on attention and comprehension* (297–327). New York: Academic Press.

———. (1988). Examen de quelques concepts éclairant la position de l'éducateur aux médias. In Centre d'Initiation aux Communications de Masse (CIC) (Ed.), *Proceedings of the Symposium Éducation aux médias, rencontre de la recherche et de l'éducation* (11–23). Lausanne, Suisse.

Anderson, J. A., & Ploghoft, M. A. (1975a). *The way we see it*. Athens, Ohio: Social Science Cooperative Center.

———. (1975b). *Television and you*. Athens, Ohio: Social Science Cooperative Center.

Association des cinémas parallèles du Québec (A.C.P.Q.). (1991). *Cinémagie*. Montréal: Association des cinémas parallèles du Québec.

Association for Media Literacy. (1991). *Media and the gulf war: A case study*. Toronto: Association for Media Literacy.

———. (1992). *The AML Anthology- Supplement, 1990–1992*. In B. Smart (Ed.), Toronto: Association for Media Literacy.

Barthes, R. (1957). *Mythologies*. Paris: Seuil.

———. (1964a). Rhétorique de l'image. *Communications, 4*, 40–51.

———. (1964b). Éléments de sémiologie. *Communications, 4*, 91–135.

———. (1966). Introduction à l'analyse structurale des récits. *Communications, 8*, 1–27.

Bazalgette, C., Cook, J., & Simpson, P. (1983). *Selling pictures: A teaching pack about representation and stereotyping*. Department of Education, Education Image Project Unit 2. London: British Film Institute.

Bayerischen Staatsministerium für Unterricht und Kultus. (1988). *Gesamkonzept der Medienerziehung in der Schule*. München: Staatsministerium für Unterricht und Kultus.

Bennet, T. (1982). Theories of the media, theories of society. In M. Gurevitch et al. (Eds.), *Culture, society and the media* (30–52). London: Methuen,

Benson, J., Hollosy, I., & Turnbull, S. (1989). *The media education statement, The arts framework P-10*. Victoria: Ministry of Education, Schools Division Victoria.

Berger, G. (1983). L'initiation aux médias: un exemple de Suisse. *Perspectives, Xlll* (2), 247–56.

Boston University School of Public Communication. (1981a). *Television literacy: Critical television viewing skills*. Boston: Dendron Press.

———. (1981b). *Television literacy: Instructor's guide*. Boston: Dendron Press.

———. (1981c). *Television literacy: Workbook*. Boston: Dendron Press.

Breton, P., & Proulx, S. (1989). *L'explosion de la communication: la naissance d'une nouvelle idéologie*. Paris/Montréal: La Découverte/Boréal.

British Film Institute. (1982). *Reading pictures*. Education Image Project Unit 1. London: British Film Institute.

————— (Ed.) (1990). *Proceedings of the meeting New directions in media education/ Nouvelles orientations dans l'éducation aux médias*. Toulouse, France.

Brown, J. A. (1991). *Television "critical viewing skills" education: Major media literacy projects in the United States and selected countries*. Hillsdale, N.J.: Lawrence Erlbaum Associates Publishers.

Canavan, K. B. (1972). *Mass media education curriculum guideline for primary school year 1–6*. Sydney: Catholic Education Office.

—————. (1975). *Mass media education curriculum guideline for secondary school*. Sydney: Catholic Education Office.

Carpenter, D., Smart, W., & Worsnop, C. (1988). *Media: Images and issues*. Toronto: Addison-Wesley.

Centre d'Initiation aux Mass-Media. (1983). *Qu'est-ce qu'un journal?* Manuel rédigé sous la direction de Gérald Berger. Fribourg: Country Centre d'Initiation aux Mass-Media.

—————. (1984). *Initiation aux Mass-Media: Méthodologie destinée aux élèves du cycle d'orientation*. Sous la direction de Gérald Berger, 3ième édition remaniée. Fribourg: Centre d'Initiation aux Mass-Media.

Centre national de la documentation pédagogique (CNDP). (1981). *Formation du Jeune Téléspectateur Actif: les dossiers du petit écran*. Paris: CNDP.

Chaffee, S. H., & Hochheimer, J. L. (1985). The beginnings of political communication in the United States' origins of the "limited effects" model. In E. M. Rogers & F. Balle (Eds.), *The media revolution in America and Western Europe* (267–96). Norwood, N.J.: Ablex.

Committee Report on the Curriculum Planning for Comprehensive Schools in Finland. (1970). *Mass communication education in the Finnish comprehensive school*. Helsinki.

Corder-Bolz, C. R. (1979). *Elementary school student's critical television viewing skills project*. Austin, Tex.: Southwest Educational Development Laboratory.

—————. (1980). Mediation: The Role of Significant Others. *Journal of Communication, 30* (3), 106–18.

—————. (1982). Television literacy and critical television viewing skills. In D. Pearl, L. Bouthilet, & L. Lazar (Eds.), *Television and behavior: Ten years of scientific progress and implications for the eighties*. Vol II: Technical review (91–102). Washington, D.C.: U.S. Government Printing Office.

Cowle, K., & Dick, E. (1984). *Teaching media studies: An introduction to methods and resources*. Glasgow: The Scottish Film Council.

Dahl, A. G. (1981). *Media education in Norway*. Oslo: Ministry of Church and Education.

—————. (1983). L'initiation aux médias en milieu scolaire. *Perspectives, XIII* (2), 213–23.

—————. (1985). *Media education for teachers in the northern countries (Scandinavia)*. Tristrand, 24–43.

De Fleur, M. L., & Ball-Rokeach, S. (1989). *Theories of mass communication* (fifth edition). New York: Longman.

Doelker, C. (1979). *"Wirklichkeit" in den Medien*. Zurich: Audiovisuelle Zentralstelle am Pestalozzianum.

————. (1992). Bildpädagogik—das chronishe Defizit der Medienerziehung. In Bertelsmann Stiftung (Ed.), *Medienkompetenz als Herausforderung an Shule und Bildung: Ein deutsch-amerikanisher Dialog. Kompendium zu einer Konferenz der Bertelsmann Stiftung* (208–17). Gütersloh: Verlag Bertelsmann Stiftung.

Dominguez, M. J. (1990). *Activos y creativos con los medios de communicacion social.* Bogota: Ediciones Paulinas.

Dorr, A., Browne-Graves. S., & Phelps, E. (1980). Television for young children. *Journal of Communication, 30* (3), 71–83.

Dorr, A., & Brannon, C. (1992). Media education in American schools at the end of the twentieth century. In Bertelsmann Stiftung (Ed.), *Medienkompetenz als Herausforderung an Shule und Bildung: Ein deutsch-amerikanisher Dialog, Kompendium zu einer Konferenz der Bertelsmann Stiftung* (69–103). Gütersloh, Germany: Verlag Bertelsmann Stiftung.

Duncan, B. (1988). *Mass media and popular culture.* Toronto: Harcourt Brace Jovanovich.

————. (1992). Media and popular culture in the classroom: Perspectives on media pedagogy. In Bertelsmann Stiftung (Ed.), *Medienkompetenz als Herausforderung an Shule und Bildung: Ein deutsch-amerikanisher Dialog, Kompendium zu einer Konferenz der Bertelsmann Stiftung* (344–56). Gütersloh, Germany: Verlag Bertelsmann Stiftung.

Eco, U. (1966). James Bond: une combinaison narrative. *Communications, 8,* 77–93.

————. (1970). Sémiologie des messages visuels. *Communications, 15,* 11–51.

Emery, W. G. (Ed.). (1993). Media Literacy [Special issue]. *English Quarterly, 25* (2-3).

Eschenauer, B. (1989). *Medienpädagogik in die Lehrplänen: Eine Inhaltsanalyse zu den Curricula der allgemeinbildenden Schulen im Auftrag der Bertsmann Stiftung.* Gütersloh: Verlag Bertelsmann Stiftung.

————. (1992). Medienkompetenz als Zielvorgabe. In Bertelsmann Stiftung (Ed.), *Medienkompetenz als Herausforderung an Shule und Bildung: Ein deutsch-amerikanisher Dialog, Kompendium zu einer Konferenz der Bertelsmann Stiftung* (323–43). Gütersloh, Germany: Verlag Bertelsmann Stiftung.

Faurie-Roudier, A., & Vallet. A. (1983). *Le langage total: expériences internationales d'éducation à la communication et aux mass media.* Collection, Communication et Société, No. 9. Paris: Unesco.

Far West Laboratory Office of Educational Project. (1980). *Inside television: A guide to critical Viewing (teacher's guide, student handbook, worksheet).* Palo Alto, California: Science & Behavior Books.

Fondation Roi Baudoin. (1993). *Télécole: Une opération d'éducation des jeunes aux médias en Communauté française de Belgique.* Bruxelles: Fondation Roi Beaudoin.

Fransecky, R. B., & Ferguson, R. (1973). New ways of seeing: The Milford visual communication project. *Audiovisual Instruction, 18* (April–May, June–July).

Gerbner, G., & Gross, L. (1976). Living with television: The violence profile. *Journal of Communication. 26,* Spring, 173–99.

Geretschlaeger, I. (1987). *International annotated bibliography on media education.* Communication and Society No: 17. Paris: Unesco.

Golay, J-P. (1988). Éducation aux médias: Rencontre de la recherche et de l'éducation. In Centre d'Initiation aux Communications de Masse (CIC) (Ed.), *Proceedings of the Symposium Éducation aux médias, rencontre de la recherche et de l'éducation* (3–10). Lausanne, Switzerland.

Grossmann, J., & Mayer, B. (1983). *Medien + Erziehung, Grundlegen, Ziele, Thesen.* Bern: Mediendidaktische Arbeits und Informationstelle (M.A.I.) der Berner Schulwarte.

Groupe de travail romand et tessinois de l'audiovisuel à l'école (GRAVE) (Ed.), (1988). *L'éducation aux médias: audiovisuel et pédagogie: Activités pour la classe.* Neuchâtel: Secrétariat du Grave.

Hall, S. (1980). Encoding/decoding. In S. Hall., D. Hobson, A. Lowe, & P. Willis (Eds.), *Culture, media, language* (128–38). London: Hutchinson.

Institut québécois du cinéma. (1992). *L'éducation cinématographique au Québec: préparer les auditoires de demain.* Montréal: Institut québécois du cinéma.

———. (1993a). *Donner aux jeunes l'éducation cinématographique qu'ils demandent.* Montréal: Institut québécois du cinéma.

———. (1993b). *L'éducation cinématographique au Québec.* Montréal: Institut québécois du cinéma.

Kahn, L. (1979). A practical guide to critical tv viewing skills. *Media & Methods,* October.

———. (1982). Television in subject areas: field-tested methods for classroom use. *Television & Children, 5* (3), 36–49.

Kubey, R., & Csikszentmihalyi, M. (1990). *Television and the quality of life: How viewing shapes everyday experience.* Hillsdale, N.J.: Lawrence Erlbaum Associates.

Lehman, R. (1980). *Centering television in the classroom.* Monona: Television Learning Ltd.

Livesley, J. (1987). *Media scenes & class acts.* Markham: Pembroke Publishers.

Livesley, J., McMahon, B., Pungente, J., & Quin, R. (1990). *Meet the media.* Toronto: Globe-Modern Curriculum.

Lowery S., & DeFleur, M. L. (1988). *Milestones in mass communication research.* New York: Longman.

Lloyd-Kohlin, D, & Tyner, K. (1991). *Media and you: An elementary media literacy curriculum.* Englewood Cliffs, N.J.: Educational Technology Publications.

Lusted, D. A. (1985). History of suspicion: Educational attitudes to television. In D. Lusted & P. Drummond (Eds.), *TV and schooling* (11–19). London: British Film Institute.

Masterman, L. (1980). *Teaching about television.* London: Macmillan.

———. (1983a). L'éducation aux médias: problèmes théoriques et possibilités concrètes. *Perspectives, Xlll,* (2), 203–12.

———. (1983b). Media education in the 1980s. *Journal of Educational Television, 9* (1), 7–12.

———. (1985). Future developments in TV & media studies: An ecological approach to media education. In D. Lusted & P. Drummond (Eds.), *TV and schooling* (87–92). London: British Film Institute.

———. (1986). *Teaching the media.* London: Comedia.

———. (1991). An overview of media education in Europe. *Media Development, 1,* 3–9.

———. (1994). En réfléchissant sur l'éducation aux média. In Le Conseil de l'Europe (Ed.), *L'éducation aux médias dans l'Europe des années 90* (5–92). Collection Education, Strasbourg: Les éditions du Conseil de l'Europe.

McCombs, M. E., & Shaw, D. L. (1972). The agenda-setting function of the press. *Public Opinion Quarterly, 36,* 176–87.

McLeod, J. M., Kosicki, G. M. & Zhongdang, P. (1991). In J. Curran & M. Gurevitch (Eds.), *Mass media and society* (235–66). New York: Edward Arnold.

McMahon, B., & Quin, R. (1986). *Real images: film & television*. Melbourne: Macmillan Company of Australia.

———. (1992). *Monitoring standards in education: Media analysis*. A report prepared for the Ministry of Education. Unpublished manuscript.

McQuail, D. (1987). *Mass communication theory: An introduction*. Beverly Hills, Calif.: Sage.

Médiacteurs. (1993). *Tout savoir sur la télé*. Bruxelles: Media Animation/Médialogue.

Media Action Research Center (MARC). (1979). *Television awareness training: The viewer's guide for family & community*. Ben Logan (Ed.), Nashville: MARC.

Metz, C. (1964). Le cinéma: langue ou langage? *Communications, 4*, 52–90.

———. (1966). La grande syntagmatique du film narratif. *Communications, 8*, 120–24.

Minkkinen, S. (1978). *A general curricular model for mass media education*. Paris: Unesco.

Minkkinen, K. (1974). *Mass media education in Finland*. Unpublished manuscript.

Minkkinen, S., & Nodenstreng, K. (1983). Finlande: plans courageux et sérieux problèmes. *Perspectives, XIII* (2), 237–347.

Ministère de l'Éducation de l'Ontario. (1989). *La Compétence médiatique. Document d'appui pour les cycles intermédiaire et supérieur*. Toronto: L'imprimeur de la Reine pour l'Ontario.

Ministère de l'Éducation du Québec. (1995). *Media files: Guide for english language arts secondary I- IV program*. Gouvernement du Québec.

Ministry of Cultural and Scientific Affairs of Norway. (1983). *Report on the course teaching mass media* (Statens Laerkurs). Oslo: Section for Continued Training Teachers.

Morley, D. (1980). *The "Nationwide" audience: Structure of decoding*. BFI Television Monograph No. 11. London: British Film Institute.

National Film Board of Canada. (1989). *Media and society*.

New South Wales Department of Education. (1984). *All about mass media education K–12*. Marrickville: Media Press.

Ontario Ministry of Education. (1989). *Media literacy: Intermediate and senior divisions resource guide*. Toronto: Queen's printer for Ontario.

Pierre, E. (1983). Une expérience française de formation du jeune téléspectateur. *Perspectives, XIII*, (2), 257–64.

Piette, J. (1985). *Une analyse des expériences et des programmes d'éducation aux médias à travers le monde*. Montréal: L'Association Nationale des Téléspectateurs.

———. (1991). Le public s'organise: censure ou éducation? In *L'état des médias*. Sous la direction de Jean-Marie Charon, Le Centre de formation et de perfectionnement des journalistes, Paris/Montréal: La Découverte-Médiaspouvoirs/ Boréal.

———. (1992). Teaching television critical viewing skills: From theory to practice to theory. In Bertelsmann Stiftung (Ed.), *Medienkompetenz als Herausforderung an Shule und Bildung: Ein deutsch-amerikanisher Dialog, Kompendium zu einer Konferenz der Bertelsmann Stiftung* (218–36). Gütersloh: Verlag Bertelsmann Stiftung.

———. (1993). *L'éducation aux médias: vers une redéfinition des rapports entre l'école et les médias*. Québec: Centrale de l'enseignement du Québec.

Pinsloo J., & Criticos, C. (Eds.) (1991). *Media matters in South Africa*. Durban: Media Resource Center, Department of Education, University of Natal.

Ploghoft, M. E., & Anderson, J. A. (1982). *Teaching critical television viewing skills: An integrated approach*. Springfield, Ill.: Charles C. Thomas.

Ploghoft, M. E., & Anderson, J. A. (Eds.) (1979). *Education for the television age: The proceedings of a national conference on the subject of children and television.* Springfield, Ill.: Charles C. Thomas.

Potter, R. L., Faith, C., & Ganek, L. B. (1979). *Channel: Critical reading/tv viewing skills.* Freeport, N.Y.: Educational activities, Inc.

Potter, R. L., Hanneman, C. E., & Faith, C. (Eds.) (1980). *TV readers skills kit.* Freeport, N.Y.: Educational activities, Inc.

———. (1981). Television behind the scene: Teachers' guide. In R. L. Poter, C. C. Hanneman, & C. Faith (Eds.), *TV readers skills kit.* Freeport, N.Y.: Educational activities, Inc.

Pungente, J. (1985). *Getting started on media education.* London: Centre for the study of communication and culture.

Reyes Tores, M. (1988). Télévision et famille: quelques expériences en Amérique latine. In Centre d'Initiation aux Communications de Masse (CIC) (Ed.), *Proceedings of the Symposium Éducation aux médias, rencontre de la recherche et de l'éducation* (38–46). Lausanne, Switzerland.

Reyes Tores, M., & Mendez, A. M. (1988). Introduction d'une éducation aux médias en Amérique Latine: Comment nous formons les enseignants au Chili. In Centre d'Initiation aux Communications de Masse (CIC) (Ed.), *Proceedings of the Symposium Éducation aux médias, rencontre de la recherche et de l'éducation* (46–49). Lausanne, Switzerland.

Saxer, U. (1992). Medien als Gesellschaftgestalter. In Bertelsmann Stiftung (Ed.), *Medienkompetenz als Herausforderung an Shule und Bildung: Ein deutsch-amerikanisher Dialog, Kompendium zu einer Konferenz der Bertelsmann Stiftung* (21–31). Gütersloh, Germany: Verlag Bertelsmann.

Saxer, U., Bonfadelli, H., & Hättenschwiller, W. (1980). *Die Massmedien im Leben der Kinder und Jugendlichen.* Zurich: Audiovisuelle Zentralstelle am Pestalozzianum.

Schermer, P. (1992). Strategische Überlegungen zur Medienerziehung in Deutschland. In Bertelsmannn Stiftung (Ed.), *Medienkompetenz als Herausforderung an Shule und Bildung: Ein deutsch-amerikanisher Dialog, Kompendium zu einer Konferenz der Bertelsmann Stiftung* (376–80). Gütersloh, Germany: Verlag Bertelsmann Stiftung.

Schramm, W. (1971). The nature of communication between humans. In W. Schramm & D. Roberts (Eds.), *The process and effects of mass communication.* Urbana: University of Illinois Press.

Singer, D. G., Zuckerman, D. M., & Singer, J. L. (1980). Helping elementary school children to learn about TV. *Journal of Communication, 30,* 84–93.

Singer, D. G., Singer, J. L, & Zuckerman, D. M. (1981a). *Getting the most out of TV.* Santa Monica, Calif.: Goodyear Publishing Book.

———. (1981b). *Teaching television: How to use TV to your child's advantage.* New York: The Dial Press.

Six, U. (1992). Medienerziehung—eine unbewältigte Aufgabe. In Bertelsmann Stiftung (Ed.), *Medienkompetenz als Herausforderung an Shule und Bildung: Ein deutsch-amerikanisher Dialog, Kompendium zu einer Konferenz der Bertelsmann Stiftung* (190–207). Gütersloh, Germany: Verlag Bertelsmann Stiftung.

South Australia Education Department. (1983a). *R-12, media studies: A curriculum document in support of media courses in schools.* Government printer, South Australia.

———. (1983b). *R-12 media studies.* Government printer, South Australia.

———. (1983c). *R-12 media lab.* Government printer, South Australia.

Southwest Educational Development Laboratory. (1979). *Elementary school student's critical television Viewer skills project.* Austin: SEDL.

Streter, T. (1984). An alternative approach to television research: developments in British cultural studies at Birmingham. In W. Rowland & B. Watkins (Eds.), *Interpreting Television: Current Research Perspectives.* Beverly Hills, Calif.: Sage Annual Review of Communication Research.

Sturm, H., Grewe-Partsch, M., Saxer, U., Bonfadelli, H., Hättenschwiller, W., Ammann, G., & Doelker, C. (1979). *Grundlagen einer Medienpädagogik.* Zurich: Audiovisuelle Zentralstelle am Pestalozzianum.

Tomasseli, K. G., & Shepperson, A. (Eds.), (1991). *Popularising semiotics* [Special issue]. *Communication Research Trends, 11* (2).

Trudel, L. (1992). *La population face aux médias.* Montréal: VLB éditeur.

Tufte, B. (1988). *Television in education.* Paper presented at the 16th Conference and General Assembly of the International Association for Mass Communication Research (IAMCR), Barcelona, July, 1988.

————. (1991). *Media education, evaluation report for the council for innovation and development in the danish folkeskole.* Copenhagen: The Royal Danish School of Educational Studies.

Tulodziecki, G. (1992a). *Medienerziehung in Schule und Unterricht.* Bad Heilbrun: Julius Klinkhardt.

————. (1992b). Medienerziehung als fächerübergreifende und integrative Aufgabe. In Bertelsmann Stiftung (Ed.), *Medienkompetenz als Herausforderung an Shule und Bildung: Ein deutsch-amerikanisher Dialog, Kompendium zu einer Konferenz der Bertelsmann Stiftung* (311–22). Gütersloh: Verlag Bertelsmann Stiftung.

Tulodziecki, G., & Schöpf, K. (1992). Zur Situation der schulischen Medienpädagogik in Deutschland: Konzepte, Materialen, Praxis und Probleme. In Bertelsmann Stiftung (Ed.), *Medienkompetenz als Herausforderung an Shule und Bildung: Ein deutsch-amerikanisher Dialog, Kompendium zu einer Konferenz der Bertelsmann Stiftung* (104–76). Gütersloh: Verlag Bertelsmann Stiftung.

Unesco (Ed.). (1977). *L'étude des médias dans l'enseignement.* Études et documents d'information, No 80. Paris: Unesco.

Unesco. (1982). *Education and the media, trends, issues, prospects: An international symposium on educating users of mass media.* German Commission for Unesco, Munich: Institut für Film und Bild in Wissenschaft und Untericht, 18-22.

Unesco (Ed.). (1984). *L'éducation aux médias.* Paris: Unesco.

Wilke, J., & Eschenauer, B. (1981). Mass media use by children and media education in Germany. Paper presented at the XXXl International Conference on Communication by the International Communication Association (ICA), Minneapolis.

Withrow, F. B. (1980). Objectives for critical television viewing skills curricula. *Television & Children, 3* (2).

WNET/Thirteen. (1980a). *Critical television viewing: Teacher's annotated edition.* New York: Cambridge.

————. (1980b). *Critical television viewing: Student's work-a text.* New York: Cambridge.

————. (1980c). *Critical television viewing: A training manual for teachers trainers.* New York: Cambridge.

5

Visual "Literacy" in Cross-Cultural Perspective

Paul Messaris

The ever-more-pervasive international flow of picture-based media raises anew a set of questions that have occupied several generations of visual scholars: To what extent is the meaning of a visual image accessible to viewers who are not familiar with the formal conventions or the cultural references on which the image is based? Does the ability to make sense of images require a visual "literacy" (i.e., a cluster of skills analogous to the syntactic and semantic competence on which verbal communication is predicated)? This chapter examines these issues with reference both to single images and to the juxtaposition of images in film or television. This discussion leads to the following conclusion: Certain formal conventions (e.g., linear perspective as a means of depicting three-dimensional space) and certain kinds of cultural allusions (especially direct references to specific visual precedents) may indeed pose interpretational problems to uninitiated viewers; however, the concept of visual "literacy" probably exaggerates the difficulties encountered by such viewers, and cross-cultural problems in visual communication seem more likely to arise from informed resistance than from incomprehension.

One of the characteristics of our age has been an increase in the frequency of international travel—and, therefore, of contact between people who do not speak the same language. A common device for coping with this situation is the pictorial sign. For example, in U.S. national parks, many of whose visitors are international tourists, places that the park service considers particularly worthy of being photographed are often marked by a somewhat schematic picture of a camera. This usage obviously stems from the common belief that pictures constitute a "universal language," whose meanings are readily accessible across the boundaries of culture and "real" language.

Although this notion may seem intuitively obvious to most people, there is a long tradition of scholarly writing that opposes it and, often, flatly rejects it. The originator of this tradition appears to have been the distinguished art historian Erwin Panofsky. In a 1927 monograph with the suggestive title "Perspective as Symbolic Form," Panofsky argued that the representational system based on linear perspective should be thought of as a set of arbitrary conventions, rather than a means of replicating the appearance of reality. This argument was derived from the fact that pictures made according to perspective principles inevitably differ from reality in a number of ways. In particular, Panofsky placed special emphasis on the observation that, whereas linear perspective involves a grid of straight lines on a flat surface, the curvature of the human retina means that straight lines are entirely absent from the images formed in our eyes. The implication of Panofsky's argument was that the ability to recognize the contents of perspective-style images must require prior learning of the style's various conventions. Nowadays, this kind of learning is often referred to as visual "literacy."

The logic behind Panofsky's thesis is not entirely sound: What happens inside the eye is not an appropriate standard by which to judge how well a picture has captured the appearance of reality. However, the more general conception of pictures as an arbitrary representational system— and, by implication, *not* a "universal language"—has long survived Panofsky's specific formulation. In the case of still images (photographs, paintings, drawings, etc.), the most influential source of this notion has undoubtedly been E. H. Gombrich's seminal book, *Art and Illusion* (1960). Much more systematically than Panofsky, this book provides a catalog of various ways in which pictures of all kinds—ranging from oil paintings to cartoons—can differ from the appearance of their real-world counterparts (if any). To this day, Gombrich's book is routinely cited as having demonstrated conclusively the arbitrariness of pictures and the consequent need for visual literacy on the part of the viewer. Ironically, however, Gombrich had actually argued against both of these assumptions in the book, and he distanced himself from them even further in the course of an acerbic exchange with Murray Krieger (Gombrich, 1984; Krieger, 1984). The fact that so many believers in visual literacy take it for granted that Gombrich is on their side may perhaps be taken as an indication of how strongly these beliefs are held. As Noel Carroll (1988) has suggested, among people who write about visual communication the notion that picture perception requires visual literacy has acquired the status of received wisdom.

This notion has also been extended to movies and television. Typical of this development is Bela Balazs's *Theory of the Film* (1970), which has probably done more than any other text to make the term film "language" a standard part of critical and scholarly vocabulary. The crux of Balazs's discussion of this term was a pair of stories about first-time viewers of film who had had trouble making sense of the medium— supposedly because of their lack of familiarity with editing and other narrative conventions. Informal anecdotes of this kind have also been used for similar purposes by other film scholars (Wilson, 1983; Worth & Adair, 1972), and a relatively small number of stories about perplexed first-time viewers of photos or drawings have been recycled repeatedly in support of the equivalent argument about still images (see Deregowski, 1980, for an excellent discussion of these anecdotes).

The presence of a substantial scholarly tradition, bolstered as it is by some seemingly telling anecdotes, may suggest that the case in favor of the visual-literacy assumption is closed. However, as the notable dissenting voice of Gombrich suggests (see also Cassidy & Knowlton, 1983; Gibson, 1982), there is reason to be cautious about accepting this assumption. In an attempt to examine this issue with appropriate skepticism, this chapter will make a distinction between two different aspects of visual literacy: first, familiarity with the *formal conventions* of visual media; second, familiarity with the *cultural content* conveyed through these conventions. Although it would be reasonable to assume that these two forms of knowledge must always interact in the interpretation of any particular image, for analytical purposes it will be useful to consider them separately.

Formal Conventions: Still Images

As we have just seen, one possible reason for assuming that picture perception requires visual literacy is the fact that many pictorial conventions involve notable departures from the appearance of unmediated reality. There are at least three major types of picture-reality discrepancy commonly found in a wide variety of pictorial styles. First, many kinds of pictures—for example, black-and-white photographs or outline drawings—contain little or no information about color and/or illumination. Second, because the real world is three-dimensional and pictures are flat, there are certain real-world "depth cues" (i.e., indicators of distance from the viewer) that no ordinary (nonholographic) picture is capable of reproducing. Finally, in a wide variety of pictorial styles—including such things as cartoons or stick figures—the shapes of human figures and other objects differ considerably from their real-world counterparts.

At first blush, these characteristics of pictorial representation may seem to constitute compelling evidence that the ability to interpret pictures must indeed depend on a prior familiarity with visual conventions. But there is more to this story than first appearances may suggest. To begin with: Although the anecdotal evidence referred to above does go along with this notion of a necessary visual literacy, the same cannot be said of much of the systematic research on these issues. As we shall see shortly, these systematic studies have repeatedly found that inexperienced viewers do not find it particularly difficult to make sense of such "unrealistic" conventions as outline drawings or stick figures. Perhaps more importantly, though, there are theoretical reasons for discounting the apparent lack of realism of many styles of pictorial representation.

The past decade has seen an explosive growth in scientific understanding of the process of vision (e.g., see Bruce and Green, 1990). Much of the groundwork for this development was performed by the late David Marr of M.I.T., whose research has led to the evolution of a new theory of visual interpretation (i.e., of what happens in our minds once an image has been formed on our retinas) (see Marr, 1982). These theoretical developments have direct implications for the visual process that concerns us here, seeing pictures.

As Marr points out, the principal goal of real-world vision is ordinarily the identification of objects and the determination of their location in three-dimensional space. In other words, the brain's task in this process can be thought of as an attempt to answer the following questions: What is out there, and where is it? According to the theory that has grown out of Marr's work, this process involves three discrete stages. In stage two, the brain answers the "where" question; in stage three, it answers the "what" question. (Perhaps counter-intuitively, the three-dimensional properties of a scene are determined *before* individual objects have been identified.) Stage one is a preliminary step in which the retinal image is prepared for further processing. Without going into technical details, it is sufficient for our purposes to say that what happens at this stage is the extraction of an outline representation of the scene recorded in the retina. It is this outline, labelled the "primal sketch" in Marr's terminology, which serves as the primary basis of object recognition and three-dimensional space perception. In other words, information about color and illumination is subordinate to the outline and does not play a substantial part in this aspect of the visual process. And this point brings us directly back to our examination of pictures.

Since "inattention" to color and illumination is a standard feature of the real-world process of perceiving objects and placing them in space, it seems reasonable to assume that the equivalent aspects of pictorial interpretation should not be hampered by the absence of color and/or shading in pictures. People should not need to learn how to interpret outline drawings, black-and-white photographs, and other pictorial styles lacking color and/or shading, because real-world vision also operates without this information. This assumption is also consistent with what Marr has called the principle of "modularity" in visual processing: To an extent that may surprise people who believe that the mind always works "wholistically," various parts of the visual process seem to be capable of operating independently of one another (see Fodor, 1983). Thus, someone can suffer pin-point damage to the part of the brain that records color and yet still retain full ability to perform other visual functions in a world of black and white (Sacks & Wasserman, 1987).

The possibility that pictures without color and/or shading may not require a prior visual literacy on the part of their viewers has been tested in several studies, with three kinds of subjects: people living in areas with limited or no access to contemporary visual media (e.g., see Cook, 1981; Dusenbury, 1990; Spain, 1983); animals (see Herrnstein, 1984, for a review); and, in a classic, one-of-a-kind experiment, a child that was deliberately prevented from seeing any pictures for the first year and a half of his life (Hochberg & Brooks, 1962). This latter study and the animal research are particularly relevant for our purposes, because we can be confident that the subjects were indeed completely inexperienced with regard to pictures. The results of this body of research, including the studies of adult human viewers, consistently support the expectation that absence of color and/or shading, in and of itself, is not an obstacle to an inexperienced viewer's interpretation of a picture. For example, the child raised without pictures was able to identify correctly virtually all of the objects in a series of outline drawings and black-and-white photographs.

Together with the theoretical observations we derived from Marr, these findings address the issues raised by the first of the three types of picture-reality discrepancies mentioned earlier. Turning to the second type of discrepancy (i.e., the contrast between three-dimensional reality and the flat surface of pictures) we encounter once again the principle of modularity in visual processing. In real-world vision, the brain's computation of the third dimension (which occurs in stage two of the overall process of identifying objects and locating them in space) is based on several distinct sources of information, commonly referred to as "depth cues." Four of these are particularly important for our purposes: (1) *Binocular disparity* (i.e., the difference between the left and the right eye's view of any particular scene). The closer an object is to the viewer, the greater this disparity will be; (2) *Motion parallax* (i.e., the amount of change that is brought about in the retinal image by any particular displacement of an object relative to the viewer). Other things being equal, objects that are closer to the viewer cause greater changes than objects that are farther away—as can be seen most clearly by looking sideways out of a moving vehicle; (3) *Texture gradients*. This depth cue comes into play when a scene that one is looking at contains regularly textured or patterned surfaces, for example, tiled floors, exposed brick walls, shingled roofs, or even such less-regular, natural surfaces as pebble beaches. In the viewer's retinal image, the more distant parts of the surface will appear more densely textured. These changes or gradients in apparent texture can therefore serve as depth cues; and (4) *Occlusion* (i.e., partial blocking of the view of one object by another object). This visual blockage is obviously a compelling source of information about the relative distance of the two objects from the viewer.

It should be evident that the final two items on this list cannot operate as depth cues in still pictures. Because all of the objects represented in a picture are equidistant from the viewer in reality, binocular disparity and motion parallax (the latter arising from changes in the viewer's position) will be the same for all of them, regardless of whatever fictional distances the picture maker may have intended to convey. If depth perception were a "wholistic," all-or-nothing process, we would expect the absence of these two depth cues from pictures to make it impossible for inexperienced viewers to infer pictured depth. In other words, we would have here a good reason for concluding that, at least as far as pictorial depth perception is concerned, visual literacy may indeed be a necessary precondition of adequate interpretation. However, this is yet another area in which modularity of visual processing has significant implications for the interpretation of pictures. In real-world vision, each of the various depth cues is capable of functioning by itself in cases in which one or more of the others are absent. It follows, therefore, that even a first-time viewer should be able to see depth in a picture when texture gradients or occlusion are present.

This prediction has been tested most directly in a study by Cook (1981). Working with informants from New Guinea, Cook found that pictorially inexperienced viewers were able to make correct inferences about the relative locations of various objects in a picture of a hunting scene, even though both texture gradients and occlusion were present only in a very rudimentary form (i.e., sparse texture and minimal overlap). At the same time, however, there are other studies of pictorial depth perception that complicate this situation. For the most part, these studies have entailed various replications of an early experiment by Hudson (1960, 1967), in which viewers were tested on a series of pictures containing either minimal occlusion or, more often, no real-world depth cues (e.g., see Ohri, 1981; see also Chen, 1991). In these circumstances, inexperienced viewers had trouble seeing depth, whereas experienced viewers tended not to find depth perception difficult.

These findings suggest that experienced viewers may be able to infer depth from certain kinds of visual information (e.g., height of an object's placement on the picture plane) that do not serve as real-world depth cues. In other words, this research appears to lead to the conclusion that there are at least some circumstances in which pictorial depth perception may require visual literacy. However, this interpretation is controversial. As critics of this research have pointed out, there are a number of plausible alternative explanations of its findings (see Hamdi et al., 1982; Kubovy, 1986; Mshelia & Lapidus, 1990). The methodological complexities at issue are beyond the scope of the present discussion (see Messaris, 1994, for a detailed examination of this matter), but it is probably fair to say that there is reason to treat the interpretation of this body of findings with particular circumspection.

We find ourselves on firmer ground, however, when we go on to confront our third type of picture-reality discrepancy, viz., the considerable differences that exist, in many pictorial styles, between the portrayed and the actual shapes of objects. With regard to present concerns, the question raised by such differences is this: What happens to an inexperienced viewer's ability to identify a pictured object when the shape of that object departs markedly from the original?

The process of real-world object identification (stage three in Marr's scheme) is less well understood than the aspects of vision examined thus far. Nevertheless, enough is known about this process to permit us to say the following: The crucial factor in the process is not the object's external shape, but its internal structure. What seems to happen in the brain's computation of object identity is a "reduction" of each object's outline (from the primal sketch) to a representation of the object's underlying structure. This structural representation is then matched against a "dictionary" of object structures in the brain's memory. Thus, regardless of how an object's perceived outline may vary because of changes in the viewer's position or the object's own activity, the "dictionary search" will always be conducted on the same basis, since the object's underlying structure will always be the same. (How exactly the brain goes about calculating this underlying structure is a complicated matter, but it need not concern us here.)

What are the implications of all this for the perception of pictures? Since underlying structure is the primary focus in the brain's final determination of an object's identity, it would seem to follow that even a first-time viewer should not be hampered by "unrealistic" pictorial shapes (e.g., cartoonlike exaggerations or simplifications) so long as the internal structures implicit in those shapes are closer to those of the corresponding real-world objects than to anything else. This possibility has been investigated directly in research conducted in New Guinea by Cook (1981) and by Kennedy and Ross (1975), who examined inexperienced viewers' ability to identify a range of "unrealistic" representational styles, including featureless outline drawings, stick figures, and incomplete sketches. Even for the seemingly least informative styles, rates of correct identification were high—in the case of human figures, close to 100 percent. As with the aspects of pictures examined earlier, then, these results support the notion that visual literacy may be less crucial for the perception of still pictures than many writers may assume.

Formal Conventions: Motion Pictures

Most of what has been said above concerning still pictures also holds for images on film or television. As far as single shots are concerned, the need for visual literacy should be even less with these media than with still pictures, since the gap between picture and reality is reduced by the presence of movement (as well as by the addition of motion parallax as a depth cue). On the other hand, when it comes to editing, we are confronted by a new set of problems, unrelated to those examined thus far. Accordingly, editing will be the principal concern of this discussion. Our focus will be on narrative editing (whether in fictional or nonfictional contexts), and, for the purposes of our analysis, it will be useful to divide this topic into two parts. First, we will examine the kind of editing that typically occurs within a single scene, in which time flows uninterruptedly forward and location remains the same. Second, we will look at changes in location and/or time frame (i.e., editing that usually occurs between scenes).

The first of these two kinds of editing entails a shift in the camera's position—and, therefore, of the spectator's point of view—in the course of a continuous event or action (e.g., cutting from one person to another in a soap opera, a talk show, a newsroom, or a televised tennis match). The interpretational task with which this kind of editing confronts the viewer will vary depending on the context, but there is one problem that the viewer is likely to face in most contexts, viz., deriving a sense of continuous space, time, and action out of the shifting viewpoints created by the editing.

Inexperienced viewers' responses to this aspect of editing have been examined by Hobbs et al. (1988), in a study conducted with a group of rural Kenyans, most of whom had had no previous exposure to motion pictures. (The rest had seen a single government-sponsored film, some time before the study took place.) The study was based on two versions of a short narrative video depicting fictional events and circumstances based on the local culture. One version of the video was recorded in a continuous, unedited shot. The other version involved the kind of editing with which we are concerned here. When viewers were tested on their comprehension of this material, it was found that the presence of the editing did not make things more difficult for them to understand.

What could account for this finding? As the study's authors, as well as other writers, have suggested (see, in particular, Comuntzis, 1987, and Comuntzis-Page, 1991), a viewer's ability to interpret the kind of editing tested in this study—commonly referred to as point-of-view editing—appears to be an extension of a more fundamental, real-world cognitive skill, namely, spatial intelligence. As conceived of by cognitive psychologists (e.g., Gardner, 1993), spatial intelligence comprises a cluster of related cognitive abilities, of which the most crucial, for our purposes, is the ability to derive a coherent sense of a three-dimensional scene out of a limited number of partial views of that scene. Anyone familiar with cognitive psychology will recognize here an area of intelligence that is typically tapped through such measures as Piaget's three-mountain task: A child is shown a certain view of a mountainous landscape and asked to indicate how the mountains would appear from a different viewing position. Although this specific situation may not have an exact parallel in film or TV interpretation (see Messaris, 1982), the general skill of spatial integration on the basis of partial views is—arguably—brought into play every time the action in a scene is "interrupted" by a cut from one point of view to another.

If this is even partly an accurate account of the basis on which viewers are able to make sense of point-of-view editing, it could also be argued that spatial intelligence must be a pervasive element in the interpretational process required by many forms of film and TV fare. This judgment is based on an analysis of the kinds of editing that a viewer is most likely to encounter in typical fictional TV programs. The analysis was concerned with the shot transitions in a convenience sample of nine TV programs: three daytime soap operas, three sit-coms, and three police/adventure shows. These transitions were classified into a number of categories, of which the only one that is relevant for our purposes was the first: a transition *within a single location, from one point of view to another.* Overall, an average of 95 percent of the transitions fell into this category. In other words, by an overwhelming majority, the kind of editing transition that a viewer is likely to be confronted with in a typical fictional TV program is precisely the kind of transition for which spatial intelligence is the relevant interpretational skill. All the other editing devices (time/space changes, flashbacks, etc., which sometimes seem to get the lion's share of attention from scholars) are in fact a tiny minority of the whole.

The creation of a coherent space/time continuum out of the fragments presented in a movie or TV program is evidently one of the central intellectual tasks that visual media demand of their viewers. However, the purpose of point-of-view editing is not always just the linking of partial views of a larger scene. A second major purpose—especially in dramatic contexts—is that of revealing characters' thoughts, intentions, and personalities. This possibility was one of the earliest discoveries in the history of explicit theorizing about the movies. Its formulation is usually associated with Lev Kuleshov and other filmmakers working during the early years of Soviet cinema. In its best-known incarnation, the so-called Kuleshov effect is illustrated in Kuleshov's experiment involving an "expressionless" close-up of the Russian actor Mozhukhin juxtaposed with a variety of other scenes, including a bowl of soup on a table, a corpse in a coffin, and a little girl playing with a toy bear. According to Kuleshov's colleague V.I. Pudovkin, to whom we owe the description of this experiment, viewers who saw these sequences without having been told about the editing responded with enthusiastic praise for Mozhukhin's acting. In other words, the editing led these viewers to see subtle changes in expression—from thoughts of food to deep sorrow to a "light, happy smile"—where in fact there were none (Pudovkin, 1958, 168; see also Kuleshov, 1974, and, for skeptical views of Pudovkin's account: Holland, 1989; Polan, 1986; Prince & Hensley, 1992).

The general category of juxtapositions explored in this experiment (and others following it) is a firmly established feature of film and TV editing, occurring most commonly, perhaps, in the conventional "reaction-shot" sequence, in which shots of a speaker or other object of interest are intercut with shots of a listener or observer. Such sequences are a typical ingredient of dialogue scenes in fiction films, as well as of nonfictional dialogues in talk shows and other TV programs, but the potential role of image juxtaposition as an indicator of characters' thoughts or reactions is probably most evident in the absence of dialogue and in those nonfictional cases in which a certain sequence of events is rearranged through editing (as in the many instances in which an interviewer's "reactions" are inserted into a TV interview after the fact). Assuming that viewers typically do use the juxtaposition of images—rather than just the facial expressions in them—as clues to what lies "beneath the surface" of characters' faces, we are confronted with another cluster of visual conventions based on a single general principle. What might be the source of viewers' ability to make sense of these conventions?

One possibility, of course, is that of previous experience with the conventions in question. On the other hand, however, this is another area in which a ready parallel with a set of real-world cognitive skills suggests itself. Although the precise visual sequence that the viewer is confronted with on the screen—a view of a character juxtaposed with a view of some object or sequence of interest to that character—may not have an exact parallel in reality, the basic inferential task that the viewer has to perform in the case of the film or TV sequence is similar to an extremely common real-life task, namely, that of judging other people's intentions from the context of their behavior. The degree to which this process is central to interpersonal communication bears some emphasis. As researchers in the areas of nonverbal communication and of person perception have noted, people's appearance, expressions, and actions are frequently ambiguous, or even completely opaque, in the absence of information about the objects or situations to which they are addressed. Indeed, Birdwhistell (1970) has argued that no facial expression or gesture has a determinate meaning out of context. The ability to take context into account in inferring thoughts and assessing intentions is consequently a vital component of any mature person's social skills. It is conceivable, therefore, that this ability—rather than any direct experience with editing conventions—may serve as the basis of the interpretational competence called for by the kind of editing we are concerned with here.

The two aspects of interpretation that we have considered so far are both concerned with piecing together a coherent sense of action, setting, motivation, and/or emotion out of the shifting viewpoints generated by the editing. In addition to achieving these mental syntheses, however, there is also another, very different interpretational task that the viewer often encounters when there is a change in point of view. Primarily in fictional contexts, but sometimes elsewhere too, a major function of changes in point of view is to inflect the emotional tone of a narrative— as when a switch to close-ups and an increase in editing speed are used to emphasize dramatic intensity.

Does a viewer need any previous experience with film or television in order to make sense of devices of this sort? A key to answering this question may be the observation that the relationship between these devices' form and their meaning is essentially *analogical*: Modulations in the emotional tone of the narrative (greater or lesser intensity, excitement, etc.) are mirrored by equivalent modulations in the editing (a move toward tighter or looser framing, an increase or decrease in the frequency of shot changes, etc.). What this amounts to is that the intended meanings of these devices are conveyed through sequences of events (coming closer or moving back; speeding up or slowing down, etc.) that embody these meanings directly, rather than signifying them indirectly through some arbitrary code. It seems reasonable to assume, then, that even a viewer who does not have prior familiarity with such devices should be able to sense their meanings without much need for reflection—provided she or he shares the cultural assumptions motivating any particular use of the devices (i.e., assumptions about the appropriate emotional tone of love scenes, scenes of violence or suspense, etc.).

The analogical character of this aspect of editing is one more reason, then, for doubting whether visual literacy is a major prerequisite of interpretation when editing does not disrupt the continuity of location and/or time frame. Our review of the various aspects of this kind of editing cannot claim to have been exhaustive, of course, but it is probably fair to say that it has given a representative account of the major functions that the editing ordinarily serves. A similar aim will characterize the second half of our discussion of editing, in which we will take up the issue of changes in location and/or time frame.

When an editing transition of this latter sort occurs in a nonfictional context, it is typically accompanied by a verbal indication of what is happening: A news anchorperson introduces a reporter at a remote location, a sports announcer analyzes the action in an instant replay, the narrator in a nature documentary tells us where and when the next segment is taking place, and so forth. There are certainly exceptions to this norm—for example, instant replays sometimes come and go without comment—but, for the most part, the presence of a verbal accompaniment means that nonfictional location/time-frame changes are unlikely to require of their viewers any special skill in deciphering visual transitional devices.

The case of fictional transitions is somewhat more complicated. There are, of course, many examples of verbal labelling of scene changes in movies and, less often, television programs. More typically, it often happens that a transition will be triggered by a line of dialogue that anticipates the new location and/or time frame. A much-analyzed instance of this occurred in *Lawrence of Arabia* (1962), in which an indoor scene of T. E. Lawrence discussing the Arabian desert was followed by an abrupt cut to a red-hot sun rising over an endless expanse of sand. This juxtaposition has often been cited as a bold experiment in the rejection of devices for guiding the viewer through the transition, because there is no fade or dissolve, no subtitle announcing the new location, no interpolated shots of the boat that brought Lawrence to the Arabian peninsula. All the same, the transition is hardly lacking in informational cues, since the dialogue that precedes the cut tells the viewer all that she or he needs to know. Indeed, in this respect the transition seems quite characteristic of standard practice in the editing of fiction.

This example is characteristic of fiction editing in another way, too. It illustrates a tendency toward stripped-down transitions (i.e., direct location/time-frame changes unaccompanied by any *visual* transitional device) that appears to be a more general norm in commercial movies. This issue has been investigated systematically by Carey (1982), in a study of location/time-frame transitions in U.S. fiction films between the 1920s and the 1970s. Working with a sample of ten films from each decade, Carey analyzed the duration of these transitions (i.e., length of time between the conclusion of action in one scene and the beginning of action in the next), as well as the nature of the transitional device, if any. He found that the period of years covered by his study had seen a pronounced shortening of the duration of transitions—from an average of more than seven seconds in the 1920s to less than a second in the 1970s—together with a simplification and eventual jettisoning of transitional devices—starting with such things as spinning train wheels or calendars shedding their pages, moving to fades and dissolves, and concluding with straight cuts.

The likely motivation for this trend is suggested by the example of *Lawrence of Arabia*. As that film's director, David Lean, had made clear (see Morris & Raskin, 1992), and as other Hollywood directors have also pointed out (Dmytryk, 1984; McBride, 1982; Rosenblum & Karen, 1979), there has long been a feeling among filmmakers that explicit markers of location/time-frame changes are redundant, since the necessary information is typically contained in the actual events of the story, either in the form of dialogue (as in the scene from *Lawrence of Arabia*) or in the evolving action. In fact, this point had been made at the very beginning of the history of narrative editing by one of the principal architects of that history, director D. W. Griffith. In the film *After Many Years* (1908), Griffith wanted to employ a direct transition between a man shipwrecked on a desert island, gazing at a locket portrait of his wife, and the wife herself, standing pensively on the porch of their house. Griffith's associates argued that the audience would need an intertitle to explain the jump in location, but he insisted that the plot line made things clear enough by itself. In the end, the direct transition did go into the film, with no ill effect on the audience's ability to make sense of it (Mrs. D. W. Griffith, 1975; see also Jesionowski, 1987).

Griffith's point has also been tested, more formally, in a recent experiment by Hobbs and her colleagues. Conducted in the same setting as their earlier research (described above), this study tested inexperienced (mostly first-time) viewers' comprehension of two versions of a short video. In one version, the story unfolded chronologically (i.e., time always flowed forward). The other version's time flow was reversed through the use of a flashback. Despite the presence of this relatively challenging structural device, there was no significant difference in levels of comprehension between the two videos. In fact, for most viewers, comprehension as measured in the study was perfect, regardless of which video they had seen (Hobbs & Frost, 1989).

These findings lend further support to the conclusion that the interpretation of location/time-frame transitions may not ordinarily require a prior familiarity with a set of visual conventions—partly because of the trend toward direct, unmarked transitions but also, more importantly, because the necessary information for understanding the transition is likely to be available in the narrative's action, dialogue, or verbal commentary, even when a transitional device such as a dissolve is also present (cf. Bell, 1992; Gabbadon, 1992). As we have seen, the need for visual literacy can also be questioned in the case of editing, which does not interrupt location/time-frame continuity, and similar skepticism seems appropriate regarding much of the representational apparatus of still images.

It must be remembered, however, that our discussion up to this point has been concerned only with the formal conventions of still or motion pictures. Even if these conventions are completely transparent to the inexperienced viewer of a particular pictorial style or type of movie, interpretation of the content conveyed through these conventions will still inevitably require a stock of cultural knowledge that might productively be termed a form of literacy. To a large extent, of course, the nature of this "literacy" is trivially obvious. It goes without saying, for example, that someone who knew nothing about life in the United States might not be able to make much sense of her/his first encounter with a U.S. TV program or advertisement. Still, there are certain situations that do raise more complex issues that deserve a closer look.

Cultural Content and Connotation of Images

To begin with, it is worth examining two kinds of "misinterpretations" that can occur because of cultural differences: on the one hand, cases in which the viewer actually misidentifies the content of an image; on the other hand, cases in which, even though identification of the content is superficially correct, response to perceived connotation is "inappropriate" (by the standards of the culture that produced the image). After we have examined each of these possibilities in general terms, we will go on to look at a more specific aspect of the problem: In both situations, but more especially in the latter one, a possible reason for the interpretational divergence from the cultural norm could be the viewer's lack of familiarity with specific visual precedents alluded to in the image. Familiarity with such precedents (e.g., Grant Wood's much-parodied "American Gothic") is perhaps the most distinctively visual component of a person's store of cultural knowledge, and it is with this aspect of visual literacy that we will conclude our discussion.

A striking instance of the misidentification of content because of cultural differences has been described by Schele and Miller (1986), in an account of the decipherment of ancient Maya inscriptions. One such inscription contained the following pair of images: on one side, the head of a woman in profile; on the other, a curving, knotted line, which seemed to pass through the woman's mouth. Unable to make any sense of this line, early scholars had dismissed its apparent connection to the woman's face and had portrayed the face by itself, detached from the line, in reproductions of the inscription. In fact, however, more recent scholarship has indicated that the two most definitely do belong together: The scene depicted in the inscription was evidently part of a ceremony of royal blood-letting, to which a Maya noblewoman would contribute by drawing a length of barbed cord through an incision in her tongue.

At first blush, this example may not seem to be telling us very much that we could not have guessed beforehand about the role of past experience in the interpretation of images: The mere fact that culturally unfamiliar objects or events can confound a viewer's understanding of a picture is hardly remarkable. What is interesting about the example, however, is not the simple presence of a misunderstanding but, rather, certain specific characteristics of the way in which that misunderstanding came about. In particular, this example illustrates two features that often complicate the process of pictorial interpretation: (1) the ambiguity or indeterminate meaning of some visual designs; (2) the viewer's consequent need for contextual information as a means of resolving the indeterminacy and arriving at a single interpretation.

The barbed cord depicted in the Maya inscription was, of course, a meaningless design to the generation of scholars who knew nothing about the ceremony in which this cord was used. But we should not take it for granted that the image of the cord would have made sense automatically to a more knowledgeable viewer. A useful analogy here might be the case of a viewer from the U.S. confronted with an image of barbed wire. In a Western movie or other similar context, we can be sure that the image would be instantly recognizable. Stripped of its context, however (i.e., reduced to a set of lines showing the wire itself and nothing else), the design might be more ambiguous, especially if the barbs were drawn to accurate scale. In other words, it seems likely (regardless of the merits of these specific examples) that cultural knowledge may sometimes affect visual interpretation indirectly, by making it possible for the viewer to draw upon the context in cases in which a visual design cannot stand on its own.

The dependence of some interpretations on context has been a recurrent finding of cross-cultural research on visual literacy. Whereas many visual designs can evidently make sense even in isolation, there are others that yield their meaning only as parts of a larger whole—and only to those viewers who are able to draw appropriate inferences from that whole. There has been some progress in arriving at a theoretical understanding of this distinction, and it is possible to make reasonably confident predictions about some of the kinds of shapes that are characteristic of each side of the divide. An account of this theory is beyond the scope of the present discussion, but an intuitive sense of the theory's parameters may perhaps be conveyed by mentioning some examples of research results that are consistent with its predictions. On the one hand, there is a wealth of evidence suggesting that no contextual setting is required for the recognition of even fairly schematic images of humans and animals, and this finding has also been extended to the case of certain isolated body parts, such as eyes (Dusenbury, 1990). On the other hand, more than one study has found that viewers often experience difficulty in trying to arrive at acontextual interpretations of lines depicting topographical features: a hill, a lake, or the horizon (e.g., see Cook, 1981; Kilbride & Robbins, 1969).

For our purposes, what is especially noteworthy about the latter findings is that the actual objects in question were abundantly familiar to the viewers in these studies, since hills, lakes, and extended views of the horizon were common features in the geographical areas in which the studies were performed. Rather, it was the relatively less familiar settings in which these features were placed that appear to have caused the viewers' difficulties. Consequently, these findings are particularly compelling demonstrations of the significance of context. In that respect, they also underscore the overall point of these comments, viz., that, aside from its direct and obvious effect on the recognizability of objects, lack of cultural knowledge can also impede visual interpretation more indirectly, by preventing the viewer's effective integration of the various parts of an image.

Whether direct or indirect, these potential consequences of cultural differences both have to do with the more rudimentary aspects of pictorial interpretation (i.e., the actual identification of the contents of an image). Even when this part of the interpretational process is not affected by cultural differences, such differences may of course complicate a viewer's assessment of the implicit or connotational aspects of an image's meaning. In fact, it could be argued that misinterpretation of cultural connotations becomes more likely when an image's "literal" content is identified without problem, because the viewer may be lulled into overlooking the possibility of other effects of culture.

A useful illustration of the role of culture in shaping the connotations of a picture is provided by Toshi Ikagawa, in an analysis of a type of landscape image that the Japanese refer to as "white sand-blue pine" (i.e., a sandy beach with dark green pine trees [Ikagawa, 1993]). Ikagawa observes that this image, which is encountered frequently in Japanese travel photography, is typically viewed with deep emotion by the Japanese (especially people of older generations), whereas to non-Japanese eyes it is likely to appear relatively pedestrian. This much could be taken for granted with any cultural icon, of course. But Ikagawa goes on to do something relatively unusual, namely, to trace in detail the historical steps through which this image acquired the meaning it has for the Japanese. For example, he notes that the white sand-blue pine landscape became a common theme in nineteenth-century woodblock prints depicting the scenic attractions of Japan; and that subsequently, under the system of compulsory education that was introduced into the country in the late nineteenth century, affectionate references to this landscape were frequently incorporated into the songs that Japanese children were required to sing in elementary school.

Such details serve to ground a particular cultural meaning in the actual processes of cultural production and transmission, and in this respect Ikagawa's analysis could serve as a model for other discussions of visual (or verbal) connotation. Even without such conceptual grounding, though, discussions of visual meaning and interpretation often seem to take it for granted that most (if not all) images are densely packed with culture-specific connotations to which an outside viewer must necessarily be oblivious. A typical expression of this view is provided by Fred Ritchin, a prominent photography critic, who has suggested that cultural differences in photographic style are analogous to the differences among languages. As he puts it: "An argument can be made for photography as a rich, multi-leveled linguistic approach, articulated differently according to the codes of each culture" (Ritchin, 1990, 99). By way of demonstration of this point, he describes his misinterpretation of the intended meaning of a picture by a Cuban photographer: Whereas the photographer had intended this picture, a portrait of a young woman in a formal gown, as a critique of "outdated bourgeois ritual," Ritchin saw the image "as sweetly romantic, a celebration of awakening individuality and sexuality"—a response which he attributes to his having come from a capitalist country (Ritchin, 1990, 101–02).

The idea that cultural differences inevitably lead to radical differences in visual connotation—and that viewers with a U.S. background need to be constantly on the alert against such a possibility—has become especially popular in the world of international advertising. A major impetus for this development was the publication of David Ricks's *Big Business Blunders* (1983), a much-cited compendium of anecdotes about international marketing efforts that purportedly went awry because of business executives' ignorance of foreign cultures. Ricks's stories span a broad range of cultures and a dazzling variety of visual malapropisms. We are informed, for example, that: a soft-drink company inadvertently offended some of its Arab customers because its labels were decorated with six-point stars, which were seen as Stars of David by the Arabs (31); a brand of baby food had poor sales in a certain (unidentified) African nation because a baby picture on the label was interpreted to mean that the product consisted of ground-up babies (31); some Asian customers object to red circles on product labels because it reminds them of the Japanese flag (33); the Singer company had to halt an ad campaign because the blue color used extensively in its ads turned out to be a local symbol of death (51); an ad campaign targeted at Brazilian consumers used a deer to symbolize masculinity, but the campaign's designers were "a bit embarrassed" to discover that "deer" is a local slang term for a homosexual (54); a company which had used an image of an owl in promotional efforts in India discovered that the owl is a local symbol for bad luck (54–55); an attempt to market a laundry detergent in the Middle East failed when the local population, used to reading from right to left, mistakenly interpreted the manufacturer's ads as implying that the detergent actually made clothes dirty (55); a U.S. shoe manufacturer whose ads showed bare feet offended potential customers in Southeast Asia where exposure of the foot is considered insulting (63–64); an ad highlighting Pepsodent's ability to whiten teeth backfired in some regions of Southeast Asia because the local population values darkly stained teeth as a mark of prestige (65); an Irish-themed beer ad featuring a man in a green hat backfired in Hong Kong because the green hat is a Chinese symbol for a cuckold (68); and so on.

The reader will undoubtedly judge for herself or himself how persuasive these anecdotes really are. However unimpeachable their veracity may be, one might still want to question the degree to which they are representative of the situations to which they refer. Furthermore, Ricks's analyses occasionally exhibit a certain tendency toward sweeping stereotypes that undermines the overall logic of his argument. For instance, he tells us that an ad in which one person calls another to say he will be late for a meeting failed in the "Latin market" because "almost no Latin would feel it necessary to phone to warn of tardiness since it is expected" (70). Not surprisingly, perhaps, the factual basis for this assertion (and some others like it) is not made clear. Nevertheless, Ricks's book has become a standard reference source in discussions of the cultural nuances of international advertising, and admonitions about the dangers of cross-cultural blunders have become routine features of this literature (e.g., O'Reilly, 1985, 17–18).

The impression conveyed by some of the writing in this area is that cross-cultural encounters are a minefield of potential misunderstandings and unintended offenses (e.g., see R. Carroll, 1988). While there can be no doubt that some kinds of images are indeed highly resistant to crossing cultural boundaries, it seems reasonable to ask whether there might be a certain amount of exaggeration in such views. In fact, as anyone who has travelled internationally in recent years cannot have failed to notice, cross-cultural image flow is ubiquitous, and instances of ready assimilation of such images seem at least as plentiful—if not actually more frequent—than the problematic cases envisioned by writers like Ricks. For example, while it may be true that Marlboro advertising failed in Hong Kong because "the totally urban people did not identify at all

with horseback riding in the countryside" (Ricks, 1983, 52), high urban-
ization and lack of horseback riding have not impeded the Marlboro man's
successful deployment in any number of other locations.

A similar point could be made about Hollywood Westerns, which have
traditionally enjoyed wide international popularity despite the fact that their
settings (both geographic and cultural) are quite remote from the experiences of most members of this international audience. In fact, when we
turn to the general area of cinema and television, we often encounter a
diametrically opposite view of cultural differences from that which seems
to prevail in advertising. Although it is recognized that genres that are
highly dependent on verbal idiom (e.g., certain kinds of comedy) do not
travel well, there is a widespread assumption that other fictional forms—
notably action-adventure movies and soap operas—can count on foreign
markets for a substantial proportion of their expected revenues (see Noam
& Millonzi, 1993). In this connection, Alfred Hitchcock—whose name
attained international status as a guarantee of quality following the release
of *Psycho* (see Rebello, 1990)—used to claim that his fondness for long
visual sequences without dialogue was a way of enhancing his films' appeal to foreign viewers (Truffaut, 1967). He took it for granted, in other
words, that the visuals themselves would not pose problems to these viewers.

If the actual international receipts of Hollywood films and television
programs are a legitimate indicator of levels of cross-cultural comprehension, we can say that there must be some validity to the assumption represented by such views as Hitchcock's. This assumption is also supported by
most of the findings in Liebes and Katz's (1990) well-known study of the
reception of *Dallas* by various subcultural groups in Israel. As these authors point out, while there were differences of approach among the groups,
there was also a common pattern of receptivity and acceptance. To be
sure, Liebes and Katz's findings have been questioned by Tomlinson (1991),
who argued that their analysis might have been insufficiently attentive to
the shadings of interpretation inevitably imparted by culture. But this criticism does not seem to be based on any *specific* shortcoming in Liebes and
Katz's conclusions, and an example that Tomlinson gives to demonstrate
the supposed cultural variability of interpretations—he cites the case of a
viewer who laughed at a TV news image of a chaotic boating accident
(54)—could arguably have been used to make the opposite point, namely,
that delight in other people's misadventures seems to be a common basis of
humor across a wide range of cultures.

To what should we attribute the seeming ease with which much Hollywood entertainment crosses cultural boundaries? One explanation—occasionally voiced by some producers of this entertainment—is that the movies and TV programs in question deal with universal themes that require no translation. However reasonable this notion may appear, it is very hard to evaluate it systematically, because cultural differences that may seem quite extreme when we look at them up close can always be made to wash out if we adopt a sufficiently abstract point of view. (For example, the actual behavior that anthropologists label "courtship" may well differ beyond recognition from one culture to another.) In any case, even if there is some validity to the universality assumption, it is worth considering the possibility that a diametrically opposite state of affairs may also be partly true.

The universality assumption is predicated on the (often unquestioned) belief that people attend only to those movies or TV programs or other forms of entertainment that are directly relevant to their own cultural circumstances. Hence also the assumption that images that are foreign to a viewer's culture will be misunderstood and rejected. And yet it should be evident, on reflection, that exploration of the unfamiliar can also be a major motive in the consumption of visual entertainment. While studies of international viewership of U.S. media do furnish examples of foreign viewers identifying with images of life in the U.S., these same studies also suggest that a common objective animating such viewership is that of cross-cultural exploration and discovery (see Messaris & Woo, 1991). Without necessarily dismissing the universality hypothesis, then, we can also say that one reason for the ease with which much Hollywood fare is received abroad is that international viewership is often actually predicated on such differences (i.e., is exploratory and assimilative) rather than being a simple search for the familiar and the known. To put this differently: It may well be the case that the ease with which an image crosses cultural boundaries is dependent not just on similarity between cultures, but also on the cross-cultural receptivity of the viewer.

It also seems likely that the nature of viewers' attitudes may explain the greater difficulty encountered by advertising (assuming that this disparity between advertising and entertainment media is not simply illusory). The mere presence of a persuasive intent might be expected to make viewers more resistant in and of itself, of course (cf. Dodd, 1987, 165), but when the persuasive attempt originates in a wealthy nation and is targeted toward a less wealthy one (as is typically the case in international advertising), ignorance of local culture can lead to resistance even when it does not affect the actual comprehension of the message (Janus, 1986, 138–41). For example, an ad for a U.S.-made soft-drink was greeted with scorn in Poland because it featured a private swimming pool. In other words, it seem likely that resentment, rather than incomprehension, may be a major reason for the difficulties that are often said to afflict international marketing campaigns.

A related point has been made by Kyoko Hirano in an extended analysis of the Japanese reaction to U.S. influence on post-World War II Japanese cinema. In line with other U.S. attempts to remold Japanese culture during the postwar occupation of Japan, extensive controls were placed on the content of Japanese films, with the aim of making them more consonant with the values of American democracy. However, although the Japanese had been receptive to American cinema before the war, they were—not surprisingly—resistant to this forced post-war importation (Hirano, 1992). Interestingly, too, a Japanese sample included in Liebes and Katz's study was the only group that did not respond well to *Dallas,* on the grounds that its cultural content was no longer relevant to the current Japanese sociohistorical situation (Liebes & Katz, 1990, 133).

In general, then, the considerations we have just reviewed suggest that it may be an exaggeration to assume that incomprehension of cultural differences is currently a major impediment to the international flow of images. Still, there are bound to be particular instances, in the course of cross-cultural communication, in which such incomprehension will arise. A study by Dumas (1988) has described an instructive case in point. Dumas compared the responses of U.S.-born and Chinese-born graduate students to a series of advertising images from which captions and all other verbal text had been removed. One of these images, taken from an ad for financial services, depicted a well-dressed, well-groomed businessman having an early morning cup of tea on a balcony overlooking a large city. This is a type of image with a long lineage in the history of U.S. advertising (see Marchand, 1985, 238–47). Beginning as early as the 1920s, this kind of scene—a prosperous-looking person (usually male) with an upper-floor view of a major city (or, occasionally, an industrial complex)—has been used as a standard device for evoking a sense of success and power. Variations of this imagery can be found in contemporary ads for such products as liquor, cosmetics, and VCRs, and Dumas's U.S. respondents were readily able to identify the image's intended meaning. However, to the Chinese respondents, who had only recently come to the United States, the connotations of wealth and power were not always that obvious. Instead, many of them constructed hypothetical scenarios to explain why this middle-aged man was having breakfast alone (Dumas, 1988).

What makes this example particularly interesting for our purposes is the fact that it involves a specifically visual cultural precedent, as opposed to more general cultural knowledge. In other words, it seems safe to assume that the U.S. respondents' understanding of the image was based not only on general knowledge about the value of penthouses, top-floor offices, and the like, but also on some prior exposure to specific ads embodying the imagery of a powerful person looking down from such a vantage point. Similar situations (i.e., cases in which knowledge of specific visual precedents plays a crucial role in the interpretation of an image) are not very hard to come by in U.S. visual media. Most obviously, this sort of situation will occur whenever one image directly imitates or parodies another. There are several widely recognized prototypes that have served as bases for such replications, perhaps the best-known being Grant Wood's "American Gothic" and the image of "Uncle Sam" that made its first appearance in James Montgomery Flagg's World War II recruiting poster. To the extent that parodies or other variants of images such as these require the viewer to recognize (explicitly) the fact that a reference to a precedent is being made, the adequate interpretation of these variants will obviously depend on a certain degree of prior exposure to the original images (or, at least, to some of their successors). From a cross-cultural perspective, it is probably this type of prior experience (i.e., exposure to the various paintings, posters, photographs, etc., that make up a culture's stock of recyclable "icons") that is the most important form of visual literacy.

Conclusions

As used in this discussion, the term *visual literacy* refers to the assumption that the ability to recognize the meaning of visual images (both still pictures and movies) is dependent on prior experience (and is therefore roughly analogous to linguistic competence). We have examined three aspects of this general topic, paying special attention to the problem of cross-cultural communication through images. First, we looked at stylistic matters: how individual still images are formed, and how their appearance relates to that of the real world. It was argued (on empirical as well as theoretical grounds) that a broad range of seemingly "unrealistic" representational practices (including the omission of color and/or shading, as well as various "distortions" of the shapes of objects) are actually interpretable solely on the basis of viewers' real-world perceptual skills (i.e., with no need for a picture-specific "literacy"). A similar argument was made with regard to the second area that we examined, the linking of images in film and television editing: Although all editing necessarily entails "impossible" violations of the continuous flow of reality, there are both theoretical reasons and some empirical support for assuming that the ability to interpret editing may be a derivative of real-world visual habits (in the case of within-scene editing) or general (not picture-specific) inferential processes (in the case of narrative editing between scenes). The final area that we examined was that of the cultural content of images. We considered a variety of images whose interpretation might pose problems to a cultural "outsider," and we concluded that visual literacy may be particularly important when an image makes direct reference (through parody or other means) to specific, commonly known visual precedents within a certain culture. At the same time, though, it was also argued that, to a large extent, difficulties in cross-cultural communication through images may have more to do with attitudinal barriers than with misinterpretations of visual content. This final observation may also be the most appropriate point with which to conclude this examination of visual literacy.

References

Balazs, B. (1970). *Theory of the film: Character and growth of a new art.* Trans. E. Bone. New York: Dover. (Originally published 1952.)

Bell, T. (1992). *Decentration as a predictor of comprehension of cross-cutting.* Unpublished M.A. thesis. Philadelphia: Annenberg School for Communication, University of Pennsylvania.

Birdwhistell, R. L. (1970). *Kinesics and context: Essays on body motion communication.* Philadelphia: University of Pennsylvania Press.

Bruce, V., & Green, P. (1990). *Visual perception: Physiology, psychology, and ecology.* Hillsdale, N.J.: Lawrence Erlbaum Associates.

Carey, J. (1982). Conventions and meaning in film. In S. Thomas (Ed.), *Film/culture: Explorations of cinema in its social context* (110–25). Metuchen, N.J.: Scarecrow Press.

Carroll, N. (1988). *Mystifying movies: Fads and fallacies in contemporary film theory.* New York: Columbia University Press.

Carroll, R. (1988). *Cultural misunderstandings: The French-American experience.* Trans. Carol Volk. Chicago: The University of Chicago Press.

Cassidy, M. F., & Knowlton, J. Q. (1983). Visual literacy: A failed metaphor? *Educational Communication and Technology Journal, 31,* 67-90.

Chen, N. (1991). *The assessment of pictorial depth in Chinese and Western paintings.* Unpublished M.A. thesis. Philadelphia: Annenberg School for Communication, University of Pennsylvania.

Comuntzis, G. M. (1987, July). *Children's comprehension of changing viewpoints in visual presentations.* Paper presented at the Visual Communication Conference, Alta, Utah.

Comuntzis-Page, G. (1991, July). *Perspective-taking theory: Shifting views from Sesame Street.* Paper presented at the Fifth Annual Visual Communication Conference, Breckenridge, Colo.

Cook, B. L. (1981). *Understanding pictures in Papua New Guinea.* Elgin, Ill.: David C. Cook Foundation.

Deregowski, J. B. (1980). *Illusions, patterns and pictures: A cross-cultural perspective.* New York: Academic Press.

Dmytryk, E. (1984). *On film editing: An introduction to the art of film construction.* Boston: Focal Press.

Dodd, C. H. (1987). *Dynamics of intercultural communication.* 2nd ed. Dubuque: Wm. C. Brown Publishers.

Dumas, A. A. (1988). *Cross-cultural analysis of people's interpretation of advertising visual cliches.* Unpublished M.A. thesis. Philadelphia: Annenberg School for Communication, University of Pennsylvania.

Dusenbury, K. A. (1990). *Inexperienced viewers' understanding of pictorial materials: The results of a survey in Lesotho, Africa.* Unpublished M.A. thesis. Philadelphia: Annenberg School for Communication, University of Pennsylvania.

Fodor, J. A. (1983). *The modularity of mind.* Cambridge, Mass.: The MIT Press.

Gabbadon, D. (1992). *Children's comprehension of flashbacks: A study of inexperienced and experienced Jamaican child viewers.* Unpublished M.A. thesis. Philadelphia: Annenberg School for Communication, University of Pennsylvania.

Gardner, H. (1993). *Frames of mind: The theory of multiple intelligences.* Tenth-anniversary ed. New York: Basic Books.

Gibson, J. J. (1982). *Reasons for realism: Selected essays of James J. Gibson.* Ed. E. Reed & R. Jones. Hillsdale, N.J.: Lawrence Erlbaum Associates.

Gombrich, E. H. (1960). *Art and illusion: A study in the psychology of pictorial representation.* Princeton: Princeton University Press.

———. (1984). Representation and misrepresentation. *Critical Inquiry, 11,* 195–201.

Griffith, Mrs. D. W. (1975). *When the movies were young.* New York: Benjamin Blom.

Hamdi, N., Knirk, F., & Michael, W. B. (1982). Differences between American and Arabic children in performance on measures of pictorial depth perception: Implications for valid interpretation of test scores based on items reflecting dissimilar cultural content. *Educational and Psychological Measurement, 42,* 285–96.

Herrnstein, R. J. (1984). Objects, categories, and discriminative stimuli. In H. L. Roitblat, T. G. Bever, & H. S. Terrace (Eds.), *Animal cognition* (233–61). Hillsdale, N.J.: Lawrence Erlbaum Associates.

Hirano, K. (1992). *Mr. Smith goes to Tokyo: Japanese cinema under the American occupation, 1945-1952.* Smithsonian.

Hobbs, R., Frost, R., Davis, A., & Stauffer, J. (1988). How first-time viewers comprehend editing conventions. *Journal of Communication, 38*(4), 50–60.

Hobbs, R., & Frost, R. (1989, October). *Comprehending transitional editing conventions: No experience necessary?* Paper presented at the Seventh International Conference on Culture and Communication, Philadelphia.

Hochberg, J., & Brooks, V. (1962). Pictorial recognition as an unlearned ability: A study of one child's performance. *American Journal of Psychology, 75,* 624–28.

Holland, N. N. (1989). Film response from eye to I: The Kuleshov experiment. *The South Atlantic Quarterly, 88,* 415–42.

Hudson, W. (1960). Pictorial depth perception in subcultural groups in Africa. *Journal of Social Psychology, 52,* 183–208.

———. (1967). The study of the problem of pictorial perception among unacculturated groups. *International Journal of Psychology, 2,* 89–107.

Ikagawa, T. (1993). White sand & blue pines: A nostalgic landscape of Japan. *Landscape, 32*(1), 1–7.

Janus, N. (1986). Transnational advertising: Some considerations on the impact on peripheral societies. In R. Atwood and E. G. McAnany (Eds.), *Communication and Latin American society: Trends in critical research, 1960–1985* (127–42). Madison: The University of Wisconsin Press.

Jesionowski, J. E. (1987). *Thinking in pictures: Dramatic structure in D. W. Griffith's Biograph films.* Berkeley: University of California Press.

Kennedy, J. M., & Ross, A. S. (1975). Outline picture perception by the Songe of Papua. *Perception, 4,* 391–406.

Kilbride, P. L., & Robbins, M. C. (1969). Pictorial depth perception and acculturation among the Baganda. *American Anthropologist, 71,* 293–301.

Krieger, M. (1984). The ambiguities of representation and illusion: An E. H. Gombrich retrospective. *Critical Inquiry, 11,* 181–94.

Kubovy, M. (1986). *The psychology of perspective and Renaissance art.* New York: Cambridge University Press.

Kuleshov, L. (1974). *Kuleshov on film: Writings by Lev Kuleshov.* Trans. & Ed. Ronald Levaco. Berkeley: University of California Press.

Liebes, T., & Katz, E. (1990). *The export of meaning: Cross-cultural readings of Dallas.* New York: Oxford University Press.

Marchand, R. (1985). *Advertising the American Dream.* Berkeley: University of California Press.

Marr, D. (1982). *Vision: A computational investigation into the human representation and processing of visual information.* New York: W. H. Freeman.

McBride, J. (1982). *Hawks on Hawks.* Berkeley: University of California Press.

Messaris, P. (1982). To what extent does one have to learn to interpret movies? In S. Thomas (Ed.), *Film/culture: Explorations of cinema in its social context* (168–83). Metuchen, N.J.: Scarecrow Press.

———. (1994). *Visual "literacy": Image, mind, and reality.* Boulder, Colo.: Westview Press.

Messaris, P., & Woo, J. (1991). Image vs. reality in Korean-Americans' responses to mass-mediated depictions of the United States. *Critical Studies in Mass Communication, 8,* 74–90.

Morris, L. R., & Raskin, L. (1992). *Lawrence of Arabia: The 30th anniversary pictorial history.* Foreword by M. Scorcese. New York: Anchor Books.

Mshelia, A. Y., & Lapidus, L. B. (1990). Depth picture perception in relation to cognitive style and training in non-Western children. *Journal of Cross-Cultural Psychology, 21,* 414–33.

Noam, E. M., & Millonzi, J. C. (Eds.). (1993). *The international market in film and television programs.* Norwood, N.J.: Ablex.

Ohri, K. U. (1981). *A study of the assessment of the pictorial depth perception of Indian children on specific depth discrimination tasks.* Unpublished doctoral dissertation. College Park: University of Maryland.

O'Reilly, J. A. (1985). *International marketing.* Plymouth: Macdonald and Evans.

Panofsky, E. (1991). *Perspective as symbolic form.* Trans. C. S. Wood. New York: Zone Books. (Originally published 1927.)

Polan, D. (1986). The "Kuleshov effect" effect. *Iris, 4*(1).

Prince, S., & Hensley, W. (1992). The Kuleshov effect: Recreating the classic experiment. *Cinema Journal, 31*(2), 59–75.

Pudovkin, V. I. (1958). *Film technique and film acting.* Trans. & Ed. I. Montagu. New York: Grove Press.

Rebello, S. (1990). *Alfred Hitchcock and the making of* Psycho. New York: Dembner Books.

Ricks, D. A. (1983). *Big business blunders: Mistakes in multinational marketing.* Homewood, Ill.: Dow Jones-Irwin.

Ritchin, F. (1990). *In our own image: The coming revolution in photography.* New York: Aperture.

Rosenblum, R., & Karen, R. (1979). *When the shooting stops . . . the cutting begins: A film editor's story.* New York: Penguin Books.

Sacks, O., and Wasserman, R. (1987). The case of the colorblind painter. *The New York Review of Books, 34*(18), 25–34.

Schele, L., and Miller, M. E. (1986). *The blood of kings: Dynasty and ritual in Maya art.* Photographs by J. Kerr. New York: G. Braziller.

Spain, S. (1983). *Factors affecting pictorial comprehension in non-literates: Results of a survey in the Gambia, West Africa.* Unpublished M.A. thesis. Philadelphia: Annenberg School for Communication, University of Pennsylvania.

Tomlinson, J. (1991). *Cultural imperialism: A critical introduction.* Baltimore: Johns Hopkins University Press.

Truffaut, F. (1967). *Hitchcock.* New York: Simon & Schuster.

Wilson, J. (1983). Comments on work with film preliterates in Africa. *Studies in Visual Communication, 9*(1), 30–35.

Worth, S., & Adair, J. (1972). *Through Navajo eyes: An exploration in film communication and anthropology.* Bloomington: Indiana University Press.

6

Expanding the Concept of Literacy

Renee Hobbs

Media literacy is an expansion of the traditional perspectives on literacy, and this chapter illustrates how media literacy pedagogy and conceptual principles connect to contemporary approaches to reading/language arts education. By broadening the skills of access, analysis, and communication to include a wide variety of messages—language, images, sound, popular mass media, and technology-based messages—the power of literacy can become fully realized as a skill essential to life in an information age.

In schools across the nation, teachers and students set aside their text-books for a few days in April of 1992 to talk about the real-world horrors that they had seen on the television news—the day after the acquittal of the police officers in the Rodney King beating trial, when the streets of Los Angeles could not contain the rioters who were filled with rage. According to Bullard (1993), "With events in Los Angeles as catalysts, classrooms have become the sites of honest conversations . . . that could be the beginning of great understanding."

In addition to discussions about racism, violence, and power, students and teachers also talked about images. For our understandings of the King beating and its aftermath were powerfully shaped by the pictures shown on broadcast news, in newspapers, and in newsmagazines. These images—first of the brutal beating of Rodney King, and then of the horrible violence, looting, and rioting that followed—were evidence of the power that the mass media have in evoking strong emotional responses. At many different grade levels, students and teachers across the nation were compelled to begin to explore the paradoxical nature of images with these powerful questions:

- Do images tell the truth?
- What meanings do different people see in images?

- How do words shape the meanings of images?
- How do the authors of images shape their messages?
- Why do images arouse us emotionally?

Reports from teachers provide examples of a variety of approaches used in discussing these issues. For example, one elementary teacher used works of children's literature about racism, and after reading, had students compare pictures from the books to pictures in newsmagazines. In a middle school, a teacher compared the language used in a radio news account of the riot compared with similar versions on television and in the local newspaper. A middle school teacher in Houston had students rewrite the cutlines to different magazine photographs to see how language shapes interpretations of imagery. A teacher in Detroit helped students analyze how entertainment television programming turned the real-life event into storytelling, as an episode of "Doogie Howser, M.D." showed how the emergency room coped with the riot, and characters in "The Fresh Prince of Bel Air" helped in the cleanup effort. High school students in Los Angeles watched the film *Boyz in the Hood* and examined how the sequence of narrative events was shaped to heighten audience identification with characters.[1]

However, it would be a mistake to think that such practices were common events in American schools, even in response to an uncommon tragedy like the Los Angeles riots. Most teachers make use of media for motivation, illustration, and enrichment, a use of media which emphasizes its value as an attractive delivery system. Only a few now use media artifacts as study objects. Why? Too many teachers believe that media—especially television—are the enemy. Some teachers find it more comfortable to stand outside the cultural world in which their students live, providing little assistance in helping students understand and interpret what has been called the "first curriculum" (Postman, 1985), the carefully designed set of messages about how the world works, how to buy products, and how to behave toward others, which television and other mass media provide to every citizen. Indeed, in 1994, it hardly seems necessary to state the evidence which shows the dominance of film, television, and other mass media products on the lives of American citizens (see Alton-Lee, Huthall, & Patrick, 1993; Howe, 1983; Kubey & Csikszentmihalyi, 1990; Weiss, 1990 for examples of recent evidence).

Just as the scholarly community is coming to appreciate the ways in which meaning is constructed as a result of the creative tension between the reader and the text, the power of mass media messages also comes from how individuals make interpretive use of them. But images have been taken for granted to serve as mere decoration, and mass media have been neglected in schools, and so students have had little instructional support in helping them analyze and think about media messages. For many years, students and teachers interested in exploring the connections between words, images, and ideas have had few resources to use. As we enter the twenty-first century, it is essential that schools be places that help students better understand the complex, symbol-rich culture in which they live.

Although equally complex, the education crisis in the United States is no better understood than the complex social, political, economic, and technological transformations which are reshaping the global communications industries. Students often do not see a connection between what they do in school and the communities in which they live. Such disenchantment with the value and relevance of education leads to failure in school. Every eight seconds a child drops out of school in the United States; 75 percent of parents have never visited their children in school; and the United States ranks low among industrial nations in its rates of literacy (National Commission on Excellence in Education, 1983). One thing is certain: our nation has been deeply hampered economically, politically, and socially by our inability to educate our citizens effectively.

What is needed is a new vision of literacy which reflects the complex communication environment in which citizens must manage. This new vision incorporates both the legacy of our rich literary and cultural heritage and the nature of contemporary symbolic expression at the beginning of the twenty-first century. This chapter examines how a new vision of literacy can be incorporated into educational resources for students and teachers. A new vision of literacy is essential if educators are serious about the broad goals of education: preparing students to function as informed and effective citizens in a democratic society; preparing students to realize personal fulfillment; and preparing students to function effectively in a rapidly changing world that demands new, multiple literacies.

What is the New Vision of Literacy?

Language is the most important element of our humanity, and yet, it is only one of a number of symbol systems which humans use to express and share meaning. Changes in communication technologies over the past 100 years have created a cultural environment which has extended and reshaped the role of language and the written word. Language must be appreciated as it exists in relationship to other forms of symbolic expression—including images, sound, music, and electronic forms of communication. Scholars and educators are coming to recognize that literacy is not simply a matter of acquiring decontextualized decoding, comprehension, and production skills, but that literacy must be connected to the culture and contexts in which reading and writing are used (Cook-Gumperz, 1986).

Consider this new definition of literacy, adopted by educators who identify themselves with the "media literacy" movement (Aufderheide, 1993, reprinted in this volume): "Literacy is the ability to access, analyze, evaluate and communicate messages in a variety of forms." Embedded in this definition is both a process for learning and an expansion of the concept of "text" to include messages of all sorts. This view of literacy posits the student as actively engaged in the process of analyzing and creating messages and as a result, this definition reflects some basic principles of school reform[2] which generally include:

- inquiry-based education;
- student-centered learning;
- problem solving in cooperative teams;
- alternatives to standardized testing; and
- integrated curriculum.

Basic Processes of Literacy: Access,
Analyze, Evaluate, and Communicate

The four processes that constitute the new vision of literacy provide a powerful frame in which to consider how people develop skills in using language and other forms of symbolic expression. For example, the ability to *access* messages connects to those enabling skills which include decoding symbols and building broad vocabularies. Access skills also include those skills related to the locating, organizing, and retention of information; using parts of a book to find information; selecting and using reference sources using print, computer, video, and other sources. The skills of access also refer to the ability to use the tools of technology, including video technology and computers. Access skills are often labeled as "information literacy," or more recently, "superhighway skills."

The ability to *analyze* messages connects to those interpretive comprehension skills which include the ability to make use of categories, concepts, or ideas; determine the genre of a work; make inferences about cause and effect; and identify the author's purpose and point of view. At the secondary level, the ability to analyze messages includes a recognition of the historical, political, economic, or aesthetic contexts in which messages are created and consumed.

The ability to *evaluate* messages concerns those judgements about the relevance and value of the meaning of messages for the reader, including making use of prior knowledge to interpret a work; predicting a further outcome or a logical conclusion; identifying values in a message; and appreciating the aesthetic quality of a work. Although the skills of analysis and evaluation are frequently conflated by practitioners of media literacy, it is important to recognize that analysis skills depend upon the ability to grasp and make effective use of conceptual knowledge which is outside the student's own perspective, while evaluation skills make use of the student's existing world view, knowledge, attitudes, and values.

The ability to *communicate* messages is at the heart of the traditional meaning of literacy, and the skills of writing and speaking have been highly valued by educators. In the last twenty years, writing has come to approach the primacy that reading has gained in the language arts hierarchy. Communication skills are diverse and, to some extent, media specific. General skills include the ability to understand the audience to whom one is communicating; the effective use of symbols to convey meaning; the ability to organize a sequence of ideas; and the ability to capture and hold the attention and interest of the message receiver. Media-specific production skills for print include learning to write letters and spell words; using correct grammatical form; and learning how to edit and revise one's work based on feedback. Similar media-specific production skills can be identified for speaking, video, and audio production.

Expanding the Concept of "Text"

While the four concepts provide a new frame for thinking about the processes involved when people create and share messages, what makes the new vision of literacy so powerful is the application of these skills to *messages in a variety of forms*. At present, reading/language arts educators focus on literature as the core of the K–12 curriculum: the short story, poetry, drama, and nonfiction are claimed to be ideal because they "motivate learning with appeal to universal feelings and needs . . . classic literature speaks most eloquently to readers and writers" (California State Board of Education, 1986, 7).

But they also may seem disconnected and remote from the experiences of students who, because of television, are "escorted across the globe even before they have permission to cross the street" (Meyrowitz, 1985, 238). Critics have claimed that, too often, a literature-based reading/language arts program "ignores the life experience, the history and the language practice of students" (Freire and Macedo, 1987, 146), and that when literary materials are used primarily as vehicles for exercises in comprehension and vocabulary development, students may become alienated from the processes of reading and writing in a range of contexts.

In the past, educators have been comfortable to disenfranchise and overlook present-day cultural products, especially television, even though many works of literature which are now considered classic or traditional began their life as popular works designed for mass audiences (Beach, 1992). But just as scholars and critics have engaged in heated controversy about what texts are appropriate study objects to be included in the canon of essential literary works (Gless and Herrnstein Smith, 1992), these debates are filtering into changes in the curriculum.

Many educators have discovered that the analysis of contemporary media can build skills that transfer to students' work with the written word. When educators permit and encourage the study of contemporary media products in classrooms, students develop skills which alter and reshape their relationship to media products. Nehamas (1992) explains that "[s]erious watching . . . disarms many of the criticisms commonly raised about television." More importantly, analysis of media texts helps students gain interest in writing and speaking, and helps nurture students' natural curiosity and motivation. Consider a story presented by Lauren Axelrod (cited in White, 1993a), a high school teacher in Houston, Texas:

> I used media literacy concepts to get my low-achievement students to tackle Conrad's *Heart of Darkness* and T. S. Eliot's *The Wasteland.* I started with an extensive analysis of the Francis Ford Coppola film, *Apocalypse Now,* and we discussed the film's narrative structure, mood, point of view, rhythm and character development. Then a team of students read Conrad while another team read Eliot. We then applied the same concepts to the short story and poem in group discussion and writing exercises. Finally, students created a videotape which com-

pared and contrasted the three works with each other. I saw students turn on to literature in a way I never saw them engage with anything in the classroom.[3]

Media education exists as an increasingly vital component of elementary education in Great Britain, Canada, Australia, Spain, and other nations. In Great Britain, the mandate includes media education as a strand within the National Standards developed in English, where students are required to study the ways in which media products convey meanings in a range of media texts (Alvarado & Boyd Barrett, 1992; Bazalgette, 1992; Brown, 1991; Buckingham, 1991; Lusted, 1991; Masterman, 1985). While still controversial among those who favor a more traditional and narrow view of "culture," scholarly work in media pedagogy has grown widely, and consensus is growing about the set of concepts, skills, and learning environments which help most to strengthen students' ability to access, analyze, evaluate, and communicate messages in many forms.

The New Vision: Key Analytic Concepts

Current approaches to reading/language arts often make use of a laundry list of concepts which inform the work of teachers and students in a classroom. Such lists are the result of adding new paradigms for learning upon older models. Layer by layer, the models now used in reading/language arts have become cumbersome and unwieldy. "The scope of English heightens the individuality of curricular patterns. . . . Teachers are left to wave the various components into a coherent pattern for themselves and their students" (Hawthorne, 1992, 116). But a simple and powerful new definition of literacy, as proposed in this chapter, makes it possible to identify the most important processes, concepts, and skills for K–12 instruction and make use of these with a wide variety of message forms, from folktales to commercials, from historical fiction to newspaper photography.

Media literacy incorporates the theoretical traditions of semiotics, literary criticism, media studies, communication theory, research on arts education, and language and literacy development. Although the conceptual principles of the new vision of literacy have taken many forms by various curriculum writers in Great Britain, Canada, Australia, and the United States, the following ideas are analytic constructs:

- All messages are constructions;
- Messages are representations of social reality;

- Individuals construct meaning from messages;
- Messages have social, political, aesthetic, and economic purposes;
- Each form and genre of communication has unique characteristics.

It is clear that the most dynamic concepts of current practice in reading/language arts instruction are wholly consistent with these key concepts.[4] But when educators include the analysis and creation of film, photographs, newspapers, radio, and television, new concepts are required to enable students to ask critical questions about these contemporary forms. A number of these concepts may be unfamiliar to reading/language arts teachers, particularly at the elementary level. For example, teachers in some communities have sometimes been reluctant to include the analysis of how messages have political or economic purposes. While it may be argued that analysis of the economics of literature is not of central value for young students, analysis of the economics of media messages is essential to help middle school and high school students understand the complex and often paradoxical nature of communicative messages in contemporary culture. It would be irresponsible to include the study of film, television, newspapers, or other mass media without providing students in grades K–12 with a paradigm to help them understand the ways in which messages have value in the marketplace and the ways in which audiences function as a commodity (Hobbs, 1994).

New Ways of Using Media in the Classroom

Technology now plays a greater role in American classrooms than in the schools of most other industrialized nations. Composition teachers, for example, often make use of word processing software which helps students prewrite, write, revise, proofread, and publish. And with multimedia software, students can create documents which combine words, sounds, images, and on-line and other information resources.

But when teachers talk about the uses of video in classrooms, they emphasize the values of enrichment or motivation, identifying television as a "lure" to make classic works more attractive, or referring to video as a vehicle to "deliver facts." Teachers often admit to using video as a "babysitter" when they are busy, overworked, tired, or when they must be away from the classroom, or when they wish to "reward" students who have completed their work (Hobbs, 1993b). Such uses of video reflect both the casual and passive ways in which we use television in the home

(Kubey & Csikszentmihalyi, 1990), and what Jerome Bruner has called "the transmission model," where learning is a process of sending information by those who know more to those who know less (Bruner, 1986). Why has the use of video technology not developed more fully in American schools? The most obvious answer seems to be because television is so ubiquitous in our homes. Years of habitual use have reinforced the belief that television is merely an entertainment media. Another is that teachers often assume that the study of television, film, and photographic imagery is unnecessary and redundant, not central to the core elements of reading/language arts.

But when television, video, and other media are used well, they can be significant teaching tools in the nation's classrooms. For example, a collaboration between WNET and Texaco Teacher Training Institute for Science, Television, and Technology involved training teachers in how to use television technology in science classes. According to researcher Ruth Ann Burns, who examined the effectiveness of the program, when television is used interactively as a component of middle school science classes, students' "writing is more creative and descriptive, and [students] displayed more ingenuity and innovation on assignments, and they were more confident and enthusiastic in class" (Studies show students, 1993, 4). This program works because, in part, it identifies teachers, not programs, products or technology, as the most significant change agents in education.

As glossily packaged and presented film, video, and advertiser-supported materials enter the school classroom, video materials are considered to be an effective way to deliver messages because everyone in a classroom is presumed to be able to decode the messages on the screen. But the new vision of literacy presented in this report is not just aimed at cultivating the relatively simple process of decoding messages—it is the sophisticated analysis, evaluation, and the active creation of messages that are the most significant, complex, and vital skills needed for survival in an information age. These take a lifetime to master fully.

Even very young students can engage in conceptual analysis and evaluation of media messages, at a time when they are still beginning to master the decoding and comprehension skills required for print. According to Resnick (1987, 31),

> the most important single message of modern research on the nature of thinking is that the kinds of activities traditionally associated with thinking are not limited to

advanced levels of development. Instead these activities are an intimate part of even elementary levels of reading . . . when learning is proceeding well.

When teachers make use of a full range of messages in developing children's literacy, higher-order cognitive skills can be integrated into the activities of very young children using media messages as study objects. This helps motivate students to master the basic accessing skills to crack the code of the printed word. These analytic concepts, already familiar to students in their work with media artifacts, can then be applied to print forms. Elementary teachers who have used this approach find that "much of the language used to view television critically is transferable to other media—noticing camera angles in photography, understanding differences between reality and fantasy. . . . There are also many connections to teaching verbal and written skills " (Lacy, 1993, 11–12).

What happens, according to British educators, is that when students critically examine a wide range of texts in both print and visual media, they develop more complex expectations about everything they read and see. "Media education is often seen as a way of defending children from television. It ought to be seen as a way of giving them high expectations of television, of all media, and of themselves" (Bazalgette, 1992, 45). Such views represent the potential of the new literacy to reshape the character of our nation's near limitless appetite for mass media products and in doing so, to help citizens reconnect to the rich storehouse of literary treasures from many cultures, past and present.

The Consequences of Expanding the Concept of Literacy

The new vision of literacy has consequences for some of the most important issues that face American educators today. As developed in the following pages, this chapter outlines how the new vision of literacy helps restore the important connection between the school and the culture, making education more relevant to the communities to which students belong. It also outlines how the new vision of literacy reflects the kind of authentic learning which occurs when reading and writing occur in contexts where "process, product and content are all interrelated" (Edelsky, Altwerger, & Flores, 1991, 9), and where language skills and language learning are conceived of as being inherently social processes, requiring direct engagement and experience tied to meaningful activity.

Building Relevance between the Classroom and the Community

The claims by now are depressingly familiar: many students actively resist the process of learning in school, and while they can decode language, they cannot infer meaning; the school curriculum is fragmented and decontextualized, promoting indifference and intellectual dependency (Diaz, 1992; Hirsch, 1989; Gatto, 1992). Fortunately, educators have already begun to respond to these criticisms by making changes in their methods of instruction: moving away from a curriculum which emphasizes facts and isolated skills and towards an emphasis on collaborative, active learning which involves complex thought and interpretation (Cohen and Grant, 1993).

Multicultural education. Multicultural education is education that values human diversity and acknowledges that "alternative experiences and viewpoints are part of the growing process" (Grant, 1993). The new vision of literacy proposed in this report is fueled by this philosophy. It promotes cultural pluralism and social equality by making changes in the processes and content of school curriculum; in doing so, it is centered on "building meaningful relationships between curriculum and life" (Pang, 1992, 67).

Carlos Cortes argues that media literacy is essential to multicultural education, noting that media literacy strengthens students' knowledge about various media forms, helps develop analytic and creative skills in responding to media, and helps students become skilled in using print, images, sounds, and other tools to express and share ideas. Cortes (1991, 153) writes, "Media can be used to stimulate students to consider multiple perspectives on current and historical multicultural dilemmas." Clearly, both multicultural education and the new vision of literacy proposed here share the goal of opening up the canon to expand the range of works which are studied in the classroom.

Not unexpectedly, much of the criticism that has developed about the inclusion of works by Hispanic Americans, Native Americans, African Americans, and others can be directed at the new vision of literacy as well, which would include works from popular culture which some critics have labeled "trash." The formal study of advertising, news, situation comedies, music television, popular music, video games, cartoons, and other popular media challenges those who value reliance on the traditional canon. Educators who believe that "good literature" is a "salve one can apply to children from the wrong side of the tracks to heal them of their background" (Beach, 1992, 554) will likely resist any efforts that attempt to make the canon more responsive to the lives of students and their communities. But John Beach recognizes that the time is ripe to examine the variety of definitions of "good literature" and suggests that instead of viewing literature as a pyramid which places classic works at the top and works of popular culture at the bottom, it should be considered "like a tree with many branches; the 'best' can be found at the tip of each branch."

ESL/bilingual education. How might the new vision of literacy affect students who come to school speaking other languages besides English? According to Porter (1990, 153), the instructional methods that are most effective in ESL/bilingual education are identical with the active learner-centered model, which the new vision of literacy promotes. Techniques which make use of "drama, songs, objects and audiovisual materials to help convey meaning and content" are highly effective.

In Portland, Maine, media artist Huey (also known as James Coleman) developed a media education program for ESL students speaking twenty-seven languages, where students make film and video using animation and live-action techniques. Portland elementary teachers "have found that Huey's approach offers their students a creative way to improve their English, their public speaking and their communication skills in general . . . and it breaks down walls between schools and communities through cable TV and closed circuit screenings and student research within the community" (White, 1993b).

Writing for the College Board, Hirsch (1989, 60) notes:

> Over and over again, teachers in ESL and bilingual classrooms have realized the power of authentic tasks to motivate communication and language learning. . . . In searching for authentic tasks and materials, many ESL and proficiency teachers are looking beyond traditional textbooks to primary sources in the language they are teaching, including newspapers, television commercials, menus, hotel receipts, children's books, and journalism and fiction.

Home-school connections. In some communities, parents are active and supportive players in the day-to-day life of the school. In too many communities, however, parents are disenfranchised partners in the educational process. In considering the relationship between the new vision of literacy and the home-school connection, it is necessary to identify the high level of ambivalence and concern which many citizens have with the ways film, television, and other mass media have shaped public discourse. Many adults believe that television has damaged the process we use to elect public officials; that mass media organizations disrupt the private lives of individuals unnecessarily; that violence in film and television programming desensitizes people and alters their conceptions of the social world; and that the values of sensationalism have reshaped culture and the arts (Bianculli, 1993).

The new vision of literacy proposed in this report is based on a fundamental truism about the purpose of democracy: in order for citizens to be engaged in self-governance, they must critically analyze and evaluate information and resources. This work is essential if citizens are to take meaningful action and make meaningful decisions on issues of concern to the community. But in a culture in which citizens see themselves as spectators and consumers, democracy is threatened. When citizens do not employ their skills of analysis and evaluation to information and entertainment products, apathy and cynicism reign.

The new vision of literacy could help encourage parents to more fully embrace their responsibilities to help their children interpret the meanings of the complex messages which bombard them every day. Too often, parents feel intimidated by the activity of the classroom, by routines which are established by educators, who may unintentionally disempower parents from embracing their own authority as interpreters of textual materials. While some parents may hesitate to voice their interpretations of a literary work, parents often feel quite comfortable discussing their interpretations of a film, a situation comedy, a dramatic series, a documentary, or an op-ed article. The new vision of literacy creates opportunities for parents and their children to re-engage with the complex task of sorting out the meanings of the messages in the environment.

Making Classrooms Centers for Authentic Learning

Educators have been discussing how to make learning more authentic since the beginning of this century, when John Dewey first began outlining how children's own activity, their work, could be a vehicle for learning. When learning is authentic, the content of classroom discourse is meaningful and relevant to students; language skills are not taught in isolation; connections between subject areas are emphasized. According to Sizer (1984), in authentic learning environments, students learn through direct experience with tasks they themselves value, with intellectual stimulation from teachers who ask thoughtful questions and provide supportive coaching.

The new vision of literacy helps nurture new relationships between teachers and students, helping rebind the current contrast that "exists between *paidia* (play) and *paideia* (education)" (Gallagher, 1992), based on the recognition that the aim of the reading/language arts teacher is to cultivate a learning environment where students bring their own naturally energetic exploration to the study of new ideas.

Student empowerment. Rather than considering language development as a series of isolated and fragmented skills, the new vision of literacy puts students at the center of the processes of accessing, analyzing, evaluating, and communicating messages. Most importantly, the new vision of literacy is centered around empowerment, defined as the "process through which students learn to critically appropriate knowledge existing outside their immediate experience in order to broaden their understanding of themselves, the world and the possibilities for transforming the taken-for-granted assumptions about the way we live" (McLaren, 1989, 186).

Consider a potential cycle where third-grade students, using a wide variety of message forms, engage in the processes of accessing, analyzing, evaluating and communicating while exploring the theme of "weather."[5] In a classroom environment which makes use of learning centers for a wide range of activities, students can *access* a variety of information resources available to them about the weather and post them on the wall. Students can discuss similarities and differences in weather coverage by their local newspaper, *USA Today, the Weather Channel,* and local radio newscasts. Perhaps the teacher can take them to a TV station where they can see how the weather graphics are created and meet and interview the meteorologist.

Working in cooperative teams, students can collect, gather, and read information from newspapers, magazines, and books about different kinds of weather phenomena (floods, hurricanes, etc). The teacher can share with them stories, poems, and biographies of people whose lives have been powerfully altered by changes in the weather, using works of children's literature. Through pen-pal letter or videotape exchanges with students from schools in South Florida or Missouri, students can learn about the recent real-world impact of weather on the lives of other children.

Again working in teams, these third-graders can *analyze* and *evaluate* the similarities and differences between the various versions of the daily weather as they appear in the news media; track the sequence of weather updates as they change throughout a twenty-four-hour period; categorize different vocabulary words used for different writing purposes: when weather is described by scientists, when children use language in their letters about floods or hurricanes, and how poets use language to describe the range of feelings weather evokes.

Students can creatively *communicate* a wide range of messages which serve to share their interpretations with others. One group of students can gather, select, and organize images to create a visual collage or wall display of the tragedy of floods and hurricanes as they affected children in the United States and around the world. Another group of students can write letters or conduct phone interviews with children in South Florida or Missouri to get a better understanding of other perspectives on the effects of weather. Students can write poetry about the feelings they experienced after reviewing TV news footage of the recent weather disasters. Working in pairs, they can videotape and edit interviews with their parents or relatives or write a description of dramatic weather experiences they've had. Students can create their own TV weather report based on data they collect themselves, developing graphics and spoken information to display their information.

Because of the breadth of projects, students will get a chance to make use of those learning modalities which are most comfortable: kinesthetic learners will choose to create the wall display, while verbal learners will choose to conduct an interview or write a letter. Effective teachers will help students to work on a wide variety of tasks to strengthen their writing, reading, thinking, listening, speaking, critical viewing, and media production skills.

Integration with other subject areas. As is clearly evident, the new vision of literacy provides a simple, process-based model that makes connections between reading/language arts, the visual and performing arts, social studies, and science. Shepard (1993, 35) explains how the new vision of literacy is an ideal tool for subject integration at the elementary level:

> If media literacy is presented to [teachers] as just another add-on, there will be little hope for its adoption. If, however, media literacy is presented not just as something that meets students' needs, but something that will meet the teacher's need to integrate the disparate elements of a broad curriculum, then it stands a good chance of becoming an important part of the curriculum. In fact, media literacy functions so well as an integrator that it would be worth using even if it were not as intrinsically important as it is.

Because mass media artifacts are relevant to science, social studies, and the visual and performing arts, as well as reading/language arts, teachers can easily make connections that stretch across subject areas by teaching with media and teaching about media.

Using new tools of assessment. When assessment is authentic, it has as its central purpose the goal of providing feedback to a child and his or her parents about the quality of the learning experience. When assessment is authentic, it mirrors the ways in which standards of quality are evaluated in the world outside the classroom: through close examination of products and performances.

For more than a century, assessment in the United States has been shaped by the needs of scholars and academics to standardize and quantify learning experiences (Gould, 1981). This has led to an atomized, fragmented view of the learning process, one conducive to "data reduction." Now, educators are coming to recognize the need to reclaim the assessment process, and as a result, diverse new forms of assessment are being used in schools.[6]

The new vision of literacy provides simple and direct opportunities to observe, monitor, and evaluate the processes of accessing, analyzing, evaluating, and communicating messages in a range of informal and formal settings. Because the creation of messages is central to the new vision of literacy, portfolio-based models of assessment are consistent with the new vision. Indeed, the premise of the new vision is based on the idea that the processes of accessing, analyzing, and evaluating messages all contribute to the creation and communication of messages, so students can make direct connections between their reading and their writing, their viewing and analysis of images, and the process of creating messages using language, images, sounds, music, graphics, and video.

The Toronto Board of Education's Benchmark Program has been using an assessment model designed to demystify educational goals and illuminate the nature of good performance (Larter & Donnelly, 1993). By combining authentic performance activities with systematic observation and holistic evaluation, teachers can assess student skills in a way that most closely matches the broad general skills that are at the core of reading/language arts instruction. For example, in one benchmark of students' ability to comprehend nonprint information and their oral communication skills, third-grade students in Toronto are asked to watch a videotape on owls and explain the major ideas in their own words. Students were found to generally lack strong skills in the comprehension of informative video, perhaps because their expectations about television shape their level of motivation and effort in decoding (Salomon, 1979). The development of standards, tied to authentic performances, which allow educators to assess the quality of students' writing, speaking, listening, and thinking skills is consistent with the new vision of literacy. The province of Ontario was the first in Canada to mandate that media literacy instruction be at least 30 percent of the reading/language arts program in grades 7–12 (Duncan, 1993). The performances of younger students from the Toronto Board of Education results suggests that students lack basic comprehension skills of information presented in video formats, pointing clearly to the necessity of direct instruction to help students in grades K–8 to learn to comprehend, interpret, and analyze a wide range of texts, including messages from television and the mass media.

Staff development issues. Teachers are just as ambivalent about media culture as the rest of the U.S. citizenry. As discussed earlier, teachers have a wide range of attitudes about the value and consequences of broadening the concept of literacy to include new materials, especially popular music, film, television, and music videos. However, teachers who have attempted to incorporate these materials into their classroom realize that students have a tremendous amount of knowledge and interest in these messages, and teachers and students can share together in the learning process.

It is not difficult for teachers to move from teaching exclusively using media for content delivery to addressing media as study objects deserving sustained analysis. Some teachers have described the process as similar to the process of "consciousness raising" about gender and race which many educators experienced in the 1970s. "It's like putting on a new pair of glasses—you see the same things [in media culture], but now I approach these messages differently," wrote one teacher.[7]

Teachers who are comfortable with whole language approaches to reading/language arts will find the new vision of literacy consistent with the practices they already use. Teachers who use traditional, teacher-directed approaches will probably enjoy the flexibility that using print, images, and sound-based materials brings, and they will find how much students can grow and learn under their own steam when they find the tasks of the classroom relevant to the world outside the classroom. Teachers who make use of skill-based approaches in reading/language arts may be able to build connections between their focus on decoding and comprehension skills and the process model of the new literacy, which places skills in the larger context of accessing, analyzing, evaluating, and communicating messages.

But German educator Dichanz (1992) writes plainly about what it takes to make the new vision of literacy a reality in schools: "It is the staff that has to translate tasks . . . into practical work, and it is that staff that has to be provided with the theoretical background for this new approach." For U.S. educators, this means that the work of staff development is best accomplished not by individual teachers acting independently, but through coordinated and sustained efforts, using resources and tools which help them gain access to new ideas and practice new strategies of managing classroom activity. Such work is well underway at the state, district, and local levels. For example, the State of New Mexico has begun a process of teacher training so that media literacy will be integrated into the high school curriculum.[8] And the community of Billerica, Massachusetts has implemented a three-year process of extensive teacher training, including the first Master's Degree in Media Literacy, in order to implement a new vision of literacy in grades K–12 integrated within existing subject areas.[9]

Conclusion

If media literacy is to emerge as a new vision of literacy for the information age, then a high degree of coordination will be required from among a range of shareholders: the scholarly community, educators in K–12 environments, parents, the publishing and media production industries, and the standardized testing industry. Given the decentralized nature of American schools, it is unlikely that such coordination will receive the support it needs, and more likely that media literacy initiatives will develop as a result of innovation and experimentation in the diverse "labs" of individual disctricts, schools, and classrooms.

A new, revitalized conceptualization of literacy makes it possible for teachers, using a variety of methods and approaches, to help students extend their analysis, evaluation, and communication skills using video production, audiotape, still photography, on-line services, and more. While media literacy holds out the promise of helping reshape teaching methods and practices to become more inquiry based and student centered, there are some dangers. It may too easily be turned, by the new technologists, media conglomerates, and publishing firms, into just another "product" to be efficiently and cost-effectively delivered by book, videotape, or satellite dish into young minds. For an institution that has historically clung to the concept of literacy as the central organizing force of education, we must respect the time it will take to create the support for sustained, rigorous, and meaningful change that is necessary for schools to embrace this expanded vision of literacy for twenty-first century schools.

Notes

1. These accounts of practice were described by teachers participating in the Institute on Media Education, 31 July–7 August 1993, Harvard Graduate School of Education, Cambridge, Massachusetts.
2. "School reform" has as many meanings as there are philosophies of education, but the author refers to those attempts to reshape the ways in which students and teachers engage with each other in order to accomplish meaningful learning. Contemporary scholars working in the tradition of John Dewey include Theodore Sizer of the Coalition of Essential Schools at Brown University.
3. Lauren Axelrod told this account while a participant at the Harvard Institute on Media Education, 31 July–7 August 1993.
4. Special issues in a number of publications point to the leadership that is currently emerging among reading/language arts educators. See the publication of the Canadian Council of Teachers of English, *English Quarterly* 25, as well as a special issue of *English Journal,* January 1994.
5. Special thanks to third-grade teacher Margaret Cowell of the Kennedy School and fourth-grade teacher Jane Kennedy of the Ditson School in Billerica, Massachusetts, for their ideas about integrated curriculum, which connects media literacy to science, social studies, and the arts.
6. The State of California, for example, recognizes a wide variety of assessment methodologies, which include many nonquantitative, performance-based tools. And in Toronto, Ontario, the Board of Education has designed a measure of elementary students' ability to comprehend nonprint information and retell it orally. This benchmark included a performance-based activity, which was of instructional value to students, used a holistic scoring criteria, and provided valuable quantitative evidence to policymakers, school administrators, teachers, and members of the community.
7. Personal communication from a teacher participating at the Harvard Institute on Media Education, 5 August 1993.
8. In 1993, state government officials met for a seminar with educators from across New Mexico to begin the process of including media literacy as a component of required courses necessary for high school graduation.
9. In Billerica, Massachusetts, the author has been privileged to help develop a comprehensive program of media education in grades K–12. Called the Billerica Initiative, the program includes large-scale teacher training, including a Master in Education Degree in Media Literacy, sponsored by Fitchburg State College and the Merrimack Education Center, as well as community outreach, curriculum development, and research on student performance. The program began in 1993.

References

Alton-Lee, A., Huthall, G., & Patrick, J. (1993). Reframing classroom research: A lesson from the private world of children, *Harvard Educational Review, 63,* 50–84.

Alvarado, M., & Boyd-Barrett, O. (Eds.) (1992). *Media education: An introduction.* London: British Film Institute.

Aufderheide, P. (1993). *Media literacy: A report of the National Leadership Conference on Media Literacy.* Washington, D.C.: The Aspen Institute Communications and Society Program.

Bazalgette, C. (1993). *Teaching for tomorrow.* Unpublished working paper, British Film Institute.

———. (1992). *Media education: Teaching English in the National Curriculum Series.* London: Hodder and Stoughton.

Beach, J. A. (1992, November). New trends in perspective: Literature's place in language arts education. In *Language Arts, 69,* 550–56.

Bianculli, D. (1993) *Teleliteracy.* New York: Pantheon.

Brown, J. (1991). *Critical viewing skills education.* Beverly Hills: Sage Publications.

Bruner, J. (1986). *Actual minds, possible worlds.* Cambridge: Harvard University Press.

Buckingham, D. (Ed.) (1991). *Watching media learning.* London: Routledge.

Bullard, S. (1993, February). Talk out student bigotry using the L.A. riots. *Education Digest, 58.*

California State Board of Education. (1986). *English language frameworks for California public schools, K-12.* Sacramento, Calif.

Cook-Gumperz, J. (Ed.) (1986). *The social construction of literacy.* Cambridge, England: Cambridge University Press.

Cortes, C. (1991). Empowerment through media literacy. In C. Sleeter (Ed.), *Empowerment though multicultural education.* Albany, N.Y.: State University of New York Press, 153.

Cohen, D., & Grant, S. G. (1993, Winter). America's children and their elementary schools. *Daedalus, 193.*

Diaz, C. (Ed.) (1992). *Multicultural education for the 21st century.* Washington, D.C.: National Education Association.

Dichanz, H. (1992). Media in the teachers' professional and personal environment. In *Media competency: A challenge to school and education.* Conference proceedings, Bertelsmann Foundation.

Duncan, B. (1993). Presentation at the Harvard Institute on Media Education, 2 August.

Edelsky, C., Altwerger, B., & Flores, B. (1991). *Whole language: What's the difference?* Portsmouth, N.H.: Heinemann, 9.

Freire, P., & Macedo, D. (1987). *Literacy: Reading the word and the world.* South Hadley, Mass.: Bergin and Garvey.

Gallagher, S. (1992). *Hermenuetics and education.* Albany, N.Y.: State University of New York Press.

Gatto. J. T. (1992). *Dumbing us down: The hidden curriculum of compulsory schooling.* Philadelphia: New Society.

Gless, D. J., & Herrnstein-Smith, B. (Eds.) (1992). *The politics of liberal education.* Durham N.C.: Duke University Press.

Gould, S. J. (1981). *The mismeasure of man.* New York: W. W. Norton.

Grant, C. (1993). Cultural connections. *New dimensions in the world of reading.* Needham, Mass.: Silver Burdett Ginn, Volume 1, 6–7.

Hawthorne, R. C. (1992). *Curriculum in the making: Teacher choice and the classroom experience.* New York: Teachers' College Press.

Hirsch, B. (1989). *Languages of thought: Thinking, reading and foreign languages.* New York: The College Board.

Hobbs, R. (1994). Pedagogical issues in U.S. media education. In S. Deetz (Ed.) *Communication Yearbook 17,* 453–56.

————. (1993a, July). *Who pays for TV? Model curriculum.* Presentation at the National Council of Teachers of English Conference, Assembly on Media Arts, Philadelphia, Pa.

————. (1993b, May) How to use TV—Not! *Cable in the Classroom.*

Howe, M. (1983). *Learning from television: Psychological and educational research.* London: Academic Press.

Kubey, R., & Csikszentmihalyi, M. (1990). *Television and the quality of life: How viewing shapes everyday experience.* Hillsdale, N.J.: Lawrence Erlbaum Associates.

Lacy, L. (1993, May). Media literacy ABCs. *Cable in the Classroom,* 11–12.

Larter, S., & Donnelly, J. (1993, February). Toronto's benchmark program. *Educational Leadership 50,* 59–62.

Lusted, D. (Ed.) (1991). *The media studies book: A guide for teachers.* London: Routledge.

Masterman, Len. (1985). *Teaching the media.* London: Routledge.

McLaren. P. (1989). *Life in schools.* New York: Longman, 186.

Meyrowitz, J. (1985). *No sense of place: The impact of electronic media on social behavior.* New York: Oxford University Press.

National Commission on Excellence in Education. (1983). *A nation at risk: The imperative for educational reform.* Washington D.C.: U.S. Department of Education.

Nehemas, A. (1992). Serious watching. In D. J. Gless & B. Herrnstein Smith, (Eds). *The politics of liberal education.* Durham N.C.: Duke University Press, 164.

Pang, V. A. (1992). Institutional climate: Developing an effective multicultural school community. *Multicultural education for the 21st century.* Washington, D.C.: National Education Association, 67.

Porter, R. P. (1990). The Newton alternative to bilingual education. In *The Annals of the American Academy of Political and Social Science,* 508.

Postman, N. (1985). *Amusing ourselves to death.* New York: Viking.

Resnick, L. (1987). *Education and learning to think.* Washington, D.C.: National Academy Press.

Salomon, G. (1979). *Interaction of media, cognition and learning.* San Francisco: Jossey Bass.

Shepard, R. (1993). Elementary media education: The perfect curriculum. *English Quarterly, 25,* 35.

Sizer, T. (1984). *Horace's compromise.* New York: Houghton Mifflin.

Studies show students tune in when teachers teach with television. (1993, April/May). *Tech Trends, 38,* 4.

Weiss, E. (1990). *100% American.* New York: Poseidon Press.

White, R. (1993a, August/September). Forming a media arts department. *The Independent, 16,* 41–42.

————. (1993b, August/September). Video as a second language: Multilingual program, Portland Maine. *The Independent,* 16.

Part III

International Perspectives

7

Media and Arts Education:
A Global View from Australia

Peter Greenaway

This paper examines the development of media education in countries outside the USA, and reflects on why a form of media education, which includes cultural literacy and social values, has not yet become a hot issue in the States. The goals and objectives of media and art education are developing similarities especially in relation to popular culture. This chapter identifies and discusses some of these common issues and their application in contemporary education.

The Value of Teaching Popular Culture

Popular culture, fed and maintained by the mass media, is probably the single most influential factor in shaping young people's perception of the world. An increasing number of educators believe media literacy is essential because it is the means by which the dominant culture is sustained and it is the source of much of our knowledge. Even though we often find ourselves saying, "I read about that somewhere," it is highly probable that we actually saw it on television or heard it on the radio. The intrusive electronic media implants ideas, expectations, and aspirations without us being aware of attending to their messages.

The particular focus of this chapter is popular culture, and particularly as related to youth. It reflects on the development of media education as it relates worldwide to American popular culture. It asks how best can popular culture be taught, by whom, and where in the curriculum, and suggests that there may be opportunity for creative ways of teaching about popular culture in the art room as well as in the media studies classroom, including creative production and/or the reworking of texts.

> Official culture as preserved in the galleries, museums and university courses de-
> mands cultivated tastes and a formally imparted knowledge. It demands moments of
> attention that are separated from the run of daily life. Popular culture meanwhile,
> mobilises the tactile the incidental, the transitory, the expendable, the visceral. It
> does not involve an abstract aesthetic research amongst privileged objects of atten-
> tion, but invokes mobile orders of sense, taste and desire. (Chambers, 1986, 12).

Mass media technology has had a substantial social and economic
impact on contemporary society, and "by the late 1950s . . . the study of
culture could no longer be reduced to an aesthetic or moral question but
involved a whole way of life" (Chambers, 1986, 203).

Television, cinema, magazines, video games, and even clothes worn,
provide the substantial influences, role models, and sources of knowledge that combine to make a popular culture. Understanding popular
culture and, perhaps more particularly, adolescent popular culture, is
therefore an essential part of any teacher's repertoire, especially those
teaching media studies.

The Canadian media educator Barry Duncan believes that

> once teachers confront the popular culture of young people, they find media-gener-
> ated issues are one of the best bridges to the world of their students. Since access to
> the media is egalitarian, and young people are its biggest consumers, teachers and
> students are on an equal footing. Particularly with general and basic level students,
> mutual media experiences may be their only common ground. (Duncan, 1988)

Teaching popular culture can be fraught with pitfalls for the unwary.
One is that some students resent critical analysis in the classroom of a
media text they enjoy in their leisure time, and see this as an invasion of
their enjoyment of the text.

Jean-Pierre Golay, a long-standing exponent for the inclusion of popular
culture in art education also points out that

> the difficulty for some teachers is to be able to realise and recognise that there is
> myth in subculture which they do not share with their students. It is hard for certain
> educated people, dealing usually with well recognised forms of art, to accept the
> emergence in sometimes fragile sub-cultures of new metaphors expressing the same
> durable truth, or of metaphors they consider low key. Sometimes it is even impos-
> sible to accept the idea that popular culture productions might be received as meta-
> phors, and not only a noise or crazy motions and grimaces. (Golay, 1988, 8)

However, by simply being aware of the likely pitfalls and sensitive to the
students use of and involvement in popular culture texts, teachers can, as
Barry Duncan suggests, build bridges between teacher and student.

One important strategy is to ask questions such as, "What is it about (insert the media text in question) that you respond to?" "Why do you think this appeals to teenagers?" and "How relevant is it to your culture?" ensuring that the discussion avoids negative criticism and value judgments by the teacher.

The Influence of American Popular Culture

Much of the western world's popular culture emanates from the USA and is often referred to as the *Coca Cola Culture*. Screens throughout the world are filled with American films and television programs and in the shops there are products, such as jeans, which have infiltrated all cultures. Recent examples would include the proliferation of American baseball and basketball sportswear. In countries other than America it is only one aspect of the popular culture, although it is often a dominant influence, especially on adolescents. My observation is that Australians have a vast knowledge of American culture compared with the limited knowledge Americans have of Australian culture. I suggest that this is directly related to the popular culture texts. (The preference for American sportswear by Australian youth is related to video clips and Nike ads).

Australians have been subjected to enormous amounts of information about America, whereas Americans' exposure to Australian culture (and for Australia read most countries) is in comparison minuscule. A revealing comparison between the two countries is that in Australia there have always been regulations requiring television stations to schedule set minimum hours of Australian-made programs; local content is an issue that has never needed raising in America. With satellite technology, Marshall McLuhan's vision of a global village has probably been achieved, but perhaps in not a way he would have expected it; he did not foresee that it would virtually be one-way traffic from America. American produces something like 97 percent of the television its citizens consume. This is only surpassed by the communist eastern bloc. (The collapse of the Soviet Union will most likely change this situation and there will probably be a substantial infiltration of American programs into this new market.) Consequently American television, like the defunct communist bloc, precludes almost entirely any outside cultural influence.

Patricia Mellemcomp writes:

> While every other industry has been de regulated, representations shown in the
> U.S. are still made in the U.S. Economics keeps the representations of other na-
> tions, on screen, on stage, and on TV, out of the U.S. with a rigid protectionism
> which the GATT will not touch, at least for now, and which is not reliant on
> ownership, conditions of production, given the Japanese takeover of two major
> studios As software for their electronic hardware. Although there are increasing
> multi national ownership. The most profitable export, the biggest industry, of the
> U.S. is representation. (Mellemcomp, 1993, 7).

Satellite technology allows Australians to watch a direct broadcast of
The NBC Today Show (albeit at 12:30 A.M.). Like other countries around
the world, Australia also has a high percentage of prerecorded popular
American programs. There would hardly be a young person in Australia
that did not know that 90210 is the Beverly Hills post code, or a child
who has not heard of Mickey Mouse or Bart Simpson. In Australia the
influence of American culture, as represented in media texts, has always
been viewed as a threat by some, and something to aspire to by others.
Australians suffered for many years from what was called a "cultural
cringe," which was basically a belief that anything from North America
or Europe would be superior to home-grown products.

A growing self-confidence in Australian-made cultural products has
resulted in a questioning of this attitude of the past. Hence, part of the
argument for media education has been made easy in Australia by media
educators pointing out the influence of outside cultures introduced through
media such as television. If Australia suffered from a cultural cringe
then America could be said to suffer from a cultural arrogance.

American popular culture is mirrored in and perpetuated and reinforced by the producers and writers of media texts. They are the dominant group that prescribes how "reality" is represented, those who own
the means of ideological production.

Those immersed in the dominant culture with nothing to compare it
with, such as foreign cultural imputs or noncommercial institutions such
as government broadcasters,[1] find it extremely difficult to see the extent
to which the media is structuring and informing attitudes and opinions.

Thus, the argument that media education should address social values
and representation is very difficult to substantiate in the United States where
media education has, so far, been related largely to media technology and
resources. This situation is slowly being redressed by the efforts of an

increasing number of concerned educators. For example, while I was in America, the National Alliance of Media Educators (N.A.M.E.) was formed.

Pedagogy

What is seen as a crucial element in teaching popular (or dominant) culture is a pedagogy that includes the making of media texts in conjunction with the analysis *this is not a new concept.* In 1977 James Donald was calling for a pedagogy that included the making of media texts in conjunction with analysis. This dual process is now seen as integral to media education.

> Practice implies initially the production of useful messages. But it is also through the practice of learning, e.g., how to use a video camera, record an interview, prepare a script, or reach a joint editorial decision that the first crucial step of revealing the human construction, the non-naturalness, of the products of the media will be achieved. The object is to reveal how the ideological messages of the mass media are put together (encoded) and to seek effective codes for the students' own messages. (Donald, 1977/1992, 81).

Donald suggests this will be achieved by practical production work and teaching for visual literacy, but stresses that his answers are only speculative. He refers to visual literacy as "a clumsy and, I hope, provisional concept," and suggests that much valuable work at the time was based on the Golay and Gauthier work with images.[2]

> Literacy is a tricky analogy, not only because it remains largely opaque itself, but because it is probably a quite different process from making sense of an image. The point is to find a way of making images "strange" (often by presenting material derived from the psychology of perception, such as ambiguous images and visual tricks and illusions) and thus reveal their multi layered significance (using concepts derived from semiology). The significance will depend not only on the content and internal form and the style of the image (lighting, colour, angle of shot etc.), but also on its context. This raises questions about the medium in which the image appears and the audience for which it is intended, as well as the relation to any other images and any accompanying text. The activity of "decoding" is thus seen to depend on not just cognitive processes and sets of conventional symbols, but crucially on the social position of the receiver. Any image may be interpreted in a number of different ways. The range of possible interpretations will reflect the economic, political, and cultural struggles and contradictions present in the audience. (Donald, 1977/1992, 81)

All that has changed in the sixteen years since Donald wrote this is that there is a more general understanding of what he was proposing and significant progress in media education theory and pedagogy.

Core Concepts of Media Education

One of the most significant milestones in the international development of media education has been the collaborative work done in the development of core concepts, principles, and theoretical frameworks. These vary only slightly from country to country and invariably include:

- representation, selection and construction;
- media texts as influencing agents of culture and dominant ideology;
- the institutions in which a text is produced;
- the function and form of media texts;
- audience (people use media, not simply consume them);
- the making of competent and articulate media messages.

These core concepts have successfully focused media education and have solved the problem of trying to write a media studies program that embraces all the identified components of the media, which include, film, cinema, video, television, books, newspapers, magazines, video clips, computer games, radio, and photography, and the categories and genres of all of the above.

Responsibility for Media Education

British media educationalist Cary Bazalgette asked some basic questions of teachers of English:

> Should media education include learning to "speak" or "write" the language of all the different media? To understand a language, both as a listener/reader and as a speaker/writer, is to be empowered. People who can communicate well have more power over their own lives, and often over other people's also, than people who can't communicate well. Knowing several languages is obviously more empowering than knowing only one. But how realistic an inspiration is this? How many forms of communication have you learned? How many are taught in schools? How many could be taught? These are not simple questions. Once the word "language" is extended from its everyday meaning of "verbal" language and applied to things like drawing and photography or radio, and we start to use terms like "reading" pictures or "writing" audio-visual texts, then the difficulties of persisting with the literal analogy become apparent. Many media teachers—myself included—have used this analogy as a polemic; to argue that understanding and using audio-visual technologies ought to be taken seriously as reading and writing verbal language. Hence we get words like "visual literacy" or "media literacy." (Bazalgette, 1991, 40)

Bazalgette is one of the many influential writers on media education who have an English-teaching background. Typical of her writing is the following, where she uses the process of taking a photograph as an illustration of how students and teachers can think systematically about the construction and consumption of media texts. She asks:

* Why am I taking this photo?
* What sort of photograph is it going to be?
* What sort of technology am I using?
* What choices can I make about what the photo will look like?
* Who is going to see the photograph?
* What do I want to show in the photograph? (Bazalgette, 1992, 202)

The illustration is very useful and corresponds with the media core concepts of agency, category, technology, language, audience, and representation. Bazalgette suggests the inclusion of snapshots, records of school events, and illustrations for teaching. The interesting omission in this otherwise excellent list is that no mention is made of someone who may regard the taking of photographs as artwork. By not including the making of a photograph as art, she is denying the use of photography as artistic self-expression. (Would she also leave creative writing or poetry out of a list of categories of writing?) I believe this to be a serious omission by many media educators coming from a language or communication studies background. They appear to shy away from anything to do with creative expression, especially when related to the visual media.

Works of art, like media texts, are reliant on various institutions for their production and consumption. A painting or photograph taken as a creative response by someone who wishes to express an opinion or emotion could be displayed in a gallery or be used as part of a media text, such as the cover for a magazine. There is increasing use of photographs in newspapers which have no news value but are simply chosen because they are aesthetically pleasing. In either context, gallery or print media, the artistic merit may be the same but the way material is consumed varies. Good graphic design, layout, and the illustrations in books and magazines are rarely consciously noticed; bad design is.

The role of art in the construction of media texts is being overlooked by some media educators. Promoting visual media literacy in America, David Considine and Gail Haley observe that,

because art is taught as a subject at school, it is often left to art teachers as a result of which other teachers seldom reinforce it by integrating it into the curriculum. Paintings and other forms of art can be analysed as social artefacts and historical documents that provide evidence of the time in which they are created or the period they depict. These representations may be accurate or misleading. They may also reflect a patriarchal culture and a social mechanism that narrowly defines the role of women. Art education must provide the opportunity for students to express themselves and communicate through their own creations. (Considine & Haley, 1992, 26)

The point made by Considine and Haley is valid and there are many media teachers who do not always consider the ways in which artworks can be similar to other media texts. The art our students consume (and live) is not only in the galleries or the art history books, and is never neatly packaged into unrelated compartments. Their art includes the animation and video clips they watch, the layout and design of the magazines they read, and the advertisements and package design they respond to. Their art can even be illegitimate graffiti.

Art education that denies the extensive application of art in the creation of popular culture, and promotes the view that art is only an elite form of creative self-expression giving no consideration to an audience other than art patrons, has little relevance today.

Obviously there is room to maneuver by both media and art educators, and it is now appropriate to apply some of the core concepts of media education to art education.

Roy Stafford is enthused about the growing convergence of media and art education in the UK:

Media education can bring to art and design developed ideas of "audience" and "institution" and other theoretical concerns as well as a willingness to grapple with new media technologies. Art [education] is riven with the same disputes about "high" and "low" culture found in English and media education generally, and the peculiar position of photography is an indication of the problem. Is it "art," a "craft," or an industrial process? Is its purpose to document or to express? By bringing together Art and media education it should be possible to push such arguments aside in favour of integrated activities in which students can apply both critical and imaginative faculties in a disciplined production framework. (Stafford, 1993, 2)

Digital imagery and its ease of "seamless" manipulation also raises fascinating questions regarding truth in visual representation. Can a photograph still be considered a documentation of an event or has it become, like a painting, an interpretation of the event?

The Relevance of Art Education to Popular Culture

One of the most significant emerging debates concerns the place of media education in any contemporary curriculum statement. Media literacy is a growing concern for all teachers and can be regarded by English teachers as a logical extension of literacy. I see it as more than this, and the more teachers who acknowledge the influence and function of the media in our daily lives, the better our education systems will be.

Art education increasingly includes production work in video, film, and photography, often referred to as media arts. This creative work has not always been considered appropriate by some media educators. However, a common approach to media education worldwide is now a philosophy of theory informed by practice.

Paul Duncum, a prolific writer on art education, is critical of art education that is not relevant to students' experience:

> It is high time that art education took a very different direction. Standing aloof and on the outside with a romantic individualistic model of cultural production, disdaining students for their tastes, believing that dominant culture represents a social decline, committed to a producer orientation, and, finally, asserting self-evident, time-honoured standards, art educators ensure that their practice remains peripheral for the great majority of students. If art education continues to be offered as a highly conservative, defensive reaction to dominant culture, it is precluded from making positive contributions. But to seek an insider's experience, with a collaborative model of production, to represent students for how they cope with the conditions imposed upon them, to acknowledge the perennial nature of dominant culture content and to recognise the changing political and social contexts in which cultural standards are established, maintained and revised are first principles for a socially relevant art education. Such an art education would both earn the right and possess the potential to contribute critically to the meanings, values and beliefs students form with dominant culture. (Duncum, 1990, 213)

The arguments made by Paul Duncum for socially relevant art education seem similar to the general philosophy of media education that dominant (popular) culture is as much a part of the cultural ideology of the art teacher as elite or high art. This raises the question of the relevance of teaching the traditional art methods of painting and drawing, using traditional materials such as paint and pencil, in the modern world of electronic image making.

In another paper, Duncum compares the creation of pictures by children with the use of pictures in society, and discusses how to make art education relevant to the life experiences of students. Even though we live in a highly visual society, many of us rarely create images. Who are the image makers outside the commercial sphere of society, say, in the family?

Dave Allen, an art educator in the UK, does not ask whether media teaching should be a part of the arts curriculum but, rather, how media teaching develops and extends our conception of art education. He acknowledges that much of the media studies teaching in UK schools is being done by teachers from English and the humanities but argues that art can, and should, offer three specific, yet related, experiences for all pupils:

1. The opportunity for making their own art work, exploring a range of media styles and conventions;
2. The opportunity to learn about cultural artifacts, conventions and histories;
3. The opportunity to explore issues of personal and social significance in more than merely propositional and discursive forms. (Allen, 1992, 427)

Allen also suggests that one of the most significant contributions of art education to English-teaching pedagogy is the concept of recognizing the importance of learning by doing and the sense of ownership and personal value, which is so important to children.

Conclusion

Discipline-based art education is not the most appropriate core art study for a relevant modern schooling system, and there is an increasing call to art educators to redefine their objectives and move toward curriculum based on the concept of a cultural literacy. The new national curriculum statement for the arts in Australia highlights

The pivotal role of the arts in the shaping of Australian identity. For thousands of years life has been known, celebrated, renewed and interpreted through spiritual expressions in the arts. Aboriginal people have always shared understanding and mutual concerns through story-telling, dance song, painting and carving. These shared symbols have been ways of transmitting spiritual knowledge and reaffirming identity. Today Australia is made up of many cultural groups which contribute to a pluralistic but predominantly English-speaking society. For all cultural groups the arts are essential for cultural continuity and they are still by which the story is told. (Curriculum and Assessment Committee Australia, 1992)

Art education must include knowledge about the way art functions at all levels of the culture. Furthermore, if an integral component of media education is to identify particular texts as influencing agents which carry culture, dominant ideology and national identity, then the goals and objectives of art educators and media educators are significantly similar. Media education is not the sole responsibility of any particular area of the school curriculum. Few media texts are produced by one person; it is more likely that a wide range of specifically skilled people contribute to the production. A similar range of specialist skills exists on any school staff. This chapter is not advocating a change in the direction of media education. Rather, it is suggesting that there are opportunities to combine and extend the converging aims and objectives of art and media education to include aspects of cultural literacy—to the mutual benefit of both disciplines, and their scholars.

Notes

1. As is the case in the UK, a large proportion of mainstream broadcasting in Australia is funded by taxpayers, and is not reliant on commercial breakcasting concerns of ratings. The two noncommercial networks, The Australian Broadcasting Corporation (ABC) and the Special Broadcasting Service (SBS), broadcast nationally under government charter for ethnic and cultural minority groups.
2. Jean Pierre Golay was the director of Centre d'Initiation aux Communications de Masse, Lausanne. He is now an honorary fellow at the School of Journalism, University of Wisconsin, and is still very active in promoting media education. In 1976 the British Film Institue (BFI) produced a set of slides and accompanying text entitled "The Semiology of the Image," which was extracted from *Initiation a la Semiologie de L'Image* by Guy Gauthier, published in France by La Revue du Cinema-Image et Son. It has probably been one of the most influential resources in the worldwide development of visual media literacy.

References

Allen, D. (1992). Media, arts and the curriculum. In M. Alvarado & O. Boyd-Barrett (Eds.), *Media education: An introduction* (426–30). London: BFI/The Open University.

Bazalgette, C. (1991). *Teaching English in the National Curriculum: Media education.* London: Hodder & Stoughton.

————. (1992). Key aspects of media education. In M. Alvarado, and O. Boyd-Barrett, *Media education: An introduction* (199–219). London: British Film Institute/The Open University.

Branston, G. (1991). Audience. In Lusted, D. (Ed), *The media studies book: A guide to teachers* (104–12). London: Routledge.

Chambers, I. (1986). *Popular culture: The metropolitan experience.* London: Metheun.

Considine, D., & Haley, G. (1992). *Visual messages.* Englewood: Teachers' Ideas Press.

Curriculum and Assessment Committee Australia. (October 1992). *National curriculum statement: The arts.* Melbourne (draft for validation).

Donald, J. (1977/1992). Media studies: Possibilities and limitations. In M. Alvarado, *Media education: An introduction* (80–82). London: BFI/Open University (originally published in 1977).

Duncan, B. (April/May 1988). Article in *Media Beat,* column in *Forum, The Magazine of the Ontario Secondary School Teachers' Federation.*

Duncum, P. (1990). Clearing the decks for dominant culture: Some first principles for contemporary art education studies. *Art Education 3,* 4 (297–15).

Golay, J. (1988). Media education: Meeting of research and education. In *Meeting of research and media education, proceedings of the symposium.* Lausanne: Center D' Initiation aux Communication de masse.

Mellemcomp, P. (Autumn 1993). *The enconologuic of global culture: Metro* (3–13).

Stafford, R. (Spring 1993). Drawing together . . . art meets media education. In *The Picture* (2).

8

Textual Pleasures and Moral Dilemmas: Teaching Media Literacy in England

Andrew Hart

Debates about the role of the mass media in the cultural and social lives of the young have raged intensely during the last decade. In the UK, it is now at the center of deep conflict over the content of English in the new National Curriculum. Many policymakers blame the media for poor literacy, the decline of the family, and increasing delinquency, while others see media education as a necessary defence against the onslaught of the media. Some educators see it as a positive and constructive process that involves pleasure, and are working for an expansion of literacy to include understanding of media processes and practices amongst young people. Attacks on the growth of media education in secondary schools have focused on the need for an allegedly value-free, "back-to-basics" English curriculum, while its enthusiasts have called for the study of a broad range of literary and media texts as proper objects of study, rather than a prescriptive literary canon. They also call for more opportunity for young people to create their own media texts through critical and practical activity. This chapter sheds new light on the current debate and its implications for the professional education and development of teachers. It draws on the author's research in English classrooms during the early 1990s, and offers new evidence about the forms of media education currently taught by English teachers. The research is now also being conducted by collaborators in Europe and in three other continents, including the United States.

Introduction

At first sight, media information and formal education have little in common. They represent quite different sets of cultural, aesthetic, and social values. According to this view in its crudest form, the only space that schools might give to the media would be to defend their students against media values. As one of the earliest English cultural writers to consider the issues put it,

everything acquired at school in the way of aesthetic and moral training is contra-
dicted and attacked by the entertainment industry. . . . The aim (of schools) is to
provide standards against which the offerings of the mass media will appear cut
down to size. (Thompson, 1964, 17–20)

Yet, in England the recently established National Curriculum for English
teaching, the Report of the Cox Committee (DES, 1989), has given the
study of media a welcome prominence. Media education is seen as part of
"the exploration of contemporary culture" (paragraph 9.4). It is recognized that media education approaches should be part of every English
teacher's practice and that "the kinds of question that are routinely applied
in media education can fruitfully be applied to literature" (paragraph 7.23),
and "media education has often developed in a very explicit way concepts
which are of general importance in English" (paragraph 9.9).

What are these questions and concepts? The main ones are helpfully
listed by Cox as "selection (of information, viewpoint, etc.) editing, author, audience, medium, genre, stereotype, etc." (paragraph 9.9). The
questions resolve themselves into "who is communicating with whom
and why; how has the text been produced and transmitted; how does it
convey its meaning?" (paragraph 7.23). If made operational, these questions would produce a form of understanding which would fit exactly the
definition of media literacy produced by the recent Aspen Institute Conference: "the ability of a citizen to access, analyze, and produce information for specific outcomes" (Aufderheide, 1993, v).

Media education is also seen as closely related to information technology. This is a potentially promising conjunction, provided that we do not
mistakenly identify information technology as limited to the use of
computers. We need to focus on a range of technologies that are used to
collect, organize, process, and circulate information. This focus is by no
means new, and it is therefore useful to look at recent developments in
teaching about information in the media.

Study of the media has been growing in popularity in English schools
at least since the 1960s. The main impetus for this growth came from
teachers of English, many of whom saw themselves as protectors of children from the "false consciousness" that the media were believed to inculcate. It was this invasion of consciousness that Marshall McLuhan
perceived in the 1960s. He saw education as a form of "civil defense"
against "media fall-out" (McLuhan, 1973, 208). Worryingly, he saw the
invasion as a subliminal one, operating beneath the threshold of con-

sciousness. In a famous phrase, he warned that the content of the media was "like the juicy piece of meat carried by the burglar to distract the watchdog of the mind" (26). This fear of the seduction of the innocent was to dominate the early years of studying the mass media.

In the 1970s and 1980s, media education grew rapidly, with the creation of new secondary-level courses in film studies, and later with new courses in media studies and national examinations at ages sixteen and eighteen. The availability of the VCR gave an enormous boost to media work, and made the study of television the dominant focus.

However, there was a tension over what kinds of texts were legitimate objects of study—those valued by teachers or those valued by students? This tension led many teachers to examine their own attitudes in more personal, less theoretical ways, and some recognized the hypocrisy in routine condemnations of what were major sources of information and pleasure for themselves as much as for their students, especially when they formed an important part of students' cultural identities.

Although media education has developed rapidly, there has not been a corresponding expansion of training opportunities for teachers. The result is that many work in isolation, with little more than examination syllabuses to guide them. Some have inherited responsibility for media courses from enthusiastic teachers who have moved on. Although some of these "substitutes" often become enthusiasts themselves, they can too easily find themselves overwhelmed by the scope of the subject and by the unlimited material from which to choose.

Because few teachers have been formally trained in media education or media studies, there is inevitably a wide variation in theoretical understanding and classroom practice. Notions of media education may vary from showing a video recording of a Shakespeare play to the critical study of media institutions and audiences. Some teachers have rejected analytical approaches in favor of creative or technical ones. Others justify the subject for its method alone, arguing, for example, that its emphasis on group work and projects develops social skills.

In spite of the diversity of aims and approaches, the importance of systematic media education has been formally recognized by being included in the new National Curriculum, with teachers of English having a central role to play. The most recent approaches to media teaching are based on a holistic framework of "key concepts," which enable a cross-media approach (see figure 8.1). This approach offers the benefit of a

FIGURE 8.1

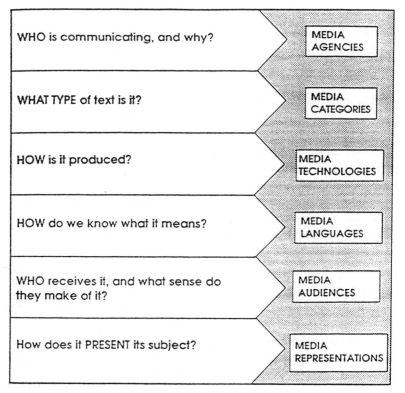

(Figure 8.1: Hart 1991, 13 and from Bazalgette 1989, 8)

framework that seems capable of moral neutrality. But it risks abandoning the high ground of moral and spiritual potential entirely.

My own research on the kinds of media work undertaken by English teachers shows a wide range of approaches to classroom work and a desire to relate learning to "real" activities (Hart, 1991; Hart & Benson 1992; 1993a; 1993b). The aim of the project was to illuminate some of the continuities and differences in media teaching styles of a small group of secondary English teachers. A small selected sample of teachers of media was interviewed. They comprised four main experiential categories, which broadly represented the current spectrum of involvement in media teaching. They were all known to the researchers and carefully chosen on the basis of their varied experience and expertise in this area of work.

Group 1: Recent graduates (two) undergoing initial training as English, drama, and media studies teachers on the University of Southampton's one-year initial training course for graduates (the Post-Graduate Certificate in Education course).
Group 2: Inexperienced teachers (two) just embarking on media teaching.
Group 3: Experienced teachers (two) new to media teaching.
Group 4: Experienced teachers (five) who had been doing some form of media education for at least five years.

We wanted to explore teachers' perceptions of media education in an English context and to discover how they saw media work relating to the other responsibilities of English departments. We also tried to document some of the perceived problems and rewards of teaching and learning about the media. We explored teachers' attitudes to media education both as a theoretical discipline and as a classroom subject; their aims for their students; the experience they brought to the work; the key concepts with which they felt most confident and the sources from which their understanding of these concepts derived; their favored resources and the ways in which these are used; and their expectations for the future of media education.

The range of experience of the eleven teachers interviewed was impressive. Most had wide and varied teaching experience, usually involving subjects other than English, and several had business or industrial backgrounds prior to teaching. Surprisingly, though, there was very little evidence of any professional experience of the media or of active engagement. A possible exception to this is that the three men all had unusually strong interests in music as performers and had varied experiences of the media through this activity.

The teachers were, therefore, generally disposed to accept new challenges and inclined to see English as a subject embracing the whole field of communication. Even so, their involvement with media teaching was sometimes patchy and determined more by accident than by conscious pursuit of a career option. Stepping into the shoes of the teacher who has left to have a baby seems to be the most common means of entry into media education.

Eight of the teachers had taught for at least ten years, and in some cases for more than twenty. None of these had any extended training in media education, but had generally approached the subject from an interest in literature and a shifting awareness of literary theory toward ideas that place reader response and a recognition that readers would benefit from reading a range of texts at the center of their approach. The other three teachers, two of whom were in their probationary year, had deliberately chosen training courses with a media or communications content. All of the teachers saw the need for further training in a subject they recognized as changing in its concepts and methods, and all valued the work of county advisers and other training agencies.

Overwhelmingly, these teachers believed that media education should be a part of students' education throughout their secondary education, and possibly before. There was very little anxiety about the subject proliferating into other disciplines and most felt secure about their own contributions to any cross-curricular initiatives. On the other hand, none of the schools concerned had yet developed a school policy for media education, and in some cases the teachers interviewed proved to be unaware of media work being done in other departments. Some expressed anxiety about attitudes of colleagues in their own departments and feared some disapproval of what was sometimes seen as the study of ephemera.

Teachers tended to express their aims in terms of helping students to make up their own minds by recognizing that media texts are constructions representing particular points of view. Most of the teachers spoke enthusiastically of the response of their students to media work. They often expressed surprise at the insights they had been able to gain into their students' perceptions and preferred modes of working. Students who were difficult to motivate often showed new strengths.

Many classes were directly concerned with cultural and social issues. Questions were constantly asked about the value of particular media texts and about the values which the texts were based on. In the process of evaluating texts, students were able to articulate a range of possible meanings and to relate their own values to others'.

Information and Values Education

Given the potential of media education for values education and the evident classroom successes highlighted by research, we would expect that media education would be embraced with enthusiasm by politicians and educational administrators. The recent discussion paper on *Spiritual and Moral Development* (National Curriculum Council, 1993) spells out in some detail the main constituents and the expected outcomes. It describes spiritual development as motivated by a search for meaning and purpose in relation to challenging life experiences and involving the growth of self-awareness and responsibility for one's own experience and identity; the development of self-respect; recognition of the worth of others and the importance of relationships; the importance of compassion, of imaginative engagement with experience, and of creative activity. Moral development is seen as based on a conscious will to behave in a morally principled way in the context of agreed social codes and conventions. It expresses itself in the making of reasoned and responsible decisions.

These descriptions of spiritual and moral characteristics may leave gaps and may not command universal assent, but the difficulty they raise is not so much ethical or philosophical as educational and pedagogical. Unfortunately, the paper has nothing to say about curriculum change or classroom methods. An important opportunity for genuine learning is being missed.

In fact, most of the goals of spiritual and moral development could be effectively reached through media education. But educational policy seems to be going in the opposite direction. In spite of the evident potential of media education in this area of values education, the government has further reduced its potential by imposing a radical change in the process of teacher training. The most successful form of initial training, the intensive one-year, post-graduate course for secondary school subject specialists, has recently produced many English teachers with specialist training in media education. But the new system announced by the government in 1992 effectively abolishes university control of such courses by insisting that each student spends a minimum of *two thirds* of their time in schools. The likely result of this for media education, as for other innovative subjects, will be that it will suffer because the experience and expertise of supervising students in media education is rarely available in schools at present.

This official neglect of media education may be because there remains great hostility from some politicians toward the mass media and toward television in particular. As in the 1960s, the media are still seen as the sources of moral and spiritual degeneration and blamed for social and cultural disintegration. For example, Kenneth Baker, who was one of the main architects of the National Curriculum as Secretary of State for Education in the Thatcher government, sees television watching as the enemy of imaginative engagement. Children, he argues, have an inner life, which needs to tapped by teachers. He quotes the poet Ted Hughes on the "world of final reality, the world of memory, emotion, imagination, intelligence and natural common sense, which goes on all the time, consciously or unconsciously, like the heart-beat" (Baker, 1988). His model of English teaching is based on the idea of cultural heritage. He wants children to be taught the literary classics.

> When I visit schools, I like to call in on English lessons and am particularly pleased if the children are being taught one of the classics. I believe passionately that the future of our language depends upon us bringing up children to appreciate its past. (Baker, 1988)

He sees this as a powerful antidote to the effects of the mass media.

> Children watch too much television. . . . I find this depressing. Literature, the reading of good books, is in many important ways a superior, richer and deeper experience than watching television. A particular feature of the written or spoken word is the unique demand it makes upon the imagination. (Baker, 1988)

He claims that watching television bypasses the imagination. It is a predominantly visual medium which makes life too easy for viewers. Only books offer readers an "engagement with language as they wrestle to create sense out of chaos and meaning out of absurdity." He concludes that "the viewer must become a reader." Here, Baker's ambiguity is accidentally prophetic. Whilst we cannot agree that students should stop watching and confine themselves to reading, we can agree that the critical skills which readers bring to literary texts also need to be brought to media texts. Media texts are too important to be ignored and understanding them may involve highly complex "reading" skills.

So, in spite of Baker's misgivings, we would expect that a proposal for revising the National Curriculum for English (National Curriculum Council, April 1993) would extend the basic mandate offered in the original (1989) version. But we would be disappointed. In the introduction to the new proposals, the Chair of the National Curriculum Council, David Pascall, proposes merely a supporting role for media education "to deliver the fundamental objective of the Order, rather than . . . as . . . distinctive areas of study." There may be as many references to media in the new proposals as in the original Order, but most of the references envisage listening tests, spoken language awareness, or elaborate comprehension exercises. Most of these references come only in the form of examples. They can be ignored. It is possible under the new proposals to omit media education from English by using other kinds of examples.

The strongest reference comes in the suggestion that "pupils should be encouraged to reflect on the language of television and radio." The context implies that "language" refers simply to words, ignoring the crucial importance of visual images in late twentieth-century communication. There is, as many English teachers have complained, a rigid insistence on the teaching of Standard English language forms and a narrow range of "cultural heritage" texts. The important "personal growth" and "cultural analysis" dimensions of English teaching, which were central to the original English Order, have been virtually ignored in the new proposals.

The new emphasis is on teaching rather than learning. Both the new English proposals and the *Spiritual and Moral Development* discussion paper share a common expectation that standards are to be taught by the efforts of teachers rather than learned through the engagement of students. The approach is didactic and expository rather than interactive and exploratory. It assumes that values are relatively static and unproblematic. It assumes that they need simply be transmitted by teachers for students to imitate. But schools may more usefully be seen as the sites of cultural struggle, where values are contested in debate and discovered through active involvement, and where students learn about and test out values for themselves in practical classroom situations. While the latest analytical approaches to media education through "key concepts" may risk creating a moral and spiritual vacuum, the new authoritarian approach to defining the curriculum risks creating a pedagogical "black hole," into which the universe of real learning may collapse.

The Privatization of Pleasure and the Iconography of Desire: A Classroom Approach to Media Literacy

A recent advertising campaign in the UK for the French aniseed-based aperitif Pernod contains ambiguities which take us to the center of the debate about spiritual and moral development. On the surface, it is exactly the kind of text which authoritarian educators would want to protect children from. It does not seek to engender spiritual and moral development, but rather the opposite. Yet, analyzing the advertisement so as to engage with the text can provide a platform for genuine learning.

One simple way of achieving this goal of engagement derives from French semiological theory developed by Roland Barthes (Barthes, 1967, 1973). Every text is conceived as a set of signs chosen for specific purposes and arranged in particular ways. Each sign and each text contain latent meanings at three levels: the denotative, the connotative, and the ideological.

In the case of a text like this one, students are asked to investigate and reflect individually on three questions which correspond to the three levels of meaning:

- What can I see in the text?
- What thoughts and feelings does the text suggest?
- What values does the text assume or express?

Other exploratory questions might be asked, in order to articulate the implied narrative surrounding the text. For example:

- What has just happened in the picture?
- What is happening now?
- What will happen next?
- What thoughts/feelings are the characters experiencing?
- Where would I find this text?

Sharing individual responses to these questions reveals a wide range of possibilities, but usually focuses on a consensus about a particular "preferred" reading (Hall, 1981), which is the dominant one in a given culture. The questions help to create a dialogue around interpretations of the text. These interpretations will show a degree of cultural uniformity but also the particularity of individual readings. In this way, students grasp that culture is realized inside each individual, rather than being something "outside." In the process of engaging for themselves with texts, they are learning about making decisions and judgements of value. They are learning to be "critically autonomous."

The image in the Pernod advertisement is a dramatically simple one. Against a dark nocturnal background, a young woman stands illuminated by a telephone and a glass of Pernod. In the corner, the brand name and the catch phrase integrated with it are also illuminated. The phrase *"Free the Spirit"* has both literal and metaphorical potential. On the literal, material level, "spirit" means simply any distilled alcoholic liquor. Metaphorically, it suggests notions of personal liberation through the full expression of inner desire. The golden glow of the yellow drink in the foreground held by the young woman is echoed by the telephone receiver in her other hand, by the glow of the surrounding telephone booth, and by the fierce brightness in the background. A burning light source is suggested in the distance. Her crucifixlike position parallels the telegraph poles which connect her with the distant perspective. She is "dressed for action," and her physical pose suggests eagerness, and availability. The arc of bright light which connects her drink to the distance parallels the line of the telegraph wire. The function of the whole image is to suggest that the drink can act like the telephone as a form of instant communication with a social reality to which the subject aspires. The validity of this reading is strengthened by other versions of the advertisement in the same series. Another version again shows a young woman with a glass of Pernod in her hand, this time gazing at a funfair in the distance. It also features the same catch phrase, *"Free the Spirit."*

"Critical autonomy" can be developed further by encouraging "negotiated" or "oppositional" readings which deviate from or subvert the "preferred" reading. So, for example, with the Pernod advertisement, rather than listening to the teacher trying to expose the deviousness and deceitfulness of the visual rhetoric, students could be asked to write as many answers as possible to the question, "Why I should drink Pernod?" This will then lead to examining the textual techniques which are used to generate the answers within the text's "preferred" reading. In order to shift away from the "preferred" reading, we can subvert the original question and ask, "Why *should* I drink Pernod?"

In the process of answering these questions, students will introduce knowledge from outside the text, thus providing a basis for questioning its rhetoric. They will be able to recognize and articulate the ideas which are embedded in the text and the values which give the product a social and cultural context. When the rhetoric has been questioned in this way, the "viewer" has become a "reader."

The Pernod advertisement is typical of the way in which the advertising industry creates "constructive dissatisfaction." Many other examples could equally well be analyzed in this way. Advertising typically offers us products as a means of escape from an unsatisfactory world into a fantastic secondary world where our dreams are fulfilled. It claims implicitly that spiritual needs can be fulfilled by material means. In the process, it tries to sell us not just a product but a set of ideas and beliefs about ourselves which have great power in our modern Western societies. One of the dangers of this process is accepting the illusion that material goods can satisfy spiritual needs.

The persuasive techniques used by advertising need special attention. Its rhetoric is relatively hidden because its propositions are put metaphorically and visually rather than logically. Its promises are only loosely associated with the product. So when the product does not satisfy the original need, we are unlikely to feel we have been deceived. We are more likely to internalize our disappointment and compensate by more consumption.

When the product fails to satisfy these needs, rather than rejecting the illusion or the product, we often become dependent on pursuing the dreams. So products have to keep offering new promises and new dreams. Advertisers know us well. They sell us products by selling us ourselves. In this way, for those who can afford to buy, a cycle of aspiration, desire, consumption, dissatisfaction and compensation is created.

The approach I have outlined centers on questions of individual responses to advertising, but media education is also concerned with many other ethical issues and many other kinds of texts. The legal constraints and codes of practice which surround the media also merit investigation. In many cases, legality and morality are not identical. It would be very interesting to explore, for example, the contradictions between the relatively permissive attitude to alcohol and tobacco advertising and health education policy in the UK. There is also a tension worth exploring between the state's acceptance of advertising as an index of a healthy economy and its desire to develop its citizens spiritually and morally.

I am not advocating more rigid controls on advertising. Nor am I suggesting that such methods can simply be exposed by teachers so as to enable students to make moral judgements which might protect them. Neither banning nor preaching is likely to be effective alone. This principle applies to the study of all media texts. Television and radio programs, newspapers and magazines, pop music and cinema all need to be approached in a way which engages with their values and acknowledges the pleasures which they offer.

Values need to be learned in an active and interrogative way rather than passively absorbed. Students need to learn how to decode culture from the inside and for themselves. The "outside" world of values must be examined through the medium of individual consciousness and identity. Articulating the implications of cultural texts makes them visible and making them visible makes them negotiable.

The role of teacher educators in this process is crucial. We need to help schools and teachers not to ignore the media, nor to condemn them, for the media cannot simply be counteracted with a forced diet of high literary culture. The media need to be approached seriously and systematically in the classroom as a way of promoting spiritual and moral development in students. "Critical autonomy" must create new "watchdogs" in students' minds in order to open up every text to questioning and reflection. Many teachers of English have the basic skills to help in this, because of their special expertise in engaging and developing the imaginations of students. Yet, we need to provide more and better training to help them in the process of decoding culture.

One of the ultimate goals expressed in the *Spiritual and Moral Development* discussion papers for schools to provide "reflective and aesthetic experience and the discussion of questions about meaning and purpose" (National Curriculum Council, 1993, 9). By bringing the worlds of media information and formal education together in a constructive way, media education offers one of the most powerful, accessible and effective ways of achieving that goal. It will involve the achievement of a literacy which is more than functional and which recognizes that information is always value laden.

References

Aufderheide, P. (Ed.) (1993). *Media literacy: A report of the National Leadership Conference on media literacy.* Aspen, Colo.: Aspen Institute.

Bazalgette, C. (1989). *Primary media education: A curriculum statement.* London: BFI.

Baker, K. (22 February 1988). *Sunday Times.*

Barthes, R. (1967). *Elements of semiology* London: Cape.

———. (1973). *Mythologies.* St. Albans: Granada.

DES. (1989). (The Cox Report) *English for Ages 5–16.* London: HMSO.

———. (March 1990). *English in the National Curriculum (No. 2).* London: HMSO.

———. (April 1993). *English for Ages 5-16 (1993).* London: HMSO.

Hall, S. (1981). The determinations of news photographs. In S. Cohen and J. Young (Eds.). *The manufacture of news* (226–43). London: Sage Constable.

Hart, A. (1991). *Understanding the media: A practical guide.* London: Routledge.

Hart, A., & Benson, T. (1992; 1993a). *Models of media education: A study of English teachers teaching media: Part 1: Overview; Part 2: Profiles and lessons.* Southampton: Center for Language in Education.

———. (1993b). *Media in the classroom.* Southampton: Southampton Media Education Group.

McLuhan, M. (1973). *Understanding media.* Falmouth: Abacus.

National Curriculum Council. (April 1993). *Spiritual and moral development: A discussion paper.* York: NCC.

Thompson, D. (Ed.) (1964). *Discrimination and popular culture.* London: Penguin.

9

A Much Debated Consensus:
Media Literacy in Israel*

Dafna Lemish and Peter Lemish

This chapter analyzes processes and issues that have emerged in developing a national curriculum in media literacy in the Israeli educational system. The need for such a curriculum was identified by media professionals, the educational establishment, and politicians. Representatives from these groups were appointed to the National Committee for Media Literacy, which produced three Media Literacy curricula that have been adopted by the Ministry of Education. In this process, agreements and alliances developed among persons whose political and ideological views differ on almost every other issue.

In practice, the national media literacy curricular guidelines are not being implemented, nor are alternatives developing which meet either media studies or educational standards of professional practice. The gaps between intention and practice suggest that there is a need for some fresh rethinking and a renewal of efforts to guide development of media education in Israel. In doing so, media professionals and educators must confront a series of issues: the definition of media studies and media literacy as a discipline; national, professional, or local control of media literacy curricula; and the role of teachers in the development of media education.

In the last decade three national media literacy curricula have been adopted by the Ministry of Education in Israel:[1] a television literacy curriculum for the elementary school system, a television and film literacy curriculum for the middle school system, and a mass media curriculum for the upper division school system. Simultaneously, teacher training programs have been developing general and specialization courses in media teaching and production, publishers have been preparing textbooks,

* This paper was supported by a grant from the Scholars Program of The Annenberg School for Communication, University of Pennsylvania, Philadelphia.

and thousands of students at all levels of the school system have begun formal study of the media. For those of us who have been seeking to advance the application of academic study and research to the field of education, the future of media studies and media literacy programs in the Israeli educational system would appear to be exceptionally bright.

While establishing curricular policies is an important step in implementing structural change in an educational system, the history of curricular initiatives suggests that the processes that develop, as well as the issues addressed, have important implications for the implementation and future development of curricular policy directives. With this caveat in mind, this chapter will analyze the processes and issues involved in establishing the media literacy programs in the Israeli educational system. In doing so, we hope that this case study will contribute as well to the recent advances in the analysis of media literacy programs (e.g., Alvarado & Boyd Barrett, 1992; Brown, 1991; Buckingham, 1990; Prinsloo & Criticos, 1991).

Achieving A National Consensus for Media Literacy

Out of the public and academic debate over the role of the media in a democratic society emerged what appears to be a national consensus calling for institutionalization of media literacy programs in schools. Achieving such a consensus is very unusual in a country whose public life is characterized by deep divisions and disagreements over most significant political and policy issues. Analysis of how this consensus was achieved reveals that alliances developed among persons whose political and ideological views usually find them disagreeing on almost every other issue. Understanding how such agreement was achieved requires focusing on the discussion of the following issues, which emerged in this debate.

Media Literacy as Ethnic Identity Issue:
Contra Americanization of Israel

Israel is undergoing a major communication "revolution"—from a limited number of public, noncommercial, audio visual sources of information and entertainment to a mixed, American-style system in which commercial and public channels compete for audiences. The delay in the commercialization of Israeli media is the result of a four-decade-long debate about the influence on the development of Israeli society of the media in general, and the American-style commercial format, in particular. The public-controlled broadcast media consists of: (1) the Israeli Broadcasting Authority, which includes three radio channels and two television stations—channel 1 has a half day broadcasting schedule, and channel 2 has an even more limited broadcasting allocation; (2) the Israeli Educational Television Station, controlled by the Ministry of Education, which shared air time with the public television channel; and (3) the military-controlled radio channel, which has a full range of programming and a very strong public following. In addition, Israel has several privately owned daily newspapers, only one of which has particularly large circulation, and a large range of interest oriented magazines (e.g., political, consumer, professional).

Since its introduction in 1992, cable television has been expanding very rapidly. As a result, Israeli based public channels must now compete with privately owned Israeli channels, as well as with the European-dominated satellite broadcasts. In mid 1993, the Second Television Channel was permitted to expand its schedule and to experiment with commercials.

The commercial television now being introduced in Israel reproduces in many respects the American style of programming. Opposition to this commercial format was one of the primary reasons for the delay in the introduction of television. In the 1950s and early 1960s David Ben Gurion, Israel's most renowned Prime Minister, and his supporters argued that American style television, with its capitalistic value system and foreign cultural attributes, would have a strong negative influence on important national effort to recreate and nourish the development of a unique Jewish Israeli culture. However, after the 1967 war, new ideological and political concerns led to the decision to include television in the public broadcasting system. Among the primary reasons for this action was the claim that through television Israel could communicate to her hostile neighbors and residents of the occupied territories. Indeed, it was hoped that the broadcast media could advance dialogue between the two peoples.

This and other political roles of public broadcasting are clearly delineated in the Broadcast Authority Law (revised, 1969):

The Authority will conduct the broadcasts for the fulfillment of the following duties:
A. To broadcast education, entertainment and informational programs in policy, society, economy, culture, science and art, in order to:

1. reflect the State's life, its struggle, creations and accomplishments;
2. to nourish good citizenship;
3. to strengthen the tie with the Jewish heritage and values and deepen knowledge about it;
4. to reflect the life and the cultural assets of all the ethnic groups of the Jewish nation;
5. to expand education and spread knowledge;
6. to reflect the life of Jews in the diaspora;
7. to promote the national educational goals.
B. To promote the Hebrew and Israeli arts.
C. To conduct broadcasts in the Arabic language for the needs of the Arabic-speaking population, and broadcast for promoting understanding and peace with the neighboring countries.
D. To conduct broadcasts to the Jews in the diaspora.
E. To conduct broadcasts abroad.

Be that as it may, the argument that television contributes to cultural imperialism and Americanization of Israeli culture continues to be raised consistently throughout four decades of debate about Israeli television. Indeed, in a May, 1993 channel 1 program devoted to evaluating twenty-five years of Israeli television, the first director of Israeli Television and a scholar of communication studies, Professor Elihu Katz stated:

> We expect to be flooded by Americanization with the (introduction of) multiple channels. . . . There is no doubt that those of us who are concerned that the creation of Israeli culture will be hurt by the introduction of American style television have a real basis for apprehension.

The demand for media literacy is an ancillary argument that has emerged in this process. It is usually proposed by those who argue for the need to "resist" Americanization of Israeli media in general, and of the media in particular. Proponents argue that media literacy is a means to confront a primal threat to the development of Israel as a Jewish State and society—an essential *raison d'etre* for most Israeli Jews. A sense of urgency characterized these arguments, a sense of "let's act while we still can" (i.e., before the irreversible trend of commercialized television is established).

Media Literacy as a Political Issue

"The People Against Hostile Communication"—so says a popular car sticker in Israel. This sticker presents the well known "kill the messenger" attitude toward the media. Such a view is given special meaning and emphasis in a society engaged in deep political conflict, such as Israel. Proponents of this view are usually identified with the "hawk" side of the political continuum—those who oppose engaging in peace processes and/or support indefinite Israeli occupation of the West Bank territories. They claim that the media are controlled by "doves," and so present biased and distorted views of political reality under the guise of objective reporting.

Israeli "doves" (i.e., supporters of the peace efforts) claim the media are biased in the opposite direction. In their view, the media are manipulated by conservative groups which oppose change and seek to advance a nonexistent "national consensus." This criticism was voiced most strongly during the period when the Likud party controlled the Israeli government and the Broadcasting Authority (1977–93). Then the media were accused of neglecting their "watchdog" role. The following quote by a well known analyst of Israeli media exemplifies this critique:

> They are changing the language, raping the words . . . so that (Hebrew) will fit the desires of a group of ignorant patriots. . . . They claim that reporters serve the enemy's propaganda. So they established a new dictionary. . . . This . . . group . . . is now (imposing) barriers of ignorance and arrogance between us and the facts. . . . Why were all these things so expected? Because sooner or later, every society which refuses to recognize the reality in which it lives, will adopt means that are meant to describe reality as it prefers to see it. Raping words is the inevitable continuation of raping facts and stupefying the public. (Summet, 1988)[2]

Though they decode news differently and find it impossible to agree on a variety of internal and foreign affairs policies (see for example Leibes, 1992), Hawks and Doves were united in their call for media literacy. Both expressed the need to demystify the news media for young people and to educate them to critical understandings of the sociology of news production as well as to the content and structural constraints on our major sources of information.

Media Literacy as an Ethical Issue

Another unusual coalition of interests was formed around ethical issues concerning media. Feminists; educators; representatives of nongovernmental organizations concerned with equal rights, child welfare, and social justice; and religious leaders have expressed alarm over the use of the media to present degrading portrayals of women, pornography, violence, and the glorification of drug and alcohol abuse. While the motivation, ideology, and claims of these groups differ significantly, they share the belief that the media function as socializing agents and that a literate audience can and should resist value systems and behaviors which undermine their ideological dispositions.

One such alliance is the cooperation between representatives of feminist and ultrareligious organizations. Both argue for the abolition of media portrayals that sexually objectify women. Both groups also lobby for the need for media literacy as a tool to educate students and to be critical consumers of the media. Advancing media literacy programs is in their view also a vehicle for social change. However, participants in this alliance are motivated by diametrically opposed motives and interests: While the former fight for complete equality for women, the latter would like to impose a strict religious regime, which will return women to their traditional role as caregiver.

A second example emerged in public discussion of a brutal murder by teenagers of a taxi driver in January, 1994. Here the media's role in encouraging and contributing to legitimization of violence was debated in the daily papers and in the broadcast media, by Ministry of Education officials as well as by Knesset's (Parliament) Education Committee, which devoted a special open meeting to discussion of potential effects of broadcast violence on youth. In all of these discussions the claim was made that schools should develop media literacy programs in order to confront the negative influences of the media on children.

Media Literacy as a Current Affairs Issue

The Israeli media's role of surveillance is crucial and problematic (Wright, 1960).[3] On the one hand, as a nation that has never known a moment of peace since establishing independence in 1948, Israelis are dependent upon and are obsessive consumers of Israeli based news media.

The most recent example of the importance of the relationship between the Israeli media and its audience can be found in the Gulf War. Then the entire population of Israel—approximately five million people—stoically followed Civil Defense instructions broadcast via radio and television: With each Scud missile attack (eighteen times within a six week period), most persons entered a room prepared in advance, sealed the doorway, put on their gas masks (for fear of biochemical warfare), and listened to the radio for further instructions and information on the events taking place. As was described by a key decisionmaker in the media industry, "in that unusual and frightening situation, the media served as an umbilical cord to the world" (Tidhar & Lemish, 1993, 112). With most of the population off the streets for weeks, the school system closed, the war taking place thousands of miles away, yet threatening our lives in a real way, there was total dependency on the media (cf. the role of the media in other survival crises, such as natural and ecological disasters).

On the other hand, the problematics involved in dependency on the media can be seen from questions such as the following, which have been raised by media scholars in Israel about the media's roles in previous wars: Did tight censorship during the harsh days of the beginning of the 1973 Yom Kippur War save the people's spirit and self confidence and so enable the country to extricate itself from near defeat? Did the unrestricted coverage of the 1982 Lebanese War accelerate the war's early conclusion? Does media presence in the occupied territories during the Intifada (uprising of the Palestinian population) encourage Palestinian violence and Israeli self restraint? Analyses of these questions produce varied and often contradictory conclusions, however, most scholars and public leaders agree that our social condition requires a literate audience of critical media consumers.

Educators who participate in such discussions add that there is a desperate need for curricula, learning materials, and pedagogical tools, which will enable classroom teachers to deal with current events in their classes in academic, nonpolitical ways. However, here it may be argued that focusing discussion and analysis on media functioning and roles may be a mechanism employed by teachers to avoid helping students to understand and perhaps to develop a clear political stance on difficult and varied issues—such as whether or not to return the occupied territories, to separate religion from state, to intervene in the military court system, or relations between Jews and Arabs within Israel. Dealing with media literacy, then, may seem like an easy "solution" to the important public debate over including discussion of political issues in the classroom.

In summary, media literacy policies in Israel developed out of pressure from the public, the educational establishment, academia, and politicians. In this broad consensus, agreements and alliances developed among persons whose political and ideological views differed on almost every other issue.

During the period in which there was a growing demand for media literacy, there was a significant lack of programs, instructional materials, or trained personnel. One of the main reasons for this situation was the fact that no undergraduate programs in communication studies existed in Israel's academic or teacher-training institutions. The entire country had one small department of communication, which granted only advanced degrees. In addition, graduates of communication and media studies programs abroad—mainly educated in the U.S.—returned to Israel to find that there was a limited number of employment opportunities.

At the same time, teacher colleges and other Ministry of Education training programs for teachers initiated pre and in service courses in media literacy for teachers. Many of these academics initiated and/or gravitated to these programs. Furthermore, as the media literacy specialty gains recognition as a legitimate branch of media studies, it is included in university programs. Thus, the development of media literacy programs has provided new employment opportunities for academics and media professionals.

Media industry officials, too, seemed pleased with the demand for media literacy programs in the schools. However, their motives may be suspect. Rather than have the public require that the media assume responsibility for the content of their broadcasts, the emphasis on media literacy meant that they were able to transfer responsibility over to the educational system.

Principles and Goals of the National Curriculum

This complex social cultural historical background explains why media literacy initiatives were supported by various interest groups in Israel. In this section we examine the process involved in establishing the goals for the media literacy curricular initiatives.

In 1990 the Ministry of Education nominated two special committees composed of educators, media studies experts, and teachers. The mandate given these committees was to create a national curriculum for media education. Following two years of discussions, the results of these efforts represent the diversity of opinions voiced in the call for media literacy. For example, the following educational goals were established for the secondary education curriculum:

- to recognize different forms of expression in the languages of the mass media and to apply them in experiences within media studies, other disciplines and in everyday life;
- to analyze communication contents and structures to which students are exposed, and to evaluate their effects;
- to know about the historical development of the mass media, to understand the effects of the current communication arena and to be able to analyze expected future developments;
- to understand the connections between contents and forms of media products in general and artistic works in particular;
- to understand that the mass media products are a result of professional and personal choices and not a neutral reflection of reality;
- to evaluate the role of media in a democratic society;
- to expose, understand and criticize the ideological and valuative aspects of mass media;
- to experience creating and producing a mass media program;
- to enjoy the creative process as well as the final product;
- to learn to accept criticism of a student's product. (Israeli Ministry of Education, 1993, 5)

Two special themes are emphasized in these goal statements. First, there is an emphasis on evaluation and criticism of products, processes, artistic values, and effects. Second, educators are instructed to motivate as well as to activate students to apply knowledge, to be critical and to be creative.

Placed in perspective of media literacy efforts, these two themes differ significantly from other media education curricula developed in other countries. For example, in summarizing media literacy efforts in the United States, Hobbs (1993) claimed that curricular goals emphasize analysis of media messages. Here students are to understand how:

- Messages are constructed;
- Messages represent social reality;
- Messages have economic, political contexts, and consequences;
- Each form of communication has unique characteristics;
- Individuals negotiate meaning in messages.

The British Film Institute's well known curriculum statement for the primary education (1989) and secondary education (1991) emphasizes a wider understanding of media agencies, categories, technologies, languages, audiences, and representations as core knowledge areas. While media education is perceived by BFI as associated with developing "systematically children's critical and creative powers through analysis and production of media artifacts" (1989, 3), little is said about the role of media literacy in a democratic society.

In contrast, South African curricular statements (Prinsloo & Criticos, 1991) call for media education to play an important role in advancing the political agenda of human rights, equality, and social change.

Examining the Israeli case within this comparative perspective reinforces the view that, while there is broad agreement on basic principles of media education (such as those articulated by Hobbs, 1993), the different social, cultural, and political agendas of countries lead to development of their own variation of media education programs. In some countries, media education serves to legitimate existing power structures and even to prevent social change. We find such interests advanced by religious parties in Israel, or the Moral Majority in the United States and England (Buckingham, 1993).

In contrast, in South Africa and Israel curricular goal statements attempt to use media education to achieve broader social and educational goals. The critical orientation of the Israeli goal statements can be attributed to the need identified by committee members to advance citizen empowerment and progressive forms of social change. In South Africa, media education is considered to be an important part of the anti apartheid movement (Prinsloo & Criticos, 1991). Here, as well as in Israel, media literacy is offered as a cure—or as a consciousness comforter—for every social ill.

Present Efforts to Implement Media Literacy Curricula

To this point the analysis of the development of the Israeli media Literacy curricula has focused attention on understanding the influence of the cultural and political context, the specific communications map, and the personal influence of specific role players on development of the educational agenda. The role of these influences is extended in the concluding analysis of issues and dilemmas developing in present efforts to implement these curricula.

The Discipline: So What Really Are Media Studies?

Should media literacy be studied as a separate discipline, or as an interdisciplinary theme? If the former, we would expect to find a cadre of media studies inspectors and curriculum specialists advancing the development of media literacy programs. On the other hand, if "everything" is communication, then media literacy themes should be found to be an integral part of language arts, civics, art education, history, and other curricula. While this issue continues to be debated in academia, it obviously has important practical implications and consequences for schools.

Those who argue for media studies as an independent discipline claim that, while it is interdisciplinary in nature, it does have its own body of knowledge, critical tools, and educational goals. Proponents argue for a more centralized model of education. To this end, they have worked to establish national curricular goals and guidelines; to develop textbooks; to gain control of the allocation of classroom hours and teacher employment; to develop teacher training programs which specialize in media studies; and to appoint the inspectorate, which supervises the implementation of these policies and programs.

Those who do not accept media studies as a separate discipline, prefer a much less structured approach. Media literacy, they claim, should be integrated where appropriate into the existing school curricula. Proponents argue that all teachers should receive some basic training in media studies, and then be reinforced by occasional in-service opportunities and production of supplementary curricular materials. When this approach is implemented, we find treatment of media related issues in high school civics classes (e.g., freedom of speech and role of the media in democracies), or in elementary school language classes (e.g., elements of a story, use of stereotypical characters, and means of resolving conflicts).

Who Controls the Curriculum?

A second, related issue questions whether development of media literacy programs should be through centralized or field based initiatives: Should media studies specialists develop and supervise implementation of the centralized national curriculum, or should local educators develop media literacy programs as local curricula, which incorporate their own and students' interests and needs?

In practice, both approaches are being implemented in Israel with mixed results. Professionals who developed the national curricula ask, "Why must educators invent the wheel all over again?" (Read: especially when they do so from an inferior position as a result of their lack of knowledge and experience?) "Don't dictate to us what is best for us," resist the local educators who create their own materials by patching together curricula, textbooks, and media materials. "Irresponsible ignorance. Would you do the same with math or grammar studies?" proclaim the former. "Educational pluralism!" argue the latter.

This debate is an extension into media studies of the general "Center Periphery" debate, which has been evolving within the Israeli educational system over the last ten years (Eden, 1986; Eden, Moses, & Ami'ad, 1992). During this period, changes have occurred in the public-private division of responsibility over education in different subsectors of the educational system (Harrison, 1993). The new policy encourages privatization of school services, creation of schools that specialize in particular curricula areas such as science or the arts, and the autonomous development of school based curricula and programs. In short, schools now have the mandate to make their own choices.

Given this trend, media specialists are best advised to attract the interest of and to work with local educators to develop school based programs. To do so requires employing: (1) media studies advisers who will work within school staffs to develop media literacy programs; and (2) the development of attractive learning materials which will be adopted in schools. In these ways, proponents of the independent media studies approach can continue to influence the development of media literacy programs in the educational system.

The Teachers

As in every innovation in an educational system, teachers are a key link in the change process. Yet, both pre and in service teacher-training programs in media education are relatively new and limited in scale at a time when the demand to incorporate media literacy in schools is growing rapidly. This gap is filled by two types of teachers: media professionals (such as unemployed journalists, graduates of film studies or advertising courses) who have no knowledge or experience in education; or their opposite, school teachers who have no knowledge of media studies or experience in media production. Both types of teachers can be found at all levels, from primary education through directors of media studies programs in teacher-training colleges. Neither type of teacher has received the professional preparation necessary to implement or to advance media literacy programs in schools.

When such teachers advance media studies in classrooms, we often find forms of media literacy malpractice in which students learn to reproduce what their teachers know best: Some students are now proudly producing sexist commercials; mistakingly learn that news broadcasts are manipulated by the "left wing" or "right wing" of the political spectrum; and elementary school students analyze cartoon stereotypes by ignoring and often reproducing—rather than criticizing—such assumed meanings as "good guys" for handsome, middle class, clean caucasians, while "bad guys" for ugly, grotesque, dirty, and dangerous noncaucasians.

In contrast, studies of media usage by children suggest principles and stages for working with students who have yet to become critical consumers of the media:

Stage One—Legitimize students' media experiences, pleasures, and knowledge;

Stage Two—Formalize this knowledge through media theories and concepts;

Stage Three—Assist students to evaluate and to be critical of their own knowledge and behavior, as well as that of the media.

Ill-informed efforts in media education such as the above examples may function in stages one and two, but rarely reach the intended goal in the third stage of developing critical skills as media consumers.

Educational Practice

Implementation of the media literacy curricula through confrontation with the above dilemmas and problems results in the following models of media literacy practice:

• In the Patchwork model, media professionals and uninformed teachers of good will patch together isolated segments of media literacy activities and materials. This process is mainly guided by convenience as opposed to implementation of a systematically conceptualized and planned program. For example, teachers use the materials or textbooks available to them from among those distributed at in-service programs; pedagogical activities or projects develop in the teachers' room, or on the phone in collaboration with colleagues who bring expertise that can be woven into the class's activities (e.g., art, sociology, or crafts). Following our metaphor, the result of this process is the patching together of unrelated activities which are may only partially achieve the educational goals. On the other, this process does facilitate the development of ideas and activities which have the potential to become innovative, context related curricular units.

• The Autocratic/Technocratic model produces programs which advance the interests of particular persons, social or political groups. Personal or political interests are applied, for example, in Ministry appointments; in authorizing institutional control and budgets for pre and in-service programs; in the advancement of particular curricular approaches; in the allocation of school appointments and teaching hours; and in the advancement of preferred materials over those approved by the professional Ministry committees. This process is a means through which persons in power impose their interpretation and control the development of media literacy in Israeli schools.

• In the Extra School Agency model, media professionals and private publishers produce and sell programs and teaching materials to schools which have not necessarily been approved by the Ministry of Education to schools.

In a period of transition from a centralized to a field based system, each of the above models is free to develop independently. The newness of the field means that there is limited guidance, supervision, or even forum for discussion and critique.

One result of the educational practice which is developing in Israel is clearly visible: There is limited evidence of implementation of the spiral curricular guidelines established by the National Curriculum Committee. According to the curricula adopted by the Ministry, we would expect to find the curriculum expanding in depth and breadth at each level of schooling (i.e., in elementary, middle, and high schools). Curricula would be organized at each stage in order to enable students to enrich their knowledge of three primary threads: the interrelationship of media, culture, and society; theories and concepts for analysis of the media; and development and practice in the use of critical media literacy skills.

In contrast, current practice leaves students (and teachers) "stuck" at all levels in the first, or at best, second stage. There seems to be but limited reinforcement and extension of learning—a result which those of us who developed the national curricula were hoping to avoid.

In summary, implementation of media literacy programs in Israel is a double-edged sword. On the one hand, there is a positive interest in development of a national curriculum. On the other hand, actions in the field are driving media literacy in a different direction: The controls applied by persons in positions of power advance implementation of their personal interpretation and interests in media literacy. Other professionals are working their way into the system through production of alternative curricular approaches and materials. Teachers are developing lessons and using materials often without professional guidance and in ways unrelated to the national guidelines. As a result, student experiences and learning are like a beginner's patchwork quilt; in the end it covers some of the subject, but does so without an integrated plan.

Professional-level implementation of the national media literacy curricula requires a parallel commitment by the Ministry of Education to induce structural changes that include policy guidelines for implementation, development of personnel at all levels—from the Inspectorate through teachers in the field—extensive allocation of school hours and investment in the development of appropriate learning materials, and ongoing formative evaluation which provides feedback to the field and leads in the further development of the media literacy program.

The complexity of processes involved in curricular development efforts and the problems and gaps described above between intention and practice suggest that there is a need for some fresh rethinking and a renewal of efforts to guide development of media education in Israel.

Notes

1. These curricula were developed by committees comprised of mass media scholars and educators. The first author was a member of these committees and has played an active role in the development of media education in Israel. She is not then a detached observer of the issues and processes analyzed.
2. The policies of the Likud-controlled government required, for example, use of the Biblical terms *Judea, Samaria,* and *Gaza* when referring to the occupied territories of the West Bank; it prohibited reference to the Arab residents of the occupied territories or Arabs living in Israel as members of the Palestinian people.
3. The "Surveillance Role" refers to the flow of information and analysis that warn the public about forthcoming environmental, military, or economic dangers. This function is usually associated with the news.

References

Alvardo, M., & Boyd-Barrett, O. (1992). *Media education: An introduction.* London: British Film Institute.

Bazalgette, C. (Ed.). (1989). *Primary media education: A curriculum statement*. London: British Film Institute.

Bowker, J. (Ed.). (1991). *Secondary media education: A curriculum statement*. London: British Film Institute.

Brown, J. A. (1991). *Television critical viewing skills education*. Hillsdale, N.J.: Erlbaum.

Buckingham, D. (1990). *Watching media learning: Making sense of media education*. Baskingstoke Hampshire: Falmer Press.

————. (1993). *Children talking television: The making of television literacy*. London: The Falmer Press.

Eden, S. (1986). *Between the "center" and the "periphery": Issues in school-based curriculum development in Israel*. Jerusalem: Ministry of Education.

Eden, S., Moses, S., & Ami'ad, R. (1992). The "center" and the "periphery" in curriculum development. *Issues in Education, 57–58*, 54–81.

Harrison, J. (1993). The growth of private education in Israel: Causes and consequences. *International Perspectives on Education and Society 3*, 193–225.

Hobbs, R. (November 1993). Paper delivered at the Media Literacy Conference of the Annenberg School for Communication. Philadelphia, Pa.

Israeli Ministry of Education. (1993). *A curriculum for the teaching of mass media in secondary schools*. (Hebrew)

Katz, E. (May 1993). (Israeli television program.)

Liebes, T. (1992). Decoding television news: The political discourse of Israeli hawks and doves. *Theory and Society 21*, 357–81.

Prinsloo, J., & Criticos, C. (Eds.). (1991). *Media matters in South Africa*. Durban: Media Resource Center, University of Natal.

Summet, G. (18 November 1988). A gun on the editorial desk. *Ha'aretz* (Hebrew newspaper).

The State of Israel. (1969). Broadcast Authority Law, revised (Hebrew).

Tidhar, C. E., & Lemish, D. (1993). Israeli broadcasting media facing the Scud missile attacks. In T. A. McCain, & L. Shyles (Eds.), *The 1,000 hour war* (111–26). Westport, Conn.: Greenwood Press.

Wright, C. (1960). Functional analysis and mass communication. *Public Opinion Quarterly 23*, 605–20.

10

Media Education for a Critical Citizenry in South Africa

Costas Criticos

Media education in South Africa has drawn on the aesthetic and academic roots of international trends in media education. Notwithstanding this heritage, there is a direction to our media education that is uniquely South African or at the very least unique to those countries undergoing similar political revolutions and national reconstruction. Our special variant has been strongly influenced by the political struggles that have sought to dismantle and oppose apartheid and its media. It also draws strongly from critical pedagogy or "people's education," which advanced a creative and generative education as opposed to the dominant consumptive and domesticating education.

Apartheid education favored passive learners who did not engage in the process of knowledge construction—instead the curricula confirmed the propaganda of the National Party regime and "naturalness" of apartheid policy.

In the late seventies and early eighties media organizations were established to support the work of community organizations and oppositional media producers who challenged apartheid media and state censorship. The Media Resource Center (MRC) is an example of these bodies. Established in 1985, it attempts to address the unequal distribution of educational media resources and skills. One of its programs, the Media Education Program, was established to promote a progressive curriculum of media education in schools. This paper suggests that "civic courage" depends on the realization of social, technical, and communicative literacy through formal and nonformal education. Furthermore, media education is a vital strategy for building "communicative literacy" in the present media and information age. Media education attempts to allow experience and the world around us to inform school knowledge—in turn this new knowledge equips students to examine the world around them and ultimately become critical citizens.

> *As the information society develops, it will not be possible to achieve the goals of citizenship, or to exercise the appropriate rights, in the absence of an information and communication system which provides the information base and the opportunities for access and participation for all citizens. (Halloran, 1990)*

*I believe schools are the major institutions for educating students for public life.
More specifically, I believe that schools should function to provide students with the
knowledge, character and moral vision that build civic courage.* (Giroux, 1992)

Introduction

According to Halloran, it is essential for citizens to be active in the
information society—this activity demands a "civic courage," which
schools ought to advance through their methods and contents. This chapter attempts to argue that media education has a crucial role to play in
support of an education for critical citizenship.

In South Africa, schools have been purposely constructed so as to disable rather than enable civic courage in our youth. Without this courage,
civil society is subdued by repressive political forces and uncharitable corporate forces. Resistance against apartheid and its ultimate demise has
been part of the growth of civil society—a society which has been strengthened by the international antiapartheid movements and national movements
such as the United Democratic Front, The Congress of South African Trade
Unions, The National Education Crisis Committee, and others. In addition
to these labor and political nodes of resistance, educational initiatives have
similarly resisted apartheid and its educational forms and attempted to
develop critical and creative skills in learners. This chapter examines the
contribution which media education makes to the development of critical
literacy. Strengthening the creative and analytical media skills of learners
has been supported by other educational initiatives, which aggregate to
develop a *critical literacy* essential for civic courage.

These emancipatory elements of media education in South Africa and
other countries undergoing national reconstruction are often not acknowledged. Awareness of Africa and its media perspective is, however, beginning to be revealed.

Media Education in Developing Countries

In 1990, the UN-sponsored Toulouse Colloquy brought together international media educationists who attempted to explore the *"New Directions in Media Education."* The significance of this meeting is that
for the first time we have attention being given to the perspective and
interests of developing countries at an international media education con-

ference. The conference participants were divided into three commissions and one of these was the *Commission III: Media Education and Developing Countries*.

In the first part of their statement the commissioners acknowledge that outside of the west, media education has a different history and form. In some of these countries media education is an interest of both school and organizations, and moreover, is concerned with both creative and analytical interests. They say:

> In developing countries, media education outside the formal educational system deserves particular attention. Educational activities of grassroots and non-governmental organizations are also especially important and the Commission wishes to stress those aspects of media education which enable individuals and groups to contribute actively to endogenous cultural development. (Prinsloo & Criticos, 1991, 298)

The commissioners' exhortations signal what we know all too well. Repression in South Africa (and in other countries) is about disempowering people through an impoverished education which has left the majority of South Africans in a political, technical, and media void. Political power, technological resources, and media access were not for black South Africans. These arenas were controlled by the white government in the interest of white South Africa. The first mature stage of revolt against this repression was realized with a counter-educational strategy—a *People's Education*—which gave critical analysis of apartheid repression. In Paulo Freire's (1972) terms, people were "*naming their world*." People's Education seeks to enable people to move from a "*magical consciousness*" to a "*critical consciousness*." This process is utilized by oppositional media, and new cultural forms to give a direct challenge to media and cultural repression.

Critical Literacy

What constitutes critical literacy? This is a literacy that incorporates literacies, which enable a person to act as a creative, active, moral, and critical citizen in a democratic society. Such a literacy will have nuances in different social environments. These environments might be a highly technological and industrialized society, a media saturated society, a rural agrarian society, or an emerging democratic society like South Africa.

The analysis and diagnosis of educational, political, technological, and media impoverishment led to many community and university-based development projects. These developments went beyond a narrow inter-pretation of literacy and numeracy to a literacy which is contextualized within the lived experiences and aspirations of people and includes tech-nical, political, and media insights. Critical literacy is not just knowing about issues, but an active and personal understanding. In my view this critical literacy is realized principally through three main literacies: com-municative, social, and technological literacy.

Social literacy relates to competencies and understandings of politi-cal and social relations; *technological literacy* relates to skills of living and acting in a technological world. This chapter is focused on *commu-nicative literacy*—a literacy which enables a citizen to be an active com-municator in multiple modes and media. It extends beyond speech and writing to the critical production and "reading" of the visual and elec-tronic media. In many cases these media frame and construct the poten-tial and limits of everyday speech and writing. I believe that media literacy is a vital competency for critical, discerning, and creative citizens in a democratic South Africa. South Africa and other countries in the global market are operated in an information age in which global nodes of in-formation power and practice have emerged to decenter the marginal, regional, and national voices. McLaren and Tadeu da Silva (1993, 48) describe those of us engaged in issues of critical citizenship as challeng-ing these nodes of power which coalesce as "empires of consciousness—regimes which structure our desires transculturally."

Apartheid Education

Establishing a civil society demands an analysis of apartheid as a precursor to national reconstruction and critical citizenry. The analytical searchlight illuminates decades of schooling constructed by the present authorities which reinforced the apartheid lie that most South Africans were inferior and in need of "special" (segregated and inferior) treat-ment. Society was segregated so that each race group had its own cur-riculum, schools, homes, hospitals, and even prisons. These ghettos of privilege and oppression ensured that people did not engage in conversa-tion or encounter experiences that would contradict the lie. In Giroux's (1992) terminology, people were forcibly constrained from "crossing the border" and South Africa was characterized by the separation and isola-tion of people, school subjects, schools, regions, work, and living spaces.

Three institutions were utilized as allies and vehicles for instituting and maintaining apartheid. These were the media, schools, and the church. Media control and censorship, Bantu education (a domesticating education for blacks), and the theological justification of apartheid by certain churches are notorious beacons of shame in the dismal history of South Africa. Ironically, it was from these quarters that apartheid was strongly challenged. Oppositional media, school resistance, and contextual theology challenged those institutions that had maintained the apartheid lie. These challenges enabled previously forbidden conversations between student and teacher, between worker and management, between researcher and subject, and between schooled and unschooled people to be energized and sustained.

The analytical process of "naming the world" of apartheid South Africa and its media environment did not go unnoticed by the State. Various State organs, especially the security services in the country, sought to crush any attempt at analysis and finding a voice. One of the most notable touchstones in this period of cultural repression was the role of Paulo Freire's works on liberation theology and education. The revolutionary climate of resistance in South Africa created a popular interest in an education which advances democracy in contrast to the domesticating education which accepts the status quo of oppression. At the heart of this emancipatory education is an epistemology which regards knowledge as being constructed by learners. These learners are *creators* rather than *consumers* of knowledge. The debate about epistemologies is not a peripheral interest, but rather a central issue that impacts on the way we teach, learn, and view our role in the educational process.

> The way we know has powerful implications for the way we live. Every epistemology tends to become an ethic, and every way of knowing tends to become a way of living. The relation established between the student and the subject, tends to become the relation of the living person to the world itself. Every mode of knowing contains its own moral trajectory, its own ethical direction and outcomes. (Palmer, 1990, 107)

Emancipatory education has an alternative epistemology which, in contrast to an objective knowing, is based on a connected knowing. This is an education which is generative, not consumptive, concerned with perception not reception, searching, not researching. In such a system intelligence is a process not a product (Stanton, 1986, 1990).

In South Africa the structures of education were designed specifically to constrain freedom. Education was divided on racial lines and the curricula were designed to reinforce the lie of white supremacy. Whites were prepared for positions of management and high technology while blacks were prepared for positions of service. In addition to school texts which perpetuated the lie of apartheid, educational methods did not give students opportunities to be critical of their own learning. Teaching styles in classrooms were typical of what Paulo Freire has called "banking education"—the depositing of knowledge into the heads of passive learners.

Oppositional (emancipatory) education—the opposite of "banking education"—flowers in harsh circumstances; it is based not on the scholarship of the textbook, but on the scholarship of inquiry—an examination of ourselves and the society we live in.

Central to these radical views of education is a valuing of personal and communal experience and a "process," or "constructive" approach to learning. The everyday environment of culture, events, biographies, and media stand as equals to the expert and textbook. In all this, experiential learning is seen as both a valuable educational strategy and a vehicle for examining the lived experiences of teachers and students. However, progressive educators, and more specifically those concerned with media education, recognize that there is more to experiential learning than mere experience. Education is about making sense of this experience. The teacher's role is to help students make sense of experience and not to do this on their behalf. They have to prepare students to "process" experience and not "consume" it. In order for experience to have any educative value it has to be arrested, examined, analyzed, considered, and negated in order to shift it to knowledge (Aitchison & Graham, 1989, 15).

For Torbert (1972, 8), experiential learning involved a reflective processing of experience and an "awareness of qualities, patterns and consequences of one's own experience as one experiences it." Indeed, the absence of this awareness might even be regarded as a form of personal or social dysfunction. A citizen or a society unable or unwilling to be critical will militate against the growth and maintenance of a vital and healthy civil society. This caution ought then to give us some clues as to how we might prepare students for citizenry—we will need curricula and methods which allow students to exercise these critical skills. In addition, schooling needs to be seen as a forum for reflecting and transforming the world and not as a monastic retreat from the world. In this way when students leave school at the end of the day they do not suspend their intellectual project.

South African Media Education

In addition to the international influence, it is from these critical and experiential modes of learning that many South African media education programs have drawn their inspiration. A progressive approach to media education is, however, not common throughout the country. In the early eighties the Transvaal Education Department (TED), responsible for white schools in South Africa's largest province, instituted film studies which were based on early British models of studying "good" films. Films became alternatives to the literature texts and were studied using the same methods. Issues of authorship, representation, audience, and power did not feature in the classroom studies. Instead, the principal characters, plots, screenplay, and technology of film making constituted film studies. In addition, only "safe" films, such as *Chariots of Fire,* were chosen, as they offered limited potential for reflection on South African society and apartheid.

Parallel to the formal curriculum initiatives of the TED, the Natal Education Department (NED) gave support to the informal and self-directed initiatives of English teachers and their associations. The Natal province can be said to be the most experimental and supportive of grassroot teacher initiatives. In addition to these two white education authorities another white authority, the Cape Education Department, and an Indian Schools authority, the Department of Education and Culture, have implemented media education programs during the last few years. The imminent establishment of a single non-racial education authority will have to come to terms with the various views and differential progress in the present bodies.

In addition to the influence of critical pedagogy on the methods of media education, other influences came from an unexpected quarter. In the late seventies and early eighties many community media organizations were established to support the work of educators and oppositional media producers who presented a direct challenge to apartheid media and the state censorship of media. The Media Resource Center (MRC), in which I am based, was one these. It was established in 1985 following a resolution of delegates at the *Media in Education and Development* conference to address the unequal distribution of educational media resources and skills in South Africa. The MRC established the Media Education Program to promote a progressive curriculum of media education in both primary and secondary schools. It hosted the first national conference on media education to gain grassroot teacher support for a holistic and progressive view of media education and *Media Matters in South Africa*, a book based on the conference proceedings, was published in 1991.

Our vision is of a media education which will make a contribution to the whole school curriculum. We regularly reassure teachers that we are not attempting to add more content to the school curriculum but rather to transform the underlying educational philosophy—a foundational rather than additional interest. Media education is not just another subject or an additional curriculum content, but a means of animating and uniting the artificial separation of school subject knowledge and the separation of the school from the outside world. It is a project in which the cultural world is explored by examining and creating media within these school subjects. Indeed, many media education programs have been designed specifically as "across-the-curriculum" activities.

The lessons we have learned from participatory video, collective media, and oppositional media in the community-based organizations have also influenced our work in media education. Workshops and exercises that we and others develop for classroom use often employ participatory and critical elements used by oppositional media activists. Furthermore, collaborative learning and social engagements enable and encourage conversations which are often silenced by social and school borders of race, class, gender and power relations.

Media Education Exercises

At the heart of our media education programs are questions. To avoid missing essential areas we have been systematic in our questions by using the British Film Institute's (BFI) six "key questions" in media education (Criticos, 1991, 230). The questions relate to an examination of technology, audience, representation, agency, category, and language. In addition to the BFI "key questions," we frame activities in the more general and unifying questions which ensure an experiential and critical encounter with media. In our media education activities the three crucial phases of experiential learning—description, analysis, and action—are evoked by the questions: What?; So What?; and Now What?

The critical and active components of learning in our media education programs are clearly illustrated in an often-repeated workshop on newspaper production. On one occasion the workshop was used with seventh-grade schoolchildren. The class was divided up into groups representing the principal activities in a typical newsroom. The paper is planned, and stories researched and written. Working in groups, these children experience the tensions of contested meaning and competition for space. The magic of the newspaper and the notion of objective reporting is undermined as the complex process that lies behind the product is revealed. The students experience first hand the industrial character of the press and the way news is "manufactured" (Criticos, 1993, 167).

The interest in public scrutiny common in participatory media was used in this workshop by magnifying the scale of the newspaper so it covered the entire wall of a school hall. Each newspaper column was printed by hand onto a roll of newsprint—a nine-column newspaper when pasted on to the wall was thirty feet wide! The students wrote more carefully since their work was now subjected to the scrutiny of their classmates and others who would come into the hall later on. An interesting development in this workshop was that the students wrote a lead story entitled, "Tuck Shop Beggars." The story relates to the practice of older students harassing young students during the lunch break while they queued at the "tuck shop" (a school cafeteria). Complaints by the young students to teachers and prefects had not been heard or taken seriously in the past—now these students planned to expose the harassment as a lead story. The newspaper would be seen by teachers and parents when the hall was to be used for a PTA meeting later on in the day. Apart from experiencing the tension of the newsroom the children also learned about the power of the press.

This example illustrates the way in which a whole class may learn. Furthermore, collaborative learning and social engagements enable and encourage conversations which are often silenced by social and school borders and thus allow for the growth and aggregation of civic courage.

Education for Citizenry in a Civil Society

Civic courage provides the possibility and potential to keep in check the ruthless intents and limitations of the market and government. Courage, however, does not emerge spontaneously or without prerequisites. It requires both information and analytical competence. One way to develop this competence is to allow students as many opportunities as possible to wrestle with moral and social issues in simulations and discussions which allow free expressions and development of critical skills in a friendly and safe environment.

Many organizations and teacher bodies are now making concerted efforts to develop materials, curricula, and educational programs which are founded on a connected epistemology and an emancipatory interest. In media education this is achieved by allowing experience and the world around us to inform school knowledge. In turn, this new (reconstructed) knowledge equips students to examine the world around them and ultimately become critical citizens.

These critical citizens, the building blocks of a civil society, a democratic nation, and government, will have learned valuable lifelong skills in school through initiatives such as the media education programs. But what is it about media education which makes it so valuable for democracy in an information and media era? In South Africa these programs ensure that

1. Students become critical media "readers" who are able to discern falsification, bias, and absences in media reportage and representation.
2. Students develop an understanding of media production. They see human agency and the manufactured nature of media below the surface.
3. Media education programs offer a safe environment in which moral and social questions can be explored. Many media exercises force students to work through perspectives of the other political view, class, race or gender.
4. The creative side of media education ensures that there is an increasingly bigger group of people who are able to give voice to their views in the various media.

South Africa's first free elections have been a baptism of fire for the newly trained media producers and users. Their skills are vital for the many civil and educational organizations engaged in voter education. In the run-up to the elections ANC President, Nelson Mandela, called on the government to relax the legal voting age from eighteen years to fourteen years. Most political analysts reject the idea as unrealistic and wrote this off as political opportunism to catch the youth vote.

While many have rejected the fourteen-year-old voter idea, there is great merit in young children learning and practicing to live in a civil society. This includes political literacy and tolerance. One such precedent is the "Kids Voting" program, founded in Costa Rica and applied in the some locations in the U.S. since 1988, which offers a curriculum to educate elementary and secondary students about important democratic principles and voter responsibility. The program, which is initiated in the run-up to the U.S. State and national elections, culminates in young children accompanying their parents to the polls on election day and participating in a youth vote, which operates alongside the adult poll. Arizona, the first state to implement the program in the U.S., has found significant improvement in voter commitment. In a survey of registered voters, 3 percent said that they voted because of the influence of their children who are involved in the "Kids Voting" program (Gandal & Finn, 1992, 6).

The Media Resource Center was commissioned to produce a voter education video for the largely rural and Zulu-speaking voters in the province of Natal. An examination of other video materials revealed that most of the videos have a paternalistic and didactic style of the "expert" (usually male) telling voters about democracy and mechanics of registration and the voting process. I attempted to move away from voting procedure toward issues which relate to critical discernment of election messages. Telling people how to vote may achieve less spoiled votes and more voters at the polls, but it is disempowering and disaffirming of the voter as a critical citizen.

The video which we produced uses the everyday experiences, skills, and competencies of ordinary people in a "soap opera" narrative style, which visits issues related to the national elections. Viewers' skills of discernment and judgment in their everyday life as critical and intelligent consumers (albeit illiterate and unschooled) are affirmed and applied to the task of discerning and making choices between election media messages and promises. Two scenarios, a family celebration of a daughter's election to executive office in a community organization and a family argument over a faulty stereo purchased by the son, raise complex issues of gender, leadership, advertising, representation, and other concerns essential for making careful choices in the elections.

Conclusion

The voter education video and other examples given in this reveal our multiple role and responsibility as teachers—roles which are often in tension with one another. Are we teachers of media or media activists? We are both! To be both, we must regard ourselves as teachers *and* citizens. The struggle for democracy in South Africa has resulted in a special form of media education. Such a media education we hope will contribute to the development of media literacy, critical literacy, and ultimately, critical citizens in the information age.

References

Aitchison, J., & Graham, P. (1989). Potato crisp pedagogy. In C. Criticos (Ed.), *Experiential learning in formal and non-formal education* (15–21). Durban, South Africa: Media Resource Center, University of Natal.

Alexander, N. (1989). Liberation pedagogy in the South African context. In C. Criticos (Ed.), *Experiential learning in formal and non-formal education* (1–14). Durban, South Africa: Media Resource Center, University of Natal.

Criticos, C. (1989). Media, praxis and empowerment. In S. Weil & I. McGill (Eds.), *Making sense of experiential learning* (207–20). London: Society for Research into Higher Education & Open University Press.

————. (1991). Developing resources for a media education program. In J. Prinsloo & C. Criticos (Eds.), *Media matters in South Africa* (224–33). Durban: Media Resource Center, University of Natal.

————. (1993). Experiential learning & social transformation for a postapartheid learning future. In D. Boud, R. Cohen, & D. Walker (Eds.), *Using experience for learning* (157–68). London: Society for Research into Higher Education & Open University Press.

Criticos, C., & Quinlan, T. (1991). Community video: Power and process. *Visual Sociology, 6 (2),* 39–52.

Freire, P. (1972). *Pedagogy of the oppressed.* Harmondsworth: Penguin.

Gandal, M., & Finn, C. E. (1992). *Freedom papers, teaching democracy.* San Francisco: Institute for Contemporary Studies.

Giroux, H. (1992). *Border crossings: Cultural workers and the politics of education.* London: Routledge.

Halloran, J. D. (1990, August). *Developments in communication and democracy.* Keynote presentation at the 17th Conference of the International Association of Mass Communication Research. Bled, Yugoslavia.

McLaren, P., & Tadeu da Silva, T. (1993). Decentering pedagogy: Critical literacy, resistance and the politics of memory. In P. McLaren & P. Leonard (Eds.), *Paulo Freire, a critical encounter* (47–89). London: Routledge.

Palmer, P. J. (1990). Community, conflict and ways of knowing: Ways to deepen our educational agenda. In J. Kendall (Ed.), *Combining service & learning, Volume I.* Raleigh: National Society for Internships and Experiential Education.

Prinsloo, J., & Criticos, C. (Eds.). (1991). *Media matters in South Africa.* Durban: Media Resource Center, University of Natal.

Stanton, T. (1986). Private correspondence from Tim Stanton on the marginal role of experiential education in mainstream education.

Stanton, T. (1990, July). *Think piece: Field experience and liberal arts education.* Paper presented at the 1990 NSIEE conference in Boulder, Colorado.

Torbert, W. R. (1972). *Learning from experience.* New York: Columbia University Press.

Part IV
Curricular and Research Perspectives

11

Media Literacy: A Compelling Component of School Reform and Restructuring

David M. Considine

Media literacy as a competency has at last begun to be recognized in the United States following examples established in the classrooms and curricula of Australia, England, and most recently, Canada. School reform/restructuring, currently shaping American education, offers a window of opportunity to integrate media literacy across the curriculum in an interdisciplinary way. Those who wish to promote the infant media literacy need to develop a management strategy that recognizes and responds to barriers and facilitators that support or subvert innovation within the culture and climate of schools as institutions. While media literacy as a concept must be explained and articulated, acceptance of the innovation will also depend heavily upon addressing the context in which change occurs, including the nature and needs of those who must embrace media literacy.

With the end of the twentieth century, now little more than a few years away, there is a growing body of evidence which suggests that the nation's schools have belatedly turned their attention to one of the most salient realities of twentieth-century American life, namely, the role the mass media plays in shaping public perception and public policy. Following examples long ago established in the classrooms and curricula of Australia, England, and most recently, Canada, individual teachers and some school systems across the country are beginning to address media literacy as both a concept and a competency. The subject is showing up in workshops, in-service programs and professional conferences of librarians, media specialists, instructional technologists, and other groups from Seattle to San Juan. Prestigious educational institutions, including the Annenberg School of Communication and Harvard University's Graduate School of Education, have hosted major think tanks, institutes, and symposia addressing the role of media literacy in both school and society. Important journals in the field of education have also begun to give space to the subject of media literacy. *Education Week* made "The Case for Media Education" (Kubey, 1991). *The Chronicle of Higher Education* used the 1992 election to publish, "How to Watch a Sound Bite: Students Need to Study Televisions Effect on Politics" (Thompson, 1992). The Association for Supervision and Curriculum Development gave four pages to a concise discussion, "Media Literacy: Educating Today and Tomorrow" (Thoman, 1993). The subject has also received coverage in major national newspapers including *The New York Times* (Rothenberg, 1991) and *The Boston Globe* (Flint, 1993). In March, 1992, media literacy was the focus of attention on ABC's *American Agenda* segment of the evening news.

Another major impetus for the media literacy movement has been the growing number of high-profile academics who have begun to articulate the need to teach students to access, analyze, and evaluate information which increasingly comes to them in iconic or visual rather than print formats. Elliot Eisner (1991) has complained that "we think about literacy in the tightest most constipated terms" and has called for a "more generous conception of what it means to know and a wider conception of the sources of human understanding" (15). Eisner connects the definition of literacy to the wide range of forms our society now uses to both produce and communicate information. President of the Carnegie Foundation for The Advancement of Teaching, Ernest Boyer, has also embraced the consequences of new communication forms. "It is no longer enough to simply read and write. Students must also become literate in the understanding of visual messages as well. Our children must learn how to spot a stereotype, isolate a social cliche and distinguish facts from propaganda, analysis from banter and important news from coverage" (1988, XXIV). Theodore Sizer is one of the leaders of the school reform movement and arguably one of the most influential educators in the country. Sizer, too, has recently begun to focus attention on the role the mass media plays in socializing and schooling our children. "Television has become the biggest school system, the principal shaper of culture . . . willy nilly, television is powerfully influencing the young on what it is to be American" (1992, 24). Noting the power of the mass media and the traditional failure of schools to address this presence and power, Sizer wonders if our education system can now "change the very nature of what it is to watch TV" (26). Finally, the prestigious

Carnegie Council on Adolescent Development, in its 1992 report, *Fateful Choices,* noted that, despite the fact that young people are surrounded by media messages, "schools have hardly begun to teach them how to view or listen critically; yet such a capacity ought to be a major component of life skills education (1992, 53).

Despite the potential of these promising developments, this is not the time for complacency. In order to protect, promote, and preserve media literacy, proponents must recognize the conditions and characteristics that for so long impeded the movement. In addition, they must respond by identifying ways in which the changing culture and climate of American education, particularly school reform and restructuring, offers a window of opportunity for media literacy to assume a central role in the educational process. The optimists who believe that success is inevitable might take a sobering look at the long, sorry history of both media and technology in education. Despite the enormous promise of successive technologies, one after another they have failed to fundamentally alter the nature of teaching and learning in the nation's schools and universities, which are change-resistant institutions of inertia (Waggoner, 1984). Nor can naive faith be placed in the apparent value of the media literacy movement. Given the increasing presence of iconic technologies and information forms in our culture, the earlier visual literacy movement should long ago have been integrated into the educational process where its relevance is manifestly obvious. Yet, in 1993 as The International Visual Literacy Association celebrated its twenty-fifth anniversary in Rochester, the organization represented little more than one or two hundred dedicated individuals, many quite brilliant, who had nonetheless, over a quarter century, been unable to build critical mass for the important ideas they represented. In the same way, the demise of the Critical Viewing Skills movement, which enjoyed some success during the 1970s, provides evidence of the need to connect media literacy as an innovation, to the nature and needs of the institution and the individuals whose response will either support or subvert it. Too many good ideas enjoy short-term fad status only to sputter and die in the day-to-day reality of education. "With its materialist consumer culture, the United States tends to consume innovations, gobble up the latest idea, not tasting or digesting the substance, just using it up, spitting it out and on to the next" (Edelsky, et al., 1991, 2).

The Aspen Institute has described media literacy initiatives at North Carolina's Appalachian State University as "perhaps the most sustained institutional effort within formal schooling" (1993, 5). The largest teacher training institute in the tenth-largest state requires undergraduate teachers to take one course that addresses the subject of media literacy and its role in North Carolina's curriculum. In addition, critical viewing skills as a competency is regarded as a core skill in the Reich College of Education. Significantly the Aspen Institute's report, *National Leadership Conference on Media Literacy,* also addresses the way these developments were promoted at Appalachian State, noting that "the success of the program reflects some useful strategies" (5). In particular, while the course in media literacy grew out of the department of Curriculum and Instruction, and the concerns of its faculty, planners recognized early in the process that they would be more successful by integrating rather than isolating media literacy as both content and competency. As such, while the main focus concentrated on one required class, faculty worked with colleagues in areas such as health education, social studies methods, and various library science courses, demonstrating the way in which media literacy addressed the goals and objectives of those disciplines. Over time, courses and program areas were modified to begin to include elements of media literacy. The experience at Appalachian State was not an accident, and it was clearly more than the result of two or three dedicated teachers serving on curriculum committees. The process by which change was facilitated was regarded with as much importance by the planners as the change itself.

Barriers and Facilitators

Conditions that support or impede the development of media literacy have been identified. Having studied media education around the world, John Pungente (1989) of Canada's Jesuit Communication Project developed a list of nine key factors that he believed were crucial for success. These included: collaboration between teachers, parents, and researchers; the development of appropriate evaluation instruments; and in-service programs at the school district level. Drawing on his experience developing media literacy in Australia, the media studies coordinator at Appalachian State compared conditions in Australian education to American circumstances, which resulted in the publication of "Media Literacy: Can We Get There From Here?" (Considine, 1990). Both documents provide useful frameworks for planners to use when attempting to implement media literacy programs and both provide a context that expands the focus from a simple discussion of what media literacy is, to a question of how the concept can be successfully presented to the diverse stakeholders involved in education, which includes of course parents, teachers, administrators, the public and students.

From Institutional Inertia to Paradigms Lost

The stratified, conservative and change-resistant nature of American education has been well documented (Cusick, 1973; Chadwick 1979). So long as those conditions remained in place, little change was likely to occur either in what was taught or how. School reform and restructuring, however, have radically changed our assumptions about American education. Major reports including *A Nation at Risk* (1983), *A Nation Prepared* (1986), and *Turning Points* (1989) have laid the groundwork for a radical overhaul of American education. The Carnegie Forum on Education and the Economy's 1986 report made this abundantly clear, saying, "We do not believe the educational system needs repairing: we believe it must be rebuilt" (14). With school systems all over the country now receptive to change, the opportunity exists for those who support media literacy to make their case.

Top-Down Management versus Grass Roots Movement

The successful history of the media literacy movement in Australia, Canada, and other countries indicates that the idea emerged from creative, independent teachers working at the classroom level. It was not imposed upon them by a centralized bureaucracy. Various departments and ministries of education later followed the example set by teachers and mandated the role of media literacy in the curriculum. Conditions in these school systems afforded young teachers greater flexibility and independence, as a result of which they had more opportunity to develop curriculum materials than their American counterparts. The school reform movement once again offers light at the end of the tunnel. Two major changes are of potential importance here. The first is the changing nature of the curriculum, best reflected in core competencies and core course documents that are still emerging and at different levels of development in each state. The second potentially significant change is the movement toward site-based management, which should place greater autonomy and decision making in the hands of teachers.

Teacher Training

It goes without saying that for teachers to teach media literacy they must themselves have been taught how to do so. While that seems obvious, the history of educational media and instructional technology in our schools paints a bleak picture of equipment and materials foisted upon teachers with little or no training (Saettler, 1968; Office of Technology Assessment, 1989). Both in-service and pre-service programs need to provide and school districts need to hire consultants who have expertise in the field. One of the greatest barriers to these developments is evident in the composition of faculty in colleges of education. With the exception of one or two individuals with some background in educational media, most education faculty have little background or training that would prepare them to respond to issues that are central to media literacy, as a result of which they are neither mentioned nor modeled in their classes. Ironically, faculty with these skills are usually present on most campuses, traditionally in areas like communication arts, where they have little contact with education faculty.

Availability of Resources

Another variable that has been crucial for the successful development of media literacy programs has been the availability of quality resources, including both print and nonprint materials. For a long period of time the only materials available even in limited ways in this country had been written or produced somewhere else. As a result, while the theoretical foundations of media literacy were addressed and relevant, the examples cited were Australian or British, and were not easily related to American media. In the last few years, however, an increasing number of materials specifically developed for American educators have come on to the market. Significantly, two of these emerged from relatively small publishers, both with strong bases in instructional technology and library science, representing an expansion of their traditional areas of interest, linking media education to educational media. Educational Technology publications released *Media and You An Elementary Media Literacy Curriculum* (Tyner & Lloyd-Kolkin, 1991). This volume was an important contribution, particularly since it veered away from the Canadian and Australian models, which had placed most of the focus on media literacy in secondary schools. Libraries Unlimited followed the next year with *Visual Messages: Integrating Imagery Into Instruction* (Considine & Haley 1992). Subtitled a "Teaching Resource for Visual and Media Literacy," the book linked media literacy to school reform and provided strategies and activities to be integrated across the K–12 curriculum.

In addition to textbooks, videotapes, resource guides, news letters, model lessons and journals are also available from several major American media literacy organizations. Of special interest are *Media and Values,* a highly professional journal that approaches media literacy from the perspective of religious education, and the clearinghouse/data bank established by the National Telemedia Council in Madison, Wisconsin. The continued growth of these resources and support groups will be vital to the success of the emerging media literacy movement.

Training of Library Media Specialists

Those who seek to promote media literacy should identify and seek out their natural allies. Since the mid 1970s, school libraries have been school media centers and those who supervise them have been library media specialists. While the media component of their training has traditionally dealt with educational media, concepts such as critical viewing skills and critical listening skills are terms and approaches most media specialists are familiar with. Linking these concepts to mass media as well as educational media is a relatively easy step with this group, which is after all, the only professional group in the public schools with any degree of substantial training in media.

Equally as important, administrators tend to look to them for advice when it comes to the question of media and technology. They therefore can be enormously influential change agents in a single school or a whole system, and they cannot and should not be ignored or bypassed in any attempt to get directly to the classroom teacher. While library media specialists are natural allies for the media literacy movement, their preparation, like that of teachers, must be modernized to include materials, content, and competencies that address the impact mass media has on children and adolescents. At the moment too little attention is given to the media that children and teens regard as important, which fosters alienation and irrelevance between the culture of the classroom and the culture of the living room. One potentially significant bridge to the two cultures that is beginning to receive some attention in both library science and media education literature is the children's picture book and conceptual frameworks for analyzing elements such as content, form, and representation (Haley, 1992; Considine et al., 1994).

Academic Elitism: High Culture and Pop Culture

Antagonism has historically existed between the educational aims of the American classroom and the entertainment aims and values of the mass media. Most academics in colleges of education and, therefore, most teachers have had little training in mass media and have little understanding of how to connect it to the curriculum or children. Mass media content is viewed as inappropriate, tasteless, and worthless. Many educators take the matter even further, regarding the mass media as competition and quite frequently as the enemy. "It ruins the imagination of young people and makes it very difficult for them to have a passionate relationship to the thought and the art that are the substance of liberal education" (Bloom, 1987, 79). "The child needs to develop a capacity for self-direction in order to liberate himself from dependency. The television experience helps to perpetuate dependency" (Winn, 1977, 7). Typically, television viewing and other media behavior of children are regarded as incompatible with literacy. Literacy, it is argued, can "counteract the visual and aural violence of the mass media" by providing "calm aesthetic satisfactions that transcend the hedonistic thrill of instantaneous and often mesmerizing exaltations" (Kozol, 1985, 177).

This response, while understandable, fails to acknowledge an important body of research that places emphasis on how children watch, rather than simply focusing on what they watch (Salomon, 1979; Dominick et al., 1979; Rapaczynski et al., 1982). The research clearly suggests that instructional intervention, or pedagogical process, can change the way young people use the media, think about it, respond to it, and accept or reject its messages. Educators who lament the passive use of the media by young people will not solve the problem by assuming the ostrich posture, attacking the media or arguing that sets should be turned off. Behind most of their concerns is the fear that mass media's mindlessness is harmful and young people need to be protected from it. Those who advocate this position need to be helped to understand that protection is more likely to come when young people are provided with the intellectual skills to become critical viewers, listeners, and thinkers. In the end, it might well be argued that critical consumption will lead to critical production. Given First Amendment protections, censoring or controlling media messages is a dubious enterprise. Even if it succeeds in affecting media content, it does little to protect young people, who will inevitably find alternative sources of information. If, on the other hand, our students are taught to become discerning consumers and users of media, it is highly likely that they will recognize and reject offensive, stereotypical, and biased media, using the dynamics of the free marketplace to assert consumer control.

Innovation Diffusion and a Concerns-Based Approach

The emphasis upon product rather than process has proved needlessly fruitless, if not fatal, in American education's traditional response to both media and technology, which is perhaps best described and detailed in *A History of Instructional Technology* (Saettler, 1968). The book represents a depressing chronicle of valid research that remains strategically relevant today, but is almost totally ignored. A 1923 study concluded for example, that "the movement for visual education will progress in direct ratio to the number of teachers who are trained in the technique of visual instruction" (Saettler, 1968, 193). A few years later, a study of the role of motion pictures in education concluded that, "however inherently effective the photoplays may be . . . it will only attain its highest degree of effectiveness when accompanied by good teaching, based on the appreciation of the real goal to be attained and of the capacity of this material to contribute to its attainment" (Saettler, 1968, 292). Tellingly, the 1923 study complained that too much teacher training with technology "has been concerned with the technique of handling visual equipment rather than the technique of instruction" (Saettler, 1968, 132).

Almost sixty years later, after more than a decade of major expenditure on computers, VRCs, video cameras, and related technology, the Director of the Institute of the Transfer of Technology to Education reported that "chalkboards, lectures and textbooks continue to dominate instruction" (Mecklenburger, 1990, 106). While some blame the technology and declare that the so-called computer revolution has fizzled or failed, we cannot blame the products of technology when the process by which they find their way into classrooms and media centers almost predetermines their failure. A quarter of a century after Saettler's book provided compelling evidence of the need for appropriate training and management strategies, the nation's colleges and universities still lacked a systematic approach to both the acquisition and application of technology. "Very few universities currently prepare teachers to use instructional technologies by modeling the use of technology in classes taught in the university . . . for most faculty in teacher education, technology is a bother, a mystery, a blur, a largely incomprehensible phenomenon" (Gooler, 1989, 20). While schools continue to acquire equipment, there is a body of evidence that documents teacher resistance (Proctor, 1983; Smith and Ingersoll, 1984; Seidman, 1986). Significantly, research indicates that teacher use of media is attitudinal (Bellamy et al., 1978). These findings make it clear that innovation cannot be imposed upon a system or injected in to it. For an innovation to progress successfully from isolated pockets of progress to critical mass, adopted and accepted by the system, those who introduce the change must carefully integrate it into the organizational culture and climate. The change must be responsive to the nature and needs of the clients or stakeholders and to the institutional context in which they work.

Computer Culture versus Classroom Culture

In the case of technologies of instruction, these concerns are seldom addressed as a result of which innovation encounters teacher resistance. Despite the promise of computer-based technology in the area of individual self-paced learning, much computer use still centers around drill and practice. The reason for this is quite evident to anyone familiar with the culture and climate of American education. The key elements of this system include batch processing of students, subject matter specialization, vertical organization, routinization of activity, and downward communication flow (Cusick, 1973). Looking at the mismatch between technology and the school as an organization, Chadwick (1979) identified several characteristics of schooling that served as barriers to innovation. In this traditional model of education, the teacher is the main decision maker, dispensing information largely through chalk and talk, to passive students, lumped together in groups, taught in formally controlled blocks of time and evaluated mainly through repetition. Technology, which promises independent activity, discovery learning, and student-centered classrooms, represents an all-out assault on these traditions. Technology's ability to transform education was clearly recognized in the report, *A Nation Prepared* (Carnegie Forum on Education and the Economy, 1986). "These technologies should make it possible to relieve teachers of much of the burden of imparting information to students, thereby freeing them for coaching, diagnosing learning difficulties, developing students' creative and problem-solving capacities and participating in school management"(Carnegie Forum, 1986, 94). For technology to actually transform American education, however, teachers and administrators must first recognize the mismatch between the nature of the technology and the nature of our schools as organizations. Only then will we be able to respond by developing systematic models for change that address the context in which change must either be accepted or rejected.

Managing the Change

Those who seek to introduce media literacy to American education would benefit themselves and the movement by developing a cohesive management strategy that addresses the nature of school as an organization. The theoretical base for this planning is evident in the literature related to innovation diffusion. At its most basic level, this approach enables planners to look at change in an evolutionary, fluid, even organic way. To change one aspect of the system inevitably results in change somewhere else. "Innovation in any component of the system almost invariably requires modification of the entire system. The basic law of ecology applies; everything is connected to everything else" (Perelman, 1988, 21). Hence, to suggest that schools begin to teach media literacy will invariably lead to a discussion about what they will stop teaching in order to make room for it. How media literacy is taught—the very fact that it is taught—can also bring about major changes. The higher-order thinking skills involved in the analysis and evaluation of information may represent a threat to many traditional educators from teacher-centered classrooms.

As media literacy has moved away from earlier protectionist modes, away from issues of aesthetics and appreciation, its new ideological concerns have had an impact on the dynamics of the traditional classroom. "It severely undermined the hierarchical role of the teacher as the accredited expert and purveyor of approved knowledge in the classroom. The teacher was no longer the arbiter of taste, but a co-partner or investigator in what was now a much more open ended process" (Masterman, 1989, 13).

Since innovation clearly has an impact upon individuals, planners must attempt to address the concerns of these clients. Workshops and faculty development programs that concentrate on the change, rather than those charged with implementing the change, are not likely to result in the successful implementing of the innovation. In the fall of 1993, The North Carolina's Center for The Advancement of Teaching began the first media literacy in-service training for the state's teachers, drawing upon faculty from Appalachian State University, Citizens for Media Literacy, a nonprofit advocacy group, and consultants from around the country. In preliminary correspondence with the faculty, the center director commented on the elements of successful training programs for teachers. "Professional development for them has meant, far too often being talked at rather than engaged in conversation by experts . . . they do not learn well unless they are active in discussion and in the learning process . . . when discourse is augmented by an illuminating or supporting hands-on activity" (Thompson, 1993).

Putting People First

Though this may seem self-evident to those involved in faculty development and in-service education, the pedagogical process must do more than engage these teachers intellectually. It must also address them as individuals, recognizing that while they may all teach the same subject or the same grade level, personality differences and different career stages may have a profound affect on how responsive they are to the change that is being proposed. One approach that has provided useful management strategies for such training has developed what has been called "adopter categories." These categories classify individuals as innovators, leaders, early majority, late majority, and resisters (Rogers & Shoemaker, 1971). By identifying which individuals in a given institution most closely approximate the salient characteristics of each group, planners are able to anticipate and organize training to draw upon the strengths and weaknesses of each. As a simple example, the venturesome nature of the innovator is useful to get an idea off the ground, but there is a substantial body of evidence that demonstrates this will not result in the adoption of the innovation without the support of those classified as leaders (Pritchard & Busby, 1991). For library media specialists and others who often find themselves charged with the task of conducting training programs, the concept offers a strategy not unlike triage. Rather than taking a shot-gun approach, which scatters ideas and concepts over moving targets, hitting some and missing others, the adopter category method offers an energy-saving means to identify individuals within an institution who are both receptive to change and likely to influence others to embrace the change.

Another useful management strategy that could facilitate the development of media literacy centers on the stages of concern about the innovation (Hall, 1979). This classification ranks various levels of concern, or engagement individuals feel about any given innovation. At the lowest level, which is called Awareness, the individual has little interest in the idea. At level two, or the Informational stage, individuals do not have much knowledge about the innovation, but they are interested and receptive. Individuals then advance through various stages, preparing for, utilizing, managing, refining, and integrating the innovation. At each stage, they are psychologically and professionally working through their level of involvement with the change. In any given school or system, teachers and faculty will be at various levels of this model in their response to media literacy. Those who wish to guarantee the success of this innovation must concentrate on much more than media literacy as content or concept; they must give equal care, planning, and attention to the concerns their clients feel about media literacy.

Clearly, teachers cannot develop media literacy in their students unless they themselves understand its components and key concepts, as well as successful instructional activities for fostering these skills. At a more basic level, however, and of equal importance to the survival of the innovation, is their need to be able to provide a coherent rationale for media literacy to their colleagues, and to the various constituencies of any school, which includes parents and administrators. Each of these stakeholders will have their own questions and concerns about media literacy. Their stakeholders need to be identified, their questions anticipated, and answers prepared. While some questions may focus on the specifics of media literacy itself, there is a generic or formulaic nature to many questions that almost inevitably emerge with any educational innovation. These base-level concerns include such questions as: How much will it cost? Who is going to teach it? Where does it fit in to the curriculum? How am I going to do this on top of every thing else? How do you test it? and How is this going to help my kid get a job?

Curriculum Connections: Building the Bridges

If media literacy is perceived as a course, rather than a competency, its impact, even if it is successfully added to the curriculum will be minimal. Housing media literacy as content, in the sanctuary of a traditional subject area like English, as has been done in Ontario, also imposes limitations on the innovation, which in reality has applications and implications across the traditional and emerging curriculum. Given the current transitional nature of American education, school reform and restructuring offers media literacy advocates an excellent opportunity to promote the initiative by linking it to core curriculum, core competencies, and developing mandates.

Rather than assuming that people have to be convinced of the need for media literacy, it might be profitable to examine mandates on a state-by-state basis to see if the skills and competencies associated with media literacy are already being addressed. In North Carolina, for example, a K–12 information skills curriculum has recently been passed. While the document never uses the term *media literacy*, the language of the curriculum clearly articulates both the rationale and the central concepts. "The sheer mass of information and variety of media formats challenges every learner to filter, interpret, accept and/or discard media messages" (North Carolina Department of Publication Instruction, 1992, 11). The goals and objectives section of the document indicates that students should be able to: (1) recognize the power of the media to influence; (2) recognize how the presentation of information and ideas is influenced by social, cultural, political, and historical events; and (3) produce media in various formats. The Minnesota Department of Education has also created a list of outcomes in the area of educational media and technology that are completely compatible with media literacy. Unlike the North Carolina document, Minnesota actually uses the term *media literacy*, and outlines numerous objectives related to it. Learners are expected to: (1) recognize the selectivity of all media in news coverage; (2) draw conclusions about the cause-effect relationships between the media's reports and the public's response; (3) recognize, interpret, and create visual images; and (4) recognize the effects of distortion, stereotyping, propaganda, and violence in visual media (Minnesota Department of Education, 1990).

These two examples provide clear evidence that media literacy and the skills it encompasses have already been accepted by the educational establishment. Both documents however, limit the concept to the relatively obvious areas of educational media and library science. As a competency, media literacy has clear connections to numerous aspects of the curriculum in terms of both subject area and instructional objectives. The core curriculum recently developed in several states reflects any number of avenues that might be successfully pursued by media literacy advocates. Virginia's World Class Education Plan, for example, says that students should be able to: (1) take care of themselves; (2) be well-informed and active members of the community; and (3) understand and care about the pleasures bestowed by culture and the arts (Bradford & Stiff, 1993). In Oregon, students are required to: (1) think critically, creatively, and reflectively; (2) deliberate on public issues; (3) use technology to both process and produce information; and (4) understand positive health habits and behaviors (Oregon State Board of Education, 1993). Increasingly, the curricula and the expected outcomes being embraced by schools throughout the country reflect recommendations made in various reports throughout the 1980s.

One of the most important studies was *Turning Points: Preparing American Youth for the 21st Century.* Dealing with the nation's middle schools, the study concluded that schools should create students "who are literate . . . know how to think, lead a healthy life, behave ethically and assume the responsibility of citizenship in a pluralistic society" (Carnegie Council on Adolescent Development, 1989). With schools now focusing increasing attention on the broad areas of information skills, health concerns, and responsible citizenship, media literacy is offered an extraordinary window of opportunity to demonstrate its relevance to the very goals that education has already embraced. In short, the most effective strategy for what might be called the selling of media literacy seems to lie in the ability of its advocates to show how it is consistent with the key concerns of American education. Those who wish to serve as change agents, operating in the vanguard of the movement, must be able to articulate this strategy.

Health Education

Now that health education has assumed a more visible and significant role in the curriculum, media literacy advocates must begin to clearly establish the relationship between the goals and objectives of health education and those of the media literacy movement. If health education classes do little more than chronicle the potentially harmful consequences of alcohol and tobacco consumption, or the dangers and risks of unsafe sexual behavior, they are not likely to change adolescent attitudes or behavior. While chemical concerns and harmful consequences are important, health education classes must also address the cultural context in which attitudes, values, and behaviors are formed.

There is simply no doubt that the mass media play an important role in the development of these attitudes. This role was acknowledged in *Fateful Choices* (1992), a Carnegie Council report which declared that "in the 1990s, the state of adolescent health care in America reached crisis proportions" (21). The study documented alarming rates of teen violence, teen pregnancy, alcohol and drug addiction, and unsafe sexual behavior. On the issue of violence, the study noted that "the television and movie industries do indeed bear a heavy responsibility for making violence appear an acceptable,perhaps even normal way of life" (165).

A task force appointed by the American Psychological Association found that "by the time the average child graduates from elementary school, she or he will have witnessed at least 8000 murders and more than 100,000 other assorted acts of violence" (Huston et al., 1992, 54). Any meaningful attempt to reduce violence in both school and society must include strategies that enable adolescents to examine these media messages and to explore nonviolent approaches to conflict resolution; approaches and alternatives that are seldom modeled in the media. This conclusion was among recommendations that emerged from *Safeguarding Our Youth,* a 1993 violence prevention conference convened by the Department of Justice, the Department of Education, and the Department of Health and Human Services.

Addressing the issue of substance abuse, the Carnegie report recommended that "advertising of alcoholic beverages and cigarettes in the media, including magazines, should cease to be directed at young people" (1992, 221). There is a growing body of evidence which demonstrates the relationship between media marketing and youth consumption. The American Medical Association recently dedicated an entire issue of their journal to a discussion of tobacco advertising and its effect upon children, with particular emphasis upon Old Joe the Camel (Fischer et al., 1991).

If marketing and, in particular, the process of targeting, renders children and adolescents vulnerable to these campaigns, educators must do more than attempt to control the messages. As much, if not more attention must be focused on the process of how these messages are consumed. Teachers must help children and adolescents recognize and understand the persuasive techniques and strategies advertisers use to attract their attention and convince them to purchase their products, irrespective of the potentially harmful consequences. Finally, the crisis in teen pregnancy and the persistent dangers of AIDS necessitate a fusion between media literacy and sex education. Perhaps in no other area is the cultural contradiction so great as in the mixed messages young people receive about sex from the media on one hand, and family, church, and school on the other. The Carnegie reported acknowledged the importance of these media messages, nothing that they "place a major role in modeling adolescent sexual behavior" (531). Exploring the messages modeled in the media, *The Journal of Adolescent Health Care* concluded that much of what adolescents learn about sexuality "does not depict the potentially unhealthy consequences of these behaviors and does not convey the need for sexual responsibility" (Brown et. al., 1990, 64). If education is to make any inroads, successfully changing the behavior and attitudes of young people, particularly those in the crucial stage of identity formation, serious and systematic attempts will have to be made to understand the way these young people use the mass media as an information source. Health education will not succeed if our classrooms and curricula continue to ignore the electronic environment that surrounds the young, constituting as it does, a major part of the cultural context that shapes their attitudes and behaviors.

Responsible Citizenship

One of the most consistent goals pervading all American education is the desire to create responsible citizens for a democratic society. Clearly, such a goal must embrace information skills and critical thinking. Responsible citizens must be able to access, analyze, and evaluate information in a variety of forms, both print and nonprint. While we live in a so-called information age, access to information should not be confused with success in comprehending that information. In fact, the speed at which information now comes to us in many ways mitigates against comprehension and clear analysis. "We are," as John Naisbitt noted, "drowning in information but starved for knowledge" (1982, 24). Naisbitt sees a society surrounded by news, but with little time or ability to process it. "We are," he suggests, "a society of events, just moving from one incident, sometimes, even crisis—to the next, rarely pausing [or caring] to notice the process going on underneath" (2). A study by the Times Mirror Center for the People and the Press described "the doofus generation whose values are lightly held and whose opinions remain ripe for manipulation" (Marin, 1990, 37). Describing the relationship between this citizen-audience and the political process, the report concluded: "Sound bites and symbolism, the principal fuel of modern political campaigns, are well suited to young voters who know less and have limited interest in politics and public policy" (37). Those who wish to foster responsible citizenship must do more that teach students to understand the three branches of government. They must provide information skills that prepare students for the information forms of their society, including the mass-mediated process that is now American politics (White, 1982; Meyrowitz, 1985; Entman 1989). Responsible citizens do more than vote; they make an informed decision. That decision must be based on access to alternative sources of information and the ability to distinguish policy from personality, issue from image. In an era of politics by sound bites, 1-800 numbers, and talk show formats, democracy is not well served if entertainment values and formats become an acceptable substitute for meaningful debate, dialogue, and discourse. For the citizens of this country to be healthy individuals and for our institutions to grow and flourish, our schools must recognize the power of media to support or subvert that process, and respond by integrating media literacy as a core competency and information skill across the K–12 curriculum.

References

Aspen Institute, Communications and Society Program. (1993). *The national leadership conference on media education.* Washington, D.C.
Bellamy, R. et al. (1978). *Teacher attitudes toward nonprint media.* Frankfort, Kentucky: State Department of Education, ERIC Document #174 197.
Bloom, A. (1987). *The closing of the American mind.* New York: Simon and Schuster.
Boyer, E. L. (1988). Preface in Edward Palmer, *Television and America's children: A crisis of neglect.* New York: Oxford University Press.
Bradford, K., & Stiff, H. R. (May 1993). Virginia's common core of learning takes shape. *Educational Leadership, 35–38.*
Brown, J., Chiders, K. W., & Wazak, C. (January 1990). Television and adolescent sexuality. *Journal of Adolescent Health Care,* 62–70.
Carnegie Council on Adolescent Development. (1989). *Turning points: Preparing American youth for the 21st century.* Washington, D.C.

————. (1992). *Fateful choices healthy youth for the 21st century.* New York: Carnegie Corporation.

Carnegie Forum on Education and the Economy. (1986). *A nation prepared: Teachers for the 21st century. The report of the task force on teaching as a profession.* New York.

Chadwick, C. B. (1979). Why educational technology is failing and what can be done to create success. *Educational Technology 19*:1, 7–19.

Considine, D. M. (December 1990). Media literacy: Can we get there from here? *Educational Technology,* 27–32.

Considine, D. M., & Haley, G. E. (1992). *Visual messages: Integrating imagery into instruction.* Engelwood, Colo.: Libraries Unlimited.

Considine, D. M., Haley, G. E., & Lacy, L. E. (1994). *Imagine that: Developing critical thinking and viewing skills through children's books.* Engelwood, Colo.: Libraries Unlimited.

Cusick, P. (1973). *Inside high school.* New York: Holt.

Dominick, J., Richman, S., & Wurtzel, A. (1979). Problem-solving in TV shows popular with children. *Journalism Quarterly 56*: 455–63.

Edelsky, C., Altwerger, B., & Flores, B. (1991). *Whole language: What's the difference.* Portsmouth, N.H.: Heinemann.

Eisner, E. (1991). What really counts in schools. *Educational Leadership 48*: 10–11, 14–17.

Entman, R. (1989). *Democracy without citizens: Media and the decay of American politics.* New York: Oxford University Press.

Fischer, P. M. Schwartz, M. P., Richards, J. W., Goldstein, A., & Rojas, T. H. (11 December 1991). Brand logo recognition by children ages 3–6: Mickey Mouse and Old Joe the camel. *Journal of the American Medical Association, 262*: 3145–48.

Flint, A. (6 August 1993). The critical eye: Educator's goal is media literacy. *The Boston Globe, 1,* 8.

Gooler D. (March 1989). Preparing teachers to use technologies: Can universities meet the challenge? *Educational Technology.*

Haley, G. E. (1992). The look of the book: The need to read pictures. *Telemedium,* 3rd and 4th quarter.

Hall G. E. (1979). *Australian Educational Researcher 7*: 2, 5–32.

Hall G. E., & Wallace, R. D. (1973). *A developmental conceptualization of the adoption process within educational institutions.* Austin, Research and Development Center for Teacher Education: University of Texas.

Huston, A., Donnerstein, E., Fairchild, H., Feshbach, N., Katz, P., Murray, J., Rubenstein, E., Wilcox, B., & Zuckerman, D. (1992). *Big world, small screen: the role of television in American society.* Lincoln: University of Nebraska Press.

Kubey, R. (6 March 1991). The case for media education. *Education Week,* 27.

Kozol, J. (1985). *Illiterate America.* Garden City, N.Y.: Anchor Press.

Marin, R. (1990). Waiting in the wings: The doofus generation. *Washington Post National Weekly Edition,* 37.

Masterman, L. (1989). The development of media education in Europe in the 1980s. *Metro 79*, 13–17.

Mecklenburger, J. (October 1990). *Phi Delta Kappan,* 105–08.

Meyrowitz, J. (1985). *No sense of place.* New York: Oxford University Press.

Minnesota Department of Education. (1990). *Model learner outcomes for educational technology and media.* St. Paul, Minn.

Naisbitt, J. (1982). *Megatrends.* New York: Warner Communications.

National Committee on Excellence in Education. (1983). *A nation at risk: The imperative for educational reform.* Washington, D.C.: U.S. National Commission on Excellence in Education.

North Carolina Department of Publication Instruction. (1992). *Standard course of study: Information skills K–12.* Raleigh, N.C.

Office of Technological Assessment. (January 1989). Power on, *Teacher training and technology, classroom computer learning.*

Oregon State Board of Education. (1993). *Working designs for change.* Salem, Or.

Perelman, L. (September 1988). Restructuring the system is the solution. *Phi Delta Kappan.*

Pungente, J. (1989). The second spring: Media education in Canada. *Educational Media International 26,* 199–203.

Pritchard, W., & Busby, J. (1991). A blueprint for successfully integrating technology into your institution. *T.H.E. Journal* special issue, 48–54.

Proctor, L. F. (1983). *Student teacher utilization of educational media.* Doctoral dissertation, University of Indiana Eric Doc. No. ED. 244 620.

Rapaczynski, W., Singer, D., & Singer, J. (1982). Teaching television: A curriculum for young children. *Journal of Communication 32*: 46–55.

Rogers E. M., & Shoemaker, F. (1971). *Communications of innovations: A cross cultural approach.* New York: Free Press.

Rothenberg, R. (6 January 1991). The mass media is the message. *The New York Times Education Life,* 4A.

Saettler, P. (1968). *A history of instructional technology.* New York: McGraw Hill.

Safeguarding our youth: Violence prevention for our nation's schools. (1993). Recommendations from the working group on media. Washington, D.C.

Salomon, G. (1979). *The interaction of media, cognition and learning.* San Francisco: Jossey Bass.

Seidman, S. (October 1986). A survey of school teachers' utilization of media. *Educational Technology,* 19–23.

Sizer, T. (November 1992). School reform: What's missing. *World Monitor,* 20–27.

Smith, C. B., & Ingersoll, G. M. (1984). Audiovisual materials in U.S. schools: A national survey on availability and use. *Educational Technology 24*: 9, 36–38.

Thoman, E. (1993). Media literacy—Educating for today and tomorrow. *A.S.C.D. Curriculum and Technology Quarterly 2*: 1–4.

Thompson, R. (1993). Personal correspondence. Available from the author.

———. (12 August 1992). How to watch a sound bite: Students need to study television's effect on politics. *The Chronicle of Higher Education,* B1 /2.

Tyner, K., & Lloyd-Kolkin, D. (1991). *Media and you an elementary media literacy curriculum.* Engelwood Cliffs: N.J. Educational Technology Publications.

Waggoner, M. (1984). The new technologies versus the lecture tradition in higher education: Is change possible? *Educational Technology 24*: 7–12.

White, T. (1982). *America in search of itself.* New York: Harper and Row.

Winn, M. (1977). *The plug-in drug.* New York: Bantam.

12

Making Media Literate:
Educating Future Media Workers
at the Undergraduate Level

Máire Messenger Davies

Students of media production, such as trainee film and video producers and journal-
ists, are required to learn about theories of mass communication and textual analy-
sis as part of their degree programs. It is argued here that any working definition of
literacy for such students must incorporate aesthetic standards, based on accepted
critical and professional media practices, and on their own personal insights and
skills. Teachers of trainee media workers need to develop theoretical frameworks for
teaching about mass media that allow for the "literary"—that is, creative—contribu-
tions of individuals to be recognized since, as teachers, their primary task is to mo-
tivate and encourage individual students. Various approaches to the teaching of mass
communication theory, both in the United States and in the UK, are reviewed from
this perspective—including cultural studies, social science, and professionalism. It
is argued that creative individuals have specific needs for their theoretical study of
the media which may not always be met in traditional communications studies cur-
ricula. In particular, production students require models of good practice and they
need the opportunity to express authentic personal reactions to media products, in-
cluding their own and fellow students' work, in appropriate critical language.

I learned something through this project I hadn't expected to. As we gave a
sneak preview of our final project today I tried to look at our documentary with
an objective point of view. I was still pretty pleased. Only I realized I couldn't
look at it with an objective point of view because we had invested a lot of time
and care in this. I have always focused more on the business aspect of television
and film, but I realized today that one derives a different kind of satisfaction
when one is part of the creative process and the final results are so good.
—Jennifer R., senior-year broadcasting student,
College of Communication, Boston University

According to Turow (1991):

> Mass communication is the industrialized (mass) production of, reproduction, and multiple distribution of messages through technological devices. Messages are linguistic or pictorial representations that appear purposeful. The word industrialized means the process is carried out by . . . conglomerations of organizations that interact in the process of producing and distributing messages. (162)

Turow recognizes that "organizations are made up of people" but, he argues, they are still primarily "goal-directed, boundary maintaining activity systems" with limited scope for individual artistic self-determination.

In working with students who want to make a career in the media industries, the teacher of mass communication soon runs into a problem with this definition of what it means to be a "mass communicator." Although a university is also a "goal-directed, boundary maintaining activity system," the responsibility of the teacher, unlike that of the corporate executive, is to the individual student. The teacher wants each student to produce the best work he or she can. Although students work in groups, particularly in production courses, they are still graded individually. In the kind of media theory classes I teach, students have to be assessed on individual written papers and exams. So important is individual assessment in a university, that plagiarism—which could also be described as an "industrial" process, recycling material produced by someone else— is the ultimate academic sin. In a university, originality is everything.

Thus, teachers of media, trying to persuade their students that the modern cultural products they are learning to produce will not derive much from their own individual inspiration or effort, are placed in a somewhat contradictory position. How does one motivate students who want to work in television, film, advertising, journalism, or media administration, to see themselves as more than a part of "conglomerations of organizations"? Should students, in the course of producing "linguistic or pictorial representations" settle for merely *appearing* purposeful? Or should these students be encouraged actually to *be* purposeful? I have no doubt that the answer to the last question is yes: there is no point in requiring work from students that is not purposeful. But for work to be purposeful, it must also be personal.

This chapter will address the issue of what "literacy in the information age" means from some personal, as well as general, perspectives. The thoughts here are prompted by several years experience of being involved in the design and production of syllabuses for teaching students about the media. Some of these students were young children, including the subjects I studied during a fellowship researching media literacy in elementary school children. This research was carried out at the Annenberg School for Communication at the University of Pennsylvania (Davies, 1993).

However, the main issues to be addressed in this chapter will be based on helping to plan syllabuses for media students in higher education— first, at the College of Communication, Boston University, and now in my present position as Director of Media Studies at the London Institute. In Boston, I was a member of the broadcasting faculty, teaching theory to undergraduates and graduates who wanted to work in television. In London I am in charge of an undergraduate degree program, which is primarily theoretical—although it is part of a school which includes vocational degrees in film/video, journalism, and photography. Students who choose the media studies degree are usually interested in working in the media, but do not want to commit themselves to a particular branch of it. They have a theoretical interest in the subject, as well as a vocational one, and a generation ago, would probably have chosen to read English. In the United States, they would, perhaps, be mass communication students.

Media studies is an extraordinarily invigorating and occasionally exhausting branch of intellectual inquiry to be in. Being concerned with ideologically contentious topics such as the production of meaning, as well as the production of money, it is a site of both metaphorical and literal struggle. Syllabus design is one of the places where this struggle is fought out. This chapter reviews some of the subject areas competing for space in the media studies syllabus—and some solutions that my colleagues and I, on both sides of the Atlantic, have worked toward, if not yet completely established.

Individual Creativity

The starting point for educational programs, as mentioned, has to be the individual student, and what he or she is being taught to do, or be. For students opting for the broadcasting program, at Boston University, we decided, after much debate, that the creative individual our students should aspire to be was the TV producer.

A number of media commentators have pointed out the creative centrality of the producer in American television. (In Britain, writers are more dominant—of which, more below). Todd Gitlin's account of Holly-wood television production, *Inside Prime Time* (1985), describes how a key individual, such as Robert Wood at CBS, was able effectively to change the whole style of programming at the network, ushering in "an age of relevance," which offered creative scope to individual talents as diverse as Norman Lear and Mary Tyler Moore. In *Prime Time Movers* (1992), David Marc and Robert Thompson describe the work of influential American TV producers, such as Lear (*All in the Family, Maude, The Jeffersons*), Larry Gelbart (*M*A*S*H*), James L. Brooks (*The Simpsons*), and Diane English (*Murphy Brown*), and question whether the industrial/technological nature of TV really exerts greater pressure against individual creativity than earlier socioeconomic systems did:

> [D]espite the gigantic constituent corporate bureaucracies of this most massive of mass media . . . the autobiographical visions of individuals did manage to break through into the television screen, just as the personal visions of artists had managed to reach expression in the older, pre-electronic arts. Were these visions mitigated or, in effect, edited by television's trilateral nature as industry, technology and art? Certainly. But when and where had art ever developed independently of other factors? (13)

In slipping the term "art" into this statement, Marc and Thompson are being provocative. Many people working in media education in the U.S. deny that television has anything to do with art, insisting that television is primarily a business. As Blanchard and Christ (1993) put it,

> Occupational [media education] programs . . . exhibit little "self-direction" or liberation from "unquestioning dependence" on the culture of the market-driven communication industry and related occupations that they serve. (63)

According to these authors, a liberal arts approach to the training of media producers is seen as potentially "subversive" by many industry employers—to the detriment of the individuals concerned, the industry itself, and the wider public interest. Blanchard and Christ set out a program of what they call the "New Professionalism," which is designed to produce "graduates [who] have been prepared to exercise *authority to shape the nature of their own work*" (my emphasis; 64). *Auteurism*—or an emphasis on the creative individual—has been acceptable in film studies since the French Cahiers du Cinema of the 1960s, and before. But, despite authors such as Marc (1981) and Newcomb and Alley (1983) championing the artistic role of the producer, the concept of the television auteur—in the U.S. particularly—

has been more difficult to get off the ground. In the UK, for a complex range of historical, cultural, and other reasons (see e.g., Rowland & Tracey, 1993), the film/television, high/low divide has been less marked—both in the culture generally, and in education.

Artistic Traditions

Robert Watson (1990), a British film educator, argues for "an aesthetic approach to the moving image" in education, and has no doubt that modern audio-visual media are art forms. He proposes that the educational home of the study of film and television is in the tradition of "narrative arts," with roots in the study of literature. For Watson this is a humanistic imperative:

> Film, which includes television and video, is a contemporary narrative art whose place on the curriculum is amongst all the arts. . . . Those arts whose place is less than assured, such as film, need the passionate advocacy of men and women who know that the creative intelligence, nourished from infancy is of the essence of human life. (149)

Watson is a film educator and, as he says in his introduction to his book, *Film and Television in Education,* "At the London School of Film Technique I received a vocational training which I have come to regard, over the last twenty years, as a model of disciplined creativity in education." There is an irony in his invocation of literary traditions to promote the cause of film. The concept of "great art"—Matthew Arnold's "the best that has been thought or said"—has fallen out of favor in English studies in recent years. As Eagleton (1983) puts it, "the so-called literary canon, the unquestioned 'great tradition' of 'the national literature,' has to be recognized as a *construct,* fashioned by particular people for particular reasons at a certain time. There is no such thing as a literary work or tradition which is valuable *in itself* " (11). Watson, though, is a production teacher, and has to deal with the real aspirations of future film makers; he thus has no intention of shooting them down by suggesting that their work will have no "value." He acknowledges the ideological problems of "great traditions," with their tendency toward elitism and "cultural imperialism," but argues that "the writers who constitute [the tradition], from Chaucer to Lawrence, have obviously given us something far more substantial than a prop for the dominant ideology. . . . I need, and think we all need, this common heritage" (134).

For Watson, this common heritage must be widened to include contemporary art forms such as film and video: "any introduction to the great art of the past is necessarily impoverished if it has not been made vivid by a lively commitment to the art of our own time" (136). From such a perspective, "literacy in the information age," for contemporary media students carries much the same requirements as literacy did in earlier ages: the meaningful understanding of their own and other people's experiences; the meaningful understanding of different kinds of texts; and the application of these understandings to producing their own texts. Like Robert Watson, I have come to believe that to be called "literate," students of film or video need to be acquainted with the traditions, genres, and significant creative individuals in the history of their medium, and to be able to combine this knowledge with their own skills and personal visions, in the business of creating new texts.

Competing for Syllabus Space

That said, there are many competing academic disciplines jostling for a place on media degree programs, all carrying their own agendas about "ideology" and "art," and the allocation of faculty appointments and resources. In Boston, with a degree that focused on production, the competition for curriculum space and for faculty posts and resources was between academic and practical/vocational courses, including business administration. In London, where the media studies degree on which I am now teaching is almost entirely theoretical (although linked with three other vocational degrees), the potential clash is between a literary-cultural studies perspective (with a subdivision between "high" culture— should we teach the Enlightenment?—or "low"—should we discuss the meanings of soap opera?), and a social science/mass communication approach, which is empirical and research oriented. Within the "studies" area, there is what often looks like a completely incompatible choice of intellectual paradigms to choose from in designing a media studies syllabus. Fiske (1990) lists more than a dozen models and theoretical approaches in his *Introduction to Communication Studies,* from Communication Theory based on engineering (Shannon and Weaver, 1949), through Semiotics and Structuralism, to Empiricism and Ideology. For the purposes of discussion here, I have reduced these to three main areas: cultural studies, social science, and professional studies.

Cultural Studies

The cultural studies approach, deriving from English literary studies, is much more dominant in British media teaching (see e.g., Alvarado et al., 1988), and reflects the historical development of the subject, in which English teachers were the first to be drafted into teaching about the media, in some cases, "thrust into something for which they felt unprepared" (Hart & Benson, 1993). However, in the last twenty years or so, these insertions into the English curriculum have developed into a major strand in both English studies and elsewhere, thanks in particular to exponents of the British school of cultural studies, such as Raymond Williams and Stuart Hall (see Turner, 1992), and the influential work on semiotics in popular culture by Roland Barthes and others in France (Barthes, 1973; 1977).

These writers and their followers have demonstrated the "constructed," "privileged," class-based nature of much of what we call "great art," and have widened the range of cultural topics permitted to be academically discussed into advertising, street signs, fashion, popular music, and even packaging. Media studies in Britain tends to be drawn primarily, though not universally, from a cultural studies tradition. This is certainly the case in the institution where I am working on syllabus design at the moment; colleagues' areas of expertise include post-war European cultural theory; the history of visual arts, including painting and photography, as well as film and television; the political economy of the mass media; and psychoanalytic and feminist approaches.

Social Science Methods

In Boston, it was apparent that the social science approach to the study of the media, using quantitative research methods and evaluating media as social and political phenomena, was more dominant in the U.S. than in Britain. Required courses included "Social Impact of Television"; "Social Impact of the Mass Media"; and "Mass Communications Research." Joseph Turow's "A mass communications perspective on the entertainment industry" (1991) belongs in some ways to this paradigm, with its emphasis on media as social and institutional phenomena. In another sense, Turow's treatment of media as more than individual products of "artistic" visions, belongs in the cultural studies worldview. Turow's colleague at the Annenberg School for Communication, George

Gerbner, has also attempted to bridge the culture/science divide with his cultivation analysis approach to popular entertainment. Gerbner argues that the persistent messages of popular television drama—particularly in their insistence on aggression and social power relationships—do spread into the culture, and profoundly affect, or "cultivate," the way TV viewers see the world (Gerbner & Gross, 1976).

However, the methodology used in cultivation analysis is drawn from social science; systematic counting of violent incidents, or of different kinds of representation on television, are statistically correlated with survey data of measures of viewers' attitudes, to demonstrate "cultivation effects." This approach has generated a great deal of research and comment in the U.S., but has not been so popular in Britain, and has been strongly criticized by some writers here (e.g., Wober & Gunter, 1988).

Nevertheless, since cultivation is a major explanatory theory in the social science field, a good media studies syllabus should include it. A media literate student would be familiar with its aims and methodologies, and would be able to recognize that counting the number of violent acts on television does not tell us what such incidents *mean* for the audience—or indeed, for the researcher/critic. The act of defining violence, for the purpose of content analysis, is itself ideologically loaded and begs the important question of what such acts are. "Violence" becomes what researchers choose it to mean, not what writers mean when they write, or what viewers perceive when they view. But it is these latter two meanings which are most central to any discussion of "literacy."

I have used this potential clash between researchers' and other people's definitions of violence as a classroom exercise on a number of occasions. Students have been required to role play a team of researchers who have to survey the incidence of violence on television over a period of time (as with the Annenberg Cultural Indicators project). Their first task is to define what they are looking for. This takes the better part of two lesson periods, and there are continuing problems of *re*definition, once they have had a look at some different kinds of violent material, such as police series, cartoons, news and "serious" drama of the kind shown on *Masterpiece Theatre.* In all the lengthy attempts at definition I have experienced with students on both sides of the Atlantic, three major points of difficulty emerge. Firstly, there is genre: "it depends what kind of a film or program it is." Secondly, there is motivation—or, to use a more literary term, *narrative function*: "it depends why the person is doing it." Thirdly, there is artistic worth: "Is violence OK if it's in *King Lear?*"

From the perspective of cultivation theory, which argues that all media violence is equivalent when it comes to producing cultivation effects, these difficulties expressed by students are irrelevant. From the perspective of aiming to produce *literate* students, who can think for themselves about the functions and meanings of their own and others' creative products, questions of genre, narrative, artistic quality, and moral relativity are central. At this point, after many exhilarating and impassioned, but indecisive, arguments, students are often tempted to give up, arguing that it is impossible to find an all-purpose definition of media violence. Then they are told that they *must* find a definition, or they won't get the funding so necessary to their department's survival. (Universities are part of the meaning-producing "industry" too.) Thus, the cultural studies lesson that moral and intellectual positions are difficult to separate from institutional practices is again underscored.

Critical approaches, such as semiotics—or "signification"—offer the student more sophisticated constructs for tackling questions of meaning than numerical content analysis. In addition, for any student learning to be "media literate," we need to offer more sensitive measures of viewer response than the number of hours people say they watch television. Sophisticated audience studies, which respect cultural and individual differences and recognize viewers' differing awareness of the codes and conventions of modern media, can provide the future media producer with a less limited image of his or her audience than the one provided by the Nielsen ratings. (See, for example, Livingstone, 1990; Ang, 1991; Hodge & Tripp, 1985). Recognizing the complexity and sophistication of viewer response is a necessary step in improved producer-education—and an important opportunity for the goals of the theory teacher to serve the interests of the production teacher and student.

When producers have high expectations of the audience, the cultural and intellectual standard of their output inevitably rises—as Lord Reith, the first Director General of the BBC, understood. Of course, Reithian ideas of raising the cultural sights of the masses may be seen as out-of-date by some. Left-wing critics, such as Terry Eagleton (1983), criticize Reithian ideas because they imply elitist value systems. Ironically, right-wing free-marketeers such as Rupert Murdoch and Silvio Berlusconi also deplore elitism, for an ostensibly different reason. In a deregulated competitive market system, the ratings—or whatever produces the largest audience—decide what gets put before the public, leading to much pessimism among cultural commentators about the culturally debasing power of mass media (Meyrowitz, 1985; Twitchell, 1992). What unites both left and right on this issue is an implicit contempt for mass audiences: an assumption that working class viewers won't appreciate high culture, or any culture that is different from what is deemed to be their own.

Media teachers have an ethical responsibility to disabuse trainee producers of contemptuous attitudes to their audiences. Insulting references to "Joe Six-Pack" and "fly-over" land, as one young broadcasting student once described all the states between the East and West coast of America to me, should be taboo, except as starting points for discussion. However, if market mechanisms are important in determining the quality of media products, then media teachers have ways of making the system work to the advantage of humanistic education. First, we can help to develop and increase the areas of discrimination and choice in young "consumers" and, hence, create a more diversified demand within the market—or as Bourdieu would have it, we can give people more "cultural capital." Second, we can educate future producers into doing the best work they can possibly do, whatever this work is, which will also increase the cultural capital made available to their audiences. It is particularly important, if we accept that this is how it works, to provide demanding and diverse media products for children (Davies, 1989; Simpson, 1989). In doing this, we can help to create what John Hartley (1992) calls "an actual or potential alliance" between producers and audiences. Writing about the radical British documentary film maker of the 1940s, Humphrey Jennings, Hartley argues that, "the possibility of a radical result requires not only radical intentions and practice on the part of the producer, but radical potential among the audience constituency" (152).

Hartley is rare among media scholars, not only in respecting the radical nature of audiences, but also in arguing, like Watson, the case for an audio-visual canon. In his essay, "The Politics of Photopoetry," he cites a long list of British television "auteurs" (mostly writers, unlike the American system, where artistically influential individuals tend to be producers). "I invoke these names," says Hartley, "in order to show that popular culture has an intellectual and aesthetic history that's all too often lost in the perennial arguments about high and low culture" (153).

Over the whole debate is the question of what the individual student actually needs, as distinct from what the academic wants to teach, and its necessary follow-up question: how is need defined? Is education about training students for specific jobs—or should it be about developing the whole person? And are these necessarily incompatible? For the student doing a degree in media—whether film, television, journalism, or theory and research—these are crucial, practical, rather than hypothetical, questions.

The Liberal Arts versus Professionalism

In their book, *Media Education and the Liberal Arts,* Blanchard and Christ (1993) challenge what they call "the myth that the liberal and the professional studies are separate." As well as producing "the well-rounded person . . . the university must pursue what the ancient Greeks saw as a fundamental purpose of education . . . the cultivation of the civic self or the political self." This, they argue, is particularly important in professional programs, "because modern professionals function as members of the ruling class; they wield power in society" (12). Blanchard and Christ agree with Watson in challenging "the myth that undergraduate pre-professional programs, including media programs that encompass newer technologies and institutional systems, have nothing of substance to offer to the liberal arts or liberal learning for the 21st century" (x).

Although the professional/liberal arts argument is usually cloaked in educational terms—the "well-rounded individual"; "the university as the home of free intellectual inquiry" versus "the need to prepare our students for the real world"; "the need for students to develop their practical creativity with start-of-the-art equipment"—the real argument, it seems to me, is about the allocation of resources, particularly faculty appointments and, increasingly, new technology. At a time of cutbacks in resources, who do we appoint?, a communications scholar with a Ph.D. in textual analysis, or someone who can teach television production? Should we devote more money to the library, and to making lecture classes smaller, or should we have a new computer lab, and a brand new editing suite? The more pragmatic voices of those who say that "technical teachers ought to have some understanding of how texts work, and computer labs could be utilized to create smaller teaching groups, so why don't we try to combine these resources?" can be drowned out in these dramatic clashes about academic "turf."

At my institution in London, there is no separation between film and video production, and theory is seen as an essential part of production courses. The "high" (film), "low" (television) cultural divide, so marked in the United States, is not reflected in the academic organization of the subject on this side of the Atlantic. This partly reflects the public service traditions of British television, (now being rapidly eroded by an unattractive market-driven, co-productionism, giving rise to hybrid and unrecognizable Euro-dramas). The BBC's original remit, stated by Lord Reith, the first Director General of the BBC, was to "inform, educate and entertain." Within this remit, it has been possible for serious dramatic writers—such as the late Dennis Potter, author of *The Singing Detective*—to do all their major work on television, and to make television a more dominant artistic form than British film. Critics seeking the heirs of Shakespeare, Congreve, or Shaw in modern Britain need to look to television writers such as Potter, Alan Bleasdale, Alan Bennett, Troy Kennedy Martin, and Alan Plater. British films which have been hits in America, such as *Four Weddings and a Funeral*, derive much of their talent, as well as (in the case of channel 4) their funding, from television. Richard Curtis, the screenwriter of *Four Weddings,* was the author, among other television shows, of the historical sitcom series *Blackadder.*

The turbulent academic waters of "media studies," incorporating literary and cultural studies; social science; politics and economics; industry and management; the creative arts and technical skills, are now becoming further muddied by the need to bring in specialists with computer skills. Departments of computer studies and engineering increasingly need to become involved in the teaching of media students. "Multi-media," using computers to generate material traditionally generated by graphic arts, or musical instruments, or even writing, is now being proposed as the up-and-coming appropriate educational mode (Laurillard, 1993).

All this is leading to an ever more elastic definition of the concept of "literacy," with "computer-literate" and "techno-illiterate" becoming acceptable phrases in educational discourse, in which the origins of the word "literacy" are becoming all but forgotten.

Aesthetics and "The Good"

In the syllabus discussions I have shared with other teachers of future producers, one concept has regularly emerged to provide a bridge between "professionalism" (skills in editing, directing, writing, and producing) and communication theory (the critical analysis of media texts and practices): this thread is what Watson calls the "aesthetic" approach. Against the mass communication model of media products as interchangeable industrial items, Watson argues that "film [which includes television] is a collaborative narrative art which we can only read in terms of specific works" (1990, 148). An aesthetic approach to teaching about the media is thus particularly relevant for future media workers since it reflects on specific products of specific individuals like themselves. Aesthetic approaches further provide potential models for trainee producers, of all kinds, and exemplary teaching aids for production teachers.

From the theory teacher's point of view, aestheticism is a useful organizing concept in addressing other questions which arise in media studies. The most useful groupings of these issues that I have found are the British Film Institute's six subject categories:

* Agencies (who produces this text?);
* Categories (What kind of text is it?);
* Technologies (How is it produced?);
* Languages (How do we know what it means?);
* Audiences (To whom is it addressed and how do we know?); and
* Representations (How does it present its subject?). (Bazalgette, 1988)

In an aesthetic approach, specific media products can be used to generate discussion about all these issues. When we address matters of content—or representation—for example, the student is asked to consider whether the work in question is believable, authentic, relevant, true. In finding answers, philosophical questions about the nature of truth; historical evidence; the reliability of personal experience as a guide to reality; the authenticity of different media forms, such as documentary film, newsreel, newspapers, and books, all have to be considered. Social science concepts of research validity can also be introduced here. A relevant recent example is Speilberg's *Schindler's List* and its representation of the Holocaust. The film was widely discussed, partly in aesthetic terms as an artistic breakthrough by a director who had hitherto been "only" an entertainer. (*Only* is a term that should not go unexamined, of course; Richard Dyer's 1992 book, *Only Entertainment*, is a useful text here.) But the film's treatment of a subject that many people believe is too awful for cinematic representation, was also discussed in terms of its truthfulness to its historical subject, and to the experiences of the people who lived through the real historical events. Newspaper coverage of the movie included interviews with survivors, and features about the real Oskar Schindler. Questions of representation raise issues of the boundaries between reality and fiction, and how we know what they are; they raise ethical questions about the legitimacy of using real events in drama—and vice versa (with news borrowing the techniques of dramatic fiction); civic questions about the rights of subjects, and of artists; about freedom of speech, and about the protection of individuals from *mis*representation.

Obviously an aesthetic approach is central to discussions of form and performance (language and technology). An aesthetic approach must address how, and how well, this product is written, shot, edited, lit, acted, designed, musically supported—the kinds of questions that always concern professional film and television makers. *Schindler's List* provides a good example of the centrality of formal questions in making broader ethical judgments. In this case, the sensitivity of the subject matter makes the formal treatment absolutely central to the critical discussion of the film; *how* do you make a film about the Holocaust? Did Spielberg "succeed" and, if so, what was the nature of his success? How much did the techniques he chose (black-and-white film; hand-held camera work; the use of real locations; the choice of cast) contribute to the authenticity or otherwise of the representation? If using a black-and-white, documentary style did create greater authenticity, why should this be? To answer *this* question, we need to move on to consider audiences. Why do they find some film techniques more convincing than others? Where do such expectations come from? Is it from experience of old newsreels? If younger audiences have no such experiences, will they "read" the film differently? An interesting examination of the changing role of film technique in creating authenticity is found in Paul Messaris' book, *Visual Literacy* (1994). It is an absolutely central question in defining literacy, particularly in the very young, who are growing up heavily exposed almost from birth to rapidly developing audio-visual techniques (Davies, 1993).

An "aesthetic" approach does not have to be a context-free, "art for art's sake" one, but can raise important questions of impact and response, again, concerning "audiences": Did this piece of media move, excite, disgust, make people laugh, cry, make them angry, make them think, set them a bad example, corrupt them? How do we know? Students, like other people, are very ready to propose that media have effects on "some people" or "certain kinds of people" but not on themselves, and good media education should help to disabuse them of this dangerous complacency. Questions of audience response when addressed in the classroom *must* include personal response.

It is a measure of the failure of our education system, on both sides of the Atlantic, that many young adults find it extremely difficult to describe their own emotions and reactions to the media products they write about academically. They can cite the details of the Surgeon General's 1972 report on the impact of television violence, but cannot find the appropriate vocabulary to describe their own reactions to *Reservoir Dogs* or *Silence of the Lambs*. This can lead to an educationally undesirable dishonesty on their part; adept at reproducing the critical opinions their teachers have asked them to read in textbooks, they hide their own opinion that it's all, to quote one student friend of mine, "a load of bollocks." (The nearest American equivalent to this expressive Anglo-Saxon phrase is, I guess, "bullshit.") Meanwhile, their own private tastes, whether in music, television, or literature, go unexamined. Any definition of literacy must include authentic, rather than borrowed, responses to media and culture. For this reason, work to be evaluated should always include personal writing.

A Personal Example

An example of personal writing that demonstrated, for me, the kind of progressive enlightenment I want to see in my students, is the quote from Jennifer R., above. It came from a journal that a class of undergraduate broadcasting students in Boston were asked to keep during a "social impact" course called *Television Culture and Society*. The journal covered a six-week unit at the end of the course, built around Shakespeare's play *Julius Caesar*. The unit had a number of starting points: first, the challenge of a colleague, who was skeptical of social science approaches to the media and didn't approve of "social impact" courses. He argued that it was impossible to teach a class about the social impact of the media and raise what he considered to be more serious cultural issues such as literary traditions, artistic values, critical analysis, and personal enlightenment. The Director of the Writing Center and I disagreed, and set out to design such a class.

The second stimulus to this unit came from one of our set texts: Mendelsohn's (1966) division of cultural products between Art ("high"),

Culture ("middle"), and Entertainment ("low"), and his accounts of the kinds of people who would appreciate each one—another "audiences" question. The project began with the class attempting to draw the lines between Mendelsohn's three categories and to decide where, within these lines, they would place Shakespeare's play—a task in which, I was pleased to see, no consensus was reached. The third starting point was the fortuitous fact that a presidential election (1992) was going on during this semester, thus raising topical issues of the transfer of political power, and the media treatment of it—topics which Shakespeare's play also raises.

The class was divided into groups of five or six and asked to work collaboratively (important for media workers) to devise a presentation based on the play *Julius Caesar*. Each individual was also asked to keep a journal about the progress of the project. The group presentation had to do two things: (1) demonstrate a knowledge of the text; and (2) show its contemporary relevance. They could use any media they liked and take any liberties they wished with Shakespeare's original; a model here was a BBC Schools Television version of the play, produced in modern dress, with Caesar as a fascist dictator, called *Heil Caesar*. An even better model, of course, is Shakespeare himself—the class was given a translation of Plutarch's account of Caesar's assassination for the purposes of comparison.

The journal had to include an entry for each session, plus a brief critical review of the play after their first reading of it (or, in the case of many students, a surprisingly revelatory re-reading of it). With the help of tutors from the Writing Center, students were encouraged to reflect on their feelings about the project, their interactions with fellow students, their responses to screenings of filmed and televised versions of the play—including the 1956 Marlon Brando version, shown in class—and, at the end of the unit, to type up a final journal in which they could reflect on the journal itself, and their own progression revealed in it. Jennifer's comments are an example of this final reflection. Her group produced a video documentary comparing *Julius Caesar* with Oliver Stone's *JFK* .

The Question of Effects

Beyond personal response lie the more general "impact" or "effects" questions. Here, the aesthetic discussion of specific texts extends into the kinds of questions raised by social scientists. Would a film like this harm the young? Cause a riot? Create racial tensions? Debase standards of civilization? Such social and moral problems are frequently concerned with questions of form. Depending on the genre, the impact may be different. If the style is perceived as realistic, the perceived effects will be stronger, or weaker, as researchers such as Robert Hawkins (1977) and Aimee Dorr and her colleagues (1990), have demonstrated. How real a media product is perceived to be is a central question in media literacy programs for young children. For children, as for adults, formal cues— such as laughter on the soundtrack, people "dressed up," people or objects doing impossible things like flying, special effects, and unusual camera techniques—are all signals as to how believable and authentic a piece of television material is perceived to be (Davies, 1993).

Structural and institutional questions about media as a mass industrial product—issues of agencies—can arise naturally within an aesthetics-based framework. Discussions about form will give rise to comment on the fact that, for example, a film has an ambiguous ending, not for intrinsic narrative reasons, but so that the production company can make money out of a sequel (*Nightmare on Elm Street, Poltergeist*). Even very young children, as with the subjects I used in the research about formal cues for reality, mentioned above, can use aesthetic cues to make pragmatic judgments about producer motives and audience response: "Computer animation— it's not real. . . . It's to make it look cool and people might think it's real and think they might get a real education . . . little kids . . . might think it was real and it isn't" (Davies, 1993).

Identifying the "Good"

Aesthetic judgments raise the question of what is worth recommending to students that they should know about and see: the thorny problem of "the canon." In my experiences of discussing syllabus content, both analytical and production teachers have found common ground in raising questions about what constitutes "the good"—although obviously, individuals disagree about the answer. One question, and answer, which cannot be avoided is: What is "good" student work? What is a "good" film or television program or photograph or journalistic story or research project, and are student standards of "good" work different from professional ones? While these questions may be avoided by the cultural relativism of writers such as Eagleton (1983), they arise daily in the media production and studies classroom and are unavoidable when it comes to grading.

Professional standards of storytelling, production, technical performance, have to be invoked in assessing a production student's work; professional standards of research, critical judgment, audience perception, debating skills, and writing, have to be used in evaluating academic work. Further, as mentioned at the outset of this chapter, the "good" (*sic*) teacher is also looking for individual creativity, the unique expressive voice, the unusual, the original, the innovative, and for individual improvement in all these departments over time. The fostering of individual creativity is partly a professional requirement but, as I have argued, it is primarily an educational one. The duty of the good teacher is to get the best work possible out of each individual student, and only secondarily (and quite a long way down the list, in my opinion) to provide a labor force for the mass media industry .

Apart from the need to have fair and consistent guidelines evaluating and grading student work, there are two further key reasons for making the study of "the good" central for media students. Firstly, the fact that it is obviously an important construct for *them*. The word is constantly used in casual debate. Following on from this, is the need for models, so that we know how to recognize the good. What does a "good" film look like, as distinct from a "bad" film? What is a "good" commercial? Can there be a "good" game show? Which examples should you show in class?

In English studies, the attempt to establish—or disestablish—a "canon" of literary works has been one of the most contentious of all topics on American—and, to a lesser extent, British—campuses, raising questions of ethnocentricity, cultural imperialism, and fears of threats to academic freedom. The case for a canon is actually very simple: you can't teach it all, so you have to make some choices. If you don't want to call it a canon, you can call it a syllabus, a curriculum, a reading list, or even just a timetable. Every teacher, including Terry Eagleton, has one. In searching for models to place before students learning the art and craft of media production, media teachers of my acquaintance tend to include works in their syllabuses which have received public, critical, historical, or professional recognition, or works that are experimental, innovative, and not widely available commercially. Thus, students can begin to understand what will be required of them as media producers—or, indeed, as critics. There is a case for including some works of popular culture with which students are familiar; works which, if not "bad" (even the most banal television sitcom demonstrates a fantastically high level of competence, as every amateur video producer knows), are conventional, format based, and uninspired. However, there are some educational dangers in doing this. First, as research student David Gauntlett (1994) amusingly points out in a *Times Higher Education Supplement* article, "any academic who attempts to talk about actual television programs risks being shown up by any regular viewer-in-the-street." In other words, students always know far more about the latest soap storylines than their teachers do. The second danger, also pointed out by Gauntlett, is pretentiousness, leading to derision on the part of students: "Little did I know that late 1970s *Doctor Who* was a triumph of postmodern self-reflexivity, semiotically thick with metatextual signifiers. I just thought it was fun." The job of teachers is not to compete with their students' knowledge of popular culture (they never can), nor to undermine it with jargon (which is doomed to fail). It is to tell them and show them things they don't know.

For example, for my media studies colleagues in London and me, a course on American media and culture presented us with a huge cornucopia of material to select from—and we have been ruthlessly, and probably arbitrarily, selective. In tracing themes of political freedom and civil rights and how these have been represented in American culture, particularly in popular entertainment, we drew on examples we considered to be relevant in terms of content, but also in terms of what we considered excellence, and what we liked; one or two of our examples were familiar to our students, but most were not. We used *Huckleberry Finn*; Toni Morrison's *Beloved* and *Jazz;* the writings of Thomas Jefferson, including the Declaration of Independence; PBS television documentaries such as *The Civil War* and *Eyes on the Prize*; the films *Young Mr. Lincoln, RKO Days,* and *Point of Order*; TV sitcoms *Murphy Brown, The Cosby Show,* and *The Simpsons*; critical writing from *The New York Review of Books, Newsweek,* and *Atlantic Monthly.* Others may differ in their selections, and they would be free to do so. But in making such selections, value judgments are unavoidable, and teachers need to be able to defend their choices to their students. There is no point in using material in valuable, and limited, class time, that the teacher does not feel able to defend. This is a waste of everybody's time and the students know it.

Making Texts Accessible

In making this almost impossible selection, we aimed particularly to bring to the attention of students examples of "good" work with which they may not have been familiar. This is particularly necessary with foreign material, or old films and TV programs not widely available in High Street video stores. Print material and photographic material is much more accessible and can be reasonably easily sought out by students themselves, with the aid of librarians. Teaching goals have been greatly hampered over the years during which media studies as a discipline has been expanding, by the difficulty of obtaining teaching and learning copies of film and video material. Availability—or more likely, nonavailability— of copies is a much greater factor in determining a film/video "canon" than any ideological biases on the part of teachers. Ironically, in this so-called information-rich age, this is nearly as problematic a situation as teaching literacy must have been before printing was invented: there are only a few precious copies of every text, which have to be jealously guarded and reluctantly passed around.

The use of video material for educational purposes is still at a primitive stage and is very much hampered by copyright laws which make it illegal, in the U.S. at any rate, to build up a collection of interesting video material taped off air. At Boston University, recordings made for educational purposes were supposed to be wiped after forty days! Destroying my precious copy of the *M*A*S*H* episode "Radar's Farewell," or of Ed's movie from *Northern Exposure,* which I have used in a variety of teaching situations, is an act of vandalism akin to burning literary first editions, in my opinion.

Thus, the term *literacy* cannot yet be applied to the study of audiovisual texts in the same way as it can to printed ones. It is not possible yet for media students to pore over, reread, access particular scenes or sections of dialogue, with film and television, as they can so easily with books. Only videos available for hire, or sale, in video shops, or some good libraries, are accessible in this way (a very limited range)—and video itself is a cumbersome medium, which can take hours of winding forward and back to identify specific passages. Only when video/film material is as accessible as books are, will Robert Watson's ideal of film and television becoming part of "the great tradition" turn into a reality— and that seems a long way off down the "information superhighway."

Conclusion: Mass Production or Individual Creativity?

As in the study of language and literature, an awareness that all cultural products are an intrinsic part of a wider socioeconomic and political system is an enlightening one. But the pragmatic and pedagogic question for the teacher of media students is: How motivating is this awareness? Will we have better or worse screenwriters, directors, producers, and managers if students are made too much aware of their own potential "irrelevance" to the production process? This question has yet to be answered—or even asked—in terms of evaluating college education for potential media workers. In the meantime, as a media studies educator, I believe that my job is to persuade students that their individual visions and skills, like the visions and skills of the people who have been set before them as examples and models, are *not* irrelevant to the production process—or, indeed, to anything that may happen to them in their future lives. What happens to them once they get jobs and become part of the Hollywood, or mass media, "machinery" is for them and their professional organizations to deal with and, when necessary, challenge. What happens to them in college is different; their college career should equip them with the intellectual skills and knowledge, and the resulting confidence, to meet such challenges. It should give them, as Jennifer put it, "a different kind of satisfaction."

References

Alvarado, M., Gutch, R., & Wollen, T. (1988). *Learning the media: An introduction to media teaching.* London: Macmillan.

Ang, I. (1991). *Desperately seeking the audience.* London: Routledge.

Barthes, R. (1973). *Mythologies.* London: Paladin.

———. (1977). *Image-music-text.* London: Fontana.

Bazalgette, C. (Ed). (1988). *Primary media education.* London: British Film Institute.

Blanchard, R., & Christ, W. (1993). *Media education and the liberal arts.* Hillsdale, N.J.: Lawrence Erlbaum Associates.

Davies, M. M. (1989). *Television is good for your kids.* London: Hilary Shipman.

———. (1993). Art and life: The function of stylistic techniques in children's perception of television reality. Report of research carried out for the Annenberg Fellowship, Annenberg School for Communication, University of Pennsylvania.

Dorr, A., Kovaric, P., & Doubleday, C. (1990). Age and content influences on children's perception of the realism of television families, *Journal of Broadcasting & Educational Media, 34,* 4, 377–97.

Dyer, R. (1992). *Only entertainment.* New York: Routledge.

Eagleton, T. (1983). *Literary theory.* Minneapolis: University of Minnesota Press.

Fiske, J. (1990). *Introduction to communication studies.* London: Routledge.

Gauntlett, D. (8 July 1994). Calling all couch potatoes. *Times Higher Education Supplement,* 1130, 13.

Gerbner, G., & Gross, L. (1976). Living with television: The violence profile. *Journal of Communication, 26,* 2, 173–99

Gitlin, T. (1985). *Inside prime time.* New York: Pantheon Books.

Hart, A., & Benson, T. (1993). The value of media education: Media teachers talking. *Journal of Educational Television, 19,* 3, 167–72.

Hartley, J. (1992). *Tele-ology.* London: Routledge.

Hawkins, R. (1977). The dimensional structure of children's perceptions of TV reality. *Communication Research 4,* 3, 299–321.

Hodge, R., & Tripp, D. (1985). *Children and television.* Cambridge: Polity Press.

Laurillard, D. (1993). Balancing the media. *Journal of Educational Television, 19,* 2, 81–93.

Livingstone, S. M. (1990). *Making sense of television: The psychology of audience interpretation.* Oxford: Pergamon Press.

Marc, D. (November 1981). TV auteurism. *American Film,* 52–81.

Marc, D., & Thompson, R. (1992). *Prime time movers.* Boston: Little Brown.

Mendelsohn, H. (1966). *Mass entertainment.* New Haven, Conn.: College and University Press.

Meyrowitz, J. (1985). *No sense of place: The impact of electronic media on social behavior.* New York: Oxford.

Newcomb, H., & Alley, R. (1983). *The producer's medium.* New York: Oxford University Press.

Rowland, W. D., & Tracey, M. (27 May 1993). *Lessons from abroad: A preliminary report on the condition of public broadcasting in the United States and elsewhere.* Paper presented to a joint meeting of the International Communication Association and the American Forum of the American University, Washington, D.C.

Simpson, P. (1989). *Children in the marketplace.* Report of British Action for Children's Television to the Parliamentary Sub-Committee on the Future of Broadcasting. London: British Film Institute.

Turner, G. (1992). *British cultural studies.* London: Routledge.

Turow, J. (1991). A mass communication perspective on entertainment industries. In Curran, J., & Gurevitch, M. (Eds.). *Mass media and society.* London: Edward Arnold.

Twitchell, J. (1992). *Carnival culture: The trashing of taste in America.* New York: Columbia University Press.

Watson, R. (1990). *Film and television in education: An aesthetic approach to the moving image.* Basingstoke: Falmer Press.

Wober, M., & Gunter, B. (1988). *Television and social control.* Basingstoke: Gower Press.

13

Multimedia Education:
Media Literacy in the Age of Digital Culture

David Buckingham and Julian Sefton-Green

This chapter argues that technological change in the form of multimedia, combined with the social uses of computers amongst young people, will begin to shift the form and content of contemporary media education toward a distinctly "post-modern" multimedia curriculum. It considers the role of computer games and other media in the formation of "moral panics," and the history and practice of media education in Britain as part of the changing response to such concerns. It outlines the theoretical basis of such an educational program, raising key issues in media education research and detailing accounts of research into the social uses of computer games and developments in domestic multimedia technology. It concludes by speculating on the nature of "media literacy" in an era of digital culture.

Techno-Panic

Early in 1993, the British public was gripped by reports of the murder of a two-year-old child. Jamie Bulger had apparently been abducted from a shopping mall near Liverpool, and then horrifically killed by two ten-year-old boys. For weeks afterward the press and TV featured analyses of the incident, made all the more gruesome as the actual moment of his abduction had been captured by video surveillance cameras. Yet, attempts to explain the killing in terms of poverty and economic recession, or the erosion of leisure provision for young people, soon gave way to another, depressingly familiar, set of arguments. For it was the media that were responsible for the murder of Jamie Bulger. Television executives were called to account, and new guidelines on TV violence were promised. The British Board of Film Classification (the industry censorship body) hastily commissioned research into the viewing habits of young offenders. TV talk shows featured teenage criminals only too ready to blame their misdemeanors on the media. Yet, at least before the killers came to trial, it was the new generation of computer games that was seen to be particularly at fault. As one commentator noted, "No feature article about the murder was complete without reference to computer games and the arcade as if, for all the world . . . such arcades should be in the dock alongside the accused" (Barker, 1993, 5). Indeed, the media were effectively condemned without trial: the question of evidence—for example, that the accused actually played computer games in the first place—was entirely ignored.[1]

The debates that followed the killing of Jamie Bulger took the familiar form of what sociologists have termed a "moral panic." The work of Geoffrey Pearson (1983) and Martin Barker (1984a and b), among others, has shown how popular pleasures, and in particular the pleasures of the screen, have been the focus of anxiety and repressive campaigns from right and left alike over the years.[2] Blaming the media provides a simplistic, reassuring explanation of events that may be too painful or difficult to face, yet it also deflects attention away from more complex underlying causes that may be much harder to remedy.

In recent years, computer games have begun to take the place of television in this popular demonology, just as television took the place of comics, and comics took the place of the cinema in earlier decades. Yet, if the focus of attention has changed, the concerns and the rhetoric in which they are expressed remain very familiar. Like television and video before them, computer games are seen to be responsible, not merely for murder and delinquency, but also for undermining children's physical, moral, and intellectual development. Thus, in the wake of the Jamie Bulger case, the press reported endless accounts of narcotized addiction and personal destruction, apparently backed up by respectable academic "research":

> One study by the University of Manchester Institute of Technology in a single school found that 60 per cent of boys and 30 per cent of girls were effectively addicted to the cult. Of the most addicted, half showed aggressive and anti-social tendencies. (*Times Educational Supplement,* 1993)

Cults? Addiction? Violence? The metaphoric fears are endless; yet the evidence (certainly in this case) is considerably more circumstantial.

Anxiety about computer games first crystallized around the public visibility of the arcade in the late 1970s and early 1980s. Leslie Haddon

(1993) has shown how the arcade came to be seen as a cause of delinquency, truancy, and addiction. In Britain a Labor MP led a campaign to curb the "menace" of video games, and in the United States the Surgeon General issued warnings about their danger, while in the Philippines Marcos simply had three hundred machines smashed to pieces (Haddon, 1993). Meanwhile, left-wing critics have issued equally familiar warnings about the effects of gender and racial stereotyping and the exploitation of children by capitalist monopolies—arguments which are often based on the same behaviorist assumptions which underpin the "sex 'n' violence" lobby (Provenzo, 1991; Buckingham, 1993a, 3–19).

There is a considerable irony in the fact that this moment of moral panic in Britain coincided with the Conservative government's attempt to remove media education from the National Curriculum—an attempt which, at the time of writing, has at least been stalled, if not defeated, by the concerted opposition of teachers. On the face of it, it is surprising that there have not been more calls for the school curriculum to redress or defend children against the effects of the media that are apparently eating away at the moral fabric of contemporary society. Yet ultimately, the government's response to these concerns has been to rush to the defence of "traditional" teaching methods, and to reassert notions of education as a means of preserving the national cultural heritage (Jones, 1992).

The form of media education that has emerged in Britain over the past two decades has moved well away from this defensive approach, and the assumptions about young people on which it is based. It offers a very different, and much more constructive, response to public concerns about the dangers—and indeed the pleasures—of popular culture. Our aim in the first part of this chapter is to outline the broad aims of media education in Britain, and to offer some brief sketches of what it might look like in practice. In the second part, we will go on to look more specifically at the implications for media teachers of new developments in communication and information technology—partly represented by computer games. We will conclude by offering some broader speculations about the nature of "media literacy" in the era of digital culture.

Media Education: Aims and Models

There is a long history of media education in different forms in the British education system. Broadly speaking, its origins lie in the subject of English. The first proposals for a form of media education were formulated by the literary critic F. R. Leavis and his colleague Denys Thompson, as part of a broader program in the "training of critical awareness" (Leavis & Thompson, 1933). The aims of teaching about media such as advertising and popular journalism were, in their terms, fundamentally defensive: they sought to train students "to discriminate and to resist" the superficial and vulgar pleasures the media were seen to afford. This notion of media education as a form of cultural "inoculation" remains a potent influence on many English teachers, despite their widespread rejection of the Leavisite approach to the teaching of literature.

More recently, this defensive approach has taken an apparently more "radical" form. Influenced by the "cultural pessimism" and elitism of the Frankfurt School, advocates of media education in the 1970s and early 1980s came to regard teaching about the media as a means of contesting the "dominant ideology" into which their students had apparently been indoctrinated (Masterman, 1980; 1985). "Deconstructing" media texts through semiotic analysis and "demystifying" the operation of capitalist media institutions were seen as means of "liberating" students from their false beliefs. Yet despite their differences in rhetoric, both approaches would appear to be based on similar notions of media power, in which young people themselves are seen as passive victims of negative influences—a view which is clearly not far removed from the "moral panics" identified above.

In the mid-1980s, however, a rather different model of media education began to emerge, which in many respects moves beyond this defensive approach. The publication of a report entitled *Popular Television and Schoolchildren* by the Department of Education (DES) in 1983 led to calls for media education as a fundamental educational entitlement for all students (DES, 1983; Lusted & Drummond, 1985). Meanwhile, the development of a common examination system at ages sixteen and above (the General Certificate of Secondary Education, or GCSE) enabled media studies to escape from its earlier position as a "low status subject for low status kids." The new, and increasingly popular, GCSE syllabuses led in turn to the publication of "Curriculum Statements" for media education by the British Film Institute, which offered highly influential models for curriculum design and classroom practice (Bazalgette 1989; Bowker 1991).

The DES report identified a broad shift away from a "set of worries about television's effects to a set of questions about television's representation of the social world," placing a central emphasis on young people's own readings and pleasures (Lusted & Drummond, 1985)[3]. This move was of course paralleled by developments in academic media studies during the same period: the "(re-)discovery of the audience," for example, in the work of David Morley, marked a fundamental break with monolithic, text-based notions of media power embodied in the theoretical work of the journal *Screen* (Morley, 1992). Significantly, however, these moves were also a response to teachers' actual experiences of teaching about the media: the notion of young people as merely "uncritical consumers," and the view of media education as a form of ideological liberation, were increasingly recognized as impossible to sustain (Williamson 1981, 1982; Buckingham, 1986). Subsequent research on classroom practice drew attention to the sophisticated and unpredictable ways in which young people related to popular media, and to the complexities and contradictions of classroom practice (Buckingham, 1990).

Broadly speaking, the model of media education that has emerged here is one which seeks to balance the recognition of students' existing understandings and competencies as "users" of media with a more formal conceptual structure. The "key concepts" contained in the BFI curriculum statements—and, in a slightly different form, in British examination syllabuses—are defined in figure 13.1 below.

It is vital to emphasize, however, that this conceptual structure should not be seen as a "body of knowledge" that is simply transmitted to students. The concepts do not specify a given curriculum content, for example, in the form of a set of indispensable "facts" or a canon of approved texts. On the contrary, they are a means of enabling students to reflect upon, and to formalize, their existing understandings and experiences of the media—both as "readers" and as "writers," as consumers and as producers—and, thence, to move beyond them.

It is this conceptual structure which has provided the basis for the extraordinary growth of media education in the past decade. The development of specialist media studies curricula at GCSE has perhaps been the most visible manifestation of this. At this level, assessment is principally through course work, involving a combination of theoretical or analytical assignments and practical production projects, often using "low-tech" media as well as video or photography. The actual content of courses is largely determined by teachers themselves, although most are likely to feature areas such as genre, image analysis, soap operas, advertising, and news—all of which may be approached both through analysis and through small-

FIGURE 13.1
Key Concepts of Media Education (Bowker, 1991)

MEDIA AGENCIES	Who produces a text; roles in production process; media institutions; economics and ideology; intentions and results.
MEDIA CATEGORIES	Different media (television, radio, cinema etc.); forms (documentary, advertising, etc.); genres (science fiction, soap opera, etc.); other ways of categorizing texts; how categorization relates to understanding.
MEDIA TECHNOLOGIES	What kind of technologies are available to whom, how to use them; the differences they make to the production process and well as the final product.
MEDIA LANGUAGES	How the media produce meanings; codes and conventions; narrative structures.
MEDIA AUDIENCES	How audiences are identified, constructed, addressed, and reached; how audiences find, choose, consume, and respond to texts.
MEDIA REPRESENTATION	The relation between media texts and actual places, people, events, ideas, stereotyping, and its consequences.

scale production work. The subject is also available at "A" level, the prestigious examination normally taken at eighteen prior to university entrance: here again, the syllabus is conceptually based, focusing on the interactions between media texts, institutions, and audiences, and includes a substantial practical component. Study of the media is also an integral part of the curriculum of other subjects, notably English, art, and technology. For example, the current National curriculum documents for English contain numerous examples of media work, both practical and analytical, which extend well beyond English teachers' traditional emphasis on newspapers or advertising (National Curriculum Council, 1991; Wollen, 1991). In all these sectors, the subject has grown at a fantastic rate, not least in response to student demand: "A" level entries have been increasing by 50 percent a year, and while there are many new media courses in higher education, they remain heavily oversubscribed (Bazalgette, 1993).

Media Education in Practice

One significant feature of the recent development of media education has been the growth of classroom research. Several detailed accounts of classroom practice are now available, which illustrate not merely the achievements, but also the contradictions, of teaching about the media (Buckingham, 1990; Alvarado & Boyd-Barrett 1992; Buckingham & Sefton-Green 1994). To give a taste of media education in practice, and to indicate some of the broader theoretical questions it raises, we will briefly outline two examples from our recent research (Buckingham & Sefton-Green, 1994). Both examples engage with different media technologies and forms of popular culture, but both were structured around the key concepts described above.

The first derives from work undertaken by year ten students on producing identity posters. These were in the form of collages, designed to illustrate students' media tastes—favorite stars, products, or programs—interspersed with images of the students themselves. In line with recent theory and critical practice[4] we wanted the students to explore representations of themselves and to reflect on how their identities are mediated through their tastes and pleasures in popular culture. The most salient point of comparison in analyzing this work was that of gender. For example, the boys' work tended to focus on a single theme—as in the case of one boy's piece, which contrasted images of his favorite WWF wrestling heroes with portraits of himself posing in the appropriate style. On the other hand, most of the girls' work was in the form of a bedroom wall style collage comprising hundreds of eclectically gathered images.

Our reflection on this work raised fundamental—and indeed awkward—questions about its meaning. What do these posters represent to their authors, and how do we as teachers make sense of them? Our aim here was not merely to enable students to "express themselves," or to engage in some vicarious romantic celebration of youth culture. On the contrary, we wanted to enable students to reflect on their pleasures, and thereby to gain a broader conceptual understanding of themselves as an audience, and of issues of representation. In the process, the interaction between the practical projects and the written work we subsequently asked them to produce was crucial—although for many students, this was the most difficult and unsatisfying part of the project. The question of how we as teachers might evaluate students' conceptual learning, and how they might evaluate their own work, is thus a central issue here. The work of Vygotsky offers one potential means of exploring these problems, although, as we have noted elsewhere (Buckingham, 1990; Buckingham & Sefton-Green, 1992), it also has significant limitations.

Our second example comes from a practical assignment on popular music, which we set as part of an "A" level course in year twelve. Following a unit based on the textual analysis of music, and of related videos and visual material, students were instructed to produce one of a range of products, including a video, a radio sequence, or an album cover. In reflecting on this work, we were particularly struck by the difference between the music magazines produced by three of the groups within the class. The first of these took an independent approach, full of dry, self-knowing irony and an informed "critical" perspective. The second appeared to be an authentic "hardcore" fanzine, which advertised local rave parties, and was written to appeal to a clearly circumscribed audience. The third magazine was aimed at teenage girls, although it displayed a level of sexual awareness unusual in magazines for this age group.

In analyzing these products, and the group processes that went into them, we came up against some fundamental questions about the social functions of judgements of taste. Students' discussions and writing about "their" music displayed a complex range of criteria, and of underlying conceptual understandings; yet the whole process was fairly fraught, not least because it seemed to involve a form of self-definition, which in turn exposed significant differences within the group, particularly in terms of class and ethnicity (cf. Bourdieu, 1984). Ultimately, this project led us to question the way in which "critical" discourse is often privileged in media education. As the language of the "indie" magazine is closer to received notions of critical competence, whereas the "hardcore" magazine is couched in an alien (and at times offensive) language, it is clear which will succeed in formal education. Yet in the process, there is a significant danger that questions about the social functions of critical discourse will become elided, and that we will merely end up validating particular class-bound forms of popular culture.

Our discussion of these projects has necessarily been brief. However, it should be clear that they raise fundamental theoretical questions—questions that in a sense revisit the "moral panics" agenda, and the anxieties over popular pleasures described above. The crucial point, though, is that we begin by considering how these agendas are established by students themselves, in their own language and in the particular social contexts of the classroom and the wider community. In the remainder of this chapter, we want to illustrate and extend this approach by considering in slightly more detail the inter-relationships between media education and the new information and communication technologies that are the focus of this book.

Techno-Culture

We want to begin, as we have suggested media education is increasingly coming to do, with the experiences of our students themselves. We want to explore the culture of computer games, in order to examine the kinds of meanings and competencies available to young people living in the age of "techno-culture" (Penley & Ross, 1991). Predictably, previous research in this area has largely been framed by the kinds of "moral panics" delineated above. It has often been based on mechanistic and behaviorist assumptions about "effects," or on superficial forms of content analysis, which involve counting instances of "stereotyping" and "violence" (Provenzo, 1991). Detailed attention to the texts of the games themselves, or to the secondary texts (such as magazines) that surround and mediate them, has been conspicuous by its absence. Yet, unless we are able to discover why children might actively seek out the games, why they might enjoy some and dislike others, we are unlikely to understand very much of what is taking place.

Part of our research here involved a series of small-group discussions with groups of children between the ages of twelve and fifteen in one North London school. It was a strange experience, not least because so much of what they said seemed so opaque—or perhaps it was simply obvious. As "outsiders," we approached the issue with a sense of a mystery to be solved: what do children see in these games, and why on earth do they like them?

The difficulty arises perhaps because the answer to that question is fairly straightforward. On one level, a couple of hours in the company of Sonic the Hedgehog will tell you most of what you need to know. In many ways, the attractions of computer games are similar to those of earlier generations of games, such as pinball. They are about developing a kind of control, about beating the machine, and about competing with oneself. And if the pleasure is less physical than pinball, it is also more cerebral: it's about choosing alternatives, discovering secrets by accident, and remembering or holding a number of things in your head at same time. Like pinball, the games do provide a very easy means of "blotting out" the self, and thereby escaping from other concerns and anxieties—without the disadvantage of a hangover the morning after.

A number of other issues emerged from these discussions, however, particularly in relation to gender. Despite the fact that many girls played computer games and possessed their own systems, there was little doubt that this was perceived by all as a primarily male domain. Rather like adult men talking about their cars, the boys' main preoccupation was with comparing the capabilities and prices of different systems. A clear hierarchy of systems emerged here—portables, super systems, mega systems, master systems, wonder mega systems—which was established partly in terms of the capacity of the disks ("meg" or "half meg"), and in terms of the potential attachments (whether you can have more than one joystick, whether you can connect it to a CD player, or even a karaoke!).

While this obsession with size and performance might be condemned as a typically male neurosis, it is clear that the quality of the games is largely related to the memory capacity of the computer. Thus, the primary criteria for judging quality were those of realism—for example in terms of the detail of the graphics, the inclusion of realistic sound effects and the smoothness of the movement—and of complexity—for example, the number of levels or options, the complexity of the rules, and the inclusion of "secret codes."

Computer magazines had an important role to play here. They helped to establish a specialist terminology, for example, for the generic classification of games (shoot-em-ups, beat-em-ups, platform games, and so on) and provided a basis for informed consumer choices (for example, about the quality of graphics, or about "presentation" and "playability"). Much of the discussion took the form of a projection, looking forward to games and systems they would be buying in the future, and awaiting the UK release of games that were currently available only as Japanese imports. At the same time, the boys preferred the "unofficial" magazines, largely on the grounds that they seemed to promote a kind of "critical consumerism," for example, by warning readers about "bodge jobs" that had been badly translated from one system to another. The boys were very aware of the high profit margins on games; and in fact most of the games in their own collections were pirate copies.

From the boys' point of view, this was a medium which was distinctively "theirs." While they acknowledged that girls might play, it was argued that they would probably use their brothers' machines; and if they owned their own system, it was unlikely to be a high-status one. Yet significantly, the "gendering" of computer games was seen to be at least partly a function of peer group talk: as one boy said, "if [girls'] friends don't talk about it, they don't talk about it."

Predictably, the girls were much less committed and enthusiastic, although they were also more reflective. Their accounts of the games they had played emphasized their predictability, although they were also keen to distinguish between the games they preferred—"fantasy ones . . . where you have to make decisions about what to do—and those which boys were seen to enjoy. According to one, "The boys like all the fast games, 'cause they don't have to use their brains . . . it's something they can do without thinking about it." They also argued that the "publicity" for computer games was "geared for boys," and that the games were largely "designed for them." Although some girls are more enthusiastic about "violent" games than the others (and this was a preference which sometimes extended to a taste in "gory" books), they were also explicitly critical of the sexism of the games: "You never see a woman on Streetfighter . . . the woman is never the heroine, she just sits there going 'help me! help me!' and he has to save her, but you never see the man in trouble and the woman saving."

The girls' comments on the games thus fed into broader criticisms of boys. These were partly on the grounds of intelligence: boys, it was argued, couldn't read, and even when they did appear to be reading—for example, computer magazines and pornography—they were only "going for the pictures." Interestingly, boys' lives were described as much more limited than their own: it was argued that girls tended to go out more, and had a wider range of interests. While boys were "hooked" on computer games, girls had "better things to do with their time."

As this account suggests, talk about popular media often serves as a means of establishing group identity and group membership, defined largely here in terms of gender: although it is important to see this, not as an inexorable process of socialization, in which young people are simply "slotted in" to existing social categories, but as a matter of active self-definition (Buckingham, 1993a). Perhaps because they did not perceive themselves to be the "primary," or at least the intended audience, the girls were much more explicit about this, and more reflective, than the boys. In attempting to explain the reasons for their sense of exclusion, the girls were inevitably more critical, both of the games themselves (for example, on the grounds of their "sexist" and violent content) and of the boys who play them. In common with many adult critics, they effectively pathologized the "fans" as mindless addicts—although it is interesting

that the boys themselves also attempted to displace the potentially negative effects of game playing onto other people, in this case "little kids"
who would fail to perceive the unrealistic nature of the material, and thus
be encouraged to imitate it.

By contrast, the boys were almost too close to the experience, and for
this reason could only define it in insiders' terms (for example, by using
the specialist terminology derived from the magazines). Yet in a sense, it
was not really in their interests to be reflective, at least in this context:
talk about the games was primarily a means of asserting group membership through the sharing of specialist expertise, and any questioning of
the pleasures of the games was only likely to disrupt this. As this account
suggests, much of the significance of the games lies not in their psychological "effects," but in the social process of circulation and use.

Yet, this is not simply a matter of interaction among the peer group: it is
also to do with the relationships between the producers and their audience.
The marketing of the games, for example, suggests that the producers have
to manage a complex balancing act between the need to retain "street credibility" and the attempt to maximize profit. The current attempt to broaden
the market, both in terms of age and gender, beyond the primary target
group of male adolescents, is thus bound to be problematic.

The broader educational implications of developments in digital technology will be taken up below. However, the games themselves clearly
offer productive material for study and for creative work in schools:
there would certainly seem to be a very interesting unit of media work
here, touching on key questions about institution, audience, and representation. Analytical work on the advertising and packaging of games
could be combined with creative planning of new games for particular
audiences. In reflecting on this work, students could be encouraged to
question received ideas about gender or "violence"—issues on which
they often have a great deal to say. Older students could be encouraged
to dissect the kinds of "moral panics" discussed above, and to evaluate
their underlying motivations.

Yet, there are also more fundamental questions here. For example, in
what sense can we talk about a computer game as a "text"? Super Mario
and his rivals would seem to be caught up in a much broader move in
children's culture to what has been termed *trans-media intertextuality*—
in effect, a blurring of boundaries between texts and between media
(Kinder, 1991). Thus, the games obviously borrow from other media

sources—from films, comics, and books; and computer game characters reappear in TV programs and in films. Yet, the games are also part of a wider system of cross-media merchandising (of posters, stickers, clothes, lunchboxes, toys, and even food); and this is reinforced by economic diversification and integration, and the increasingly complex patterns of cross ownership among media corporations. We are rapidly reaching the point where it is impossible to talk about these media separately, or even to begin by focusing simply on texts.

In combination with other forms of digital technology, particularly hypertext, the popularity of computer games implies a fundamental change in notions of reading and authorship (Tuman, 1992a & b). Computer games are not obviously "authored," nor are they "read" in the same way as books or even television programs. The increasing availability of re-production technology—computers, video recorders, photocopiers—has resulted in a massive increase in piracy and copyright theft, which may eventually undermine the notions of intellectual property that were the basis of print culture. New production technologies may also be contributing to this fundamental blurring of the distinctions between consumers and producers; and their availability in schools and perhaps increasingly in the home also has profound implications for the content and pedagogy of media education.

Toward the Age of Multimedia

The term *multimedia* derives from the integration of information and communication technologies—a process which has been growing apace in recent years. Basically, multimedia offers the possibility of encoding different kinds of analogue information (sounds, such as music and speech, and images, including moving images) in digital form, so that they can be handled by the computer. Thus, it is possible to "scan" still images or frames of video, or to "sample" musical sounds, and then use the computer to edit, combine, and manipulate them. Until recently, these possibilities were only available to professional media producers with access to expensive and complex technology. Yet they are now increasingly accessible to users of personal computers (PCs), both in education and in the home.

Perhaps the most familiar example of multimedia is the "interactive" compact disc—often referred to as CD-ROM (compact disc, read-only memory)—which currently seems poised to begin a major move into the domestic market. The CD allows you to store enormous amounts of information of various kinds, and to gain random access to it. Significantly, this includes a range of different types of media—not simply written text, but also still and moving images, as well as spoken and musical sounds. These different information media are rendered in digital form, and often combined using hypertext.

Despite the arguments of some enthusiasts, this is not immediately going to replace the book. However, titles in the Voyager catalogue (ranging from literary classics to a combined film and text of *A Hard Day's Night*) and their proprietary adaptation of the HyperCard system enable you to do many of the things that you can do with books much more efficiently and easily—such as cross-referencing, reading at your own pace, and choosing your own way through—as well as offering the added benefits of sound and moving images. To date, interactive CDs have been used mainly for encyclopedias and dictionaries, which are primarily about information retrieval, and where their benefits are much more obvious, not least in terms of physical bulk. Yet recent work in this field suggests that the technology also possesses considerable potential for generating new artistic and fictional forms. The interactive CD offers very different possibilities in terms of narrative, for example, that move beyond a traditional linear structure—and there are signs that this is beginning to influence the approach of "older" media, for example, in some children's television. Thus, we have seen the advent of "CD novels"—although in many ways, the book has become a somewhat inadequate model or metaphor for what is possible here.

However, the interactive CD remains primarily a "consumer" technology, in that it offers new ways of storing and retrieving existing information—and this seems to be the way it will be marketed to domestic consumers. As has been argued elsewhere in relation to hypertext, this is "interactive" only in the sense that it allows the reader to choose different paths through that information (Tuman 1992a & b). As we have implied, this in itself significantly changes what is normally meant by consumption, or by reading, certainly in relation to moving images, where linear reading has been very much the norm (at least before the advent of video). Yet ultimately, this is a rather spurious kind of "interactivity": it generally fails to provide the potential for readers to contribute their own information or ideas, and restricts them to choosing from a predetermined range of possibilities.

However, other developments in multimedia offer much greater creative possibilities. Rather than simply consuming different kinds of texts, users can manipulate existing texts and create their own. For example, the development of digital sound recording technology has already revolutionized the music industry, but is now becoming an affordable option for home use. Two of the most popular "home entertainment" computers, the Atari and the Amiga, led the way with MIDI. This is a simple process that turns sounds from an instrument into a digital code. The code is visually displayed on screen and can be "edited" in a variety of ways far more precisely than with a razor blade and tape or by copying. You can sample existing sounds, regularize rhythm or tempo, repeat phrases or beats, and combine up to eight tracks. The only limitation of MIDI is that the code can only be played back on the same instrument that you started with. With a modern synthesizer and MIDI one person can produce "whole," integrated songs or tracks working on their own: modern Techno and House music are produced using this technology, and many composers in more "traditional" fields also make extensive use of it. As it becomes possible to compress larger and larger pieces of information, musicians will be able to transform live sound from any source directly into digital information which can be manipulated in even more sophisticated ways. This kind of technology will soon be much more widely available for the domestic user.

Another example of multimedia production is image manipulation. It is now possible to buy, for a couple of hundred dollars, a scanner and related software which can enable you to input and store almost any picture you want. Color scanners are less than a thousand dollars, and you can buy a "still video" camera for half that price, with which you can take pictures directly onto disk. Add to this the images available on commercially produced CDs and you can do almost anything to any image you like, combining, cutting, fixing, and falsifying. The main limitation at present is "output": color printers are just beyond domestic reach.

In the last year or so, it has also become possible to use the computer to edit moving pictures. Again, the current technological limitation is storage size, since even a small piece of film is very large in digital format. However, processes like Apple's "Quick Time" now make desktop editing feasible; and the input device only costs a couple of hundred dollars. The related software allows you to edit video in ways that you could only achieve previously with expensive equipment like Quantel and paintboxes. You can play around with the images and add sound or special effects tracks. For example, you can use a program called "Morph," which is a version of the much lauded technology that did the transformations in *Terminator 2,* and just about every commercial currently showing on TV (Clarke, 1993). The limitation at present is that these films are not full size and can't be played back on video, but there is no reason to think these difficulties will not be overcome.

Significantly, these developments build upon technologies that have already become much more accessible for the domestic user. Video recorders are now available in something like 75 percent of British homes with children, and despite the recession, around two million portable video camcorders are currently being bought in the UK every year, predominantly by families with children, and by no means only by middle-class ones.

On one level, then, these technologies could be seen simply as an extension of those which are already widely available. The marketing of "home video," for example, employs many of the ideological themes which have been developed in marketing still cameras and "home movies," most notably the emphasis on family harmony. However, although there is as yet little research, it is clear that the uses of video technology are much more diverse and idiosyncratic than this would suggest. Video permits a more conscious, and potentially subversive, manipulation of commercially produced media texts, for example, through "sampling" and re-editing material recorded off-air, and digital multimedia radically extends these possibilities. The large numbers of children now growing up with video will clearly have a very different relationship with broadcast television than the generations that preceded them.

Potentially, these new production technologies may begin to abolish distinctions between readers and writers, or consumers and producers. Combined with the gradual fragmentation of the major broadcasting institutions, and with much greater reliance on freelance labor throughout the media industries, they may be contributing to a blurring of the division between "amateur" and professional production.

Of course, it is possible to overstate these utopian ideas about the coming of media democracy. Whatever the potential of the technologies themselves, their social impact will depend on wider social forces. On the one hand, they might indeed be seen to permit more democratic access to information and more egalitarian forms of communication. Yet on the other hand, they may simply be part of a more disturbing move toward social fragmentation, in which collective leisure is increasingly privatized and forced back into the home (Buckingham, 1993b).

Multimedia Education

Nevertheless, these developments do seem to offer significant new possibilities for media education, both in terms of practical production and in terms of analytical work. The status of practical media work has changed quite significantly over the last decade, partly as a result of changes in how media education itself is defined, but also in response to the increasing accessibility of new production technologies, particularly video and desk-top publishing. Multimedia represents an important extension of this: and even smaller schools have already invested in the hardware that would be necessary to run multimedia programs, although it may not be currently used in this way. The ability to "sample" and manipulate material in a range of media, and the much greater control over the editing process that is possible with multimedia, are particularly significant here. Rather than regarding practical work in media production as rare, one-off opportunity, it becomes possible to think in terms of drafting and redrafting. Multimedia brings closer the notion of practical work as a form of writing, which is fully integrated with other kinds of media work. By implication, it also points to an expanded notion of writing in English, whereby students use computers to generate compositions or productions that integrate different media.

The interactive potential of multimedia also offers much greater possibilities for analytical work. For example, many teaching materials in media education are based on enabling students to manipulate given images and texts and to see the consequences of what they have done.[5] Yet, the use of print-based media means that only a limited number of alternatives are on offer, and the end result often takes the form of a rather uneven collage. Multimedia may offer an approach to analysis which is much less cut and dried, and much more genuinely exploratory. It offers a potentially infinite range of options, much greater opportunity for experimentation, and a more "polished" final product.

The crucial need, however, is to ensure that production remains a collaborative, social process. One of the important arguments about information technology in English has been the notion of the computer screen as a public forum, and as the focus of group talk. Similarly, in the case of multimedia, we need to avoid lapsing back into the notion of the isolated individual creator in silent communion with the screen. The ability to present one's work to others is vitally important—and here there is a need to invest in screen projection and good quality sound. As with educational television, mediation is vital for learning: the process should be one of dialogue between the student, the screen, the teacher and other students.

In the current context of underfunding, and of moves to return the curriculum to a pre-electronic era, these kinds of possibilities can seem fanciful. Yet in the last ten years, the advent of domestic VHS video recorders in schools has radically altered classroom practice in a whole range of curriculum areas. Multimedia is already here, and its diffusion is likely to prove much more rapid. If we are to ensure a genuinely interactive approach, and to enable students to explore the creative potential of the technology, we need to keep ahead of the game.

Literacy in a Digital Age

Clearly, the development of multimedia needs to be seen in the context of broader social and cultural changes—at least some of which are increasingly defined by the glib and sweeping term *postmodernism*. In some ways, these technologies do seem to represent a tangible manifestation of the theoretical claims, not just of postmodernism, but also of poststructuralism and "reader-oriented" literary theory, with its notion of the "active reader" and the "death of the author" (Tuman, 1992b). Likewise, postmodernist accounts of youth culture have drawn attention to the changing nature of consumption, and the blurring of distinctions between production and consumption—which we have argued are particularly manifested in computer games and multimedia (Kinder, 1991; Nava, 1992).

Optimistic accounts of these developments tend to stress their democratic potential, as a means of increasing the power and autonomy of consumers. "Sampling," for example, would seem to make a mockery of copyright and of capitalist notions of intellectual property and, hence, to undermine the power of media institutions. Likewise, although he doesn't use examples from new technology, Jim Collins's (1989) description of the post-modernist text seems tailor made for interactive multimedia:

[T]he post-modernist text constructs *polylogic* rather than dialogic relationships with "already saids," where the relationship between past and present coding is based on interaction and transformation instead of simple rejection. (134)

Collins and others argue strongly for a rejection of elitist and sterile oppositions between high and popular culture: postmodern culture is seen here, not as a reflection of alienation and meaninglessness, but as vibrant, diverse, and creative. This kind of analysis not only offers insights into "texts" like *Sonic the Hedgehog* or *Last Action Hero*: it also begins to describe the process of "consumption/production," which is made possible by the "interactive" nature of digital texts, in which we are simultaneously "readers," "writers," and "players."

As this ambiguity suggests, the meaning of "digital literacy" is wide open to debate. As other contributors to this book indicate, the notion of literacy is itself a heavily contested one. Nevertheless, recent research has pointed to the need for a broader definition of the term, which acknowledges that it is inevitably embedded within particular social relationships and practices (Buckingham, 1989). The nature of literacy—or, more accurately, of literac*ies*—is culturally and historically diverse and changeable. Any contemporary definition of the concept, and any educational programs based upon it, must include the understandings and competencies that are developed in relation to "new" communications technologies, in addition to "older" technologies such as writing and print.

Our account of the uses and potential implications of these technologies has inevitably been somewhat speculative, although we have attempted to ground our arguments in research and in educational practice. Theoretical accounts of this area are currently proliferating, although the empirical research which might serve to substantiate them remains very limited. Both academic and popular writers veer wildly between apocalyptic warnings and utopian optimism, yet the arguments are often extraordinarily abstract. If educational responses to these developments are to be at all informed and constructive, they will need to be based on thorough empirical investigation. To this end, in our current research, we are beginning to explore in more detail the questions we have begun to raise here. By introducing such technology in media classrooms, we are hoping to discover what happens when members of the "cyber generation" become multimedia producers in their own right—for example, by producing expanded books using the narratives of computer games and the technology of hypertext, or using image manipulation and morphing programs to create family albums and montages of self-portraits. By giving the students time and space to experiment, and to bring their cultural experiences to the technology, we hope to explore how their "writing" challenges our concepts of literacy.

Notes

1. For a more complete account of this case, and the ensuing controversy around "video violence," see Buckingham (forthcoming). There is a significant parallel here with the case of Michael Ryan, who in 1987 shot sixteen people in the small town of Hungerford, in the north east of England. See Duncan Webster (1989).
2. Provocative comments on the current panics are contained in Barker (1993).
3. This is apparent in some of the contributions to Lusted and Drummond (1985), particularly those of David Lusted and Richard Dyer.
4. For example, the work of Jo Spence (1986), or Cindy Sherman (1984).
5. Many of the photoplay exercises produced by the British Film Institute and the English and Media Centre in London use this approach.

References

Alvarado, M., & Boyd-Barrett, O. (Ed.). (1992). *Media education: An introduction.* London: British Film Institute/Open University Press.

Barker, M. (1984a). *A haunt of fears: The strange history of the British horror comic campaign.* London: Pluto.

Barker, M. (Ed.). (1984b). *Video nasties: Freedom and censorship in the media.* London: Pluto.

Barker, M. (April 1993), Sex, violence and videotape. *Sight and Sound,* 10–12.

Bazalgette, C. (Ed.). (1989). *Primary media education: A curriculum statement.* London: British Film Institute.

———. (23 April 1993). *Times Educational Supplement.*

Bourdieu, P. (1984). *Distinction: A social critique of the judgement of Taste* (Nice, R., trans.). London: Routledge and Kegan Paul.

Bowker, J. (Ed.). (1991). *Secondary media education a curriculum statement.* London: British Film Institute.

Buckingham, D. (1986). Against demystification. *Screen, 27*(5), 80–95.

———. (1989). Television literacy: A critique. *Radical Philosophy, 51,* 12–25.

———. (Ed.). (1990). *Watching media learning, making sense of media education.* Basingstoke: Falmer.

———. (1993a). *Children talking television. The making of television literacy.* Basingstoke: Falmer.

———. (1993b). *Changing literacies: Media education and modern culture.* London: Tufnell Press.

———. (forthcoming). *Screening effects: Rethinking the regulation of children's viewing.* Manchester: Manchester University Press.

Buckingham, D., & Sefton-Green, J. (Spring 1992). In other words: Evaluating media learning. *English and Media Magazine, 26,* 31–37.

———. (1994). *Cultural studies goes to school: Reading and teaching popular media.* London: Taylor and Francis.

Clarke, N. (28 May 1993). Morphing. *MacUser,* 78–79.

Collins, J. (1989). *Uncommon cultures: Popular culture and post-modernism.* London: Routledge.

Department of Education. (1983). *Popular television and schoolchildren.* London: Her Majesty's Stationery Office.

Haddon, L. (1993). Interactive games. In Hayward, P. & Wollen, T. (Eds.), *Future visions: New techologies of the screen* (123–47). London: British Film Institute.

Jones, K. (Ed.). (1992). *English in the National Curriculum: Cox's Revolution?* London: Kogan Page.

Kinder, M. (1991). *Playing with power in movies, television and video games from* Muppet Babies *to* Teenage Mutant Ninja Turtles. Berkeley: University of California Press.

Leavis, F., & Thompson, D. (1933). *Discrimination and popular culture.* London: Chatto and Windus.

Lusted, D., & Drummond, P. (Ed.). (1985). *TV and schooling.* London: British Film Institute.

Masterman, L. (1980). *Teaching about television.* Basingstoke: Macmillan.

———. (1985). *Teaching the media.* London: Comedia.

Morley, D. (1992). *Television, audiences and cultural studies.* London: Routledge.

National Curriculum Council. (1991). *English: Non-statutory guidance.* York: National Curriculum Council.

Nava, M. (1992). *Changing cultures; Feminism, youth and consumerism.* London: Sage.

Pearson, G. (1983). *Hooligan: A history of respectable fears.* London: Macmillan.

Penley, C., & Ross, A. (Eds.). (1991). *Technoculture.* Minneapolis: University of Minnesota Press.

Provenzo, E. (1991). *Video kids: Making sense of Nintendo.* Cambridge, Mass.: Harvard University Press.

Sherman, C. (1984). *Cindy Sherman.* Munich: Shirmer/Mosel.

Sight and Sound. (April 1993). Editorial 3 (4), 1.

Spence, J. (1986). *Putting myself in the picture.* London: Camden Press.

Times Educational Supplement. (20 August 1993).

Tuman, M. (1992). *Word perfect: Literacy in the computer age.* London: Falmer.

———. (Ed.). (1992). *Online literacy: The promise (and peril) of writing with computers.* Pittsburgh: University of Pittsburgh Press.

Webster, D. (1989). Whodunnit? America did: Rambo and post- Hungerford rhetoric. *Cultural Studies, 3*(2), 173—93.

Williamson, J. (1981/2). How does girl number 20 understand ideology? *Screen Education, nos. 40,* 80—87.

Wollen, T. (Ed.). (1991). *Media in English at key stage 3.* London: British Film Institute.

14

Living with the Tiger:
Media Curriculum Issues for the Future

Robyn Quin and Barrie McMahon

*Century 21 approaches and we face new challenges in media education. The informa-
tion age is changing the social and technological context of the media. The increase in
the volume and velocity of information and images hurtling around the globe makes
obsolete our old ideas about time and space, history and geography. The new technologies are fast, exciting, and promise unlimited access to information. But sensation
and information do not equal knowledge and wisdom. Students need to be educated
both by and about the new technologies if they are to develop the necessary frameworks for understanding the information they get. This raises the issue of media literacy and media education for the new generation.*

*This chapter argues that curriculum approaches in media education must move be-
yond text-based analysis of closed visual narratives and into the neglected areas of audiences and their technological environment. It is time that the new technologies joined
the press, cinema, and television as objects of criticism, analysis, and evaluation in the
classroom. This chapter offers a flexible and accessible theoretical curriculum model
that addresses issues of text, context, and audience in teaching about the new media.*

The family decides that a mere television set is not enough, so they
buy a wall screen, a television that covers one entire wall. As their finances improve they replace the second, third, and fourth walls with
similar screens, so now they can sit in the middle of the images. Then
they add a ceiling screen and, finally, a screen that gleams beneath their
feet. Now at last, they have wall-to-wall, floor-to-ceiling television—
100 percent television. But the family does not have to suffer the boring,
repetitive programs pumped out by the networks. Their television room
picks up thoughts and fantasies and renders them as three-dimensional
images. That which is not real becomes real.

Inevitably the children in the family become addicted to the television room. They spend increasing amounts of time in the room and their parents' concern is heightened when they begin to notice strange smells emanating from the television room. They hear deep, muffled roars within, and yet every time one of them opens the door to see what the children are up to, the images on the screen are harmless. Usually the children are watching the Mad Hatter's tea party scene from *Alice in Wonderland.*

As time passes, it becomes increasingly difficult to get the children to leave the TV room. In desperation the parents announce plans for a family holiday to the Grand Canyon. Far from being thrilled, the children protest and are resentful. The parents, however, are insistent. The children negotiate just one more night of viewing. Later that same night, the parents smell again the strange stench that has been worrying them and hear the deep muffled roars from within the room.

Suspecting that *Alice in Wonderland* is a camouflage for something more sinister, the father bursts into the room. He sees—and it's the last thing he sees—a huge tiger padding toward him. FADE TO BLACK.

The next day, the neighbors are puzzled. The car is in the driveway, packed and ready to go, but there is no sign of the family. The concerned neighbors enter the house. Tentatively, they open the door of the TV room and, as usual, the children are there enjoying the Mad Hatter's tea party. One of the neighbors notices something on the floor. It is the remains of the father's wallet—chewed. End of story.

This story is not original. It was written many years ago by Ray Bradbury, but it is retold as a parable for the twenty-first century (Bradbury, 1952). The television room with its six screens is a metaphor for the video display unit, the front-end technology of computers, bulletin boards, education packages, broadcasting and satellite systems, telephone communications, and games.

Those who worry about the effects of the media often behave like the man with the tiger outside the door who thinks that the tiger is the only problem. He forgets that the problem is not so much the beast itself, but what he is going to do about it. A tiger is an appropriate symbol for the media, particularly the emergent interactive technologies—colorful, exciting, fast moving, and sometimes violent. The tiger is not outside, however, it is in the same room as us and our children. The average school student shares her mind and living space with a crowd of media tigers, so the question now is, "What, if anything, should we or can we do about it?"

The Issues

The intention here is not to cast the media in the role of a monster responsible for all sorts of social ills, the supposed depravities of which pose a special threat to the young. The content of a particular program or video game might sometimes be a cause for concern, but criticism which never leaves the sex and violence orbit misses the point. Of far greater concern are the cultural values and ideologies promoted by the media across a whole range of texts: advertising, news, current affairs, family comedies, cartoons, and electronic games—in fact all the programs that we enjoy. Let us not deny that the media offers us pleasure. The networks would broadcast grand opera twenty four hours a day if it would bring an audience. Nintendo would market mathematics programs if they would sell. The media's profits are directly related to our pleasures.

The media's pursuit of profit has had major implications for childhood. At some time in the last twenty years we put our children to bed. When they woke up in the morning they were not children any more, but a demographic entry point for marketers who, determined to turn children into consumers, invented pester power. The new consumer is under 4'5" and is called Jessica or James, Andrew or Amy. Jessica and James place themselves firmly in the front of the supermarket cart and point to the goodies they saw on the television yesterday. Mothers burdened by a job, lack of time, and sometimes a guilty conscience hand the purse strings to the whining piece of humanity in the cart. There are 32.8 million Americans aged between four and twelve years (12 percent of the population). They spend (or have spent on their behalf) $140 billion a year. Kids sell films, records, video games, computer programs, and fashion. *Home Alone 2* made $70 million in its first week of release, an even more startling statistic when you consider that 80 percent of the tickets were sold to children at half price.

In the lead up to the twenty-first century we face new challenges in media education. The social and technological context of the media has changed with the coming of the information age. The increase in the volume and velocity of information and images hurtling around the globe makes obsolete our old ideas about time and space, history and geography. Today we wear tiny computers on our wrists which break seconds into tenths and time is measured not in minutes but by the multimillion divisions of the atomic clock. History is no longer a succession of events recounted in a newspaper. Satellite links and computerized image transmission mean that television news can bring us instant updates on many more events than we could ever fit into some neat idea of the progress of history. Networks dissolve geography. In the space of a few short minutes we can cross from a sentimental hometown story to a horrific war a continent away, and from there to a Coke commercial and onto a video clip of Madonna disrobing. The enormous growth of data transmission over the telephone lines from one computer to another makes huge amounts of information available instantaneously, cheaply, and uncontrollably. It is as easy and as cheap, especially if one has access to the education networks, to talk to someone on the other side of the globe as it is to the next-door neighbor. Virtual reality will signal the death of geographical distance. Because virtual reality systems operate on lists of co-ordinates rather than specific photographic data, they can operate in real time on today's telephone lines. Two people on opposite sides of the world can slip on a headset and a Polhemus bracelet, connect their computers, and instantly see a representation of each other. They can walk around, beside, or through each other. It is not inconceivable that together they can take a trip via virtual reality through the streets of Rome. Significantly, what the users talk about and the images they swap are outside the jurisdiction of national boundaries and, therefore, national laws.

The new technologies are fast, exciting, and promise unlimited access to information. But sensation and information do not equal knowledge and wisdom. The electronic media fragment the experience of life. They crowd sensation and information in a way that is unique to our time. The communications revolution drowns us in data and invites us to confuse data with information. Data is not information, and information is not knowledge. Knowledge most certainly is not wisdom. They are quite distinct points on a continuum, and while the information explosion showers us with data, wisdom seems thin on the ground. Students need to be educated both by and about the new technologies if they are to develop the necessary frameworks for understanding the information they get. This raises the issue of media education for the next generation: its goals, methodology, content, and relevance.

The Role of the Educator

What can we as teachers contribute as we co-exist with our students in this image-based, information culture? As teachers we cannot ignore the power of this new culture—satellite television, virtual reality, video games, computer games—in defining and constructing students' sense of identity, politics, and culture. The purpose of media literacy education is to give students an informed and critical understanding of the media, its techniques, and impact. For many years progressive teachers have argued for the importance of student experience as the central component in developing a critical pedagogy, and yet many have ignored the ways in which student experience is shaped by the new technologies of the media. Today computerized interactive video games are, to use the hackneyed phrase of more than one Australian educator, "where the kids are at." More than seven in ten households in the United States own a Nintendo set (Estes and Thomas, 1993). It is time to rethink our conceptions of media literacy and appropriate curriculum in the context of the new technologies.

Before sketching what a media literacy program for the next decade might look like, it must be emphasized that there is no fixed body of knowledge which constitutes media education. The role of the teacher in educating about the media is to produce the *conditions* for understanding a changing world and giving students the power to make informed, critical decisions about their relationship to the media. Successful media education involves an empowerment of learners, essential to the creation and sustaining of an active democracy, and of a public which is not easily manipulable, but whose opinion counts precisely because it is critically informed and capable of making its own independent judgements (Giroux, 1989, viii).

Curriculum approaches in media education must move beyond text-based analysis of closed visual narratives and into the neglected areas of audiences and their technological environment. For example, in interactive video games we are seeing the first evidence of computerized communications technology which is socializing the next generation on a mass scale. In Australia there has already developed the public assumption that such games are harmful. The editorial of the major national daily recently stated: "The proposal of the Commonwealth's chief censor . . . that video games should be subject to the same classification as films is welcome and timely. . . . The most serious aspect of such imports (the games) is the increasing number that are sexually explicit or violent, or both, and which could have a disastrous effect on young and impressionable minds" (*The Weekend Australian,* 1993, 9).

Someone should tell the chief censor he has no chance. Modems, networks, and bulletin boards spell the end of terrestrial boundaries. Messages originating in one country and transmitted to another via international networks will be outside the jurisdiction of the receiving country's regulatory laws. The new communications systems will be answerable only to the consumer. We need education and not regulation. What is at stake here is not the amount of time or money spent on the games but the cultural values and ideologies constructed and reinforced by this aspect of the image culture. It is time that interactive video games joined the press, cinema, and television as objects of criticism, analysis, and evaluation in the classroom.

Curriculum Methodology: An Illustration

Textual analysis remains a useful starting point in the analysis of any media product, but it is only a starting point. Studies of production and reception are equally important in developing an informed understanding of the nature and role of the media. Textual analysis begins with a study with the text's construction—the symbols, the narrative, and the encoding of the media message. Such analysis, if rigorously undertaken, will uncover the workings of the text, its preferred reading, and its position within dominant ideology. Textual analysis alone, however, will not reveal the sense the viewer is making of the text. Given the absolute centrality of the user in interactive technology, the next generation of methodologies for media education need to be able to embrace both the text and the audience. Research has demonstrated that audiences are not passive recipients of media messages. Rather, they actively and unpredictably construct diverse and sometimes contradictory meanings for the identical text. The particular meanings the audience constructs around the text will be dependent upon the discourses, knowledge, prejudices, or resistances available to the audience members (Morley, 1980, 7). The audience member, whether viewer or game player, is active in the construction of the text's meaning and the importance of his/her role should not be understated.

Effective media teaching should foreground the issue of values and acknowledge differences and antipathies between individuals and between subcultural groups. Part of the teacher's task is to make students aware that they do have positions, attitudes, and values which they bring to bear in their interaction with the media. These pre-existing values and attitudes will influence the meaning that students make of their media experiences. The reason for foregrounding the issue of values in media education is not to make students either value free or full of "correct" values, but to recognize the politics of their own position. Such an understanding is a prerequisite to making comparisons and judgements about their own and wider community values. To say that values matter is not to say that students must believe in our values. It is to say that "you have to come out of this classroom believing that you have to make choices and that those choices have consequences." It is the ability to make informed choices that is the condition for critical autonomy.

Having established that each of us has a political position in relation to the texts, it is possible to explore the interpretative frameworks employed by media audiences in their understanding of any media text. This exploration will raise issues about the relationship between viewer's interpretations and their social position (gender, race, age, socioeconomic position); issues of pleasure and textual signification; issues of textual determination vis-à-vis the possibility of resistive readings.

Taking one of the new technologies—interactive video games—as an example, the starting point of analysis might be the value systems developed and reinforced by the games, the subject positions constructed for the players, and the interface between the values of the game world and the values of our culture. The characterization, narrative structure, plot, and resolution in various video games raise issues about the representation of gender, race, and age. Consider for a moment the gender orientation demanded and reinforced by interactive video games. Textual analysis will reveal some now well-understood elements of stereotyping, such as the gender roles within the text.

Most of the games offer a male point of view and stereotypically masculine forms of pleasure (Fiske, 1987, 203). They are action oriented, climax focussed, and control dependent. The games offer immediate gratification or punishment and narratively they work through metaphors of conquest, domination, and control. While they offer valuable opportunities for learning technological mastery, the games generally support very traditional ideas about gender roles. In *Night Trap,* released by Sega, scantily clad women are tortured and mutilated by aliens. *Custer's Last Stand,* an underground game, features the raping of squaws. In another game, accessed by a faxed driver's license, the user directs the sexual antics of a cartoon female. Admittedly these are extreme examples from the sex/violence continuum of games available, but even the highly popular

Super Mario Brothers 3 features a princess in need of rescue. Regardless of the resolution of the games, the female characters remain in their traditional assigned positions as victims or prizes. Part of the analysis, therefore, is to go beyond the closed text, into the cultural dimensions pertaining to the ways in which the texts are used. Here it is the cultural dimension of pleasure, particularly whose pleasures and the types of pleasures, that is to be examined. The next question to ask is about the consequences of what has been revealed.

One consequence of the gender bias in the narrative is the possibility that the video games, by sustaining gendered social identities, provide boys with basic computer skills that girls are denied. Research supports the contention that video games develop skills in comprehension, reasoning, logic, hand/eye co-ordination, and decision making (Estes & Nolan, 1993). But research also indicates that girls and boys have very different relationships with interactive video games. Girls play less often than boys, are less skillful, and less engrossed in the games. This has implications for the development of computer skills in girls and flow over effects into girls' relationships with other forms of technology (Wajcman, 1981). Sherry Turkle, in *The Second Self: Computers and the Human Spirit,* argues that these differences in approaches to the games are the result of early socialization of children into roles as hard or soft masters. Boys, she says, are "hard masters," looking for ways to control the simulated world on the screen; girls are "soft masters," more likely to look for ways of accommodating its rules. Most video games definitely require hard mastery if the player is to score and will therefore reinforce the social behaviors practiced by the hard masters. The games reinforce the stereotypical position that technology is a male domain and that females operate effectively only within the emotional domain.

Designing Appropriate Curriculum

Outlined below is a simple theoretical curriculum model for improving students' understanding of the media (figure 14.1). To argue the need for teaching skills in visual literacy is to imply that the media are never transparent. If the video screen were simply a window on the world, then the study of it would be as pointless as studying a pane of glass. The case for teaching visual literacy rests upon the idea that the media are actively constructing reality rather than neutrally transmitting it.

What follows is work in progress and should be considered as such. Secondly, the model is only a framework for curriculum design and is meant to be used as a guide to the development of course content and teaching strategies. It should not be seen in prescriptive terms, but as a base for adaptations.

FIGURE 14.1
The Model

Context
- community issues
- student backgrounds
- active audiences

Aims
- transferral of learning
- importance of the parents
- negotiating aims

Strategies

KNOWLEDGE	→	ISSUE	←	BELIEFS VALUES
research		(negotiated)		ethical considerations
current texts				cultural expectations
historical texts				alternative belief systems
student responses				moral judgments
data				
alternative representations				
critiques				

Outcomes
- identifiable
- achievable
- valuable

Evaluation
- student oriented
- continual

Aims

We need to generate high order outcomes for our students so that they will be able to function as effective and informed critics long after they have passed beyond the classroom walls. Our aim is to make media literacy a lifelong process. To this end the teaching/learning of media literacy skills should be a partnership between the players in the field. The central player is the student but, there are also the media themselves which carry a great deal of material about their own activities and both assume and help to create a public which has a serious interest in media issues.

The second players are the parents and teachers, many of whom have an anxious interest in the media and its effects. Both groups need to be educated too if they are to move beyond simple and ineffectual calls for greater regulation and censorship. Part of the urge to leap to simplistic solutions is many of those in the groups of educators and parents have not had the opportunity to work through that basic media comprehension problem that was alluded to in the earlier part of this chapter—the need to establish an awareness that we, as consumers and critics, occupy a political position. We need to be aware of this, to be able to articulate it, so that from there, we can arrive at conclusions about our own interpretations and those of others. Parental involvement, therefore, has to be informed involvement, and we must not underestimate either the energy that this will absorb or the rewards that it will bring.

Outcomes

Although there has been some educational resistance to an outcomes-based approach to education, there is gain providing the outcomes are stated in knowledge-based and conceptual terms rather than purely mechanistic terms. We need to decide what it is that we want students to be able to do if we are to be in a position to evaluate the extent to which the aims have been achieved. Without this there is limited scope for diagnosis and remediation. The outcomes need to be identifiable, reasonable, achievable, and valued as worthwhile by both students and teachers. If the issue in question was to be the representation of women, possible outcomes might be:

- The students will be able to identify the visual techniques used to create the image of the perfect woman, for example, lighting techniques, airbrushing, soft focus, frame position, female's pose.

- The students will be able to identify the relationship between the choice of specific images of women in advertising and the target audience for the product.
- The students will be able to illustrate with relevant examples the ways in which stereotypical images of women serve the economic and social interests of particular groups in the community.

The Two Contexts

There are two contexts that need to be taken into account—those of student and of the text. First we need to recognize the diversity of background and experience that young people bring to their media experiences. Children are not passive, vacant-eyed dupes soaking up everything they see. They are audiences and as such are active and ceaseless producers of meaning. Although a media text may offer an audience positions from which to view the world, these positions are not immutable (Hodge & Tripp, 1986, 159). They are often disputed, argued with, integrated, modified, negotiated, or even ignored. We need to pay attention to what the students are bringing to the text and acknowledge that their readings of a program may be very different from our own but equally valid. We need to encourage students to negotiate their own meanings, argue back with the media in their own terms, and make sense of the media's values in terms of their own.

Within this context, we need to recognize the importance of pleasure. Students enjoy their media experiences and consider them to be a valuable and important part of their culture. The context of media education needs to be an acceptance of this aspect of their culture, not a denigration of it. If the hidden agenda is to get the children to turn off the television and throw away the computer games, then the teacher will be chewed up and spat out like the father in the opening story. That father would have lived a little longer if he had gone into the TV room and watched for a while with the children.

The second context is that surrounding the text, or as is more likely the case, the series of related texts. The traditional categories of the political, the economic, and the social are useful when approaching the concept of intertextuality. Part of the political context are the key debates that may be surrounding the texts at any given time. For example, in the illustration that has been provided in this chapter, key related debates have centered around censorship, sex, and violence. The individual's position within these debates, even if unacknowledged, will affect the meanings that are constructed from the texts.

A key economic question, beyond that of target audience, markets, monopolies, and merchandising tie-ups, is the overarching question of whose economic interests are being served, including those of the customer. These will contribute to shaping the meanings that are drawn from the texts. Either included in the economic context or as a fourth category are the institutional contexts. Matters related to policy, funding, and means of text production and distribution affect the meanings that are given to texts. Matters of policy and consequent government funding determine, for example, that chamber music as a medium has quite a different meaning from the medium of the video parlor.

The social contexts embrace the social circumstances of the users *and* the texts, particularly the status positions of the latter. As media educators we are well aware of the different meanings that can be drawn from texts because of their status differentials, that the texts of the literature class have a different meaning from those of the media studies class because of their status.

Strategies

Successful media literacy teaching will necessarily be innovative because of the relative infancy of this form of education. Media literacy critiques the experiences of today, yesterday, and tomorrow. It will draw from history and from other disciplines, but currency of the experience is an overriding concern. This prerequisite demands strategies that are relevant to the everyday and issue oriented. Teachers need to be prepared to tackle a range of priority issues, from the local to the global.

The earlier advocacy in this chapter was to focus in on the ideological issue, that connection between text and audience. In the classroom the starting point may be text or audience or both, through addressing the contexts previously outlined. The starting point is of marginal consequence providing it has interest and relevance. It could be tomorrow's news or a traditional entry point such as examining a still advertising image which raises issues of the representation of women in the media: issues of exploitation, implicit violence, passivity, aberrant sexuality, consumerism, and stereotyping. The visual text that follows in figure 14.2 is an entry point to the wider issues of knowledge, beliefs, and values.

FIGURE 14.2
Integration of Knowledge Base with Values

KNOWLEDGE	BELIEFS AND VALUES
research findings	ethical considerations
current textual examples	cultural differences/expectations of the representation of women
historical representations of women	feminist perspectives
student responses to selected images	moral judgements

The purpose of the image analysis therefore goes well beyond straight deconstruction, which by itself may lead to intellectual dead ends such as simple blame apportioning or moralistic hand wringing. The danger of deconstruction without the broader fields of study is that beliefs and values are seen as different terms of camouflage for prejudices and assumptions.

The urge to hastily apportion blame so the problem can be quickly dismissed might be counterbalanced if we also draw upon alternative pro-social representations of conflictual violence in the media. For example the Australian film *Shame* draws on the genre expectations of the American western but twists them decisively away from the western's masculine culture of violence.

Although violent in parts, *Shame* works a feminist inflection of the western. *Shame* portrays an ensemble of women uniting to defeat socially structured and sanctioned violence. This is quite unlike the traditional lone western hero majestically cleansing the social order and reinstating the status quo. *Shame* demonstrates that the status quo is not always either right or desirable and that women have the power to change it.

Evaluation

We need to implement a continuous process of monitoring, critical reflection, and action that will enable us and our students to measure the extent to which our intended outcomes are being achieved and to identify areas requiring attention. An important aspect of this monitoring process will be dialogue between students and teachers about their responses to and concerns about their everyday media consumption. Such dialogue should be a means of continually updating the methods that are being used by all as part of their media lives. For example, if one reflects back to the outcomes outlined earlier, the first framework for analysis that is available to the learner would be little more than an identification framework (the first outcome). A diagnostic sign for the teacher that the learner's framework was becoming more sophisticated might be that there is now consciousness about the assumption of "normality." Feedback may indicate to the teacher that the notion of normal behavior or normal depictions is indeed a fundamental problematic. Another sophistication to the learner's analysis model would be to be able to identify significant anchors to the meanings—to see, for example, the anchor that statistics give to meaning by providing credibility, the anchor that documentary gives to meaning again by being more credible than drama.

The purpose of evaluation is to prepare our students for the next phase of their life long experience in learning about their media. If educators are successful, it will be their media irrespective of who owns it.

Conclusion

Let us return finally to the opening story. It was science fiction fantasy forty years ago, but with the advent of the technology of virtual reality the time is fast approaching when we will be the central players in an electronic world of movement, smells, sensations, and changes in temperature. Our students will not have the skills necessary to survive, contribute, and prosper in this new world of substitute realities unless we consciously strive to make them media literate.

References

Bradbury, R. (1952). "The Veldt." In *The illustrated man*. London: Rupert Hart-Davis.
Censor Fights Back. (7/8 August 1993). *The Australian*.
Estes, N., & Thomas, M. (Eds.) (1993). *Rethinking the roles of technology in education*. Austin: The University of Texas at Austin.
Fiske, J. (1987). *Television culture*. London: Methuen.
Giroux, H., & Simon, R. et al. (1989). *Popular culture, schooling and everyday life*. Toronto: Ontario Institute for Studies in Education Press.
Hodge, B., & Tripp, D. (1986). *Children and television: A semiotic approach*. Oxford: Polity Press.
Morley, D. (1980). *The nationwide audience*. London: British Film Institute.

Turkle, S. (1984). *The second self: Computers and the human spirit.* New York: Simon and Schuster.
Wajcman, J. (1991). *Feminism confronts technology.* Cambridge: Polity Press.
The Weekend Australian. (7/8 August 1993): Editorial, 9.

15

Media Literacy in the Home:
Acquisition versus Deficit Models

Roger Desmond

This chapter presents an argument for media education in the home, supervised by parents and caregivers. Definitional issues in media literacy are reviewed, as is literature that addresses the relationships among television watching by elementary school children and academic achievement. A critical period is posited (from age three to age seven) where heavy television viewing may lead to an erosion of several skills underlying academic achievement. The results of an in home intervention program are presented, which demonstrate the efficacy of "customized" books featuring the names and faces of readers in increasing first and second graders' knowledge of the television industry and awareness of the conventions of TV production. Results are discussed in terms of the future of media education in the United States.

The purpose of this chapter is to explore the concept of media literacy by determining how it has been defined by advocates, educators, and researchers; to assess its potential as a stimulant for further theory and research; and to present preliminary results of a project designed to initiate media education in the home. While issues surrounding the topic are vast, I will confine myself to one important dimension of the concept, the place of entertainment television in the lives of elementary school children, and its hypothesized impact on their academic achievement. While the advocates of education for media literacy express diverse definitions of the concept, a recent conference on the topic at the Aspen Institute yielded a definition that the majority of attendants could support: "A media literate person can decode, evaluate, analyze and produce both print and electronic media" (Hobbs, 1993).

The analysis component of this definition goes beyond simple textual literacy; there is also an ideological aspect as well. Such things as the economic and political climate surrounding the negotiation of meaning are particularly stressed by advocates and scholars outside of the United States (Davis, 1993). The production aspect of the definition suggests that an operational test for literacy is an awareness of the production codes and conventions of each medium. How, for example, the depiction of people *thinking* might be conveyed on television (slow motion, voice over), in radio (the use of "dreamy" music), and in print cartoons (balloons over the heads of thinkers). In one sense, the choice of the term *literacy* for these cognitive skills has added some confusion to research and advocacy in the field; even though print literacy is the mediation of thought by language, there are crucial differences between print literacy and the sub skills required to comprehend a televised narrative. Joshua Meyrowitz states flatly, "Understanding visual symbols has nothing to do with literacy" (Meyrowitz, 1985). To underscore the ease of accessibility of television, he offers evidence from ratings demonstrating that adult programs are enjoyed by children, and vice versa. It is important to note that Meyrowitz uses the term *visual literacy* somewhat interchangeably with media literacy, as do others (Messaris, 1991). Curiously, the medium that has occupied the most attention by researchers and advocates is television, although concern has been expressed regarding video games, film, rock lyrics, and comics (Provenzo, 1991).

Those critics who argue that media literacy is not the same as literacy are correct in their rejection of the issue of metaphoric correspondence; the elusive television isolate, upon first confronting an action adventure, has no linguistic symbols to decode, no letters to recognize, no grammatical rules to master in order to recognize that someone is chasing or being chased. One of the consequences of applying the literacy label is an automatic invocation of print as the logical opposite of video. The opposition emanates from a belief that video experiences displace reading. Regardless of the validity of the claim, there is accumulating evidence of interdependence among media in the construction of narratives by viewers and readers. Marsha Kinder makes a strong argument for interdependence in her study of intertextual relationships among books, television, video games, and film in the construction of the Teenage Mutant Ninja Turtle narrative (Kinder, 1991). Another author suggests that this intertextuality is facilitated by the growing tendency of cross ownership of media: the comic, the movie, and the toy are all made and marketed by the same media agglomerate (Turow, 1992). We can acknowledge differences among media without rejecting the notion of media literacy. If the metaphor has substance, it will emerge in its explanatory power and the extent to which people recognize the problems that gave rise to the metaphor at the outset.

Evidence for the Efficacy of Intervention

There are two components of the definition implicit in the opinions cited earlier: teaching people to be critical consumers of entertainment and advertising fare, and teaching them to gain more insight and information from what they watch. In terms of the former position, a recently developed curriculum for high school students lists at least three general components of television literacy: (1) awareness of one's own relationship with the medium, including awareness of viewing habits and the categories of programming; (2) understanding the television industry and the conventions of television production; and (3) the critical function, including awareness of the stereotypic distortion exhibited by many entertainment programs and the ways in which programming shapes our social customs and attitudes (Singer & Singer, 1992). In a recent survey and evaluation of twenty-six critical viewing intervention and research programs for school children across the world, virtually every effort described embodies one or more of these three dimensions (Brown, 1991). Television is seen as a powerful force that needs counteracting with special training; to be a "critical" viewer is to be well trained in a kind of Deweyan skepticism.

Much less developed is the latter view of media literacy: improving the skills of viewers in extracting more from the content than they typically do. While there has been some recent activity in this realm, the focus has been on those with some type of cognitive impairment, such as learning disabilities or emotional disturbance (Sprafkin, Gadow, & Kant, 1988; Sprafkin, Watkins, & Gadow, 1990). One study of the impact of viewing instructions on retarded adolescents and nonretarded fourth graders found that forewarning them that they would be tested subsequent to their viewing produced no effects, but for both populations, instructions to watch "for fun" resulted in fewer propositions learned from the program than for all other conditions (Raynolds, 1991). While the majority of critical viewing programs have been conducted with children of pre-school or elementary school ages, one educator provided "ideological decoding" training for adults, and concluded that a program in how to "read between the lines" of television portrayals of politics, news events, and social issues was successful in elevating critical viewing skills in college students, but his evidence is entirely anecdotal (Brookfield, 1986). In a more formal investigation, seventh graders demonstrated more extensive learning of content from educational television programs than did controls, using a classroom lecture approach (Von Kolnitz, 1986). The effect was particularly pronounced for students with high intellectual abilities (teacher designated). Taken together, what these studies suggest is that it is *possible* to increase the amount and kind of information that people extract from television; whether these changes transfer to the context of everyday viewing and whether they can overcome earlier resistance to effortful viewing remain as unsolved problems for future research.

In this context the work of Gavriel Salomon and his concept of AIME (Amount of Invested Mental Effort) is relevant; although there is convincing evidence that young viewers' and readers' investment of mental effort mediates what they learn from either source, there is a need to clarify the role of mental effort for a definition of media literacy (Salomon, 1984). The conclusion of several studies suggest that television is often seen by viewers as inherently easier to decipher than print, which is why they expend less effort in viewing, but as one critic points out, researchers often globalize television, ignoring the vast differences among its formats and programs that they would acknowledge with respect to reading (Neuman, 1991).

Mindfulness is another concept that has been studied in regard to effort. When a sample of adult viewers were instructed to watch television from a variety of perspectives they perceived more complexity in plots and characters than did viewers who were told to "just relax" (Langer & Piper, 1988). Mindful viewers also remembered more details than did the mindless viewers. The literate viewer allocates AIME in the necessary amount for the appropriate category of program and learning goal, just as a reader allocates more AIME for a textbook than for a comic. In Langer's terms, literacy is positively related to mindful viewing. Along with the critical function, then, we must include the concept of efficiency in a definition of media literacy: the literate viewer is one who can derive an adequate amount of information from each opportunity.

An additional dimension that has not been addressed in the media literacy literature is the set of skills involved in applying prior knowledge to the content of a film or TV program, and the related skill of applying the fruits of media literacy to world problems. In this regard, viewers and readers confront similar problems: both must be able to apply prior knowledge to a text or program to acquire new meanings, resolve ambiguities, account for missing information, and to determine what schema must be called into play. In the case of a young viewer of crime shows, prior knowledge of a "cops 'n' robbers" script for television programs will determine the amount of novel information that can be acquired (Collins, 1983). In the application of media derived information to social situations, a kind of "editor" is necessary or the cultivation of media-distorted information can occur (Morgan & Gross, 1983). For the heavy viewer of prime time television, the world is exaggerated in many ways— the literate viewer knows the difference between a satire like "The Simpsons" and a documentary about family life. In the majority of school reading programs, the distinction between fantasy and reality is applied much more diligently to books than to film and television.

At this point, our evolving definition of media literacy has grown to five dimensions: (1) awareness of one's own relationship with media; (2) knowledge of how media organizations shape their fare, and the conventions of production for each; (3) a critical ideological awareness; (4) the role of effortfulness; and (5) relationships among prior knowledge, media comprehension, and the "real" world. As Brown's (1991) survey reveals, existing critical viewing programs for children have concentrated much more on the first three than on the last two.

Rationales For Media Literacy Interventions

As Brown's (1991) review of the critical viewing programs of the 1970s and 1980s illustrates, the majority were established along definitional lines one through three. Since they grew out of a fear of television related child deficiencies, I shall designate their collective properties as the *deficit* model of media literacy. In light of the expansionist connotation in definition elements four and five, these will be designated as the *acquisition* model of the concept. The primary rationales for intervention that have been invoked under the deficit model are:

1. Television erodes academically related skills including reading ability, concentration, and attention.
2. Television watching causes aggression.
3. Entertainment television is the source of sexual and ethnic stereotypes.

4. Advertising elicits poor consumer habits in children, including the adoption of "junk" foods, and renders them extremely susceptible to advertising claims.

Rationales for an acquisition model are less evident; there is a growing number of academics who believe that people could learn to gain more from TV viewing than they do now. The work of Salomon, as interpreted earlier in the discussion of effortfulness, is certainly suggestive as an impetus for a new kind of intervention.

In terms of the first rationale, which concerns the erosion of academic skills, an extensive and contradictory literature exists on this problem. The most consistent finding is a negative correlation between TV viewing by school-age children, with a magnitude of slight to moderate (Reinking & Wu, 1990). In an exhaustive review of this research, Comstock and Paik (1991) conclude, "There is no question that the amount of time spent viewing television by American children and teenagers is negatively associated with their academic performance" (86). Later, they attribute causality to key variables in the equation: "The evidence supports a three factor process in which large amounts of viewing not only (a) displace skill acquisition but also (b) interferes with further practice, or skill development and maintenance, and (c) lower the quality or value by decreased capacity of practice done in conjunction with television (136).

Beyond mere displacement and reduced practice capability issues, there are other sources of concern surrounding issues in academic achievement. Among the numerous methodological problems that recur in the measurement of the relationship of environmental factors to academic achievement is that few studies have examined children's pre reading learning before first grade; Singer et al. (1988) found that kindergartners and first graders who were heavy viewers of television were less capable early readers one year later than were their lighter viewing counterparts, even when variables such as S.E.S. and I.Q. were controlled for. In short, the real damage done by television may very well occur *before children begin school, and are therefore masked by the assumption of initial equality at grade one.* In a review of television viewing and skills associated with reading, two scholars argue that heavy viewing may operate to decrease attention focusing, increase impulsiveness, and discourage task persistence in young viewers, which they label as "concentration deprivation" (Beentjies & van der Voort, 1991). Impulsiveness and task persistence have been studied in an interrupted time series experiment; six year olds whose viewing was reduced demonstrated decreased impulsiveness during a six week period (Gadberry, 1980). Less perseverance has been found after a long in school viewing period (Salomon, 1984). Children's ability to wait quietly is negatively associated with heavy viewing, particularly when viewing was not mediated by parents or teachers (Singer, Singer, & Rapazynski, 1984; Singer, et al., 1988). The term *concentration deprivation* is frustrating because it connotes a general mindlessness resulting from prolonged viewing, for which there is scant evidence. It is clear that the several sub skills outlined above are part of the concept concentration, but there are other areas of concern. Among these is the preschooler's ability to visualize characters and events in a written or spoken story in a manner that allows for memory, reflection, and internalization.

In other words, the child may begin to "frame" narratives in a televisionlike manner, where *events* are more important than motives or the inner states of characters in stories. An ongoing study of children's story comprehension suggests that six year olds who saw audiovisually presented stories based more inferences about the story on characters' appearance and actions than did those who read stories (Brown, 1988). It is clear that the possibility of "narrative deprivation" needs further investigation. A large part of reading comprehension is the ability to reflect on the events and inner states of actors in a story, and as Singer has suggested, the pace of television does not allow much time for reflection (Singer, 1983). There is also evidence of a tendency for "scripted" television viewing to interfere with comprehension of viewing (Collins, 1983). Finally, in a three-year panel study of children aged six through nine, the heaviest viewers of television comprehended less of a program immediately after viewing than did lighter viewers, and this effect continued throughout the second year of the study. When the sample was analyzed after year one, the relationship between viewing and comprehension was the most pronounced (Singer, et. al., 1988). Taken together, these results suggest that heavy viewing during a hypothesized critical period (from age three to age six) may have negative implications for both television and reading story comprehension. Until there is more research directed at the early reader viewer, the bulk of evidence points to television viewing as one of several factors in the decline of reading comprehension in the past decade. As has been argued for viewing and aggression, it is also important to consider the aspects of these relationships that may be masked in the aggregation of results and debates over effect sizes; one disruptive child in a classroom may produce a chain reaction of tremendous import for the entire class (Kubey, 1992). Similarly, one poor reader may demand inordinate amounts of time from a teacher at the expense of other students.

Aggression

Although the primary rationale for American intervention programs has been television's potential impact on learning and achievement, there are other areas where the dual-edged sword of criticism and enhancement of learning have been applied. Aggression is one candidate for modification of television effects; the majority of critical viewing programs have attempted to heighten children's awareness of the unreality and inherent danger of televised aggression. One intervention that has been praised because of its focus on media depicted aggression and its consequences for imitation is Huesmann's program (Huesmann et al., 1983), but even in light of his success, he warns about the intractibility of aggressive media content. In light of the persistence of the viewing aggression relationship in young heavy viewers, there is no evidence or reason to believe that an in school intervention will reduce the magnitude of the association.

Sex Role and Ethnic Stereotyping

Other areas where arguments for effective intervention have been advanced include gender and ethnic stereotyping. Virtually all of the critical viewing programs in Brown's (1991) survey address gender and race issues, but again, from a deficit or protectionist perspective. In the case of both gender and ethnicity, we can say that virtually every intervention program reviewed has demonstrated gains in awareness of television stereotypes and stereotypic and inaccurate portrayals. As is also the case with every program, we cannot say whether these gains persist beyond the few days, hours, or weeks in their evaluation periods, or whether children transfer these lessons to everyday viewing.

Advertising Awareness

The same conclusion is true of advertising, but there have been many more programs with similar results: impressive but short term gains.

Several studies have shown increased awareness of and cynicism about advertising claims and persuasive strategies as a function of classroom interventions (Anderson, 1980). Advertising is so ubiquitous and such a common viewing experience for young children that lessons that address it are relatively simple to formulate, and are intuitively attractive to advocates of critical thinking.

Clearly, the most research attention under the deficit model in American media systems has been devoted to the relationships among TV viewing and academic achievement. While other dimensions of media literacy are present in numerous intervention programs, it is in the viewing-learning dimension where we can say that there is unequivocal support for some type of program to correct the deficit.

Who Should Intervene?

An assumption that dominates the literature on media literacy and education is that the classroom is the most appropriate place where instruction should occur. Virtually every intervention program has taken place in a school setting; paradoxically, it is teachers and administrators who have historically been the opponents of media literacy instruction in the United States. As one journalism educator frames the issue: "Part of the reason that media education is largely absent in this country is that there are many demands for curricular attention in the public schools, and media studies is often seen either as a frill or as an extracurricular activity best conducted as adjunct to the classroom, say on the school paper" (Dennis, 1993). A frequent complaint from school administrators is that if media literacy is instituted, something else that is important will have to be subtracted from the curriculum.

There is also a relatively large literature that concerns the role of parents and siblings in the mediation of television (Abelman, 1987; Desmond, Singer, & Singer, 1990). The most outstanding conclusion of this research is that parental styles of discipline (both generally and television specific) are powerful determinants of the amount of television that children watch and the extent to which they imitate its content. There is also evidence that family communication patterns about television reinforce certain aspects of content learning (Singer, et al., 1988). Finally, older siblings provide information regarding television programs (Morgan, Alexander, & Shanahan, 1990). Apart from research evidence supporting the value of family communication in mediating television's effects, there are pragmatic arguments for parents as teachers of media literacy: the home environment provides for extended learning and repetition of content that geometrically exceeds available classroom time; parents have the means and the authority to limit and restrict television viewing by their children; and finally, parents are aware of the specific behaviors that their children exhibit across the parts of their day.

An Investigation of a Media Literacy Intervention in the Home

In light of issues raised in the previous review, I created an intervention and an evaluation of the program which was designed to provide for early media education in the home. The program was developed for first and second grade children in an inner city environment where resources for classroom media study were unavailable. The goal was to provide for parent child interaction about television throughout one semester, with a minimum of teacher involvement. The specific goals of the study were:

1. To assess the state of children's knowledge about four dimensions of media literacy: The reality of entertainment television, knowledge of television terminology, awareness of the conventions of film and television production, and awareness of advertising techniques.
2. In light of the evaluation, to create a series of take home story books that would feature the individual reader as a character in a drama or narrative that would provide attractive and highly salient vehicles for specific lessons in these selected areas of media literacy.
3. To evaluate the efficacy of these story books over the span of one semester.
4. To initiate some components of media education based on an acquisition model.

One weakness of the majority of early media education (critical viewing) programs is that they employed short term pretest posttest designs that would only measure immediate recall of lessons. Another is that the typical stimulus for intervention was a series of classroom demonstration/lectures, or specially produced videos that provided limited child input and parent-child interaction in the home, where most TV viewing takes place. I developed the customized books for a previous project with Head Start children, and found that children of this age love to see and read about themselves and their friends in a colorfully illustrated story book that belonged to them.

The Sample

Seventy three children (thirty male, forty-three female) were recruited from an inner city Philadelphia public school; approximately 80 percent of the children were African American, the remainder were Asian or Caucasian. Forty children were first graders; thirty-three were in second grade.

Study Design and Procedures

The design was a pretest/posttest field investigation with a control group. Test groups were drawn from three classes; one group each of first and second graders were given stimulus books, and a control group of first and second graders were given nonpersonalized books. Pretests were administered to all participants in September, 1992. Three books were presented to students in October, November, and December. Posttests were administered in February of 1993.

Test items. Pretests/posttests had four sections:

1. Perceived Reality—A ten-item scale was used that had previously demonstrated adequate reliability in a large scale study of children of this age group (Van Der Voort, 1991). Example: "In cartoon shows on television, sometimes you see a Ninja Turtle throw someone ten feet into the air. Can very strong men do that in real life too?" Responses are coded "yes," "no," or "sometimes".
2. Television Knowledge—A six-item index used in a previous longitudinal study measured children's understanding of television terminology and key concepts such as audio and video, animation, props, advertising, and the like. This multiple-response index has predicted more global awareness of television with a similar population (Singer, et al., 1988).
3. How Television Works—Five open ended questions tapped children's understanding of special effects, for example, "How do TV programs make a building look taller or shorter than it really is?" This was employed in several longitudinal studies, and has been found to be correlated with actual comprehension of TV programs that children watch (Desmond, et al., 1990).
4. Knowledge of Commercials—This ten-item index has been used in several long term investigations, and has been found to be a good predictor of advertising comprehension, using a variety of indicators (Singer, Singer & Rapaczynski, 1982). Example, "Does 'batteries not included' mean you have to buy the batteries yourself?"

Personalized books. Each child was provided with three books concerning how television "works" to achieve meaning. In light of pretest results, I endeavored to produce stories that incorporated those aspects of media education that were most deficient in the sample, and one book that represented an attempt to embody the acquisition model by suggesting that TV programs could be investigated through library research and through interaction with adults.

Book one was *Watch with Care,* which presented a scenario of a show and tell day in the classroom, and focused on one child who was disappointed with a toy she had ordered as a result of watching a commercial. Her disappointment stems from the fact that the toy is much smaller than it looked on TV. The teacher explains the concept of "close up" camera shots by showing the children how a close up zoom lens can magnify objects. This lesson inspires children to make their own commercial in a class skit for a kite called "Superkite." In the voice over, the narrator says that the kite can fly higher and faster than an airplane. The teacher suggests that such exaggeration is tempting when advertising a product, and that care must be exercised when evaluating any commercial.

Book two is titled *A Battle in the Neighborhood,* and opens with a visit from a documentary film maker who has produced a program about a revolutionary war battle. Children inquired about how the characters appeared to get shot and bleed, and the excitement of the battle. The director explains how she used props such as artificial blood and smoke machines to add authenticity to the battle. She invites the children and their teacher to her studio, where they see demonstrations of editing and special effects, and they see how camera angles can influence judgments of size and importance.

The third book, *Watch and Look it Up,* opens with two children watching a program on the Discovery channel that depicted dolphins and dolphin communication. At school the next day the children ask their teacher if dolphins can really "talk." She suggests that they go to the library and find information about the subject, which they do. This leads to a discussion of the fantasy-reality dimension of other things they have seen on TV, such as werewolves, unicorns, and flying horses. Throughout this story, the importance of verifying information through a variety of sources is stressed.

Each book was twelve pages, with high-quality illustrations. The opening page featured illustrated images of each child in the class. Books were distributed in school, and a survey of parents revealed that the mean number of parent child readings was 3.44 over a four-month interval. Parent acceptance was high, with nearly 100 percent agreeing that the books elicited discussions about the topics.

Results

Difference scores from pretest to posttest were computed with a series of one way anovas using grade levels as independent variables; dependent measures were the four indices outlined above. In terms of perceived reality, no significant between group differences were found. Inspection of group means revealed slight gains for all groups.

Television knowledge, a measure that reflects awareness of the television industry and terms associated with general television knowledge, was significantly increased beyond controls for second graders ($F = 4.91$, $d.f. = 2.57, p < .01$) but not for first graders. Group means are displayed in table 15.1:

TABLE 15.1
Mean Change Scores for All Dependent Measures

Variable	First Grade	Second Grade	Control (First and Second Grade)
Perceived Reality	.77	1.01	.93
Television Knowledge (General)	1.46	4.39*	.63
Knowledge of TV Production	.39	2.52*	1.21
Commercial Knowledge	.88	1.11	1.32

* (significantly differs from controls, $p<.05$)

Knowledge of television production was also increased by personalized books ($F=4.67, d.f.=2, 62$, $p<.01$) for second graders, but not for first graders. There were no significant gains for the measure of advertising awareness in any condition.

Discussion

In light of the stated objectives of the intervention, there is reason to pronounce it a qualified success. Two of the four dimensions of media literacy were significantly increased by take-home materials with no classroom explanation or exercise. Results for both general knowledge of the

TV industry and awareness of the conventions of television production were most pronounced for students in the second grade. Reasons for the age-grade advantage center on the relationships among print literacy, media literacy, and the development of critical thinking. A large body of literature suggests that children of this age begin to exhibit evidence of internalization of abstraction, increased speaking, reading and writing ability, and nonelicited question asking during the seventh and eighth year of life (Sprafkin, et al., 1992).

Each of the three books represented an attempt to improve childrens' ability to distinguish television reality from fantasy. There is no evidence that suggests that this goal was realized. In this sample, initial scores on the reality measure were quite low; a follow up question was asked at the pretest stage, "If someone gets shot on TV, do they really die?" Thirty-four percent of the first graders and 19 percent of the second graders answered, "Yes," although some who said "yes" would say, "but they come back to life." It is clear that at this stage of development, conceptions of TV reality are in flux. There is probably no at home intervention that can significantly accelerate this process for children of this age, although there is evidence that for older children, an extended classroom curriculum can increase this cognitive skill (Sprafkin, et al., 1990).

The results for the perception of advertising are disappointing; one book dealt specifically with a commercial theme, yet there was no appreciable gain in consumer sophistication in these children. Again, this aspect of television awareness may be better achieved in a classroom environment, with some "hands on" exercises. Nevertheless, in future home interventions, more emphasis will be given to this dimension, as it lends itself to personalized narratives.

The gains that were achieved using this approach did not come from the content of the books alone; reports from parents indicate that these materials *initiated* family conversations about television, that in turn led to heightened awareness during subsequent TV viewing. It is possible that this process increases metacognitive strategies for understanding the world of television (Desmond, et al., 1990). While this research did not probe amount of viewing or content discrimination, future research should look at the impact of family talk on critical viewing. The fact that even controls gained in knowledge is important; controls got the same essential stories as test subjects. While it would have been ideal to have a "no treatment" control, there were simply not enough children or resources to include one; it was important to test the personalization dimension because if the controls gained equally, the cost of delivery of these books would have been vastly reduced. It is apparent from these results that it is the personalization that made parents and children want to spend time reading them. There is every reason to believe that personalized texts will prove effective in other domains of learning such as health, values, social studies, or in any domain of knowledge where parental interaction might make a difference.

The Future of Media Literacy

The discussion of the intervention described above does not represent an argument to shift media literacy from the school to the home. Instead, they are offered in support of a multifaceted strategy for achieving the objective. A child who is exposed to one of the excellent school curricula that now exists and who brings the discussion home has a better chance of understanding the medium of television than a child who is exposed to a singular approach. If the hypothesis of the critical period outlined earlier is correct, the school home "united front" is vital for children in the first two grades. But what of the implementation of an acquisition model alluded to in the introduction to this chapter? The book titled *Watch and Look it Up* represents a preliminary attempt to implement this model. Ultimate goals for young children are to stimulate a consumer to conduct research for further information about a topic seen on television; provide "templates" for guided viewing; suggest guidelines for evaluating news stories and documentaries; to elicit questions for parents, teachers, and caregivers concerning what is seen and is not seen on entertainment television; and in general, provide for ongoing interactions between television and other sources of information and entertainment.

Presently, a number of school systems in the United States use Whittle's Channel One in the classroom as a source of current events information for high school and junior high school students. It is fashionable in some educational or scholarly circles to attack Channel One for its superficial coverage of international news, its consumer orientation, and most of all, its package of commercials for jeans, acne remedies, and fast foods. An acquisition model lesson plan for Channel One could be an assignment that will invite viewers to suggest what stories are not likely to be covered on the program, or to suggest how the program would be seen by teenagers in Costa Rica, or any emerging economy. In short, the acquisition model represents an attempt to elevate mental effort by reframing existing media content and thereby elevating mental effort during viewing. Conversely, inviting students to create a video script for an important novel will elevate attention to reading in order to retell the essential elements of the story in a visual mode. Visualizing great literature is certainly the goal of many an English teacher in contemporary American classrooms.

Moving beyond the American model, Canada and Australia have implemented significant programs of media education. Their successful implementation is one factor in the development of a media literacy movement in the United States, led primarily by educators with occasional support by television networks and cable operators, and PBS affiliates in the larger cities. The major difference between the path to implementation in the U.S. and other countries is that in the U.S., there is far less consensus among the scholarly community for a need for media literacy intervention, and paradoxically, there is a greater reliance on the academic community for approval of such programs. The result is that grant proposal approvals and endorsements for the activists from the research community have not been forthcoming. One important reason for this tension is that media educational activists have focused on the deficit model, promoting their programs as prophylactics for a host of diseases that have not been supported by existing media research. There is no doubt, however, that media literacy as an educational movement is "in the air." In 1992 alone there were numerous national and international conferences on the topic; two at the Annenberg School For Communication at the University of Pennsylvania, and at the Aspen Institute in Maryland, in Guelph, Canada, and Bitburg, Germany.

What is clear from the interactions of researchers and activists at these meetings is that the goals of the groups have been so different, and their educations have differed so much, that necessary dialogue among them will be a long time coming. One issue that has the potential to unite them is the temporary abandonment of the deficit model, and a shift toward an acquisition model.

One problem inherent in such a shift is that the deficit model gets good press; media literacy activists are the first to admit that public fear of negative media effects is a politically correct entry into program acceptance by school administrators and parents (Davis, 1992). Ultimately, an acquisition model would provide a framework for questions regarding issues such as: (1) transfer of information to new contexts—how lessons from home entertainment and in school viewing are or could be applied to other domains of learning; (2) mental effort—how can viewers, listeners, or users of cd rom, electronic games, and the like be stimulated to allocate more effort and attention to important content?; and (3) can visual media production synthesize knowledge from other forms (e.g., scriptwriting elicits the author's research for script detail), which in turn may lead to reading skill and practice? These and other issues related to skill and information acquisition have the potential to unite the concerns of researchers, educators, and activists in ways that may prove fruitful for both producers and consumers of education.

What Research is Necessary?

The controversy surrounding the deficit model makes it a central priority for further research. The summary of work in the relationships among television viewing and academic achievement cited earlier suggests that what we specifically do not need are more cross sectional, correlational studies of relationships among leisure tv viewing, reading, and virtually every other indicator of scholastic achievement. Those data are in. What is necessary are some investigations that can assess the size of these relationships for significant population subgroups, and most important, nail down or at least disambiguate causality. A beginning step would be some longitudinal work. Earlier in this chapter a hypothesized critical period was invoked in an attempt to resolve some consistent lines of investigation into the relationships among media use and task persistence, practice in reading, math, and other areas which may result in lowered abilities at later ages, where most of the current research is concentrated. If, as Anderson (1992) speculates, "It is possible that because young children find tv viewing easier than reading, that tv viewing displaces small but crucial amounts of leisure reading at the most critical ages" (9), it is imperative that a time series design with data points across the pre-school years into grade three be employed. The work of Gadberry (1980) demonstrates the possibility that this work can be done, but her interrupted time-series analysis focussed on only a few weeks of restricted viewing.

Huesmann and Eron's (1986) investigation (over twenty years between measurements) of early viewing and aggression demonstrates the "pay-off" of a longitudinal approach, but what is needed to resolve the causal role of early TV viewing is more frequent measurement of a difficult to-measure population in the most formative of years.

A second area of research concerns the entire notion of passivity; as Anderson (1992) points out, we lack a conceptual definition of this state, therefore pioneering efforts at conceptualization and operationalization are necessary. Passive viewing is one of the key elements of the deficit model in lay circles and popular writing; as such, it has been used to justify a need for media literacy. Even as a fuzzy concept, it is integrally linked with a number of important issues in cognition. It is possible that ultimately, a psychophysiological approach could yield a proxy, but early efforts have not paid off.

Among other gaps in our knowledge about television's relationship to education that were discussed earlier in the context of established knowledge is the issue of amount of viewing. It has seldom been adequately measured, but even with differential measures, it has traditionally been an independent variable. As such, the use of it has yielded a number of qualifiers of negative effects based on heavy viewing; even skeptics such as Neuman (1991) allow that it is heavy viewers who suffer the greatest deficit. If one of the goals of media literacy is to reduce the deficit, it is imperative that research designs examine the impact of viewer training on amount and kind of viewing. There is an implicit assumption in the media literacy movement that critical viewing can alter everyday patterns of viewing, but little evidence for or against the assumption. Previous work suggests that the context most amenable to viewing modification is the family (Bryant, 1990). The role of the family in mediating television comprehension and enjoyment has long been investigated in the traditions of effects research, phenomenological and cultural studies, but is seldom discussed with respect to media literacy. Since the viewing done at home is the major concern of the deficit arguments, the role of the family context in reinforcing and originating media education is crucial. What is needed are methods of providing systems models of media education, and theoretically sound evaluations of those methods.

The research agenda for the acquisition model is far less certain. As noted earlier, the issue of transfer is salient for educators and researchers: transfer of insights and information from television to other domains of knowledge, transfer of world knowledge to television, and transfer of media education from schools to everyday viewing. An important initial effort might examine the benefits of television scriptwriting as an exercise and as a measure of learning. Are scripts generated by the media educated richer, more complex, more informative, more "visually literate" than those written by untrained writers? With respect to education issues, would a term paper be written and researched with more quality and thoroughness if it were assigned as a documentary script?

The majority of forecasts regarding the future of media in the past few decades have fared miserably, primarily because they were made in the economic "blue sky" of the 1950s and 1960s, when all things were possible (Desmond & Jassem, 1986). In the harsher light of the current global economy, poorly designed and administered programs of media literacy will go the way of marching bands and instruction in the arts—"extras" quickly and easily sliced from school budgets. Those that survive will require hard data on effectiveness from the research community, a difficult requirement in light of the schisms between researchers and educator advocates presented earlier. A great deal depends upon whether some good research is forthcoming; earlier suggestions represent a few possibilities, but theory building of the amount and kind witnessed in the search for connections between television and aggression or advertising and social behavior are necessary. In the past twenty years, a number of models of the processes were developed, competition among them was partially resolved, new branches of the effects framework emerged, and just recently, recommendations have been heeded to some extent as evidenced by the Children's Television Act of 1990. If the same sort of concentrated labor is exhibited by investigators of media literacy, the necessary funds, coordination of efforts, and concomitant publicity may provide support for media education from all of its many constituencies.

References

Abelman, R. (1987). Child giftedness and its role in the parental mediation of television viewing. *Roeper Review, 9* (4), 217–226.

Anderson, D. R. (May 1992). Television, children and education: Issues for research. Paper presented to the Annenberg Conference on Television and Education, Philadelphia.

Anderson, D. R., & Collins, P. A. (1988). *The influence of children's education: The effects of television on cognitive development.* Washington, D.C.: U.S. Department of Education.

Anderson, J. (1980). The theoretical lineage of critical viewing curricula. In J. Bryant & D. Anderson (Eds.), *Children's understanding of television* (297–330). New York: Academic Press.

Beentjies, J. W., & van der Voort, T. H. (1991). Children's written accounts of tele-vised and written stories. *Educational Research and Development, 39*: 15–26.

Brookfield, S. (1986). Media power and the development of media literacy: An adult educational interpretation. *Harvard Educational Review, 56* (2), 151–70.

Brown, J. A. (1991). *Television critical viewing skills education.* Hillsdale, N.J.: Erlbaum.

Bryant, J. (1990). Introduction. *Television and the American family.* Hillsdale, N.J.: Erlbaum.

Collins, W. A. (1983). Interpretation and inference in childrens' television viewing. In J. Bryant, & D. R. Anderson (Eds.). *Childrens' understanding of television* (125–50). New York: Academic Press.

Comstock, G., & Paik, H. (1991). *Television and the American child.* Los Angeles: Academic Press.

Davis, J. (1993). Media literacy: From activism to exploration. Paper presented to the National Leadership Conference on Media Literacy, Aspen Institute, Queenstown, Md.

Dennis, E. E. (15 April 1993). Fighting media illiteracy. Lecture to the School of Journalism, Indiana University.

Desmond, R. J., & Jassem, H. C. (1986). Mass communication theory and new me-dia: assumptions in light of technical change. In B. Ruben (Ed.), *Information and behavior.* New Brunswick, N.J.: Transaction Publishers.

Desmond, R. J., Singer, J. L., & Singer, D. G. (1990). Family parental communica-tion patterns and television influence on children. In J. Bryant, (Ed.). *Television and the American family.* Hillsdale, N.J: Erlbaum.

Gadberry, S. (1980). Effects of restricting first graders' TV viewing on leisure time, I.Q. change and cognitive style. *Journal of Applied Developmental Psychology, 1,* 161–76.

Gadow, K. D., Sprafkin, J., Kelly, E., & Ficarotto, T. (1988). Reality perceptions of television: a comparison of school-labelled learning disabled and non-handicapped children. *Journal of Clinical Child Psychology 17,* 25–33.

Greenberg, B., & Reeves, B. (1976). Children and the perceived reality of television. *Journal of Social Issues 32,* 86–97.

Hobbs, R. (1993). Defining media literacy. Presentation to the Aspen Institute Na-tional Leadership Conference On Media Literacy: Queenstown, Md.

Huesmann, L. R., & Eron, L. D. (1986). *Television and the aggressive child: A cross-cultural perspective.* Hillsdale, N.J.: Erlbaum.

Huesmann, L. R., Eron, L. D., Klein, R., & Fischer, P. (1983). Mitigating the imita-tion of aggressive behaviors by changing children's attitudes about media vio-lence. *Journal of Personality and Social Psychology 44* (5), 899–910.

Kinder, M. (1991). *Playing with power in movies, television, and video games.* Ber-keley: University of California Press.

Kubey, R. (20 November 1992). Personal communication.

Kubey, R., & Csikszentmihalyi, M. (1990). *Television and the quality of life: How viewing shapes everyday experience.* Hillsdale, N.J: Erlbaum.

Langer, E., & Piper, A. (1988). Television from a mindful/mindless perspective. In S. Oskamp (Ed.). *Television as a social issue* (247–60). Beverly Hills, Calif.: Sage.

McMahon, M., & Quin, R. (1992). Knowledge, power, and pleasure: Directions in media education. Paper presented to the Second North American Conference on Media Education, Guelph, Ontario.

McLuhan, M. (1964). *Understanding media: The extensions of man.* New York: McGraw-Hill.

Messaris, P. (1991). Visual literacy: What is it? How do we measure it? Paper presented to the Fifth Annual Visual Literacy Conference: Breckenridge, Colo.

————. (In press). Does TV belong in the classroom? Cognitive consequences of visual "literacy." *Communication Yearbook 17.*

Meyrowitz, J. (1985). *No sense of place: The impact of electronic media on social behavior.* New York: Oxford.

Morgan, M., & Gross, L. (1983). Television viewing, I.Q. and academic achievement. *Journal of Broadcasting 24,* 117–33.

Morgan, M., Alexander, A., & Shanahan, J. (1990). Adolescents, VCR's and the family environment. *Communication Research 17,* 83–106.

Neuman, S. (1991). *Literacy in the television age: The myth of the TV effect.* Norwood, N.J: Ablex.

Provenzo, E. (1991). *Video kids: Making sense of Nintendo.* Cambridge: Harvard University Press.

Raynolds, C. T. (1991). The effects of viewing instructions on the recall of a television story by mildly retarded and nonretarded individuals. E.D.D. dissertation, Columbia University.

Reinking, D., & Wu, J. H. (1990). Reexamining the research on tv and reading. *Reading Research Quarterly 29,* 30–43.

Salomon, G. (1984). TV is easy and print is tough: The role of perceptions and attributions in the processing of material. *Journal of Educational Psychology 76,* 647–58.

Singer, D. G., & Singer, J. L. (1992). *Creating critical viewers.* Denver: Pacific Mountain Network.

Singer, J. L. (1983). Psychologists look at television: Cognitive, developmental, personality and social policy. *American Psychologist 38,* 826–34.

Singer, J. L., Singer, D. G., Desmond, R. J., Hirsch, B., & Nicol, A. (1988). Family mediation and childrens' comprehension of television: A longitudinal study. *Journal of Applied Developmental Psychology 9,* 117–40.

Singer, J. L., Singer, D. G., & Radaczynski, W. S. (1984). Family patterns and television viewing as predictors of children's beliefs and aggression. *Journal of Communication 34,* 72–89.

Sprafkin, J., Gadow, K., & Kant, J. (1987–88). Teaching emotionally disturbed children to discriminate reality from fantasy on television. *Journal of Special Education 21,* 99–107.

Sprafkin, J., Watkins, L., & Gadow, K. (1990). Efficacy of a television curriculum for emotionally disturbed and learning disabled children. *Journal of Applied Developmental Psychology 11,* 225–44.

Sprafkin, J., Gadow, K., & Abelman, R. (1992). *Television and the exceptional child.* Hillsdale, N.J.: Erlbaum.

Turow, J. (1992). Story telling in the age of media synergy. Paper presented to the Second International Media Ecology Conference: Mainz, Germany.

Van Der Voort, T. H. (1991). Children's written accounts of televised and written stories. *Educational Research and Development 39,* 15–26.

Von Kolnitz, D. (1986). The effect of critical television on the performance of seventh grade students. Ph.D. Dissertation, University of South Carolina.

Williams, T. M. (1986). *The impact of television: A natural experiment in three communities.* New York: Academic Press.

16

In Favor of "Bad News": An Experiment in Teaching the Role of the Press in Israel[1]

Tamar Liebes

This chapter documents the design and the trying out of a project for teaching the role of an autonomous and critical press (and electronic media) in a democratic society. The teaching focuses not on the importance of "higher values" such as freedom of speech and the publics' right to know, but on the functionality of public criticism for the existence and well-being of the society. The project described here is one in a series of projects for teaching media literacy experientially, planned by a team of communication researchers in Jerusalem, headed by Professor Elihu Katz, and based on the principle of building on students' existing skills and knowledge, in an attempt to expand these skills to less famil-iar realms. The project both proves the hypothesis that children understand the function of critical exposure in their own school society, and arouses awareness for their tendency to deny the legitimacy of public opposition—that of an anti-establishment press—in the larger society. Students are actively engaged in playing journalists and, more important, in having to account for the implicit criteria they have used for the selection of particular sources and news items. The context of media literacy proves efficient for the studying of the principles of active citizenship in democracy.

School curricula tend to discriminate against teaching the role played by the mass media and the press in democratic societies. Programs for the study of mass media do not usually involve democracy, and the role of mass media in modern democracies is marginal to the teaching of the role of citizenship in democracy (Katz, 1992). This separation leads to forget-ting the essential and necessary link between the two, expressed by the principles of the right (and the duty) of citizens to know, and the freedom of expression of different opinions over which the press is in charge.

This segregation between democracy and communication in the school curriculum arises from ascribing democracy to the study of political science and history, and communication to the study of the popular art. Thus, the principles of pluralism, opposition, and freedom of expression (incorporated in the curricula in the study of the role of citizen), tend to be demonstrated in class on an interpersonal level, on the assumption that the principles *that* operate in society may be acted out within a small group. The study of the mass media, on the other hand, ignores the crucial function of the media and the press in providing an anti-establishment voice in democracy, focusing instead on the more glamorous cinematic and televisual drama and on the generation of creative activities.

Analyzing the news is also perceived as too close to politics, and therefore the teachers are wary of it. When teachers do engage directly in analyzing the messages of press and television, the aim is to "protect" the students from manipulation by the mass media who are selling the viewers class, ethnic, and gender stereotypes, life styles and social ideals (Gitlin, 1980; Hall, 1985).

The loss in focusing on the exposure of media manipulation in programs of media literacy is the reinforcing of the public's existing suspicion and discreditation of television and press reporting, and of the journalists themselves. At a time when journalists, not to mention television reporters, operate under constantly increasing heavy pressures which, in turn, create a continuous erosion of the concept of objectivity of journalistic reporting, the challenge is to advocate the independence of journalism without delegitimizing the profession as such.

The particular form that the pressure on the press is taking in Israel at present is more similar to the situation in the United States than it has been in the past. Up to now, pressures on the press freedom were mainly political, with the government and the military establishment trying to control the journalists, often under the guise of worrying about the potential for compromising Israel's security (Goren, 1976; Negbi, 1985). The commercial pressures of competition for advertising, and of monopoly ownership, have hit only recently, with the drastic change in Israel's communication environment. The explosion of local papers, the closing down of ideological and minority papers, and the introduction of cable television and a second public television channel have forced serious newspapers and the BBC-like first public channel to compete with tabloids and local news, and with television drama. At the same time, the concentration of media ownership—with three families in control of the second channel as well as the major newspapers—introduces a new threat to journalistic freedom of expression (Caspi & Limor, 1993).

This process of ever growing commercialization of the media everywhere makes for a greater temptation for media literacy teachers to concentrate on the raising of consciousness to "how they manipulate us"—pointing to cases of inexactitudes, breach of the individual's right to privacy, sensationalism in reporting, and over dramatizing. This is throwing out the baby with the bath water by pulling away the public support on which the press relies, and adding to the risk to the survival of a free and critical press, which, in spite of its weaknesses, continues to serve the public's interest.

In other words, what is lacking is educating for the value of opposition and of criticism in a democratic society, represented by the concepts of parliamentarism and free press (Mosse, 1975). The objective is to bring about a legitimization of the press through the acknowledgement that the press and the mass media are the realization of the public's right, and duty, to know.

What complicates the situation for teachers and students is that the public's suspicion of the press arises not only, not even especially, in cases when the media fails to do its job (and there is no lack of such cases), but in cases when it does (Liebes and Ribak, 1991a & b). The phenomenon (in no way limited to Israel, as shown in the American film "Medium Cool") is expressed by the nationalistic bumper-sticker campaign "the people against hostile media," which challenges the right of the media to question the presumed consensus. True, it is not pleasant to see on television an angry mass attacking Arab passers-by in the Jerusalem market, following a terrorist attack, or for American viewers to watch an American air attack on a civilian shelter in Baghdad. Some of the viewers prefer not to watch, arguing that such behavior is not representative of "normal" reality (Liebes, 1992). But this expectation of the mass media to reflect what is "normal" or normative—whether genuinely naive or hypocritical—fails to recognize one of the media's main functions; it ignores the media's role in exposing exactly those events which *are* exceptions, or which do deviate from the rule in order to prevent the recurrence of deviations and thereby to reaffirm (in some cases to reflect over, and change) the norms (Lazarsfeld & Merton, 1971). Showing "bad news" on television is, therefore, not meant to undermine society, but to serve the public's interest by warning against the abuse of power, and thereby acting as a control mechanism over the government, the military, or other centers of power.

Paradoxically, educating for seeing through media manipulation, therefore, may protect the establishment against criticism, and play into the public's wish for blindly trusting the government. In such cases the public's urge to escape from freedom is channelled into hostility against the media exactly when it is not manipulated by the establishment.

Educating for the Value of Opposition through Media Literacy

Education for the principles of democracy under the label of "communication" has an advantage over other kinds of programs for the study of democracy. Communication raises the students' interest and curiosity; democracy is more of a problem. The experience of headmasters and teachers, and of bodies who initiated programs for the study of democratic principles, shows that abstract discussions don't work, and that sometimes students develop antagonism toward what seems to them like empty slogans.

In what follows I will describe a pilot project, developed by a team of communication researchers in Jerusalem headed by Professor Elihu Katz,[2] designed with two purposes in mind. The first was to study the degree to which adolescents in Israel understand the function of opposition in general, and the function of a critical press in particular. The second was to develop a teaching tool for learning the function of a critical press (including electronic journalism) in democracy.

The project is one in a series of experiential projects in media literacy, all of which draw on the existing resources and capabilities of the students, and apply these to areas in which the students are less well equipped. In its present form, the project described in this chapter is designed for high school students (aged fourteen through eighteen), and was tried in a number of schools. It requires work in groups, with group leaders trained for the program, and is based in every stage on the active participation of the students.

The Educational Aims of the Project

The program attempts to teach two principles. The first is the functionality of criticism. The idea is to focus not on the abstract principle of the freedom of the press, but on its usefulness for the existence and well-being of the society, what is sometimes called the function of serving as democracy's "watchdog." The emphasis on functionality, not on values, was the result of our suspicion (which proved justified) that the adolescents would be cynical about the moral value of concepts such as the freedom of speech, and could be more easily reached through an appeal to its instrumental use.

We start with the assumption that the role of the press is to defend the citizen from the risk of the government's abuse of power. This function is based on the understanding that every elected government is motivated by the interest of continuing to be in power, and is therefore, inasmuch as it is up to itself, inclined to provide the public only with information that serves this purpose (Keane, 1991). It follows that, rather than causing damage to the society, exposing deviations from social norms is a means of protecting the citizen from ignorance about the manner in which his or her affairs are (mis)managed. Journalists have therefore a mandate to guard the interests of individuals and groups in the population by exposing deviations from values, norms, and agreed procedures, as a controlling mechanism over the government and the power centers, and as means for repairing and limiting deviations on the part of the establishment.

The second principle the program teaches is that the necessary condition for providing crucial information to the public is the autonomy of the electronic communication and the press and their independence from the government (in particular, in societies with a public, BBC-like electronic communication), from commercial companies who in turn depend on government (for favorable taxation etc.), and from advertisers (who do not wish to antagonize any group in the population, and may veto what seems an unpopular issue).

A Two-Stage Project—From School Society to Society-at-Large

In order to achieve these two educational goals, we developed a two-stage program. In the first stage the students learn the functions of public exposure in the school society, and in the second stage they apply the principle of critical exposure to the larger society.

Preceding from the familiar to the less familiar was founded on our assumption that teenagers have only little interest in social and political issues, and tend toward conformism and reluctance to criticize when faced with national issues.[3] We expected the students to feel freer and more confident in criticizing what is happening in their own realm, about which they feel more qualified, and we assumed they could then be more prepared to learn the analogy between the function of publicity in the well-known school environment and in the whole of society.

Stage One: Learning the Importance of an Independent Media and Defining Criteria for the Selection of News Items and Sources— for Broadcasting in the School Society

The program was tried in secular Jewish schools of average educational level, with students of middle and lower-middle-class families, of both Eastern and Western origin. In the first session, classes were divided into groups of ten to fifteen students. Members of each group were asked to prepare news items about an issue that concerned their school for a radio (or a television) newscast, which would be shown to the whole school.

In order to compare the product of a communication institution that depends on the government with that of an institution with a higher degree of freedom, we entered into the game a manipulation in the figure of the headmaster. The headmaster appeared in one of the two groups at the beginning of the session, and expressed his assurance that the group members would represent the school in the best manner while not planning to interfere in the editorial considerations. In the second group there was no interference on the part of the school establishment during the process of the journalistic work. At the end of the work the items were presented to the other group members.

The second part of the session opened with a request to cut the number of items to be included in the broadcast to half the original number, "because of the time limitations of the news program." And most important, the students were asked to define the criteria that guided them in the inclusion (or the rejection) of particular items. The choice of items for inclusion was done first individually, later in couples (who had to come to a consensus through argument among themselves), and, finally, by the whole group. Some of the items produced were particularly critical toward failures of the school management or of school teachers, or presented difficult social issues (of integration, absorption of immigrants from Russia, etc.). Other items celebrated the successes of the school.

The criteria for the choice of items and for deciding on the order of appearance in the broadcast were recorded.

Stage Two: Learning the Importance of an Independent Media and Defining the Criteria for the Selection of News Items and Sources— on the National News

For this session we chose one news event—a terrorist attack on a crowded holiday beach (Liebes & Bar-Nachum, 1994). It was an attempt to carry out a mass massacre that could have ended in a large-scale disaster. Twelve terrorists came from the sea in two rubber boats. One was caught at dawn north of Tel-Aviv, after it ran out of fuel. The other landed three hours later at a beach south of Tel-Aviv, after a fast navy boat failed to capture it. The beach, crowded with bathers, was not evacuated. The army was activated only after the terrorists were on the beach. Only the confusion of the terrorists, who were surprised by their own success (Ha'aretz, 31 May 1990), and ran into the sand dunes rather than shooting at the bathers, prevented a tragedy. Reporting of the event was censored, roadblocks were erected on the main roads, creating a wave of rumors and panic in the public. There was no coordination between the actions of the army and the police, and local initiatives were taken by enterprising citizens.

The task in this session was to edit a news item about the attack from various television and press interviews we collected. Only half the number of sequences could be used for the item. The students had to choose among the Chief of Staff's description of the event, the Prime-Minister's compliments for the army's successful action, the demand of an opposition member of parliament for a committee of inquiry to investigate the failure of the military, a senior navy officer's claim that Israel lacks speedboats fast enough for capturing the kind of boats used by the terrorists, and the beach manager who took the initiative of quietly ordering the lifeguard to evacuate the beach once he saw the boat approaching. In parallel to the process the students went through in the editing of the school news, they were asked again first to edit the item individually, to convince one another about the best choice of sequences, and to finally arrive at a group decision, and to argue why certain sequences and not others were included in the item.

Our assumption that the students would be more critical when reporting about the school was verified. The subjects chosen for the school newscast included management failures in the handling of the new immigrant students (from Russia and Ethiopia), of the over-crowding of classrooms, and of classroom heating; teachers' preferential treatment of certain students, sexual harassment, and the system of examinations were all discussed. The students argued that without exposure things would not change, and that there is a need to draw the headmasters' and teacher's attention to the issues that need improvement.

The editing of the terrorist story, on the other hand, went in the establishment direction. The participants hesitated to include statements which cast doubts over the functioning of the army, the police, or the government, or that indicated the need to draw the right policy lessons from the near-miss attack. Thus, for example, the demand of the opposition member to nominate a committee of inquiry was not included by any of the groups (although it had supporters in the individual choices), because he was suspected for having "political motives," because as an opposition member, "he is against the state." In spite of the fact that the reporting in the media started only once the event was over and the terrorists were overcome, the criteria for editing the item tended to the direction of the importance of calming the people, and preserving the national morale, and the possible damage to the state's image. Generally it was assumed that the army would draw the right conclusions and correct its weaknesses without outside pressure.

The project turned out to have unforeseen side benefits in two areas. First, individually, students acquired some experience in writing and video production, and, with it, a sense of the journalistic profession. Second, for the interaction among students and teachers in the school, the school newscast created an agenda for discussion for issues which, although partially known, were not necessarily seen as a problem, and were not discussed systematically before. In some cases these discussions brought about initiatives for change.

Critical Exposure vis-à-vis the School Management: Escape from Opposition vis-à-vis the National Elites

The greater readiness of students to expose the weaknesses in the management of the school than to examine critically the more distant social of power is not necessarily self-evident. Public criticism of the school management may result in punishment, unlike the criticism of failures in the political or military establishment. Why, then, did we assume, and indeed prove, that the students would display more criticism toward their close environment than toward the establishment? The answers seems to be that the students: (1) have a daily and close acquaintance with the school management, which prevents a process of mystification of the leadership: (2) feel more confidence and professionalism concerning issues which are connected with school; and (3) are directly involved in, and see the relevance of issues such as students' rights, learning systems, and teacher/student interaction.

The reasons for the repressing of criticism concerning national issues show the reluctance of a large part of the population toward criticizing the establishment, especially in security issues. Such issues, as proved in the United States in the context of Vietnam and the Gulf wars, raise longing for national integration, for reassurance, and a wish for a promise that everything is under control, which exereses itself in hatred of arguments in the Parliament and of "hostile media" (Mosse, 1975). To this may be added an aspiration for a simplified perception of the political reality, in black and white terms.

The educational challenge in our program is to find a way to overcome the intuitive and understandable wish for unity, security, and for mapping the world in terms of a division between "them" and "us" in favor of an open debate about "us," or our leadership, which may be unpleasant to listen to but crucial for a mature society that is able to face rather than to deny where it goes wrong. Our project, limited as it is, attempts to raise awareness to the problem, and, through that, to contribute to a change of attitude. We do so by: (1) linking the first part, where students act as journalists on home territory, demonstrating understanding of the function of critical publicity, with the second part, where as editors of nationwide news, they become diffident of opposition; and (2) careful analysis of a case study of docile press coverage (the beach attack), pointing to the price of ignorance and denial.

No doubt the press is expected to fulfill, and does fulfill, other functions, as is made evident in the analysis of the press and television coverage of the beach attack. Raising national morale, calming the public, and contributing to social integration are functions taken over by the press and television in any social crisis, such as war, terrorism, or natural disaster. In periods of relative calm the media act in varied roles such as entertainers and personal advisors (the radio's usefulness in giving advice, for instance, may be equal to its usefulness as news carrier). When these functions of the press are accepted as legitimate, it becomes easy to prefer the media to look after social integration rather than to arouse dispute. In the terrorist event presented here, as well as, on a much larger scale, in the Gulf War, the media may have contributed to the morale, but the information provided by journalists was misguided, inaccurate, and wrong.In the two cases, Israeli and American journalists failed their clients in their watchdog roles. The argument that the clients would have rather not known the whole truth at the time (because it would have shaken their faith in their leaders, and disturbed their false peace of mind), is irrelevant. If journalists are professionals, they should act in the best interests of their clients (Katz, 1989).

Notes

1. Author note: I would like to thank the Kahanoff Foundation for its generous support of the development of a series of projects for the teaching of media literacy, one of which is the project described here. I am also indebted to the Scholars Program of the Annenberg School of Communication, at the University of Pennsylvania, for the opportunity to further conceptualize the idea of oppositional decodings of journalistic framings. A companion paper—"What a relief": When the press prefers celebration to scandal—appeared in *Political Communication, 11*, 35–48.
2. The other members of the team were Professor Yaron Ezrahi, Dr. Ziona Peled, Dr. Izhak Roeh, and Professor Dov Shinar and Dr. Tamar Liebes, who were in charge of the project designed to teach the role of media in democracy.
3. In Israel, the psychological preparation for compulsory army service at the end of high school strengthens this pro-establishment tendency.

References

Caspi, D., & Limor, Y. (1993). *The mediators: The mass media in Israel 1948–1990*. Tel-Aviv: Am Oved.

Gitlin, T. (1980). *The whole world is watching*. Berkeley and Los Angeles: The University of California Press.

Goren, D. (1976). *Secrecy, security and the freedom of the press*. Jerusalem: Magnes press.

Hall, S. (1985). Encoding/Decoding. In S. Hall, D. Hobson, A. Lowe, and P. Willis (Eds.), *Culture, media, language* (128–38). London: Hutchinson.

Katz, E. (1989). Journalism as profession. Paper presented at a meeting of the Centre for the Study of Journalism at Tel-Aviv University.

Katz, E. (1992). The legitimacy of opposition: On teaching media and democracy. Paper presented at the Bertelsmann conference on Media Competence, Gutersloh, Germany.

Keane, J. (1991). *The media and democracy.* Cambridge, UK: Polity Press.

Lazarsfeld P., & Merton, R. (1971). Mass communication, popular taste and organized social action. In R. Schrammm, & D. Roberts, (Eds.), *The process and effects of mass communication* (459–80). Urbana: University of Illinois Press.

Liebes T. (1992). Decoding television news: The political discourse of Israeli hawks and doves. *Theory and Society 21,* 357–81.

Liebes, T., and Ribak, R. (1991a). A mother's battle against the news: A case study of political socialization. *Discourse and Society 2,* 203–22.

———. (1991b). Democracy at risk. *Communication Theory 1,* 239–52.

Liebes, T., & Bar-Nachum, Y. (1994). "What a relief": When the press prefers celebration to scandal. *Political Communication 11,* 35–49.

Mosse, G. (1975). *The nationalism of the mass: Political symbolism and mass movements in Germany.* New York: H. Fertig.

Negbi, M. (1985). *Paper tiger.* Tel-Aviv: Sifriat Poalim (Hebrew).

Part V

Perspectives on Computer, Information, and "Museum" Literacy

17

Can Computers Turn Teaching Inside-Out, Transform Education, and Redefine Literacy?

W. Lambert Gardiner

This chapter describes a personal odyssey of the author (Can Computers Turn Teaching Inside-out?), a theoretical approach to education that emerged from this odyssey (Can Computers Transform Education?), and a reconsideration of the concept of literacy within this alternative educational system (Can Computers Redefine Literacy?).

The odyssey explores three successive visions of the use of the computer in education (Outside-in Vision, Inside-out Vision, Interactionist Vision). Those visions could be considered as based, respectively, on three metaphors of the computer in education—computer as source, computer as tutor, computer as prosthetic.

The theoretical approach explores three other metaphors of the computer in education—computer as positive prosthetic, computer as production studio, and computer as corpus callosum. Those visions, based on teaching as an inside-out rather than an outside-in process, could serve as a foundation for an alternative educational system.

Traditional education is based on the limited concept of literacy. Stretching the concept of literacy to embrace media literacy and computer literacy continues to privilege print and to preserve an antiquated educational system based on talk-and-chalk (proliferating literacies). The alternative educational system, implied by the theoretical approach presented here, would be based on the acquisition of skills in using our various communication tools (acquiring skills). Language is only one of those tools.

Can Computers Turn Teaching Inside-Out?

Once upon a time, long long ago, I played professor of psychology at Concordia University, teaching 700 day students in the matinee and 700 evening students in the late show. After five years, my courses evolved into books, which made me obsolete. There was no point in standing reading them until my tenure was up in the year 2000. So I took a decade off to explore alternative styles of living and learning.

This decade crystallized into a book called *The Psychology of Teaching* (Gardiner, 1980), in which I argued for a shift from the traditional concept of teaching as an outside-in process (that is, I know something, you don't, and I'm going to pass it on to you—the psychic transplant operation I had been conducting for those five years) to teaching as an inside-out process (that is, you have a certain intrinsic potential in there and I from out here may be able to help pull out this potential by arranging congenial environments for your growth).

When I published this book, advocating that teaching be turned inside-out, I didn't know how to do it. However, this does not prevent an academic from publishing. My colleagues at GAMMA Institute (Groupe Associe de Universites de McGill et Montréal pour l'Etude de l'Avenir), a future studies think tank, and at the Department of Communication Studies in Concordia University, lured me out of my premature retirement and kindly invited me back into the academy after such a long sabbatical. Through my work with them studying the human impact of new information technologies (and especially with hands-on experience of working with computers) I am beginning to get a glimpse of how we may finally turn teaching inside-out. The short answer is that we recruit our new electronic colleagues to perform the outside-in, information-providing aspect of teaching to set us free for the inside-out, inspiration-creating aspect of teaching. This chapter is the long answer. It could be considered as a progress report on my project for *this* decade.

Computers in Education—Outside-in Vision

My first vision of the use of computers in education was based on an electronic data terminal, which I carried around with me so that I could get information from databases over its built-in modem. Fast Eddy (as I called it) and I were partners. As in any partnership, there was a division of labor. As in any division of labor, each of us does what he(she) can do best.

What can Fast Eddy do best? He can memorize. He already *knows* dictionaries, thesauruses, encyclopedias, bibliographical sources like Psych Abstracts and ERIC, the contents of many major newspapers over the last several years, and many other vast sources of information. Some day, he will have the Library of Congress at his (sorry, my) fingertips. I'll never know a millionth of what he *knows* now. Nor would I ever want to. Why clutter up that very personal home computer between my ears (that is, my brain) with all this content? Why become a computer when I can buy one? What remains for me to do? Fast Eddy's full name is Electronic Data Terminal. Note his middle name. Data is a very low-level form of content. Data must be put into context to yield information, which must in turn be put in context to yield knowledge, which must be put in context to yield understanding, which must be put in context to yield wisdom. Eddy is good at content and I am good at context. Or, to use my earlier terms, he is good at the outside-in, information-providing aspect of teaching and I am good at the inside-out, inspiration-creating aspect of teaching. By assigning the mechanical aspect of content to the machine, the person is freed for the human aspect of context and can thus move up the hierarchy from data to information to knowledge to understanding to wisdom.

This division of labor was my first simple-minded notion of the appropriate relationship between the teacher and the computer. It is simple-minded because it simply slots the computer into the traditional outside-in framework of education. This has typically been the fate of the computer as used in education to date. In trying to understand the unfamiliar in terms of the familiar, new technology X is seen as old technology Y with difference Z. Film, for example, was first viewed (and therefore used) as theater in front of a camera so that a play can be preserved and re-presented later. Television was, in turn, viewed and used as a box in which to bury old movies, so that they can be viewed in one's own home. The fuller unique potential of each medium began to be realized only when it had escaped this limited *rear-view mirror* perspective.

The computer is now going through this initial phase. It is being used as a new box in which to bury old media. It is being view as Y (familiar thing) with difference Z. Because it is such a versatile machine, there are a number of rival Ys. For example, the computer is viewed as a typewriter with memory, a television set you can talk back to, a telephone to talk to other computers as well as people, and so on.

This first vision of computers in education, based on Fast Eddy, falls within the metaphor of computer-as-source. Some would argue that we do not need more information—we are already inundated with information. Indeed, many would argue that information overload is the major problem of our post-industrial, information-based society. To use the computer like this is like throwing water to a drowning man. We need means of assessing information rather than more information to assimilate. We should be supplying students with better *shit detectors*—to quote Ernest Hemingway (Plimpton, 1963)—rather than providing teachers with bigger shovels.

If the computer is assimilated to the outside-in tradition, it will simply continue to do, more efficiently, what has been done before. However, some would argue that much of what has been done before, in the name of education, is not worth doing. If it is not worth doing, then it is not worth doing—no matter how efficiently. If you are going down the wrong road, it does not matter how briskly you are travelling along it. There is a need for something completely different. This brings us to my second vision of the use of computers in education.

Computers in Education—Inside-Out Vision

This vision is perhaps best introduced, somewhat whimsically, by telling a story of three wise men bringing gifts to a child—or to anyone who has ever been a child.

The first wise man is Jean Piaget. His gift was a theory, which does for ontogenetic development (from child to adult) what the theory of Charles Darwin did for phylogenetic development (from animal to human). He has provided us with a three-dimensional description of human development in all its length, breadth, and depth.

The second wise man is Seymour Papert. His gift was a language. A student of Jean Piaget, he developed a computer language called Logo, designed to enable computers to facilitate human development, as described by his teacher.

This language was first *taught* to a mechanical *Turtle* attached to a keypad. A child (of whatever age) would type "FORWARD 40," and the Turtle would take forty turtle steps forward, leaving a trace of its trip with a pen on a paper on the floor. The child may then type "RIGHT 90," and the Turtle would turn 90 degrees to the right. Using four basic words in the Logo language (FORWARD, BACK, RIGHT, LEFT), the Turtle can be instructed to draw any shape on the paper.

Let us imagine that a child has commanded the Turtle to draw a triangle, then a square, then a pentagon, and so on. The child may already have discovered the Total Turtle Trip Theorem, that is, regardless of the shape of the figure, the Turtle must turn a total of 360 degrees to get back to the position in which it started. This is only one of many insights into geometry the child could get using only those four simple words.

Let us say that the child now wishes to teach the Turtle how to draw a circle. The Logo teacher may encourage the child to *think Turtle*. This could help the child realize that the Turtle will have to go forward a little, then turn a little, over and over again. Few children would have the patience to key in "FORWARD 1," "RIGHT 1," 360 times. No child would be willing to repeat this chore every time he/she wanted the Turtle to draw a circle. This brings us to the third wise man.

The third wise man is Guy Montpetit. His gift is the distribution to the general public of a disk containing the Logo language. A student of Seymour Papert, he returned home to Montreal to found Logo Computer Systems Inc. (LCSI) to manufacture and distribute software containing the Logo language. The mechanical Turtle on the floor can be replaced by a triangle on a screen and the keypad with a keyboard. A disk, supplied by LCSI, could be considered as the *mind* of the Turtle. It mediates between you at the keyboard and the Turtle-triangle on the screen.

This disk solves the two problems mentioned above. The first problem of repeating "FORWARD 1, RIGHT 1" 360 tedious times is solved by simply typing "REPEAT 360" (FORWARD 1, RIGHT 1). REPEAT is another Logo word which the Turtle *understands* because it is programmed into the disk. The second problem of repeating this process every time you want a circle is solved by teaching the Turtle a new word. This is done as follows:

```
TO CIRCLE
REPEAT 360 (FORWARD 1, RIGHT 1)
END
```

The first line of the program, "TO CIRCLE," tells the Turtle that you are about to teach it a new word, which will be called CIRCLE. The second line, "REPEAT 360" (FORWARD 1, RIGHT 1), teaches it the *meaning* of the word CIRCLE. The third line, "END," tells the Turtle that you have finished defining the new word. Now, when you want a circle, you simply type "CIRCLE."

The Logo language invites students into a *microworld*. By exploring this microworld, they can discover certain principles underlying the real world. One textbook, *Turtle Geometry* (Abelson & diSessa, 1987), takes the student from his first few tentative Turtle steps through Euclidian geometry and Newtonian physics to Einstein's theory of relativity.

Whereas the first vision is too outside-in, this second vision is too inside-out. It is a step in the right direction, since it shifts emphasis from the secondary process of outside-in conditioning to the primary process of inside-out growing. However, a further step is necessary. The theoretical basis of outside-in teaching is behaviorism, with its emphasis on conditioning from the outside; the theoretical basis of inside-out teaching is humanism, with its emphasis on growing from the inside. We all know, of course, that we are simultaneously growing from the inside out and being conditioned from the outside in. The behavioristic thesis and the humanistic antithesis, therefore, require a synthesis. The interactionism of Jean Piaget, based on a long lifetime of brilliant research in developmental psychology, provides a theoretical basis for an optimal orchestration of inside-out growing and outside-in learning. This brings us to my third vision of the use of computers in education.

Computers in Education—Interactionist Vision

This third—and current—vision of computers in education attempts to suggest how computers can best contribute to this *optimal orchestration* of growing and learning. It is based on a program called HyperCard (or any of the equivalent programs for the various computer platforms). No one—including Bill Atkinson, who wrote it, Danny Goodman (Goodman, 1993), who wrote a 1144-page handbook for it, and John Sculley, who agreed to include it free with every Apple Macintosh computer he sold—seems to know exactly what HyperCard is. This is a good sign. It means that it may be something genuinely new, since it can not be described as old technology Y with difference Z. Perhaps the computer has finally found its novel niche among the media.

Having said that HyperCard can not be adequately described even by the people most intimately associated with it, I will not fall into the trap of trying to describe it. However, I will illustrate its use by examples. It's better to show than to tell.

Imagine a stack of cards representing all the paintings in the Metropolitan Museum of Art. There is a device which selects subsets of those paintings—for example, pointillist paintings, or paintings by nineteenth-century French artists, or paintings with ships in them, or pointillist paintings by nineteenth-century French artists with ships in them. There is also a device for sorting those paintings—for example, in the order in which they were

FIGURE 17.1
The Pocket Museum

Link to information about painting

Link to information about artist

Link to 'blow-up' of indicated part of painting

[The buttons on the painting are transparent and become opaque
only on pressing a combination of keys on the keyboard.
Each of the linked cards can, of course, link to further cards.]

completed. On each painting there are buttons which link you immediately to cards containing information about the painting, or about the artist, or which provide blow-ups of various parts of the painting (see figure 17.1). Each card may contain further buttons which link you to yet other cards—for example, a button on a technical term within the *painting* card, which links to a card containing a definition of this term, or a button on an asterisk within the *artist* card which links to a card containing a footnote to that statement. This *footnote* card can, of course, link to other footnote cards, which explore the subject in more and more depth.

You need imagine no further. Such a system is already available. The *cards* are stored as 54,000 frames on a videodisc, which can be viewed on a large color monitor and, thanks to HyperCard, in any order the visitor to this *pocket museum* desires. It takes little imagination to visualize similar videodiscs which invite students to explore any domain of human knowledge.

This third vision could still be viewed as an invitation to a student to explore *microworlds*. However, whereas the microworlds of the first vision are all content with no context, and the microworlds of the second vision are all context with no content, the microworlds of this third vision embeds the content within a context.

Such preprogrammed videodiscs, which invite students to explore various domains of human knowledge, will play an increasingly important role in education in the future. However, this interactive videodisc technology will also invite students to create their own personal videodiscs. I am currently using HyperCard to create a shell for such creations.

Imagine a stack of cards which contain all your personal notes and images, favorite quotes and anecdotes, sources and resources, the books you have read and the papers you have written, the lectures you have heard and the speeches you have delivered. That is, a sort of silicon clone of yourself. Let us call it the Siliclone. The Siliclone can be best represented as a filing-cabinet, with ten drawers, and an in-out box on top, which enables you to put information into the drawers and to pull information out of them (see figure 17.2).

Imagine the following scenario. You press the in-box button and have the following conversation with your computer:

What drawer do you want to open?
You click "sources."
What is the name of the author?
W. Lambert "Scot" Gardiner.
What is the title of the book?
The Ubiquitous Chip: The Human Impact of Electronic Technology.
Where, by whom, and when was it published?
Hudson Heights, Quebec: Scot & Siliclone, 1987.
What are the keywords?
INFORMATION FUTURE FEAR HOPE.
(The relevant four keywords from a dynamic system of about 100 keywords which I use to organize information within the Siliclone.)
I am now entering this information into your siliclone.

You now press the out-box button and have the following conversation with your computer:

What keyword(s) do you want me to look for?
FEAR and FUTURE

FIGURE 17.2
The Siliclone

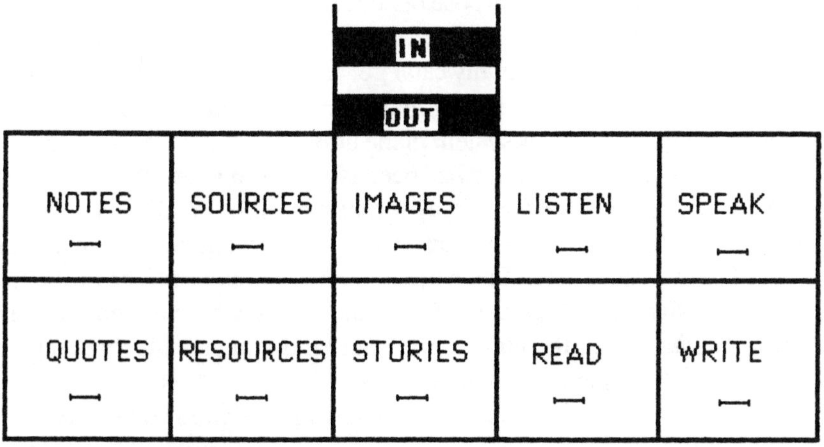

NOTES	SOURCES	IMAGES	LISTEN	SPEAK
QUOTES	RESOURCES	STORIES	READ	WRITE

In which drawer(s) do you want me to look?
ALL
I am looking—here they are.
(The computer searches through all the drawers, finds all the cards which have been keyed to both FEAR and FUTURE—including the one you have just entered—and puts the stack of cards in the out-box.) *This* system is not yet available but I'm working on it.

Can Computers Transform Education?

The previous section has a familiar ring. This is not the first technology which has been touted as a means of transforming education. Each wave of technological innovation washes on the shore of education, recedes, and then is swept over by the next wave. Will computers join the teaching machines, television sets, and other dust-gathering devices which have promised—and failed—to transform education in the past? Skepticism is entirely appropriate. Once bitten, twice shy; often bitten, very shy. However, I have a guarded optimism that this time the technology will become powerful (and cheap) enough to finally turn teaching inside out, and thereby transform education.

Whatever the technology, however powerful and cheap, it should not determine the course of education. Machines are simply means to desirable and feasible ends of persons. The appropriate role of technology in education can be understood only within the larger context of the purpose of education.

A larger vision of the purpose of education which I find helpful is that education is the process in which a person acquires the operating manual for our species. When I got my car, I got an operating manual; when I got my computer, I got an operating manual; when I got my brain (the most complex and mysterious system in the universe), there was no manual. I kept waiting for it, thinking it had been issued by another department and got lost by Canada Post. Halfway through my life, I realized that it was a do-it-yourself job. So I've been writing my own operating manual. It is based on the assumption that a brain is a brain is a brain. The difference between Margaret Mead and Albert Einstein (or whoever you think has most fully realized the human potential) and you and I is that they acquired a better operating manual.

The problem with the use of computers in education so far lies not so much within the machine itself, but within the metaphors of the machine in our minds. The major metaphors of the use of computers in education—computer as source, computer as tutor, computer as prosthetic, and so on—are all within the outside-in framework of traditional teaching. Computer as source is simply a device from pouring yet more information into the student; computer as tutor is a mechanical simulation of outside-in teaching which is mechanical enough already; computer as prosthetic allows people with sensory-motor problems to be stuffed full of information just like everyone else. The rest of the chapter describes three metaphors within an alternative inside-out framework of teaching, and the concept of education as the acquisition of the operating manual.

Computer as Positive Prosthetic

My three visions of computers in education, as described above, could be considered as based, respectively, on those three outside-in metaphors—computer as source, computer as tutor, and computer as prosthetic. However, the third vision has a twist which enables us to escape the outside-in framework. It is based on the metaphor of computer as *positive* prosthetic. It does not supplant some biological system which is defective, but supplements a biological system which is working perfectly well. This metaphor implies a synergy between natural and artificial intelligence. It is the metaphor used, not in the familiar artificial intelligence

(AI) tradition in computer science, but in the intelligence amplification (IA) tradition (Rheingold, 1985).

Acquiring the operating manual is largely a matter of learning how to use tools (the word *acquiring* is judiciously chose to stress the fact that it is an *inside-out job*). As the wonderful genetic potential—given to all members of our species as a conception-day gift—unfolds, we reach out for tools which help us realize this human potential. Education could be considered as the process of augmenting the information in the zygote, which represents the experience of our species, with the information we each acquire in our individual lifetimes. There are extragenetic tools (outside the genetic code) and there are extrasomatic tools (outside the body) (Sagan, 1977). The computer is the latest, and most dramatic, extrasomatic tool. It extends the function of the brain as the telescope extends the function of the eye and the car extends the function of the leg. It is a powerful positive prosthetic. To refuse to use this tool is to try to outsee the telescope and to outrun the car.

Communication tools constitute a large subset of our tools. If you consider media as involving the storage and transmission of information and if you classify tools as extragenetic and extrasomatic, then those two dichotomies yield a taxonomy of four generations of media (figure 17.3). In speech, storage and transmission are both extragenetic; in print, storage is extrasomatic; in video, transmission is extrasomatic; in multimedia (the emerging generation of media around computers), both storage and transmission are extrasomatic. Each generation supplements rather than supplants the previous generations. One must therefore acquire the tools of all generations (see figure 17.4). To ask which of those generations is best is like asking whether it is better to walk, cycle, drive, or fly. Each is appropriate in different contexts—I walk to Hudson to get my mail, cycle to the Willow Inn for lunch, drive to Montreal to the university, and fly to Europe.

Computer as Production Studio

Traditional education confines itself to the first and second generations of media—talk-and-chalk. Most discussion within education about the third generation concerns the detrimental effect of television. The criticism of television is largely based on the fact that the child is a passive consumer. Recent innovations in video technology have, however, resulted in what

FIGURE 17.3
Four Generations of Media

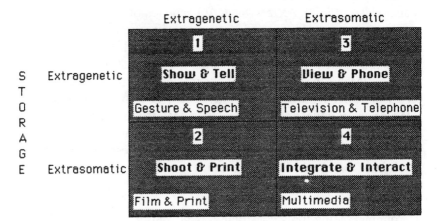

FIGURE 17.4
Classification of Explaining and Understanding Skills

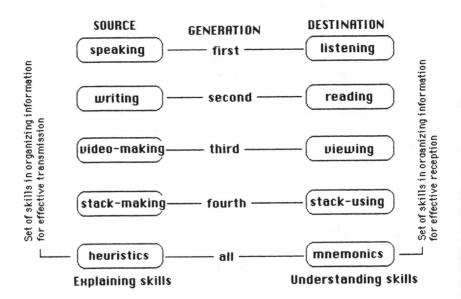

one of my students, Nathalie D'Souza, describes as the revolt of the couch potato. Four tools—two in general use already and two starting their penetration—have served as empowering devices to facilitate this revolt:

Remote control. This enabling device permits you to switch channels without getting off your couch. Thus, you can more easily browse, graze, as well as eat—the three major styles of acquiring information. You do not have to watch commercials, but can simply switch channels until they are over. You are, however, still confined to the programs which happen to be currently on the air.

Videocassette recorder. The videocassette recorder (VCR) permits you to watch what you want to watch when you want to watch it. Each of the buttons on the VCR can be identified with some aspect of button power, as indicated in figure 17.5. Button power has become such an intrinsic part of our daily lives that the three-year-old child of a friend of mine would say, when he wanted anything, "Press the button, Daddy!"

Interactive videodisc player. Records far outsold audio cassettes. However, when domestic products moved beyond audio to video, video cassettes far outsold videodiscs (the video analogue of records). What had happened in the interval? People had shifted from being passive consumers to active producers or, at least, to use Alvin Toffler's term, *prosumers.* They preferred the format which gave them more button power. We will soon see the comeback of the videodisc, in an interactive form. It will overtake the videocassette because it will offer even more button power. You will not only be able to cycle back and forth over the linear presentation of the VCR, but you will be able to access any of the 54,000 images in any order instantaneously. HyperCard is the prototype of the front end mediating between you and the videodisc which makes this possible.

Desktop video production (DTVP) studio. The next step is the development of a large storage medium on which one can write as well as read. Such a medium, already available in the CD-ROM, will be the basis for a Desktop Video Production Studio. CD-ROM disks, only a little larger than the 3½ floppy disks, contain the equivalent of about 300,000 pages of information. Many households already have a VCR, a Camcorder, and a computer. The addition of HyperCard, a scanner, an optical character reader, and various devices to link those elements into an integrated system would provide a domestic DTVP studio. Such a system would complete the process of transforming the domestic consumer into a producer. The revolt of the couch potato will be over.

The author is currently writing a HyperBook based on HyperCard (Gardiner, 1994). This is just a little less silly than making a traditional book. However, it is an intermediate device, for those who do not have a $2,000 computer to read the electronic version. It embodies the principles of HyperCard and thus invites people to learn those principles within the familiar and friendly (books are very user-friendly) context of a book.

This is a small step toward the DynaBook, conceived by Alan Kay (Goldberg, 1979; Kay & Goldberg, 1977). As the saga of the incredible shrinking chip continues, computers will become even smaller and faster and cheaper and smarter and friendlier. It is easy to imagine, before the end of this century, each child with a personal pocketbook-sized device. It flips open to reveal a screen on the top and a keyboard and a rollerball (a sort of built-in mouse) on the bottom. You slip in a card, like a credit card, which permits you to read a book, see a movie, or explore a domain of knowledge. When tired of it, the children trade them with friends (as they now trade sports cards). This electronic device will no doubt be called a Binary Operating-system for the Organization of Knowledge (B.O.O.K.). This is not some far-off future. I have in my wallet a debit card, of the same size and shape as a credit card, which contains 800 pages of optical memory. Blank disks will enable students to build satellite brains (siliclones) so that they can establish a synergistic relationship between the natural intelligence of the person and the artificial intelligence of the machine.

Computer as Corpus Callosum

The operating manual for our species is, more precisely, an operating manual for the nervous system of our species. This is the only one of our subsystems which can be "operated" directly. The two major categories of media, print and video, could be identified with the left and right hemispheres of the brain, responsible, respectively, for creating a conceptual and a perceptual map of the objective world (figure 17.6). Schools and universities traditionally emphasize the function of the left hemisphere. That is, they teach us how to build a conceptual map of the world and they focus on print media. Little effort is concentrated on the function of the right hemisphere. That is, we do not learn how to use image-based media to build a perceptual map of the world. Indeed, as discussed above, television (the most ubiquitous image-based medium) is often condemned as harmful to education.

FIGURE 17.5
Various Button Powers Offered by the VCR

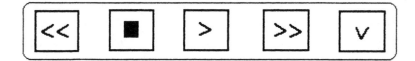

REWIND – the power to look at a video (or any part of it) as often as
you wish
STOP –   the power to have the video wait till you have dealt with
interruption or to look at a single frame
PLAY –   the power to play a video any time you chose to see it
FAST FORWARD – the power to zip past (or zap out) commercials
RECORD – the power to time-shift (record now – play later) or to
make your own video

FIGURE 17.6
"Media"ting Between Subjective Map and Objective World

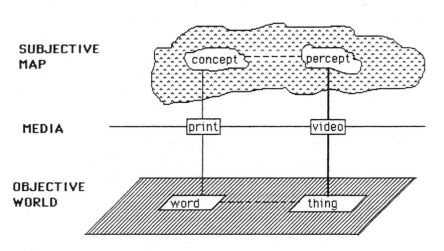

The computer, loaded with HyperCard, could be considered as the corpus callosum, the tissue linking the two hemispheres. Each card can contain words and/or images. Thus HyperCard serves as an integrative device. The corpus callosum is an even more apt metaphor because it links the cortex (responsible for thought) to the rest of the nervous system (responsible for action). Each card also contains buttons, which allows the user to interact with the computer. Thus HyperCard serves as an interactive device. Education will then provide the whole operating manual—for the left hemisphere, for the right hemisphere, and for the corpus callosum, which links the two hemispheres to one another and to the rest of the body.

Can Computers Redefine Literacy?

Proliferating Literacies

Education was described above as the process by which we each augment the phylogenetic information of our species, which we acquire as a conceptual-day gift, with the ontogenetic information we acquire in our individual lifetimes. Basing traditional education on the three Rs embodies the insight that the acquisition of communication tools is central to education. It is tempting to extend this language of "literacy" to the third and fourth generations of media, by talking of video literacy and computer literacy, respectively. However, this continues to privilege print, to perpetuate a limited concept of literacy as the foundation of education—the three Rs, and to preserve an antiquated educational system based on the first two generations of media—talk-and-chalk. The concept has been associated with print (the second generation of communication tools) for the many centuries of print-dominated media and thus can not easily be extended to cover the third and fourth generations which have emerged relatively recently.

Each of the metaphors described above implies a different literacy. Using the computer to access and explore databases through a modem, to create a microworld, or to create a stack of interlinked cards each require different skills. None of them could be considered as literacy in the strict sense of acquiring a language. It is becoming less and less necessary to learn a computer language to use computers. People are increasingly "driving" computers, leaving tinkering under the hood to programmers who have learned the languages which computers understand. Just as we do not speak of car literacy when a person learns to drive, so we should not speak of computer literacy when a person learns to use a computer. As we move from an industrial society, with its infrastructure of transportation, to a post-industrial society with its infrastructure of informatics (network of computers linked by telecommunications), it is useful to learn not only to drive a car but to "drive" a computer through cyberspace.

Acquiring Skills

A spate of recent books struggles to update our language about language, as we are challenged by the threats and opportunities of the emerging electronic communication tools. Seymour Papert (Papert, 1993) suggests that we use "letteracy" to describe what is traditionally called literacy, reserving "literacy" as a broader term to embrace both print and electronic media. Jay David Bolter (Bolter, 1991) suggests "writing space" as a broader term which embraces memory as the writing space for speech, paper as the writing space for print, and the screen as the writing space for video and computer technologies. Gregory Ulmer (Ulmer 1985; Ulmer, 1989) explores the application to education of "grammatology." This term was proposed by Jacques Derrida to refer to all marks with meaning to distinguish it from the limited subset of such marks called "writing." However, each of those new terms—*letteracy, writing space, grammatology*—are associated with the second generation of print. Creative analogies from the familiar (print technology) to the unfamiliar (electronic technology) is a good intellectual strategy. However, preservation of print-based language helps perpetuate the hegemony of print established over centuries of unchallenged dominance.

It would be better, perhaps, to talk simply of the acquisition of communication skills as one gains competence with our various communication tools, with the tools of the second generation simply a subset within the toolkit. This would not only encourage the use of the tools of the third and fourth generations, but also of the first generation. Back to the basics would really be back, not to the three Rs, but to the real basics, the first generation of communication. Speaking and listening have been squeezed out of the curriculum by writing and reading. Listening is least-listed and most-practiced in traditional education. Thus education would be based on the acquisition of the explaining and understanding skills of all four generations of media (see figure 17.4).

References

Abelson, H., & diSessa, A. (1987). *Turtle geometry: The computer as a medium for exploring mathematics.* Cambridge, Mass.: MIT Press.

Bolter, J. D. (1991). *Writing space: The computer, hypertext, and the history of writing.* Hillsdale, N.J.: Lawrence Erlbaum Associates.

Gardiner, W. L. (1980). *The psychology of teaching.* Monterey, Calif.: Brooks/Cole.

———. (1994). *This book is about this book: Invitations to multimedia.* Hudson Heights, Quebec: Scot & Siliclone.

Goldberg, A. (1979). Educational uses of a Dynabook. *Computers and Education 3* (4): 247–66.

Goodman, D. (1993). *The complete Hypercard 2.2 handbook (4th edition).* New York: Random House.

Kay, A. C., & Goldberg, A. (1977). Personal dynamic media. *IEEE Computer 10* (3): 31–41.

Papert, S. (1993). *The children's machine: Rethinking school in the age of the computer.* New York: HarperCollins.

Plimpton, G. (Ed.). (1963). *Writers at work: The Paris Review interviews (2nd series).* Harmondsworth, Middlesex: Penguin.

Rheingold, H. (1985). *Tools for thought: The people and ideas behind the next computer revolution.* New York: Simon & Schuster.

Sagan, C. (1977). *The dragons of Eden: Speculations on the evolution of human intelligence.* New York: Ballantine.

Ulmer, G. L. (1985). *Applied grammatology: Post(e)-pedagogy from Jacques Derrida to Joseph Beuys.* Baltimore: Johns Hopkins University Press.

———. (1989). *Teletheory: Grammatology in the age of video.* New York: Routledge.

18

Interactive Technology in the Classroom: A Case Study with Illiterate Adults

Micheline Frenette

In addition to skills in reading, writing, and computing, technological literacy has become necessary for people to participate fully in society. However, literacy classes for adults rarely include a technological component. This article describes a case study on the introduction of an interactive cable technology in beginner, intermediate, and advanced literacy classes during a school year. The goal of the study, guided by a transactional view of people and technology, was to understand the importance of context and users' personal visions in the appropriation of a new technology. Qualitative methods were employed, in particular participant observation and individual and group interviews. The paper documents how a system initially designed for the domestic sphere was used in a classroom setting. It also describes how literacy students view technology through the prism of their personal apprehensions and expectations, including their attachment to the traditional school model and the perceived devaluation of literacy skills suggested by the introduction of technology as a new means of communication. Several recommendations for the design of technology appropriate to the skills and needs of an illiterate clientele and for the creation of pedagogical aids for the literacy classroom are presented. The findings are also discussed in relation to a recent report on adult literacy and technology by the United States Office of Technology Assessment.

Although illiteracy may be defined technically in terms of schooling achieved by an individual (with fifth grade often used as a benchmark), it is possible and in fact desirable to view literacy more broadly in relation to a person's life goals. Thus, a UNESCO commission in 1958 defined illiteracy as "the incapacity to read and write, whilst understanding, a simple text related to one's daily life" (UNESCO, 1990, 7). In 1978, the notion of "functional" illiteracy was introduced to designate "a person incapable of exercising any activity for which literacy is required in the interest of the proper functioning of his social group and community and also to allow him to continue reading, writing and computing in view of his own development and that of his community" (UNESCO, 1990, 7). Illiteracy is more common in industrialized countries than one would think. Canada is no exception, since a survey in 1987 revealed that, in the province of Quebec alone, an estimated 10 percent of the population was fully illiterate and 18 percent functionally illiterate (Brunel, 1990).

The lack of reading and writing skills has far-reaching consequences. For example, several aspects of daily living, such as grocery shopping, are problematic for those who do not master the written language. Not surprisingly, illiteracy is also closely linked to unemployment and poverty. The real problem then, for illiterate individuals, is not being able to participate fully in the intellectual and economic life of society as it stands, while the demands of the labor market keep rising steadily. Employment and Immigration Canada[1] foresees that in the last quarter of the twentieth century, 64 percent of all new jobs will require at least twelve years of schooling (Brunel, 1990).

Moreover, the evolution of traditional modes of communication brings an extra challenge to illiterate individuals, that of coping with technology itself. Consider the radical changes that television is undergoing, adding to its traditional lifelike programming a plethora of other communicative functions, which require a fair level of literacy from its users. A recent report by the Office of Technology Assessment of the United States Congress entitled *Adult Literacy and New Technologies: Tools for a Lifetime,* aptly summarizes the situation:

> Today a whole new information infrastructure is emerging; access to it depends on understanding and using a variety of technologies. Just as the inability to read has often isolated people from the mainstream of society, technological "illiteracy" threatens to marginalize those who lack technology access. (OTA, 1993, 89).

The OTA report presents several arguments in favor of technology for adult learners in general, and illiterate students in particular, while realistically pointing to some limitations of technology in this respect (OTA, 1993). Surprisingly, however, literacy courses (both in Quebec and in the United States) rarely include educational activities with a technological component. Three years ago, it was resolved to tackle the problem of how the traditional objectives of literacy classes, that is, reading, writing, and computing, could be joined with the goal of introducing students to new technologies.[2] We decided to experiment with an innovative interactive cable system (Videoway[RegTM]) that extends the role of television and stands as a precursor of the information superhighway, delivering videotext, videogames, electronic mail, and interactive television to the home.

The Videoway (VW) system met five criteria that had been identified for the selection of a technology suitable for experimentation with illiterate individuals:

1. *User-friendliness*. The Videoway system was designed for home use by the general public and young children use it with ease; all the functions are activated by a simple remote control device similar to the one used to control the television set.
2. *Connections with real life*. Television is a medium used daily by an overwhelming majority of Quebecers, including the economically disadvantaged. The Videoway system also gives access to a broad spectrum of information services of general interest (weather, lottery results, and others).
3. *Educational potential*. Several educational products dealing with languages (French and English), mathematics, science, history, and other subjects, are offered on the Videoway system.
4. *Flexibility*. The products are presented in a variety of formats including tutorials and videogames. Videoway also provides an interactive television channel which offers viewers the opportunity to alter the content of a program while it is being broadcast (e.g., answer a question during a quiz, choose an interview topic during a talk show, select the viewing angle during a hockey game, and others).
5. *Affordability*. The system is available on a monthly basis with a small supplement ($5 U.S.) to the basic cable subscription ($17 U.S.) and does not require a massive technical investment.

In 1991, an exploratory study using focus groups had been conducted with some thirty men and women between twenty-three and thirty-seven years of age from introductory and advanced literacy classes with a view to exploring the potential of this interactive cable technology for their needs (Frenette, 1991). Although the participants made suggestions to improve the technology, and rightly so, their enthusiastic response convinced us that the Videoway system had been a good choice. However, we felt that only an extended experimentation with illiterate individuals would enable us to formulate a coherent set of recommendations for the development of specialized services for this clientele. Therefore, a project was set up to explore the potential of Videoway technology for literacy classes during a full school year. Specifically, three literacy teachers were to become familiar with this interactive system and integrate it within their classroom practice in the manner they judged appropriate. The theoretical stance of the study may be compared to the transactional viewpoint, inspired by cognitive psychology (e.g., Clark, 1988), which leads us to consider technology from the perspective of the interaction between media and user. As such, the personal vision of the user and the social context within which the experience takes place are of paramount importance. Thus, the study's goals were to document what happens when a domestic technology is transferred to the classroom, and to understand what technology means for illiterate individuals. Indeed, the point of view of less fortunate social groups with regard to communication technologies is not often heard. The chapter relates the highlights of this study on illiterate adults' appropriation of an interactive technology in the hope that the findings may benefit others who wish to introduce technology to literacy students. This account also provides an opportunity to discuss the conclusions of the OTA report on technology and illiteracy in the light of these findings.

The Experiment

The Social Milieu

The experiment with Videoway technology in literacy classes took place during the 1992–93 school year in a community center located in Hochelaga-Maisonneuve, a division of the city of Montreal. This French-speaking neighborhood has 53,000 inhabitants, of which a high percentage are economically disadvantaged, living on welfare or unemployment benefits. In some sectors, half the population is considered illiterate. On the other hand, this working-class neighborhood is also known for its dynamism and community initiatives. For instance, a low-budget restaurant founded and operated by volunteers is often cited as an example of citizen involvement. One such nonprofit organization, located in a building which used to be an elementary school in the heart of the neighborhood, is the PEC (Community Education Pavilion), founded in 1972. It houses several clubs and associations of interest for residents (e.g., senior citizens' groups, lodging and food cooperatives, community radio, citizen action groups, etc.), as well as literacy classes, which fall under the jurisdiction of the local school board.

A Portrait of the Literacy Classes

The objectives pursued in these literacy classes are to develop reading, writing, and computing abilities on the one hand, and to foster the students' personal and social development, on the other, that is, raising their self-confidence, showing them practical life skills, and broadening their cultural horizons. The three teachers who agreed to participate in the study were responsible for two beginner groups, two intermediate groups, and two advanced groups, respectively.

The *beginner* (B) group was comprised of two sub-groups: (1) mildly retarded individuals in the morning class (some of whom were nonfunctional illiterates whose concentration was very limited); and (2) a slightly stronger group attending the afternoon class, that is, illiterates who were almost functional with a longer attention span and capable of some abstraction. With respect to reading abilities, the teacher responsible for the morning group distinguished three competence levels: students incapable of reading but who could recognize letters; those able to read single words by syllabic decomposition; and those able to read simple sentences. As for writing skills, very few students at this level were able to produce even simple sentences. Competence levels in mathematics were somewhat more varied: some students were limited to addition, while others could perform multiplication and division.

Students in the *intermediate* (I) group were able to understand almost every word taken singly when reading a text, but experienced difficulty in grasping the overall meaning. With respect to writing, they were able to produce words and simple sentences, but they often relied on a phonetical transcription. In mathematics, they could resolve some common problems encountered in daily life, drawing on basic notions such as addition and subtraction. Some intermediate level students had difficulties in concentrating.

Finally, the students in the *advanced* (A) group were able to read with some ease, though there were important individual differences. Thus, the global meaning of a text might be lost for some, while others were able to discuss a book they had read. All the students were able to write sentences, but the quality of composition and the length of the written material varied considerably; while some could write at most a few sentences, others wrote texts a few pages long. With respect to their mathematical abilities, the students had a good understanding of basic operations.

At the time of the experiment, there were seventeen students registered in the beginner classes, twenty-seven in the intermediate classes,
and twenty-three at the advanced level. Thus, some seventy students were
taking literacy classes four half-days per week. Adults in their twenties
mixed with those in their fifties, but most of the students in the various
groups were between thirty-five and forty-five years of age. Women made
up the majority in the intermediate and advanced groups (nineteen to
eight, and twenty to three, respectively), while men were slightly more
numerous in the beginner group (ten men for seven women).

The three literacy teachers viewed technology not as an end in itself,
but as a tool to meet their educational objectives. As such, they saw three
complementary roles for Videoway technology in the literacy classroom:

1. *To practice reading, writing, and computing skills* in a novel fashion using video-games and interactive television (ITV).
2. *To serve as a practical resource* of renewable texts and videos for introducing students to a wider variety of contents related to everyday life.
3. *To demystify technology* by giving students hands-on experience with a
   system that foreshadows technological developments in the home and that
   could also serve as a stepping-stone to more advanced technologies.

Methods

The teachers each received three Videoway consoles, which were in-
stalled at the rear of each classroom, such that the teacher could monitor
the screen from her desk in the front. The consoles consisted of a four-
teen-inch color television monitor and a Videoway terminal, both of which
were encased in a wooden box placed on the top of a desk. Each console
was also equipped with a headset and a remote control device. The decision to divide the terminals among the three classrooms (as opposed to
sharing them in a common locale) was made by the teachers, who favored a "workshop" approach, that is, students would take turns at the
terminals while the remainder of the class worked on other assignments.

Extensive support was foreseen for the participating teachers. They were
given literature describing the functions and contents of the various components of the Videoway system. The teachers could also communicate at
any time with the research team and the technical team to obtain material
and documentation or to order an interactive program on the network.
Moreover, they were provided with cable and Videoway services in their

homes, free of charge, for the duration of the project in order for them to become familiar with the technology in a leisurely fashion. In accord with the goal of understanding the point of view of illiterate students and literacy teachers, the methodology was decidedly qualitative as recommended by Patton (1987). This positions the project within a user-oriented perspective of program evaluation as defined by King, Morris, and Fitz-Gibbon (1987). Two methods of data collection were employed: (1) participant observation of illiterate adults during their work sessions with the Videoway system in the classroom; and (2) monthly interviews with the students and teachers respectively, both individually and in small groups. The final report was accompanied by a lengthy companion volume containing detailed recommendations for the adjustment of all the interactive services in relation to the needs of illiterate individuals and literacy teachers. Data from all sources have been pooled to provide an overview of the more significant findings.

Three Classes: Three Learning Experiences

Prior to describing the students' personal reactions to the technology, this section of the results will present an overview of how the system was used in class, considering in turn the contents and the pedagogical methods privileged by the teacher in regard to the information services (comprising videotext and videogames) and interactive television, respectively. The fact that the three teachers led their respective classes into very different learning experiences with the same technology underscores the relevance of the transactional viewpoint to understand the relationship between people, technology, and context. Indeed, it is interesting to consider how a technology designed initially for the home takes on a whole new dimension when it is brought into the school setting.

Information Services in the Classroom

In all three cases, the teachers' first concern was to initiate and sustain students' motivation, although their approach in doing so reflected the characteristics of their groups as well as their own personal teaching style. Indeed, the teachers differed as to the information services they selected for use in class and the manner in which the services were used.

Videogames of all sorts were the main information content employed in the *beginner* classes. For instance, the teacher used games which fostered visual discrimination and spatial orientation in students with learning difficulties and games of spelling, arithmetic, and strategy for the more academically able students. Some general information services (weather, television schedule) were also employed in these classes, mainly for the acquisition of vocabulary. For her part, the *intermediate*-level teacher emphasized the other information services, especially contents relevant to the interests and life situation of her students. For example, she elaborated a pedagogical activity pertaining to osteoporosis, drawing on a service related to lifestyle information. The*advanced*-level teacher employed for the most part language and mathematics games, as well as some practical information services. Nevertheless, she also attempted to accommodate student interests by employing, for example, the horoscope service as a reading or verb conjugation exercise.

The learning sessions with the information services were usually held once or twice a week and lasted on average one hour, but they could be as short as twenty minutes or extend for half a day. As with any classroom activity, teachers have pedagogical decisions to make with respect to grouping on the one hand *(individual, small group, or collective)* and to degree of supervision on the other *(guided or nondirective learning)*. Given the limited reading skills of *beginner* and even *intermediate* students, the information services were initially used in the context of collective lessons. For example, for a general knowledge game, the teacher would gather the students around the monitor, read the questions out loud, establish a consensus for the choice of an answer, and activate the remote control device. Later on, students often worked cooperatively in teams of two. In fact, this grouping was the most common overall. It was all the more interesting when stronger students were placed with slightly less able ones in the performance of a common task. On the other hand, the teacher of the *advanced* classes favored individual sessions.

Whatever the grouping, the teachers usually favored guided learning activities over free exploration. Thus, a typical learning exercise with the Videoway system consisted of distributing a questionnaire which the students had to answer by consulting the information services. One teacher favored the development of a single theme in class over a few days and gave out the Videoway questions, in advance; when the students located them, they were better prepared to answer successfully. Thus, the work sessions on the terminal served as reinforcement for the learning of academic content and helped them become familiar with the technology in a rewarding fashion. After the "workshops" using Videoway, the teachers monitored what progress had been made in terms of both academic content and skills with the technology and planned the next work session accordingly. In addition, the intermediate and advanced students wrote their personal impressions in a notebook at the end of each Videoway session, with a view to developing their writing skills and their ability to synthesize ideas.

Interactive Television in the Classroom

Given that watching an interactive television (ITV) program requires a form of participation which might be difficult for some illiterate individuals (e.g., reading questions on the screen and answering them within five seconds), the *beginning-* and *intermediate*-level teachers made limited use of it in class. However, they took advantage of student interest in a series on popular psychology to introduce them to this component of the Videoway technology. On the other hand, the *advanced*-level teacher could explore a greater variety of interactive programs with her students, given their better reading skills. For the most part, she chose contents the educational character of which was explicit, for example a quiz on history. She also scheduled a dramatic episode where the viewer has to identify the correct spelling of certain words used by the characters which appear on the screen.

In general, the *beginner* groups experienced ITV in the collective mode. For her part, the *intermediate*-level teacher favored individual watching, with or without prior preparation. Nonetheless, she felt that the experience was more gratifying when the students were sufficiently prepared to answer questions correctly. At the *advanced* level, small group watching was the preferred mode. The teacher would order two successive broadcasts of the same program so the students took turns watching them in small groups, which made them feel more secure. In the case of the history quiz where the viewer obtained a score, the teacher first prepared a general talk on the topics of the episode to be broadcast (i.e., Vietnam, the Titanic, etc.), but students met with little success. Subsequently, she supplied them directly with the questions and answers beforehand, so that the ITV session served to reinforce the newly acquired knowledge.

In short, we notice that teachers pulled out the specific services that matched their needs and organized different learning experiences around the technology. Thus, the Videoway system, selected partly because of its multiple services, did accommodate a variety of learning trajectories when transplanted into the classroom. However, information services (both videotext and videogames) blend more easily into classroom practices than ITV because the former are under direct user control, whereas interactive television is constrained by a broadcast schedule.

Students' Appropriation of the Technology

From a transactional viewpoint, a key element in the successful appropriation of a technology is the user's personal state of mind in approaching that technology, which determines to a great extent how it will be used. In other words, the most sophisticated technology may not be used at all or largely underutilized (which is just as regrettable), while a simpler technology may in fact allow the user to make important strides in achieving his personal goals. Given that the literacy students, as characterized by the teachers, were usually resistant to any kind of novelty, it was especially important to understand their point of view since it would color their encounter with technology. This section will share insights on the positive and negative aspects of technology as experienced by the literacy students. Surprisingly, participants as a group were relatively homogeneous in their attitudes since no differences as a function of sex or age were apparent.

The Benefits of Technology

The students identified four kinds of benefits following from the introduction of technology into the classroom, two of which are related more directly to academic goals (the facilitation of cognitive skills and the sustainment of motivation), while the other two concern personal development and social skills. When appropriate, quotes from the participants are used to convey their personal vision more forcefully.[3]

Cognitive skills. It was through the reading practice and mental calculations they were engaged in to operate the Videoway services that the students made progress in their learning. The students themselves acknowledged the educational value of such activities. When the technology allowed the practice of reading skills on contents with an immediate relevance for students (such as information pertaining to osteoporosis), all the conditions for an optimal learning experience were brought together. Specific cognitive benefits sometimes also accrue from using a technology per se. The beginning-level students, for example, showed a greater than usual level of concentration while playing video games (e.g., up to an hour). In addition, one of the teachers noted progress over the weeks in the problem-solving strategies used by students during these games. The teacher attributes this phenomenon to the material's engaging interactive dimension and to the appropriateness of the task for students' intellectual abilities.

Sustaining motivation. While many students showed strong personal involvement in their learning process, others were clearly less interested; some were actually compelled to attend literacy classes by the welfare services. Therefore, sustaining motivation in class was a primary concern of the teachers. Indeed, negative attitudes can exercise a heavy toll on the group's morale and deplete the teacher's energies. Therefore, any method likely to raise interest was welcomed by the teachers. In this regard, overall appreciation of the technology on the part of many students encountered at all three levels was encouraging.

It's good for elementary school (i.e., their level) 100%. (B)

There are some good ideas in there. (I)

Everything is good. It's very interesting. (A)

One indicator of intrinsic motivation was the spontaneous use of the terminals outside class hours; during their free time, most students opted for the games, but a few students also browsed through the system for practical information (i.e., personal ads, stain removal, etc.).

Interactive television had the greatest appeal across all three groups; it was found to be motivating and especially suited to the learning needs of illiterate individuals.

It was fun. There's more action. It's more lively. (A)

We have to hear things. We're not visual enough yet for the words. So if we hear someone, we have a better chance of understanding what it's about. (I)

The illusion of interacting with the characters or hosts in the program added a personal dimension that was an important source of motivation for the literacy students compared to reading texts in the information services. In addition, the relative ease of operating ITV, as compared to navigating among the information services, contributed to student confidence vis-à-vis the technology.

Personal development. The pride experienced from being able to master the Videoway technology is equal to the challenge it poses for illiterate individuals, some of whom likened it to a computer.

> It gives us an independence from the teacher. We learn to deal with the machine by ourselves without the teacher standing by our side. It's an independence that is good for us. (I)

According to the teachers, learning to use this new tool played a role in increasing the self-confidence of some students who displayed special personal initiatives (i.e., consulting a dictionary at home). Moreover, the novel aspect of the technology in the classroom motivated some students to express their personal opinion more often than usual. Viewed in the light of enduring passivity and dependence on the part of students, these minor manifestations of autonomy were viewed as significant by the teachers.

Social dynamics. Introducing Videoway technology into the literacy classroom also provided some individuals the opportunity to display new social behaviors. The beginning-level teacher in particular observed a great deal of interaction and collaboration among the students during the game sessions. Furthermore, some students who were familiar with the system displayed leadership qualities in helping others out which they did not manifest during regular classes. The fact that this teacher favored a collective mode of working with technology seemed propitious for the development of social skills.

The Reservations toward Technology

Although many students had a very positive response to the introduction of technology in the classroom, a certain number of them did have strong reservations about it. From our understanding, these are related to the fear of novelty, to self-doubt, and interestingly, to a deep attachment to the traditional school model.

Fear of the unknown. Resistance to change is often cited as an impediment to the integration of technology in general (e.g., Nickerson, 1981). Therefore, it is not unusual that the literacy students should have felt some apprehension about the arrival of technology in the classroom, given that routine activities already represent some challenge for them. As teachers had predicted, anything new is likely to be viewed with suspicion.

> VW is like the unknown. You press the remote but you can't know what will come up on the screen. You don't even know what you're looking for in reality but with TV, when you press channel 2, you know you're getting channel 2. (A)

This fear of novelty was sometimes expressed in the opinion that the Videoway system had been designed for younger people because they are more familiar with computers. Others simply avoided this new situation for fear of encountering failure, as one of the older students explained.

> The person who doesn't understand VW, do you know why? They say it's not interesting, that they don't like it. Well it's because they don't know how to use it and they don't want to say so. Take me for instance. For 30 years I didn't admit I couldn't read. I would be in a meeting and I would say to other people that I forgot my glasses. It's the same thing with *the machine.* (B).

Lack of self-confidence. Not unexpectedly, the experiment confirmed that illiterate adults need a longer time to feel at ease with the system than the general public. It appeared that inferiority feelings and a lack of self-confidence sometimes interfered with their exploration of the technology. It is difficult for people with formal instruction to imagine the challenge faced by individuals who lack reading skills, when they encounter a technology for the first time, even if it has been designed for the general public. Heartfelt reactions expressed by some students give us a glimpse into their personal experience.

> I don't understand anything at all. . . . You need a computer course . . . I panicked with the arrows. (A).

> It's all right for someone in 6th or 7th grade, who already knows how to read and write. But for beginners like us, it's too "strong." We are already lacking something, so you need to start at the beginning and show us slowly. (I)

As a result, the importance of good planning to foster success in the initial learning stage cannot be overstated. If students are not comfortable with the technology from the beginning, their feelings of insecurity are likely to be heightened because they usually have no prior experience with technology to help them work through a problem. Since illiterate students often doubt their personal capacity, it is not unusual for them to assume responsibility for any difficulty encountered with the technology, which only serves to deprecate their self-image further.

> I didn't answer in time. I wouldn't blame the thing (i.e. VW) though, because we're the ones who are not fast enough. (B)

Attachment to the traditional school model. Notwithstanding the fact that the services were not perfectly suited for an illiterate clientele, there was a deeper attitudinal phenomenon very revealing of their own outlook on school and learning that colored their encounter with the Videoway system. In effect, many illiterate students displayed an attachment for the traditional school model they had experienced in their youth, albeit only for a short period. This "school" schema, through which technology is evaluated, involves four components:

1. *Focussing on the three Rs.* Pedagogical objectives in a traditional sense (reading, writing, computing) were primordial in the eyes of many literacy students. Their goal in attending classes is to master those very skills they did not acquire in school the first time around. As a consequence, technology may be seen to have no connection whatsoever to these goals.

> In school, I prefer to read and write. School is school. (I)

This reaction in fact echoes Nickerson's (1981) comment that the perceived devaluation of hard-won skills may be an impediment to the integration of technology for any learner. Given the personal efforts some of the participants need to summon in order to improve their reading and writing skills, their reaction is quite comprehensible.

2. *The presence of a teacher.* The importance of the teacher was paramount in the minds of most literacy students. Beyond the feeling of security provided by her presence, she is perceived as an essential guide in helping them to understand school material. She also acts as a motivator who prompts them toward a greater personal effort than if they were left to work by themselves. Viewed from this vantage point, technology, whatever its objective merits, was not comparable in their eyes.

> The teacher is very patient. She can explain things five or six ways so that we understand, but that (i.e., the technology) won't repeat for you. You can't ask it a question. (A)

> There is a big difference between doing a dictation on the terminal and doing a dictation with the teacher. With the technology, if you make a mistake, it's under-

lined and then you correct your mistake. In two seconds, "bing bang," it's over. But with the teacher, it has to be more intense, more worked through.(I).

Without the technology, we have to make an effort because the teacher requires it from us. (A)

In short, the students did not seem in the habit of independent learning and relied heavily on the teacher to sustain their motivation and to help them understand the subject matter. Students in one group in particular had the mistaken impression that the introduction of a technology might eventually lead to the disappearance of the teacher. Understandably, and unlike the others, they were hostile toward the technology. Thus, the classroom may be a good context to introduce literacy students to the more demanding educational components of interactive cable technology, as long as the presence of the teacher is not threatened in any way.

3. *Sticking with paper and pencil*. Nickerson (1981) also mentions that user conceptualization of a system and unfounded assumptions about what is required by the system are other potential impediments to the successful integration of technology. Indeed, a fairly common assumption among the literacy students was that they learned better when working with traditional tools (pencil and paper) than with technology. In a group less satisfied with the experience for instance, one finds a shared belief that individuals who use a system like Videoway find themselves de facto in a cognitively passive situation. Thus, several students had the impression that interactive programs "do their work for them" and are less beneficial than working with pencil and paper.

Videoway is easier than looking something up in a dictionary. The computer gives you the answer, whereas when you look in the dictionary, you get to practice reading. You can't do that with the technology. (A).

4. *The company of other students*. Lastly, group support is such an important benefit of coming to class for the adults that some participants were afraid of being isolated from the other students by technology.

I don't like to be alone with the machine. (I)

It's better when someone is with you. (A)

We are reminded here of Nickerson's (1981) and Rice's (1984) remarks about feared dehumanizing effects of technology as a common response to text-oriented new media. Some ideas about the design of videotext and classroom pedagogy naturally come to mind in response. Printed texts per se may be no more personal than electronic texts and it is the writing style as such that serves to convey warmth. Designers of videotext may be well advised to emphasize the affective tone when appropriate to help learners in general overcome this obstacle. For literacy students, the judicious enhancement of text with graphics may further personalize the information in a meaningful way.

Acknowledging students' social needs through peer tutoring and team collaboration can also help create a positive climate around technology in the classroom. Learners can also use electronic networks to share information and communicate with learners or tutors in other locations, which would help counteract the notion that technology necessarily isolates people. In this regard, it is puzzling that the project teachers who, on the one hand, were extremely sensitive to the social dynamics among the students, did not take advantage of electronic mail to foster communication activities among students.

In short, illiterate individuals have developed their own *weltaschaung* through which they view technology. It would appear desirable to take their personal viewpoint and in particular, their mental representations of school, into account when designing services and material for literacy students. As suggested by Clark (1989) and other authors, the principles of developmental psychology can be fruitfully applied to the design of technology even for adult learners. For instance, Whiteside and Wixon (1985), borrowing from Piaget's theoretical perspective, remind us that learning proceeds by assimilation (integrating new information within established mental schemata) and accommodation (gradually transforming existing schemata to better interpret new facets of reality). Yet, they point out, technology designers seem to do little to connect with learners' existing schemata. In this case, establishing links between electronic learning and traditional learning might go a long way in helping illiterate individuals view technology as a learning tool. Following this same line of thought, Carroll and Rosson (1987) suggest making or describing a system as similar as possible to something familiar. For instance, a simple starting point may be to identify designated services with icons of pencils and books. In the next section, some of the other recommendations for improving the technology that were formulated in response to the participants' reactions will be outlined.

Recommendations

This project allowed us to pinpoint certain essential conditions for illiterate individuals to realize their potential through the use of technology. For the benefit of researchers and educators who foresee similar experiments with technology in literacy classrooms, this section will share the main recommendations of the study with respect to the optimal design of technology and the necessary pedagogical complements for classroom use. Finally, the OTA report will serve to put this study in perspective with respect to similar experiences in the United States.

Design of Technology for Literacy Students

Design of information services. The optimal design of interactive technology for illiterate users involves nothing less than the intensification of basic design principles, that is, the contents must be *very* relevant and the presentation must be *extra* user friendly. With regard to the first point, the content of several information services had a clear pedagogical relevance because they were consistent with the major objectives pursued by the literacy teachers:

• *the development of language and mathematics skills* through the use of tutoring programs or games;
• *the acquisition of knowledge related to daily life* (government services, household maintenance, mechanical repairs, etc.); and
• *the development of various cognitive skills related to learning* such as memory and concentration as well as strategy and logic.

However relevant the contents, only an excellent mode of presentation is likely to entice both students and teachers to take advantage of them. This dimension takes on acute importance with literacy students because an inappropriately designed service constantly reminds them that they do not read well and further undermines their self-confidence. Four complementary aspects of the design of an interactive technology might be considered with a view to optimizing its services for an illiterate clientele.

1. *General appeal of the presentation.* The visual presentation should be constructed so as to provide an agreeable experience for users. Among the elements which contribute to making information services attractive for illiterate individuals are: (1) overall simplicity of page display; (2)

pleasing graphics; (3) vivid and harmonious colors; and (4) humorous cartoon characters.

2. *Ease of use of a given service.* With respect to use, navigation through the system needs to be not only user friendly, but illiterate-user friendly. Among the facilitating elements which should be reinforced are: (1) a navigational track clearly indicating the steps to follow; and (2) user-controlled page scrolling; (3) a permanent exit option.

3. *Ease of comprehension of the contents.* Different system components should facilitate user comprehension of contents at a basic level for informal use. Certain elements in this regard are especially important for illiterate users: (1) vocabulary within their grasp; (2) iconic symbols to support textual information; and (3) simple sentences.

4. *Specific pedagogical features.* In addition, certain characteristics could contribute to the improvement of the pedagogical potential of an information service. In a school setting, it is important for students to be able to: (1) choose among finely graduated difficulty levels; (2) receive positive reinforcement when answering correctly; (3) correct themselves in case of error; and (4) have access to help mechanisms (i.e., definitions, suggestions).

Design of interactive television. Interactive television was greatly appreciated by the illiterate students because of its dynamic and engaging aspects. However, ITV was not used as much as the information services by the teachers in the classrooms. In large measure, this can be imputed to broadcasting constraints which render it a much less flexible tool for a school setting. This is unfortunate because the OTA report points out that many adult learners, unable to use text for information, have developed alternative skills for understanding, organizing, and remembering information that draw on imagery, sound, and spatial memory (OTA, 1993). Therefore, given future technological developments, it is worth underlining ITV's potential for the illiterate population and pointing to some adjustments relative to the content and the design of interactive programs that could help meet their learning needs.

As to *content,* the creation of interactive programming dealing with varied topics consistent with the interests of illiterate individuals (eg., health, family finances, etc.) would be beneficial. Thus, most of the participants in our first exploratory study (Frenette, 1991) displayed a keen interest in a pilot interactive program about grocery shopping intended for illiterate individuals. This program featured a young, economically disadvantaged couple who overcomes problems at the grocery store. The story serves as a context to explain how to read food labels and to give savings tips. Viewers could verify their understanding of this information by answering questions and obtaining supportive feedback.

Just as importantly, the *design* of interactive programs needs to accommodate the reading and comprehension capacities of an illiterate clientele by incorporating special features (e.g., simple vocabulary both written and spoken, sufficient time to respond, acknowledgment of group viewing situation, etc.). The optimal design of information services and interactive television is a necessary condition for the successful appropriation of technology by illiterate individuals, but it appears to be insufficient. The project also underscored the importance of developing pedagogical aids for the classroom, in addition to well-designed technological products, to favor a meaningful integration of technology into teaching and learning practices.

Pedagogical Aids for the Literacy Classroom

Although designers usually expect interactive technology to be self-standing, there is a long school tradition of using written material that needs to be acknowledged. From our observations in school settings in general, it has often been the case that inertia rapidly sets in when new users are left on their own before they are "on a first-name basis" with the technology. In the case at hand, the need for pedagogical material and pedagogical support for both teachers and students was strongly documented.

Pedagogical material. Working with Videoway technology in the classroom allowed the teachers to identify which type of pedagogical material would be most useful so that the interactive system would fit well into the school setting. In this regard, three principal tools were seen as highly desirable: (1) a detailed *reference document* (such as was used in the project) describing the contents of information services and ITV programming; (2) a *teacher's guide* that highlights specific contents and suggested learning activities intended for an illiterate clientele; and (3) large *posters* of the menus and of the remote control device.

Caroll and Rosson (1987) make a very relevant suggestion to assist learners in mastering a new system. They propose that training material should be in accordance with real-world goals and not system functions. In this case, it would involve for instance designing a guide that corresponds to a teacher's concerns (i.e., "How to plan a French lesson with the Videoway system," etc). Teachers also expressed the need for pedagogical material conceived specifically for the students. It is important to create tools and activities that allow the students to combine activities on electronic learning systems with reading and writing on paper. A daily log such as was used in the project, for example, can help illiterate students to become aware of their personal progress with the technology. Removable stickers of letters, key words, and icons related to the technology would also be useful for beginning students.

Pedagogical support. The project teachers made a pioneering effort in experimenting the technology alongside their regular teaching duties, but they experienced some difficulty in doing so. Dealing simultaneously with their own appropriation of the technology and assisting that of their students appears to take its toll on teachers unaccustomed to working with technology. Therefore, in planning future projects, it is very important to allocate a sizable portion of resources for teacher support. For instance, training sessions for teachers are highly recommended. These sessions should include classroom management techniques and simulations of pedagogical activities adapted to the needs of illiterate students. System options of special value for the classroom, such as pre-programming of frequently used services, should be highlighted. Teachers also need to know they will have easy access to a congenial and reassuring resource person after the training sessions for trouble shooting. Finally, regular meetings and networking among teachers using the system would provide them much valued psychological and pedagogical support.

Comments on the OTA Report

The report on adult literacy and the new technologies published by the Office of Technology Assessment is of direct relevance to the issue at hand. Since there is little research available on technology with illiterate adult learners, this paper provides the opportunity to comment on its conclusions based on the findings in our own study. The report begins by listing several advantages of technology for adult learners in general (OTA, 1993, 8).

A first advantage of technology would be the possibility of *reaching adult learners outside the classroom.* This is certainly a worthwhile objective for illiterate adults as well, but given the extensive support that was needed for both students and teachers to become familiar with a domestic technology, it appears essential to foresee a supportive system. Indeed, readers may have found it paradoxical that interactive technology which is praised as enhancing autonomous learning, was used mainly within structured activities in this project. In this regard, we are reminded by Rogers (1983) that reinvention is a common, indeed desirable, aspect of how people adopt new technologies. In addition, this finding suggests that the goal of autonomous learning of illiterate individuals through technology should be situated in a long-term perspective.

Two other major advantages of technology for adult learners according to the OTA report are *using learning time efficiently and individualizing instruction* since learners have control over features such as pace, repetition or extra explanation. In principle, illiterate adults could benefit from these same features to optimize their learning. However, participants in our study did not appear to be in the habit of self-learning. Therefore, it appears that this individuation would need to be supported by an excellent design (in the sense of making technology extra simple and very progressive) and by support and structure from their immediate environment. Adults attending literacy classes may have faith in teachers, but no experience whatsoever with technology and if so, they cannot be expected to transfer this confidence immediately.

A fourth advantage of technology for adult learners underlined by the OTA report is that of *sustaining motivation*. Indeed, technology enjoys a social status in addition to being novel and engaging for many adults who like the challenge of mastering the "machine." This motivating potential was confirmed as well for many illiterate participants in the study. However, there is an interesting twist on the point made by the authors of the report that technology-based learning environments do not resemble those of past school failures (and thus favor adult learners). In this study, a number of literacy students expected traditional school methods and believed in them. As a consequence, technology may be judged unfavorably when viewed through the lenses of the traditional school model, unless a special effort is made to help students see the connections between traditional learning tools and electronic tools.

Finally, as the OTA report points out, technology can provide *access to information tools*. On this point, we wholeheartedly agree provided that the contents are anchored in the life reality of the economically disadvantaged who make up a great number of illiterate adults.

The OTA report goes on to identify *specific benefits of technology for literacy students,* each one of which is commented upon [in brackets] (OTA, 1993, 204):

- *Learners like the tools.* [But not all learners, since in fact personal and social dynamics can generate heavy resistance to technology.]
- *Information tools help teachers but do not replace them.* [But the students need to be reassured on this point and the teachers themselves need help in appropriating these new tools.]
- *Information tools do meet some of the special learning needs of adults with low literacy skills.* [Indeed some advanced technologies such as voice recognition and touch-screen interface may be ideally suited for illiterate learners but the reality of the educational world leads us to put affordability into the equation, especially with a view to home learning. This project led to the formulation of lengthy recommendations for the adjustment of an interactive cable technology which may be less flexible at this point in time, but is already widely accessible and harbors the promise of future technological developments in the home.]

Finally, the report indicates some *limitations of technology for literacy learners* (OTA, 1993, 204–05); the first three were supported in this study while the two other points appear quite relative:

- *Technology can be intimidating to some learners.* [Indeed some students in the project expressed strong reservations about technology and we have attempted to understand their personal vision in this regard].
- *Tools require learner investment.* [Indeed, this point is largely documented in our study.]
- *Information technology requires new skills of teachers.* [This point is also a major conclusion of the study.]
- *Technical problems with hardware and software are common; special expertise is often needed to get technology working optimally.* [It was not the case with the relatively simple cable technology we chose to experiment with. Therefore, one has to legitimately wonder about the reliability of sophisticated technologies and the technical support required when planning to introduce these into educational settings. This caution needs to be stressed for the literacy milieux since a breakdown may be more intimidating for both teachers and students.]
- *Decisions about technology implementation often must be made by trial and error.* [Although there is always some unpredictability, costly mistakes can be avoided. Needless to say, research has a very important part to play in this regard and we believe the present study may assist others' decisions in some modest way. Indeed, we hope that summative and formative research will be regularly included in educational projects with a technologi-

cal component to help further our understanding of the dynamics involved in the appropriation of technology by illiterate individuals.]

Conclusion

This experiment demonstrated that there are many potential advantages of an interactive technology like the Videoway system for literacy classes. Notwithstanding the numerous adjustments that need to be made, the system's components—videogames, videotext, and interactive television— proved to be very stimulating for learning. Games in particular sustain motivation and introduce novelty. The use of videotext services is itself a reading activity, the content is renewable and feedback is immediate; for its part, interactive television allows for learning in a user-friendly and dynamic fashion. The ideal learning situation is created when the contents are relevant to students' personal needs and appropriate for their reading skills. In other words, *the what and the how* of technology are intertwined.

We also observed that a technology must lend itself to diverse modes of usage in the classroom. Thus, the Videoway system was used individually, in pairs, as well as collectively and provided nondirective or guided learning activities, although the latter type was definitively favored in the project. Also, it was employed at different moments of the learning process, either as a stimulant or as a reinforcement. In addition, Videoway technology, conceived for home use by the general public presented a sufficient enough challenge for illiterate students to serve as an introduction to technology in the broad sense of the term (i.e., infra-red signal, menu hierarchies, etc.), thereby performing the demystification role initially desired by the teachers.

Through this project, illiterate individuals and literacy teachers had the opportunity to express their apprehensions and their expectations with regard to technology. The appropriation of a technology follows different paths, and illiterate individuals, far from comprising a homogeneous clientele, display a variety of experiences and attitudes. Global appreciation of technology is not only linked to the academic level of the student or the teacher's pedagogical style, but it also relates to several other factors, such as group dynamics, individual motivation, student representations of the nature of learning, and expectations vis-à-vis school. In comparison with other learning milieux for adults, these factors may take on added importance in literacy classes.

Once again, it is necessary for a technology to merge with the personal and pedagogical objectives pursued in the classroom and, above all, to be rooted in the lives of illiterate adults. Indeed, the ultimate goal of introducing technology into schools is to provide students and teachers with a better means to achieve their goals, and not as an end in itself. Therefore, in planning future educational projects with technology, decision makers should be aware of the day-to-day reality of literacy classes and the personal investment required by teachers and students to appropriate technology in a meaningful way. Proactive design of technology anchored in users' needs and life context would avoid the situation of having to retrofit technology to fit those needs.

The transactional viewpoint privileged in this case study serves to remind us that technology will be viewed and evaluated through different lenses when moving from home to school. The system then becomes the focus of a group of people involved in a common goal over a period of time, and as such, undergoes minute scrutiny. This stands in contrast to the alternate domestic situation of numerous individual users with a myriad of lifestyles where technology may or may not be a central object. As a result, certain features which are inconsequential in one context become critical in another (i.e., possibility of self-correction, acknowledgment of group viewing), and the absence of such key features, may signal the premature ending of the technology's career in that particular setting.

Considering what was learned in this exploratory project on the interaction between illiterate individuals, teachers, and technology, we can only concur with Rice (1984) that case studies are a useful approach to understand users' point of view. Thus, it is hoped that other literacy projects will benefit from this endeavor and that other studies will eventually complete and enrich the findings. In terms of social equity, it appears imperative for illiterate citizens to have the opportunity to gain sufficient familiarity with the new information technologies to be able to judge for themselves if and how they are relevant to their life goals. The investment necessary for their participation, however great, is worthwhile if we are to prevent illiterate citizens from being stranded on the service roads of the information superhighway.

Notes

1. Employment and Immigration Canada is the federal ministry responsible for prospective studies on the economics of the labor market, the implementation of

training programs for the workforce, the enforcement of labor laws and immigration policy, as well as the management of unemployment benefits.
2. Two studies on technology and literacy (1991, 1994) were conducted by the "Laboratoire de recherche sur les nouvelles technologies" (*Research Laboratory on New Technologies*), Department of Communication, Université de Montréal, in collaboration with Vidéoway Communications Inc. in Montréal. The long-term study was made possible by the added financial support of the "Ministère de l'enseignement supérieur et de la science" (*Ministry of Graduate Studies and Science*) of Quebec.
3. Student quotations were translated literally in an attempt to preserve the tone of the original statements in French, which were not always syntactically correct. The letters (B), (I), and (A) refer to a subject from the beginner, intermediate, and advanced literacy classes, respectively.

References

Brunel, M. (1990). *Année internationale de l' alphabétisation: Proposition d' interventions municipales* (*International year for literacy: A proposition for municipal interventions*). Unpublished manuscript, Recreation and Community Development Services, City of Montreal, Montreal, Quebec.

Carroll, J. M., & Rosson, M. B. (1987). Paradox of the active user. In J. M. Carroll (Ed.), *Interfacing thought: Cognitive aspects of human-computer interaction* (80–111). Cambridge, Mass.: MIT Press.

Clark, R. E. (1988). The contributions of cognitive psychology to educational technology. In J. Y. Lescop, (Ed.), *Technologie et communication éducatives* (21–33). Ste-Foy, QC: Télé-Université.

———. (1989). Current progress and future directions for research in instructional technology. *Educational Technology Research and Development, 37,* 57–66.

Frenette, M. (1991). *Une étude exploratoire du potentiel de la technologie Vidéoway pour les adultes analphabètes* (An exploratory study of the potential of Videoway technology for illiterate adults). Unpublished manuscript, Department of Communication, Université de Montréal, Montreal, Quebec.

———. (1994). *L'appropriation d'une technologie interactive par des adultes analphabètes, Vol. 1:* Bilan. *Vol. 2: Recommandations.* (The appropriation of an interactive technology by illiterate adults. Vol. 1: Report. Vol. 2: Recommendations). Unpublished manuscript, Department of Communication, Université de Montréal, Montreal, Quebec.

King, J. A., Morris, L. L., & Fitz-Gibbon, C. T. (1987). *The assessment of program implementation.* Beverly Hills, Calif.: Sage.

Nickerson, R. S. (1981). Why interactive computer systems are sometimes not used by people who might benefit from them. *International Journal of Man-machine Studies, 15,* 469–83.

Office of Technology Assessment (OTA). (1993). *Adult literacy and new technologies.* Washington, D.C.: U.S. Government Printing Office.

Patton, M. Q. (1987). *The use of qualitative methods in evaluation.* Beverly Hills, Calif.: Sage.

Rice, R. E. (1984). Evaluating new media systems. In J. Johnston, (Ed.), *Evaluating the new information technologies* (53–71). New Directions for Program Evaluation, No. 23. San Francisco, Calif.: Jossey-Bass.

Rogers, E. M. (1983). *Diffusion of innovations.* N.Y.: Free Press.
————. (1986). *Communication technology: The new media in society.* N.Y.: Free Press.
UNESCO. (1990). *L'Action mondiale pour l'education-Année internationale de l'alphabétisation.* (*World action for education—International year for literacy*). Paris: Educational studies and documents No 42.
Whiteside, J., & Wixon, D. (1985). Developmental theory as a framework for studying human-computer interaction. In H. R. Hartson, (Ed.), *Advances in human-computer interaction, Vol 1* (29–48). Norwood, N.J.: Ablex.

19

Network Literacy in an Electronic Society: An Educational Disconnect?

Charles R. McClure

Significant changes in the communications infrastructure are affecting the very fabric of society as information technologies are able to provide an incredible and seemingly endless array of information resources and services. There is an educational discon-nect between the rapidly developing communications technologies and information resources available to the public, and the public's ability to use these sources. While the gulf between those who are network literate and those who are not continues to widen, the educational community remains largely oblivious. The manner in which edu-cational and societal issues related to network literacy are addressed and resolved will have a significant impact on how society evolves, how notions of literacy and a literate society evolve, and the degree to which societal equity can be enhanced. The library community has the opportunity to make a significant contribution to the resolu-tion of these issues. This chapter puts forward strategies to develop Internet/NREN as a vehicle for: (1) "reconnecting" different segments of our society; (2) promoting a network literate population to ensure social equity; and (3) enhancing the role of li-braries and the education community to accomplish these objectives. **

> *We're all connected by communications miracles. It's the people, still fumbling with the Switch Hook Flash who are stuck in the Stone Age.* (Gleick, 1993, 26).

The skills required to use the switch hook flash on one's telephone pale in comparison to the skills and knowledge that are needed to use resources and services in the evolving National Information Infrastruc-

---

* This chapter is a shortened and edited version of "Network Literacy in an Elec-tronic Society: An Educational Disconnect" (1993), in *The Knowledge Economy: The Nature of Information in the 21st Century* (137–78). Queenstown, Md.: The Aspen Institute, Institute for Information Studies.

ture (NII) and the Internet/National Research and Education Network (NREN). While some people begin and others expand and refine their network skills and competencies, the vast majority of the public has no skills related to using these new communications technologies and many live in fear of a passing thunderstorm that might force them to re-learn (again) how to reset the LCD time displays on their VCR or microwave.

There is an educational disconnect between the rapidly developing communications technologies and information resources available to the public, and the public's ability to use these resources. An elite few, typically academics, researchers, technology enthusiasts, and "network junkies," are network literate. While the gulf between these network literate "cybernauts" and those who are not continues to widen, the education system continues to be largely oblivious. Individuals in this emerging electronic society primarily "learn on their own" to be productive in and empowered by this new environment, or they are being left behind.

Significant changes in the communications infrastructure are affecting the very fabric of society. Information technologies in telecommunications, cable television, wireless satellite transmissions, the Internet/ NREN, and others now provide an incredible, and seemingly endless array of information resources and services. Experts knowledgeable about these technologies tell us that future uses and applications are limited only by one's imagination (The Info Highway, 1993). Network literacy, the ability to identify, access, and use electronic information from the network, will be a critical skill for tomorrow's citizens if they wish to be productive and effective in both their personal and professional lives.

The NII, an amorphous term for the collection of these information technologies and the infrastructure that supports them, appears to be taking shape (U.S. Congress, 1993a). We are moving toward establishing an ubiquitous electronic network that connects different information technologies to endless streams of digital data throughout the country and the world. Indeed, the "network" is an evolving term that includes these various computer, telecommunications, cable TV, and other technologies.

Meanwhile, the telephone, telecommunications, and cable television companies are battling for the rights (and the profits) for wiring individual homes into a massive array of information providers, resources, and services (Stix, 1993). But while the battle for connecting individual homes to this evolving information infrastructure is still developing, it is clear that the Internet/NREN already provides a great deal of connectivity throughout the country and will have a significant impact on society. Indeed, the "networked society" is already taking shape.

While the technology developments related to networking are significant and draw much attention, there is also an infrastructure that supports these technologies. The nontechnological aspects of the infrastructure includes the human resources, political and social processes, organizational support, and the tools (both physical and attitudinal) that people need to use the new technologies. The technological infrastructure that supports the Internet/NREN continues to grow at a much faster rate than our knowledge about how to use the network—to say nothing of the switch hook flash—the network's impacts, its uses, and its effects on organizations and individuals.

Despite the traditional role of libraries in providing a range of information resources and services to the public, inadequate Federal policy and planning has been done to assist libraries transition to the networked environment. Nor has there been adequate planning or assistance to the public in learning how to use and access these electronic resources. Making these resources available to the public, learning how to communicate and use the network, and insuring network literacy among the population is critical to the success of the NREN and to the people in the networked society.

In our fascination with the new information technologies, we have given inadequate attention to how society will migrate to this networked environment. Will the networked society result in excluding a range of services and opportunities to those who are unable, for whatever reason, to move to the networked environment? Who will be responsible for educating people to use the networking technologies and take advantage of the wealth of resources currently available and yet to be developed? How will the public participate in decision making about technology applications that will affect the fabric of their society if they are network illiterate?

The purpose of this chapter is to explore educational and societal issues related to network literacy. How we address and resolve these issues will have a significant impact on how society evolves, how notions of literacy and a literate society evolve, and the degree to which social equity can be enhanced in this country. The country must develop strategies to develop the Internet/NREN as a vehicle for: (1) "reconnecting" different segments in our society; (2) promoting a network literate population to ensure a social equity; and (3) enhancing the role of libraries and the education community to accomplish these objectives.

Networked Information Resources and Services

The term *networked information* applies to a vast range of electronic information and services now available through the Internet. It is not the purpose of this paper to review the extent and nature of these resources and services since others (Krol, 1992; LeQuey, 1993) already have done so. There are thousands of discussion groups; databases and sources to access information from governments, commercial providers, and other individuals; sophisticated scientific applications; books and journals in digital format; electronic card catalogs of many libraries throughout the world; weather reports and restaurant guides; and much, much more.

Information that has been networked, that is, made accessible via one of the over thousands of worldwide networks comprising the Internet, puts new dimensions on the impacts and uses of information (see following section). But uses and applications of the Internet have gone far beyond ordinary electronic mail (e-mail). To cope with the vast amounts of information available over the network new communication techniques and information resource discovery tools are available and being used, (Brett, 1992) including:

- *Listservs and discussion groups*: users who share a common interest in a particular topic can subscribe to a listservs where a message posted to that list will be sent automatically to everyone subscribing to that list. There are thousands of such lists on every conceivable topic imaginable. For example, there is a PUBLIB listserv in which individuals exchange information related to public library activities. Someone can post a note to such a listserv and immediately have it sent to thousands of other people interested in that topic.
- *File Transfer Protocol (FTP)*: individuals and organizations have placed vast amounts of information on file servers at many different sites around the world; using FTP, users can log-in to a remote computer system, identify a particular file, and retrieve that file directly into their computer. For example, a file containing *Alice in Wonderland* at Project Guttenberg can be FTP'd to an individual's personal computer to be read whenever desired.
- *Telneting*: once an address is known for a particular database, the user can log-in to a remote database and search that database for information; for example, users from around the world can log-in to a data base at the Library of Congress and determine the current status of legislation.

- *Gophers*: this technique identifies files on the Internet by keyword searching, connects the user to the desired file, and the identified file then can be searched and downloaded (if desired) directly into their computer. For example, within a gopher program, users might search on the term "environmental pollution" locating twelve different data bases covering that particular topic, users can select one they wish to search and be seamlessly connected to that database.
- *Wide Area Information Server (WAIS)*: a WAIS is similar to a gopher in that both identify and access remote databases; a WAIS, however, ranks the likelihood that a particular database has the information one needs and can do full-text searching of multiple databases.

These, of course, are only some of the services and techniques that people can use to identify, access, search, and obtain a wealth of information over the Internet. Krol (1992) and Kochmer and NorthwestNet (1993) are two of the best guides currently available for how to use and search the Internet.

This environment promotes a very pluralistic, albeit, constantly changing and chaotic approach for accessing and using information in a networked setting. And while there is still much need for more "user friendly" programs and services over then network, and while some of the issues related to privacy, intellectual property rights, pricing of services, and acceptable use of the Internet (to name but a few of the issues) remain thorny and contentious, growth and use of the Internet proceeds exponentially.

For example, one recently developed service is called AskERIC, which is an Internet-based question answering service for teachers, library media specialists, and the education community. It is supported by the Department of Education through the ERIC Clearinghouse at Syracuse University ("AskERIC: ERIC and the Internet Continued," 1993). By sending an e-mail message over the Internet with the request for information to <askeric@ericir.syr.edu>, users can obtain a response, usually within twenty-four hours, about virtually anything related to education. In addition, the librarian answering the question at the ERIC Clearinghouse may direct the user to additional Internet resources, provide digital information from the ERIC database, or attach a range of additional information in his/her electronic response to the user.

The impacts of having access to and use of the Internet are extensive. One business executive commented:

The Internet gave us the power to do something significant and the ability to do it quickly. In business terms its a first-quarter success. We can work quickly with experts around the world and we can get rapid feedback on early revisions. It improves our customer support, which increases our income from sales. (Levin, 1993, F3)

Another example of impact comes from a television manager in Omaha, Nebraska:

> My daughter was scheduled for surgery in October of 1991 for correction of scoliosis (curvature of the spine). In late summer of that year, I decided it was important to learn more about scoliosis. A library catalogue search over the Internet led me to discover that another daughter had symptoms that could mean our family was affected by a serious hereditary disorder. . . . I used a specialized Internet service, WAIS, that let me search multiple databases. The bibliographies led me to physicians who knew how to diagnose and treat it. *The Internet may have saved my daughter's life!* (author's emphasis). (Stix, 1993, 105)

Health care delivery over the evolving NII is another example where rapid changes will occur. The Consumer Interest Research Institute (1993) concluded that powerful new information technology applications are emerging which can make home based health care surprisingly effective:

- *Computer based medical records.* Computer based medical records are a "foundation technology" that will make possible a wide range of new applications. They will record and store patient information including patient problems, test results, orders submitted, treatment plans, X-rays and other images.
- *Health information and communication systems.* Easy consumer access to health information will be crucial for making a disease prevention/health promotion strategy work. Consumers will have greater health information available to them at home including clinical advice about specific diseases, information on their own conditions, access to their own medical records, disease prevention/health promotion information geared to their individual health status, etc.
- *Diagnostic and therapeutic expert consultation.* By 1995, expert systems are likely to be used increasingly on physician's workstations for consultation and quality control. . . . In the late 1990s they will be linked to the electronic medical record and knowledge bases that will advise the practitioner on the logic and medical literature supporting specific decisions. (12–15)

These experiences and visions—as well as thousands of other "success stories"—dot the Internet landscape. The new communication techniques, and the resources and services available over the Internet, will continue to change the way we work and live. Those not connected or unable to use the Internet, however, may find themselves increasingly disadvantaged in the workplace, dealing with daily issues, being an informed citizen, and in living a quality life.

A Policy Perspective on the Internet/NREN and Literacy

Although the intent of this chapter is not to provide a policy analysis of the Internet/NREN and of literacy, it is interesting to juxtapose a brief overview of these two areas. There have been few efforts to consider relationships between these two policy areas. Yet, the successful development of the NII will require both a new expanded information policy system and network literacy throughout society.

Internet/NREN Background

The Internet is a currently existing, operational network of networks. The NREN is a program, a concept, and a vision of an interconnected future. The Internet was not created at a single point in time, but has been an evolving structure since the late 1960s. The term NREN is often used as shorthand for a ubiquitous, national network connecting computers, people, databases, digital libraries, and a host of other resources residing on the network.

Projects underwritten by the Defense Advanced Research Projects Agency (DARPA) in the mid to late 1960s resulted in the ARPANet, an experimental packet switched computer network that began in 1969. ARPANet provided both operational functionality as well as an opportunity for further research into advanced networking technologies. The Transmission Control Protocol/Internet Protocol (TCP/IP) emerged from the research in the ARPANet environment. These protocols allowed the concept of the Internet, a network of interconnected computer networks of all sizes—from local area networks (LANs) to wide area networks (WANs), to become a reality. Lynch and Preston (1990) and McClure et al. (1991) provide overviews and history of the Internet.

In the mid to late 1980s, the National Science Foundation (NSF) funded several supercomputer sites to serve as national supercomputer resources and developed a high-speed backbone network (NSFNet) to connect them. This initiated the second phase in national network development. NSF also coordinated a tiered structure of interconnected computer networks by funding the establishment of regional, or mid-level, networks. These regional networks interconnected educational and research organizations, institutions, and their individual computer networks, and they provided access and connection to the NSFNet backbone. The NSFNet backbone is one of several federally funded backbone networks, connected together through the Internet.

The Internet is not only a United States computer network, but a truly global network, connecting an estimated 12–14 million users on thousands of networks. In recent years, the Internet has shown tremendous growth in number of users, networks connected, and traffic. Rutkowski (1993) details this tremendous growth and predicts that exponential growth of the Internet, in terms of users, connected networks, network hosts and registrations, and traffic will continue for the foreseeable future.

Now in the early 1990s, the Internet is in another transitional stage. The NSF has been reducing its subsidies to the regional networks in recent years and is guiding the Internet towards privatization and commercialization. Privatization means that the Federal government will no longer subsidize directly network services and connections. Commercialization will allow the lifting of current restrictions on traffic flowing over the network and acceptable use of the network will not be limited to network traffic supporting research and education. The direction and character of the moves toward privatization and commercialization have sparked widespread debate within the networking community (DeLoughry, 1993).

As a federally funded, multi-agency initiative, the principal goals of the NREN program are: establishing a gigabit network for the research and education community and fostering its use; developing advanced networking technologies and accelerating their deployment; stimulating the availability, at a reasonable cost, of the required services from the private sector; and serving as a catalyst for the early deployment of a high speed general purpose digital communications infrastructure for the nation. Despite these goals, the NREN means different things to different people. The policy debates will continue, but network literacy issues have yet to be raised and receive adequate attention.

Current and Proposed Internet Policy Instruments

The *High Performance Computing Act of 1991* (P.L. 102–194) authorized the creation of a National Research and Education Network. After several years of legislative action, the Act was signed into law in December, 1991. McClure et. al. (1991) provides a comprehensive legislative history of the Act and related legislative initiatives. In the Act, the NREN is one of several components in a high performance computing and communications program. In the FY 1993 proposed budget for the high performance computing program by the Office of Science and Technology, only 15 percent of the funds are allocated to the NREN. The majority of the funds are targeted at the High Performance Computing Systems and the Advanced Software Technology and Algorithms components.

Section 102 of the Act describes the NREN, and section (b) specifically discusses "access" to the network:

> Federal agencies and departments shall work with private network service providers, State and local agencies, libraries, educational institutions and organizations, and others, as appropriate, in order to ensure that the researchers, educators, and students have access, as appropriate, to the Network. The Network is to provide users with appropriate access to high-performance computing systems, electronic information resources, other research facilities, and libraries. The Network shall provide access, to the extent practicable, to electronic information resources maintained by libraries, research facilities, publishers, and affiliated organizations.

While public access is prominently mentioned in this section, the sense of this section is severely compromised by phrases such as "as appropriate," "with appropriate," and "to the extent possible."

The Clinton administration has expressed commitment to advancing the information infrastructure and increased deployment of information technology in the cause of education, research, and national competitiveness. A February, 1993 policy statement states (Clinton & Gore, 1993):

> Public investment will be provided to support technology that can increase the productivity of learning and teaching in formal school settings, in industrial training, and even at home. New information technologies can give teachers more power in the classroom and create a new range of employment opportunities. Schools can themselves become high-performance workplaces (14).

Regarding the importance of "Information Superhighways:"

> Access to the Internet and developing high-speed National Research and Educational [sic.] Network (NREN) will be expanded to connect university campuses, community colleges, and K-12 schools to a high-speed communications network providing a broad range of information resources. Support will be provided for equipment allowing local networks in these learning institutions access to the network along with support for developing of high performance software capable of taking advantage of the emerging hardware capabilities. (35)

The policy paper goes on to discuss the importance of using the new information technologies and the national network for enhanced economic competitiveness; making a range of government information and services available of the network; and expanding access to the NREN.

In the Spring of 1993, Representative Boucher (VA) introduced, H.R. 1757, the *High Performance Computing and High Speed Networking Applications Act*. The bill was renamed the *National Information Infrastructure Act of 1993* when it passed the House in Summer of 1993. Section 2 (3) states:

> High performance computing and high-speed networking have the potential to expand dramatically access to information in many fields, including education, libraries, government information dissemination, and health care, if adequate resources are devoted to the research and development activities needed to do so.

Section 2 (5) states:

> The Federal Government should ensure that the applications achieved through research and development efforts such as the High-Performance Computing Program directly benefit *all Americans* (author's emphasis).

And Section 305 (b) states that the program will

> train teachers, students, librarians, and state and local government personnel in the use of computer networks and the Internet. Training programs for librarians shall be designed to provide skills and training materials needed by librarians to instruct the public in the use of hardware and software for accessing and using computer networks and the Internet.

This bill is important since it includes language supporting training issues for networking, extending the role of libraries and the education community in developing and operating the national network, and promoting the development of networking applications and demonstration projects. The bill recognizes the importance of assisting individuals move into the networked society successfully. As of August, 1993 the bill has passed the House and awaits Senate action.

Literacy Policy Perspectives

Policy instruments related to literacy have evolved from a number of agencies and initiatives. For example, the *Adult Education Act* (P.L. 89-750) promotes the development of a range of basic literacy programs to adults; the *Library Services and Construction Act* (P.L. 88-269) provides for Department of Education grants to states for public library services such as literacy programs; the *Omnibus Trade and Competitiveness Act* of 1988 (P.L. 100-148) amends the *Adult Education Act* to provide literacy programs and amends the *Education for Economic Security Act* to authorize mathematics and science education programs.

In general, however, these initiatives provide support and funding for the individual states to create and run a range of "literacy" programs. It is unclear how successful these efforts have been. Some have argued that there is no accountability from the states regarding these programs and that the results have been mixed at best (Bishop, 1991). Moreover, these efforts typically concentrate on: (1) improving adult reading skills; (2) promoting math and science education; and (3) job training—not on network literacy of information problem solving skills.

For example, one of the National Education Goals that resulted from the meeting between President Bush and the state governors in 1992 (U.S. Department of Education, 1992), was that by the year 2000,

> Every adult American will be literate and will possess the knowledge and skills necessary to compete in a global economy and exercise the rights and responsibilities of citizenship. (xi)

Currently, it is estimated that there are some 30 million functionally illiterate Americans in this country. Thus, how this goal will be accomplished is unclear. How these adults will be "literate" in a networked society and what might constitute such literacy is also unclear.

Probably the most important recent policy instrument related to literacy is P.L. 102-73, *The National Literacy Act of 1991*. A major thrust of this law is its creation of the National Institute for Literacy. Section 102 (3) states:

> A national institute for literacy would (a) provide a national focal point for research, technical assistance and research dissemination, policy analysis, and program evaluation in the area of literacy; and (b) facilitate a pooling of ideas and expertise across fragmented programs and research efforts.

The Institute can also award action grants to be given to volunteer groups that provide literacy training. Because the Institute is still in its infancy, it is unclear how successful it will be in dealing with the plethora of literacy problems and policies.

Literacy policy and support at the Federal level is uneven, at best. Recently, in Spring, 1993, the Clinton administration proposed the elimination of $8 million in literacy projects from the *Library Services and Construction Act*, Title VI. For fiscal year 1993, that program accounted for some 250 awards, administered by state and public libraries. In the overall scheme of the U.S. federal budget, $8 million may be trivial. But in terms of support for dealing with literacy issues, $8 million is significant.

In perhaps the best recent analysis of policy issues related to literacy, the U.S. Office of Technology Assessment (1993) concluded:

> The Federal response to the problem of adult illiteracy consists of many categorical programs—at least 29, perhaps many more, depending on the definition used—that in some way aid adult literacy and basic skills education. Although the individual programs have solid records of accomplishment, together the create a Federal role that is complicated, fragmented, and insufficient, and which, by it very nature, works against development of a coordinated Federal adult literacy policy. (127–28)

Federal policy instruments related to literacy issues are limited to a very traditional interpretation of "literacy." Overall, the literacy policy framework can be best described as one that has been given much rhetoric but has received very limited direct support.

Assessment

Until the Clinton administration, the federal policy framework for creating the Internet/NREN has emphasized the development of new networking technologies and creating a "level playing field" for the private sector to develop the network. Inadequate policy exists supporting public sector uses of the Internet/NREN. The library and education community had minimal input and impact on developing the NREN plan. The policy framework has promoted the use of the Internet/NREN among researchers and scientists working primarily on "grand challenges" rather than developing it as a "public right" to which all citizens are entitled. This may change with Clinton administration policy initiatives and the introduction of H.R. 1757 in March, 1993.

Moreover, development of the Internet/NREN is uneven. Gigabit transmission speeds are being developed, while the typical American classroom has no telephone line to connect to the network; some individuals have free (oftentimes subsidized) use of the Internet, and others must pay

significant fees; the gulf between network literacy and illiteracy continues to widen; and overall, large segments of the population appear likely
to be by-passed as the networked society evolves. How society will migrate to this networked environment is unclear.

Interestingly, the Department of Education has limited involvement in
the deployment and planning of the NREN or the NII. Despite some
recent activities for promoting literacy and the passage of PL 102-173,
there is only beginning understanding of literacy in an electronic age or
for the networked society. Inadequate thought appears to have been given
to the educational roles of national networking or how the network could
be used to enhance the country's educational institutions.

Federal policy related to literacy is very decentralized and dependent,
to some degree, on a host of private initiatives and local efforts—all
largely uncoordinated. In addition, literacy policy is best characterized
as developing basic reading and writing skills. Moreover, "OTA finds
that technology is not a central consideration for most literacy programs"
(Office of Technology Assessment, 1993, 15.) Literacy in terms of information literacy, information problem solving skills, or network literacy
are not considered in the existing policy framework.

Apparently, the belief is that public uses of the network will occur
naturally with little or no Federal, state, and local planning and support.
Either the private sector will provide for public uses and educational
applications, or the library and education community will marshall the
resources needed to move the population into the networked environment. *Somehow, someone,* or *some* institution, will assist the country
move to the networked environment and provide access to information
resources, services, and holdings in an electronic format.

Information in a Networked Environment

There is considerable discussion and debate about what networked
information is, how it's access or lack of access affects a range of societal activities, and how information can be best managed to improve
societal productivity. Generally, information is considered as data or signals that affect the uncertainty state of an individual. That is, for something to be considered as information, it must either make the individual
more or less uncertain about a particular situation or phenomenon
(Whittemore & Yovits, 1973, 222).

As a resource, information is unique in that it has a number of characteristics that separate it from traditional types of resources (adapted from Yurow, 1981, 54):

- The information is not used up by being used;
- The information can be possessed by many persons simultaneously.
- It is difficult to prevent persons who wish to do so from possessing particular parts of information, or acquiring information without paying for it.
- The value of information for a particular consumer often-times cannot be determined until the information is disclosed to that user.
- Information can become obsolete, but it cannot be depleted.
- Frequent use of information does not wear it out.
- The technical units of measurement of information (e.g., bits, packets, etc.) lack meaning and fail to carry meaning for the consumers of that information.

Thus, information fails to follow traditional aspects of a "resource," making it difficult to develop policy for how best to acquire, manage, and use it in a basic market economy such as that in the United States.

This description of information, then, raises the issue of the degree to which it might be best considered as a public good. Some information might be best seen as "public," that is, belonging to the public at large (e.g., much of the government information produced by the U.S. Federal government); other information might best be seen as "private," that is, owned by an individual and either kept for that person's own use or sold if a market price can be determined.

More recently, the notion of value added has been applied to information as a conceptual approach for better understanding its characteristics (Taylor, 1986). In this model, a range of different value added services and processes can be added to information as a means of enhancing its usefulness. For example, an author writes a book, to add value to that book, she hires someone to produce an index for the book. A publisher adds value to the book by having it copyedited, and so forth.

Understanding these basic attributes of information is important if we are to understand educational issues and concerns related to information in a networked society. One significant change from traditional notions of information to information in a networked environment is less emphasis on information as affecting the uncertainty state of the individual to information as an empowering tool. Such an empowerment tool, when properly managed, and when appropriate value added process are attached to the information, can assist an individual make better life decisions and contribute to the overall productivity of a society.

Networked Information and the New Literacy

The term *literacy* means many things to different people. In recent years, different types of literacies have been proposed and defined. Introducing the term *network literacy* into this already confusing array of terms and definitions requires some discussion of the various terms and how they are being used.

Types of Literacies

With the range of services and resources available over the Internet, what constitutes literacy given this evolving networked society? P.L. 102-73, *The National Literacy Act of 1991*, Section 3, states:

> The term "literacy" means an individual's ability to read, write, and speak English, and to compute and solve problems at levels of proficiency necessary to function on the job and in society, to achieve one's goals, and develop one's knowledge and potential.

This notion of literacy is the traditional view—and one that is increasingly out of date.

Computer literacy, for example, is an additional extension of traditional literacy, requiring that individuals can complete basic tasks on a computer such as word processing, creating and manipulating data on a spreadsheet, or using other types of software. The notion of "media literacy" recently has been introduced (the entire statement is reprinted in chapter 3 of this volume) and is described as follows (Aufderheide, 1993):

> Media literacy, the movement to expand notions of literacy to include the powerful post-print media that dominate our informational landscape, helps people understand, produce and negotiate meanings in a culture made up of powerful images, words and sounds. A media literate person—and everyone should have the opportunity to become one—can decode, evaluate, analyze and produce both print and electronic media. (1, v)

Thus, media literacy is a step beyond traditional notions of literacy although it does not specifically mention computing skills or skills/knowledge related to locating, processing, exchanging, and using information in a networked environment.

Probably the most encompassing notion is "information literacy." The Association for Supervision and Curriculum Development stated in a 1991 resolution (Breivik, 1992):

> Today's information society transcends all political, social, and economic boundaries. The global nature of human interactions makes the ability to access and use information crucial. . . . Information literacy, the ability to locate, process, and use information effectively, equips individuals to take advantage of the opportunities inherent in the global information society. Information literacy should be a part of every student's educational experience. (7)

Although it might be assumed within this definition, the resolution could be strengthened to make clear that information literacy includes an "ability to locate, process, and use information effectively" *regardless of delivery mechanisms and the type of format in which that information appears*, that is, to be literate, one must be literate with both print and electronic formats.

Hancock (1993, 1) provides additional detail describing information literacy, concluding that "education systems and institutions must take seriously the challenges of the Information Age. This includes restructuring the learning process to reflect the use of information in the real world, [and] changing the role of the teacher from presenter of prefabricated facts to facilitator of active learning." Information literacy thrives in a resource-based learning environment rich in a variety of print and electronic information.

Ochs, et al. (1991) provide an excellent literature review of information literacy. Figure 19.1 describes a very useful set of goals and objectives related to developing information literacy skills (Ochs, et al., 1991). The goals and objectives were developed in the context of undergraduate student skills and knowledge, but they are useful in expanding our thinking toward network literacy skills. Moreover, the objectives on this list suggest the importance of such skills in not only higher education, but as basic skills for leading a productive life in a networked society.

Although the objectives listed in figure 19.1 tend to be "library-oriented," they offer an excellent perspective on what types of generic skills we need to be teaching the public if they are to be productive in a networked environment. But, at the core of the notion of all the various literacies is the idea of "information problem solving skills."

FIGURE 19.1
Information Literacy Program Goals and Objectives*

A. Understand the role and power of information in a democratic society; students can describe and understand:
- how scholars and researchers use information and keep currently informed;
- how practicing professionals use information and keep currently informed;
- how the use of information can improve the quality of scholars' and professionals' work;
- the commodity nature of information; who generates, controls, and uses information. In particular, the role that governments play in the dissemination and control of information;
- the costs of misinformation, the possibilities of abuse and its consequences.

B. Understand the variety of the content and the format of information; within their discipline, students can:
- distinguish popular from scholarly treatments of a subject;
- distinguish between primary and secondary sources;
- define various standard formats for the storage or scholarly information, e.g., print, microform, optical, floppy and compact disk, and magnetic tape;
- evaluate the quality of information and the usefulness of the content and format of a particular information tool based on relevant criteria.

C. Understand standard systems for the organization of information; within their discipline, students can:
- define types of databases and their organization, e.g., records, fields, and the retrieval function/process;
- recognize that different types of reference sources lead to various forms and formats of information;
- define standard terms such as bibliographic citation, periodical index, abstract, and citation index;
- differentiate between the types of materials typically represented in a library's catalog and those that are not;
- determine the index structure and access points of print or computerized information resources.

D. Develop the capability to retrieve information from a variety of systems and various formats; within their discipline students can:
- construct a logical plan to organize their search for information;
- describe the difference between controlled vocabularies and keywords and use both efficiently in their search strategy;
- effectively use logical operators (e.g., and, or, not) to link their search terms and intersect concepts in various electronic information systems;
- understand and apply the concepts of truncation and field qualification in various electronic information systems;
- describe and use appropriate services which are available to assist them in locating information;
- successfully navigate within the libraries they use;
- accurately interpret bibliographic citations from print and computerized information resources and locate the materials they represent;
- operate a standard personal computer, develop mastery of certain programs/software, and maintain a working awareness of others.

E. Develop the capability to organize and manipulate information for various access and retrieval purposes; within their discipline, students can:
- use a bibliographic file management package to organize downloaded citations and personal files of references;
- conduct their own needs assessment, based on relevant criteria, to identify suitable software packages appropriate to a given application;
- use electronic spreadsheets to reformat and analyze numeric data which has been either downloaded or manually entered into the package;
- use a word processing package to format papers, reformat downloaded references and construct bibliographies;
- write correct bibliographic citations for books, journal articles, and conference reports.

*Source: Ochs, et al. (1991, 93–97).

Literacy and Information Problem-Solving Skills

These skills, or the "Big Six Skills," as described by Eisenberg and Berkowitz (1990), suggest that people should successfully solve problems and make decisions by being able to engage in six key information problem-solving activities (see figure 19.2). People involved with the Internet recognize the importance of such skills in training and education programs. What they sometimes fail to recognize, however, is the importance of developing Internet skills within the contexts of: (1) real need; and (2) the overall information problem-solving process.

The first context is real need: curricular, life, or work. While it is certainly possible to learn skills in isolation, practice and research confirm that people learn best when the use and purpose are clear. Students can probably learn to communicate via e-mail or to access a NASA database, but they will eagerly engage and internalize these skills if they see how they directly relate to their school assignments, personal interests, or work requirements.

The second, and often overlooked, context is information problem-solving process itself. Computer and telecommunications technologies are supposed to extend our abilities to solve problems. That sounds fine in the abstract, but what does it really mean? Again, practice and research tell us that when people understand how specific skills fit into an overall model or process, the power and usefulness of the specific skills are expanded.

Task definition is step one of Eisenberg and Berkowitz's Big Six approach to information problem solving. Electronic communication is also a powerful tool for consulting with others about the best strategies for seeking information (step 2), to locate and access the information itself (step 3), to extract relevant information (step 4), to present the results (step 5), and to seek reaction to your work (step 6). Therefore, it is essential to design and deliver Internet and technology training within the overall problem-solving context.

The two contexts, need and process, provide the necessary anchors for meaningful technology training—and increasing network literacy. This is true regardless of whether those receiving the training are students gaining their first glimpse of the Internet, unemployed workers involved in retraining programs, or corporate executives seeking to stay on top of emerging technologies. Figure 19.2 offers examples of how Internet capabilities can be placed in the Big Six information problem-solving con-

FIGURE 19.2

Internet Capabilities in an Information Problem-Solving Context

The Big Six Skills©	Internet Capability	Application
1. Task Definition		
1.1 Define the problem	E-Mail	to seek clarification from teachers
1.2 Identify information requirements of the problem	E-Mail	to consult with group/team members
	Discussion/Interest Groups (listservs, newsgroup)	to share and discuss concerns/questions/problems with persons in similar settings or with experts
2. Information Seeking Strategies		
2.1 Determine the range of possible sources	electronic libraries, data centers, resources	to be aware of options, to determine possible and priority sources
2.2 Evaluate to determine priority sources	WAIS, Gopher, various Internet resource guides	to determine possible resources, to search for types of files and databases available
	use of AskERIC, NICs	to consult on resources, files, databases
	E-Mail	to consult with group/team members
	Electronic Discussion Groups (listservs, newsgroups)	to request recommendations from persons in similar settings or from experts
3. Location and Access		
3.1 Locate sources (intellectually, physically)	Archie, Veronica	to search for the location of specific files or databases
3.2 Find information within sources	WAIS, Gopher	to search by subject within/across sites
	Telnet, Remote login, ftp	for remote access to computers and electronic libraries
4. Use of Information		
4.1 Engage (read, view, listen)	download and file	to get the relevant information from a remote
4.2 Extract relevant information	transfer, ftp	computer to your own
5. Synthesis		
5.1 Organize information from multiple sources	E-Mail	to share drafts and final communications
5.2 Present information	Listservs, newsgroups	to share papers, reports, and other communications
	Electronic Journals	to present papers and reports
	Ftp and Gopher sites	to archive reports, papers, products
6. Evaluation		
6.1 Judge the product (effectiveness)	E-Mail	to gain feedback
6.2 Judge the process (efficiency)	Listservs, newsgroups	to gain feedback

Source: Michael B. Eisenberg, Director, ERIC Clearinghouse on Information & Technology, School of Information Studies, Syracuse University, Syracuse, NY 13244

text. These are, of course, just some of the options. The chart is easily modified as new Internet functions and resources are made available or as teachers and students find new ways to apply existing capabilities.

Notions of information problem solving and the Big Six skills can be used to enhance our conceptualization of various types of literacies and how they are related to each other. Of concern is: (1) we cannot wait until college for such skills to be obtained; (2) for those who have not gone or do not intend to go to college, how would they obtain such skills; (3) the degree to which members in the education and library community, themselves, have such skills and could impart those skills on others in the general public; and (4) a range of additional skills, unique to the network, need to be added to the list.

Recasting Notions of Literacy

Recasting information literacy notions into the networked society are mind boggling. Project Literacy U.S. estimated that as many as 23 million adult Americans are functionally illiterate, lacking skills beyond the fourth-grade level, with another 35 million semiliterate, lacking skills beyond the eighth-grade level (White House Conference on Library and Information Services, 1991). It must be remembered that these numbers consider literacy in a print-based society, and not in a networked society.

Figure 19.3 suggests a possible approach for thinking about literacy in a networked society. At one level, an individual must be able to read and write—traditional notions of literacy. At another level, the person must be technically literate, for example, be able to operate computer, telecommunications, and related information technologies. At a third level, people need media literacy, and yet at another level they need network literacy. All of these types of literacies can be cast in the context of information problem-solving skills.

Papert (1993) explores the importance of redefining literacy in a networked society. He discusses "knowledge machines" that provide children with interactive learning opportunities that include virtual reality, and an ability to have freedom to explore and interact in an electronic knowledge arena:

> School will either change very radically or simply collapse. It is predictable (though still astonishing) that the Education Establishment cannot see farther than using new technologies to do what it has always done in the past: teach the same curricu-

FIGURE 19.3

Thinking About Literacy Concepts

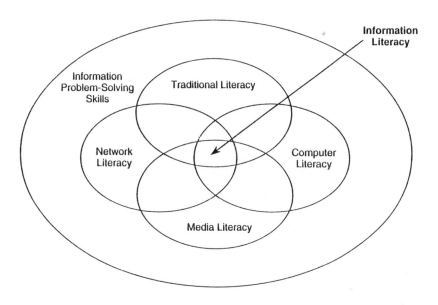

lum. . . . I would go further: the possibility of freely exploring worlds of [electronic] knowledge calls into question the very idea of an administered curriculum. (50)

But what Papert does not tell us, is what, specifically, are the skills and knowledge that these children will need to be literate in this networked environment, and how will they be taught these skills?

A beginning discussion piece for the knowledge and skills that might comprise network literacy for the general public include:

Knowledge

• Awareness of the range and uses of global networked information resources and services;
• Understanding of the role and uses of networked information in problem solving and in performing basic life activities;
• Understanding of the system by which networked information is generated, managed, and made available.

Skills

• Retrieve specific types of information from the network using a range of information discovery tools;
• Manipulate networked information by combining it with other resources, enhancing it, or otherwise increasing the value of the information for particular situations;
• Use networked information to analyze and resolve both work- and personal-related decisions and obtain services that will enhance their overall quality of life.

Such knowledge and skills cannot be seen as "supplemental" to traditional literacy, but rather, part of a reconceptualized notion of literacy in an electronic society.

These skills and knowledge are targeted at the *general* public for *network* literacy. Likely as not, they will require other "literacies" to already be in place (see figure 19.3). Additional knowledge and skills certainly can be included in this beginning list. But even these knowledges and skills listed above, while seemingly basic and rudimentary to the already network literate, will require national commitment and a range of programs if they are to become commonplace in society.

Answers to what constitutes network literacy and how network literacy relates to other types of "literacies" requires immediate attention and research. But as more information services and resources are networked, those individuals who, for whatever reason, cannot access and use them will be severely disadvantaged in society. They may be unable to obtain good jobs; they may not be able to communicate effectively with governmental units; they may not be able to exploit a range of self-help or entertainment services available over the network; and they may become disenfranchised from mainstream societal goals and values. Implications from such a widening gulf between the network literate and the illiterate are significant and require our immediate attention.

Information in the Evolving Networked Society

Even those who are creating the networked society cannot predict how it will evolve. It is still too early to determine how the public can best be connected, which applications will be most useful to the public, how to determine which types of services should be made publicly available and which will be costed, and what might differentiate roles among the government, the public sector, and the private sector in developing and operating the Internet/NREN.

What we do know, however, is that information in this evolving networked society may have different characteristics than information in the pre-networked society. The following aspects of information in a networked environment will require us to re-think educational programs to insure network literacy.

Pervasiveness of Electronic Information

Increasingly, information is in a digital, electronic format. Currently, information tends to be: (1) created in electronic format and then, if necessary transferred into a paper format; or (2) created in electronic format and never migrated into a paper format. The vast majority of Bureau of the Census data, climate and weather data beamed down from satellites, and a range of research data will never be migrated into a paper format. Thus, increasingly, users of information will either have to identify and access information in electronic format or they will be unable to use it at all.

Convergence of Information Technologies

The computer that sits on my office desk is: (a) a computer; (b) a C-D Rom reader; (c) a fax machine; and (d) a world-wide telecommunications node? To refer to this machine as a "mere" computer is an insult! Increasingly, it has become almost impossible to determine where a telecommunications technology, a computer technology, and other information technologies begin or end. Mergers among cable TV companies, computer companies, software producers, and telephone companies testify to the fact that the new information technologies will be multitasked and seamlessly combine many technologies into one package.

Transferability of Digital Information

Related to the convergence of information technology is the transferability of digital information. Once information is in a digital format, it can be transferred, manipulated, edited, revised, and sent through endless transmitters and receivers. A digital picture of the Mona Lisa can be enhanced, changed, "brushed up," or otherwise manipulated, sent over a network, downloaded, and "brushed up" again with existing software. Once information is digital, it can go anywhere, to anyone, at any time. Society will be in a sea of information and only those information services and products that meet real needs, offer true user-friendly software, and make life easier (as opposed to more difficult) will prosper.

Information for Electronic Services Delivery

To date, emphasis has been placed on delivery of electronic information rather than delivery of electronic *services*. Dumping gigabites of data on the network is not the same as providing services to successfully use that information in one's daily life. The ATM machines at the local banks, however, are only the beginning. Increasingly government services, for example, will be delivered through a range of electronic kiosks and directly to the home (McClure, et. al., 1992). Shopping, financial services, entertainment, public education, and other services will be common place on the network. Individuals unable or unwilling to take advantage of these electronic services—especially government services—will be increasingly disadvantaged.

New Information Navigational Skills

In the short term, people will be forced to "drink from firehoses" as a glut of information resources and services overwhelm them. New information navigational skills on the network will be a prerequisite for successful use. Already, it is clear that if individuals cannot use a "gopher," a WAIS, or "telnet" to a "FTP site," they will be hopelessly swallowed in a sea of information and resources—drowned, as it were, in information. Traditional navigational tools such as the card catalog at the library, the Sunday weekly newspaper listing of television programs, or reliance on one or two "key" newspapers or journals will be grossly inadequate to identify and retrieve networked information.

"Bottom's-Up" Information Services Development

Due in part to some of the above characteristics, individual infopreneurs have it in their power to develop, test, market, and distribute a range of information products and services. Such services and development efforts have been largely in the domain of large companies. No more. The nature of the information technology allows amebalike developments by individuals with curiosity, perseverance, and good ideas. The rapidly expanding Community Networking movement is a good example of this phenomenon (Civille, 1993). Individuals who wish to take advantage of the new technologies, who know how to operate them, and see possible applications, can develop these services from their home—both to enhance the quality of their life or for economic gain.

Filtering and Synthesizing Information

With the glut of digital information, filtering and synthesizing that information and determining which information is needed in what situations will be a critical concern for individuals in the networked society. The only way to deal with such large amounts of information is to develop mechanisms to filter and synthesize it. Such information retrieval techniques will have to be uniquely individualized in their design. "Profiles" of the information needs of individuals will be converted by "knowbots" that scan the network for specific types of information of interest to the individual, synthesize that information, and report it in a timely and organized fashion. Knowledge management will be much more important than information management.

Information in Search of People

In the past, it has been extremely difficult for individuals to "publish" their ideas or make them widely available to a large audience. In the future, the problem will be the reverse. There are thousands of messages posted on Usenet discussion groups today that are never read; endless papers and articles that are posted on the network are ignored; and hundreds of unread e-mail messages are deleted from reader files every day. The network has made it easy to produce and send information; the problem is to get people to read or review the information service or product sent them. The tyranny of information overload, despite sophisticated filters and synthesizing devices, is likely to be resolved by ignoring most information.

Privacy Protection

Because of many of the characteristics outlined above, the networked environment will increase the difficulty in protecting individuals' privacy. The *Privacy Act of 1974* (5 U.S.C. 552a) and the *Computer Matching and Privacy Protection Act of 1988* (P.L. 100-503) provide a number of important safeguards to insure that the government, or others, do not divulge certain information about individuals. The success of these policies in the networked environment, however, is unclear.

New information technologies, and the increased use of authentication devices to confirm transactions between sender and recipient (especially for certain personal services e.g., social security information) will strain our ability to keep private information about ourselves to ourselves. Without adequate policy and enforcement, governments and commercial firms can easily maintain files of "personal data" linked to specific individuals that can be matched to other files to produce, for example, composite "buying patterns" that includes specific types of purchases by specific individuals, demographic information about that person's household and income, and other types of information.

Issues and Implications

Literacy in, and for, an electronic society will require a major overhaul and rethinking. As the educational system currently operates, it is ill-prepared for the challenges it faces in migrating individuals from a print-based society to a digital, networked based society. There are a number of issues that will need to be addressed if we are to move successfully into a networked society where all members of society have "an equal playing field" to be empowered by the network.

Increasing Awareness of the Importance of Network Literacy

The first issue that must be addressed is increasing the awareness of government policy makers (at all levels of government) and the public at large that notions of literacy have changed, and will continue to change in the future. Literacy cannot be defined simply as the ability to read and write at a fourth-grade level. It includes a range of technologically based skills as well as information problem-solving skills.

Increasing awareness is linked to demonstrating the importance of networked literacy and the impact of network literacy on:

• The individual's ability to operate successfully in a networked environment;
• Society's ability to empower the individual to be a productive member of society;
• The economic productivity of the country and the ability of the United States to compete successfully with a knowledgeable and technically skilled workforce.

Such impacts will have a significant affect on how well this country will maintain leadership not only in industry, but in health care, manufacturing, delivery of services, and the individual's pursuit of happiness.

Reaching Agreement on What Constitutes Information and Network Literacy Skills and Knowledge

A major impediment to developing programs for increasing networking literacy in this country is that we have been unable to operationalize skills, competencies, and knowledge that could constitute "network literacy." Debate continues about how best to define and measure traditional notions of literacy—to say nothing of networked literacy. Yet, until we can operationalize the term network literacy, we certainly will not be able to teach it and determine the degree to which individuals have gained such skills.

And as suggested by the opening quote to this chapter, the existing level of knowledge and skills of most people in this country (to say nothing world-wide) in dealing with the new information technologies is abysmal. The reality is that if you cannot read, you cannot use the network. Reaching agreement on what literacy skills are essential for the public will require much coordination between Federal, state, and local governments, private foundations, and others. Unfortunately, many of these same individuals, themselves, are unfamiliar with what the network is and how it works.

Revising the Federal Policy Framework

The brief overview of policy related to the Internet/NREN and literacy suggests that a significant disconnect exists. Not until the proposed H.R. 1757, *High Performance Computing and High Speed Networking Applications Act* has there been some linkage between development of the Internet/NREN with education and training concerns. While the linkage between the development of the network with education is laudable, H.R. 1757 still does not address literacy issues, that is, educating the general population, or in some cases, retraining the population to be able to work and live in "Cyberspace" (Communications, Computers and Networks, 1991).

A Federal policy initiative that has as its objective to develop a program that will train or retrain—or even make available—network literacy skills to the population, is essential. Such a policy could also coordinate and organize the efforts for developing network literacy at state and local governmental levels. Such a policy framework would need to bring together the efforts of a number of Federal agencies such as the Department of Education, the National Commission on Libraries and Information Science, the Department of Agriculture Extension Service, and the National Literacy Institute, to name but a few.

In addition, a revised policy framework for this area needs to recognize the importance of libraries in promoting network literacy and serving as a vital link between networked resources/services and the public. Recent research suggests that the library community is beginning to redefine its roles and responsibilities to move more effectively into the networked society (McClure, Moen, & Ryan, 1993). But a clear mandate by Federal policy to coordinate the education and library community to work together in this area is essential.

Reinventing Education and Libraries for the Networked Society

There has been considerable discussion about "reinventing" a range of services and institutions in this country. The Clinton administration, for example, is attempting to reinvent government. Education and libraries are additional institutions desperately in need of being reinvented. *A Nation at Risk* (U.S. Department of Education, 1983) identified a raft of problems with the American education system. Now, in 1993, there is general consensus that those problems still exist, and if anything, have only become worse. Many libraries lack infrastructure, public support, and leadership in visioning their role in the networked environment (McClure, Moen, & Ryan, 1993).

Hughes (1993) notes that the intensified commercialization of the network, the lack of attention to public uses of the network, and our inability to confront issues related to educating the public for the networked society will result in

> an acceleration of the decline, or in some places the death, of the public education system. It simply won't be able to compete for the attention of students. And those parents who want a decent education for their kids will get it—commercially. Including offerings over the infotainment net. And then will act to stop or reduce taxes for a broken public system. Which will further decline. And in the long run be reduced to educational welfare for the have nots.

Schools and libraries may not be able to continue what they have always done in a networked environment since the networked environment is substantially different than the traditional school and library environment. These two institutions need to be reinvented, they need to rethink their roles and services in a networked society, and they need to determine their responsibilities for transitioning the public into the networked society such that individuals are empowered and advantaged.

Libraries can serve as an electronic safety net for the American public to insure basic access to electronic information. Public libraries are especially well-suited to assume this role as they already serve such a role in a print-based society. Not only can they provide access to electronic information and provide connectivity for those otherwise unable to link to the network, they can also provide training and education to the public at large in how to access and use networked information. Despite the lack of federal policy supporting libraries to move into this area, there is evidence that such can be accomplished with adequate planning and resource support (McClure, et al., 1993).

Creating a Level Playing Field Between Public and Private Interests

Increasingly, development of the Internet/NREN appears to be a commercial venture. The Bush administration promoted commercial development of the Internet/NREN, and it appears that the Clinton administration will continue this policy—although with some restrictions and modifications (U.S. Congress, 1993b). Investment from the private sector in the national information infrastructure certainly is welcome and appropriate. Such an investment, however, cannot be made without also supporting public and educational uses and access to the network.

We cannot afford the development of a national network that provides unlimited access to entertainment, home shopping, and other commercial activities—with hundreds to interactive multi-media channels that are all pay-for-view or pay for access (Hughes, 1993):

> TCI, US West-Time-Warner, At&T and the MCI's of the world are now falling all over each other in the race to push the pipe in your front room, entertain you to death, interactively. . . . This administration is urging these "private companies" on as a way to build the infrastructure. . . . But, with the tidal wave of entertainment/home shopping interactive telecom via fiber, ISDN, cable about to wash of the US, the "serious" Internet is going to look like a tiny mountain rivulet in comparison. I think we [U.S.A.] are in for some gigantic problems.

Commercial applications cannot be developed to the exclusion of public applications and uses of the network. Public service and educational applications on the network for the nation's elementary, secondary, and vocational schools, as well as independent learners, must be nurtured and promoted.

There are, however, areas where both the public and private sectors have mutually supportive goals. The goal of educating the public to be network literate certainly can be supported by all. From the public sector perspective, network literacy will be a prerequisite to operate effectively in society. From the private sector perspective, there must be a network literate population, or there will be no market to purchase the new and innovative gadgets that continue to be introduced. These, and other common goals must be recognized so that partnerships between the two groups can be formed.

Promoting Research

A range of research initiatives related to educational matters are needed to facilitate the transition into the networked society. Research initiatives in the following areas are needed:

- *Policy research*: two key thrusts can be identified in this area. First, we need a comprehensive policy analysis of existing policy in the areas of Internet/NREN development, literacy, electronic privacy, and related policy instruments. Secondly, we need to develop and assess policy options that have as an objective the provision of educational initiatives to prepare individuals to be productive members in the networked environment.
- *Applied research*: a range of social and technological topics related to educating for the networked environment remain to be addressed. Do what de-

gree are those who are network literate more or less productive on what types of tasks? What variables affect the development of network literacy in individuals? Would cost savings result from delivery of networked government services, for example, if we had network literate individuals in society?

- *Descriptive studies*: baseline data is needed that describes the number and types of users of the existing network. What are the demographic characteristics of users and non-users of the network? What trends can be identified in terms of the use of the network among the various population segments?

- *Program development*: currently, it is unclear what types, how many, and from which sponsoring agencies and institutions will be needed to educate and retrain the population to be productive members in the networked environment. Further, we have yet to understand how best to marshall the new information technologies to help us promote network literacy in our schools, workplaces, and at home.

The above topics are intended to be suggestive, not comprehensive. What government agencies, foundations, or other organizations will be able to take leadership in this area for promoting such research? At the moment, however, we are woefully ignorant about topics related to how information can be best managed and used in a networked environment.

The Need for Vision

Probably the most important challenge for exploiting information in a networked environment is extending our horizons of what is possible and developing new visions. A vision is a "dream" of what the network should be in the future and how people and institutions will use that network. A vision statement is a description of a possible future state or set of functions for developing a network literate society. Getting the "vision thing" right requires that it address (Lee, 1993) :

> [people's] physical and economic well-being, their social need to be treated with respect and dignity, their psychological need to grow and develop, and their spiritual need for meaning and significance. (28)

Vision statement development requires us to make explicit our assumptions about the future and to envision a future state of the networked society in light of these assumptions and in light of societal goals and resources.

A primary purpose of such visioning is to describe and explore *visions* of what constitutes educated individuals in a networked society. In terms of strategic planning, we need to develop a range of possible visions, identify those that are most important and which would benefit society the most, and then take appropriate steps to insure that the vision evolves as defined. A vision statement provides a target at which we can move toward, a vision of what we would like to occur, and suggests resources needed to reach that vision.

In the policy process, vision statement development is a precursor to setting mission, goals, objectives, and tasking programs to accomplish the objectives. It is essential that this development precede the traditional activities of strategic planning to insure the development of visions, to encourage stakeholder groups to think in terms of new opportunities, and to define possible states of being that would be especially appropriate for the networked society.

In thinking about developing a vision for the education and library community, stakeholders need to:

- State societal assumptions under which the vision is based.
- Identify societal assumptions under which the vision is based.
- Identify institutional assumptions under which the vision is based.
- Recognize impacts, benefits, constraints, and limitations of the vision for individual segments of the society.
- Consider resource needs to realize the vision.
- Produce draft vision statements for public debate and discussion.

Group processes among a broad range of stakeholder groups regarding these points are essential as they encourage policymakers to consider factors that will affect the success of the network in the future, possible services that should be provided given changing environmental conditions, and to better identify and accomplish educational objectives.

For example, one vision of education in the networked society is to have public libraries all connected to the national network. Any person could access the array of information resources and services simply by using the "network room" in the library. Students could work interactively on lessons, adult learners could tap into endless instructional tools and persons providing support to use those tools. Virtual learning communities (Schrage, 1990) can form and grow.

Electronic resources or all types and forms would be publicly available for those who cannot connect from the home. Librarians and educators would serve as electronic intermediaries, navigators, and instructors—

being actively involved in assisting people best use the network. Parents, students, adult learners, educators, and others could work interactively and inter-dependently on projects and activities that we can only begin to imagine now. The public library, as a non-partisan, publicly supported institution, with strong local community ties, is well-suited to serve in this role.

This, of course, is just one of many possible visions. Minimally, the key stakeholder groups that need to participate in such a discussion are information providers from the commercial and public sectors, government policy makers, educators, librarians, parents, and individuals and firms that design instructional materials and equipment. Constructive policy debate among these groups (and possible others) in terms of visioning has not occurred. Discussions about how the network *should* evolve, how people *should* be able to use the network, and how individuals will be *empowered* by using the network (as opposed to entertained) are essential.

Reconnecting Society

Maintaining the status quo for network development will insure an ever-increasing gulf between the network literate and illiterate. Those disempowered from using the network, those without access to a network "safety net," and those who simply are bypassed by the network, will be increasingly disadvantaged and unable to lead productive work or professional lives. As suggested by the recent report resulting from White House Conference on Libraries and Information Services (1991),

> as dependence on information grows, the potential increases for emergence of an Information Elite—the possibility of a widening gap between those who possess facility with information resources and those who are denied the tools to access, understand, and use information. . . . Today, now more than ever, information is power. Access to it and the skill to understand and apply it—increasingly is the way power is exercised. (6)

To not be on the network, to not be able to use networked information, and to not take advantage of a range of networked information services and resources will insure second-class status in this society.

But "information gaps" in our society are widening. Increasingly, various population segments are disenfranchised from accessing information due to race, gender, family income, geographic location, and a host of other reasons. A report issued by the Freedom Forum Media Studies Center states (Pease, 1992):

> Neglecting the needs of minorities and others who may be underserved [in the networked environment] would only exacerbate their disenfranchisement from the information marketplace, said Julius Barnathan, senior vice president for technology and strategic planning of Capital Cities/ABC, Inc. "There's no concern for the minority, for the people who live in rural communities," he said. "We find that education and illiteracy are getting worse, not better. So we need an information system to do one thing: educate. We've got to educate people so they can use these devices." (8)

Disparities between the richest and poorest segments of the society continue to widen; and social equity issues, that is, the degree to which all people may legitimately make the same claims on social resources, are exacerbated by the evolving NII (Doctor, 1993).

Moreover, to the degree that information in the network is available to some and not to others, we may witness the development of a hyper-pluralistic society. The hyper-pluralistic society is one that is composed of thousands of small interest groups that know only of limited pieces of information and are unable to understand and assess larger societal concerns. They typically are interested in only one or two issues or topics and develop skills—either in the print or in the network world—to support that interest. Making it easier for "like-minded" people to maintain communication, as suggested by Cleveland (1991, 40) can exacerbate this hyper-pluralistic society.

Such impacts from the networked environment are difficult to predict, but require thinking and debate *now*. Information in a networked society takes on characteristics and impacts that we are only now beginning to identify and recognize. There is an educational imperative to assist individuals—be they in school, in the workforce, or at home. They need to know much more than how to use the "switch hook flash" on the telephone. They must learn how to use this network, exploit the digital information for personal growth, workforce advancement, and national economic productivity. Development of formal policy and programs to support this re-tooling of American society is essential.

Technology in general, and the development of the NII in particular, must be seen as a dynamic social and cultural phenomenon. As Winner (1993) notes, one view of technological change is as a pump for economic development. But it can also be seen as loom from which the fabric of society can be reweaved. He argues that policymakers thus far have inadequately considered "what Walter Lippmann called the public philosophy—a vision of the purposes that bring us together in society in the first place" (B2). Network literacy, reconnecting society, and insuring social equity in an electronic society are parts of this public philosophy that still require attention, public policy debate, and resolution. This challenge is one that we cannot ignore. If we fail to act, fail to accept this challenge, the various segments of our society will become increasingly disconnected and intolerant of each other. It is a challenge that will require a long term program and resource commitment. But perhaps most importantly, it will require a commitment to *people*, a commitment to provide equal opportunity to all members of society, and a commitment to promote the self-worth and individual productivity of *all* members of society.

References

AskERIC: ERIC and the Internet continued. (1993, Spring). *ERIC/IR update, 15*, 1.

Aufderheide, P. (1993). *Media literacy: A report of the National Leadership Conference on media literacy*. Washington, D.C.: The Aspen Institute.

Bishop, M. (1991, Winter). Why Johnny's dad can't read: The elusive goal of universal adult literacy. *Policy Review, 55*, 19–25.

Breivik, P. S. (1992, March). Information literacy: An agenda for lifelong learning. *AAHE Bulletin*, 6–9.

Brett, G. H. (Ed.). (1992, Spring). Accessing information on the Internet [special theme issue]. *Electronic networking: Research, applications, and policy, 2*.

Civille, R. (1993, April 15). *The spirit of access: Equity, NREN and the NII*. Paper presented at NET '93, Washington, D.C. (Available from Center for Civic Networking, P.O. Box 65272, Washington, D.C. 20035.)

Cleveland, H. (1991, Winter). The knowledge imperative: The revolutions of know-what, know-how, know-why, and know-who. *The Aspen Institute Quarterly, 3*, 8–45.

Clinton, W. J. & Gore, A., Jr. (1993, February 22). *Technology for America's economic growth, a new direction to build economic strength*. Washington D.C.: Executive Office of the President (mimeograph).

Communications, computers and networks: How to work, play and thrive in Cyberspace. (1991, September). (Special theme issue.) *Scientific American, 265*.

Consumer Interest Research Institute. (1993). *21st century learning and health care in the home: Creating a national telecommunications network*. Washington, D.C.: The Institute.

DeLoughry, T. J. (1993, May 19). Colleges and telephone companies battle over future of the Internet. *The Chronicle of Higher Education, 39* (37), A25–27.

Doctor, R. D. (1993, April 13). *The national information infrastructure: Social equity considerations*. Paper presented at the Center for Civic Networking Conference: From Town Halls to Civic Networks, Washington, D.C. (mimeograph).

Eisenberg, M. E., & Berkowitz, R. E. (1990). *Information problem-solving: The big six skills approach to library & information skills instruction*. Norwood, N.J.: Ablex Publishing Corporation.

Gleick, J. (1993, May 16). The telephone transformed—Into almost anything. *New York Times Magazine*, 26–29+.

Hancock, V. E. (1993). *Information literacy for lifelong learning*. Syracuse, N.Y.: Syracuse University, ERIC Clearinghouse on Information Resources and Technology (ERIC Digest EDO-IR-93-1).

Hughes, D. (1993, May 23). Highways of the mindless. [Posting to com-priv@psicom discussion list, Hughes offers other insights on the development of the network in: J. Leslie. (1993, May–June). The cursor cowboy, *Wired, 1,* 62–65+].

The info highway: Bringing a revolution in entertainment, news and communication. (12 April 1993). *Time*, 47–58.

Kochmer, J. & NorthWestNet. (1993). *The Internet passport: NorthWestNet's guide to our world online*. (4th ed.). Bellevue, Wash.: NorthWestNet.

Krol, E. (1992). *The whole Internet: User's guide and catalog*. Sebastopol, Calif.: O'Reilly and Associates, Inc.

Lee, C. (1993, February). The vision thing. *Training, 30*, 25–34.

LeQuey, T. (1993). *The Internet companion: A beginner's guide to global networking*. Reading, Mass.: Addison Wesley.

Levin, J. (1993, May 17). Getting caught up in the Internet: More area firms are plugging into the world's largest computer network. *The Washington Post*, F3.

Lynch, C. A. & Preston, C. M. (1990). Internet access to information resources. In M. E. Williams (Ed.), *Annual Review of Information Science and Technology, 25*, (263–312). New York: Elsevier.

McClure, C. R., Bishop, A., Doty, P., & Rosenbaum, H. (1991). *The national research and education network: Research and policy perspectives*. Norwood, N.J.: Ablex Publishing Corporation.

McClure, C. R., Moen, W. E., & Ryan, J. (1993). *Libraries and the Internet/NREN: Perspectives, issues, and opportunities*. Westport, Conn.: Meckler Publishing Co.

McClure, C. R., Wigand, R. T., Bertot, J. C., McKenna, M., Moen, W. E., Ryan, J., & Veeder, S. (1992). *Federal information policy and management for electronic services delivery*. Washington, D.C.: U.S. Congress, Office of Technology Assessment (available through ERIC Clearinghouse as ED 366-353).

Ochs, M., Coons, B., Van Ostrand, D., & Barnes, S. (1991, October). *Assessing the value of an information literacy program*. Ithaca, N.Y.: Cornell University, Mann Library (available through ERIC Clearinghouse as ED 340385).

Office of Technology Assessment. (1993). *Adult literacy and new technologies: Tools for a lifetime*. Washington, D.C.: Government Printing Office.

Papert, S. (1993, May–June). Obsolete skill set: The 3Rs: Literacy and letteracy in the media ages. *Wired, 1,* 50.

Pease, E. E. (Ed.). (1992). *Citizen's information service roundtable: Plotting a course for information and democracy in the 21st century*. New York: Columbia University, Freedom Forum Media Studies Center.

Rutkowski, A. M. (1993, Spring). Internet metrics. *Internet Society News, 2* (1), 33–38.

Schrage, M. (1990). *Shared minds: The new technologies of collaboration*. New York: Random House.

Stix, G. Domesticating cyberspace. (1993, August). *Scientific American, 269*, 101–10.

Taylor, R. S. (1986). *Value-added processes in information systems*. Norwood, N.J.: Ablex Publishing Corporation.

U.S. Congress. House Committee on Science, Space and Technology. (1993a). *National information infrastructure act of 1993: Report to accompany H. R. 1757*. Washington, D.C.: Government Printing Office [H. Rpt. 103-173].

————. (1993b). *Hearings on the national information infrastructure*, 6 May 1993. Washington, D.C.: Government Printing Office.

U.S. Department of Education. (1983). *A nation at risk*. Washington, D.C.: Government Printing Office.

————. (1992). *National education goals report 1992: Building a nation of learners*. Washington, D.C.: U.S. Department of Education, National Education Goals Panel [1850 M Street NW., Suite 270, Washington, D.C. 20036].

White House Conference on Library and Information Services. (1991). *Information 2000 library and information services for the 21st century: Summary report of the 1991 White House conference on library and information services*. Washington, D.C.: Government Printing Office.

Whittemore, B. J., & Yovits, M. C. (May–June 1973). A generalized conceptual development for the analysis and flow of information. *Journal of the American Society for Information Science, 24*, 221–31.

Winner, L. (4 August 1993). How technology reweaves the fabric of society. *The Chronicle of Higher Education, 39* (48), B1–B3.

Yurow, J. W. (Ed.). (1981). *Issues in information policy*. Washington, D.C.: National Telecommunications and Information Administration [NTIA SP-80-9].

20

Literacy in the Information Age School: Skills for Lifelong Learning

Carol C. Kuhlthau

The three basic charges of education in a democratic society, to prepare students for the workplace, for citizenship, and for human interaction, change substantially in the information age. The information-age school is charged with preparing children to lead full, productive lives in a technological environment that is characterized by vast amounts of information and rapid change of events. Literacy in the information age calls for competency in using information to address problems and make decisions that require deep understanding within a dynamic environment.*

Education in a democratic society is charged with preparing children for the workplace, for citizenship and for daily human interaction (Dewey, 1944). The skills needed for success in each of these areas changes radically in the information age.

The automated workplace requires very different skills than the industrial workplace. Zuboff (1988), of Harvard Business School, has studied changes in the skills expected of managers, clerical, and plant workers. She finds that the automated workplace calls for critical judgments and abstract thinking. Decisions require use of computer-generated information rather than information gathered from direct personal contact with the problem situation. There are fewer individualized tasks and more team projects. In addition, the automated workplace requires fewer work-

---

* Based on a presentation made for the Tenth Anniversary of the School of Communication, Information and Library Studies, Rutgers, The State University of New Jersey, and The John P. and Alice McCarthy Commons Lecture in Children's Libraryship at the University of Texas Graduate School of Library and Information Science, February, 1993.

ers resulting in serious unemployment, displacement, and the necessity of repeated retraining for new jobs. Students need generic and transferable information skills for the automated workplace.

Citizenship and participation in the democratic process, also, has changed in important ways. Stotsky (1991), of Harvard School of Education, notes increasingly low participation in the democratic process, particularly at the local level of government. Students need to be prepared for the public discourse that our society requires and for taking responsibility for the processes of democracy at all levels. Technology has changed the ways people keep informed. This prompts problems, such as agenda setting and incomplete "sound bites," and even bias and distortion. Students need skills for gathering information in a technological environment to participate in the civilized conduct of civic discourse.

Preparation for daily living and human interaction recalls Naisbitt's (1982) warning of the need for "high touch" in a "high tech" environment. Goodlad (1983), of the Institute for School Renewal at Stanford, stresses the need for a sense of civilization in preparation for participation in the human conversation. An understanding of what it means to be human in a technological age is becoming more critical each day. Students need preparation for difficult ethical decisions and an appreciation of the spiritual dimension of human life. There is a need for basic human values, such as concern for family living, nurturing children, and appreciation for variety and tradition in a multicultural society.

The technological information age is characterized by vast amounts of information and rapid change of events. We live in an amazingly dynamic environment that alters our ways of knowing and becoming informed. In all aspects of our daily lives, we experience an increase of rapidly transmitted information. In a real sense, information technologies are extensions of the mind affecting the way we think and learn. In McLuhan's (1964) terms, like the car and airplane, as extensions of the foot, have changed our concept of space and time, new information technologies, as extensions of the mind, alter our concept of understanding and learning. These extensions bring both promise and problems. Speedy travel has altered our concept of community and our sense of neighbor, some would argue, not always in enriching ways. In a similar way, information technologies expand our access to information but do not necessarily lead to depth of understanding and increased knowledge.

Television, of course, is the most pervasive information technology, reaching a broad spectrum of the population. Additional information technologies offering vast databases of indexes and full texts have become commonplace in our libraries, schools, workplaces, and homes, with new applications emerging constantly. Electronic networks advance one system, a giant global library, with rapid delivery from one location to another through fax and e-mail. The National Research and Education Network (NREN), a vast interconnected network of electronic systems referred to as the "highway of the mind," is close to becoming a reality. In fact, for many people, use of information technologies have become a part of their daily routine.

While these information technologies expand our access to information some serious problems are surfacing related to the use of information. One critical problem in an information-rich environment is that of an overwhelming amount of information, often referred to as overload. Information technologies intended to expand our knowledge may result in an overload of information that can inhibit understanding and meaningful learning. Overload prompts trivialization and shallow processing and actually may increase rather than decrease uncertainty and confusion. The tendency to skim along the surface of the novelty of the moment results in distraction and boredom.

How do we prepare children for learning in an overloaded, information environment? Education plays an important role in preparing all students for access to the "highway of the mind" by developing skills for lifelong learning in an information-rich environment. These skills incorporate a knowledge of the process of information use, particularly for addressing problems that require deep understanding. Education for the information age calls for restructuring schools in fundamental ways.

The concept of an information-age school calls to mind classrooms filled with the latest computer and video technology for advancing instructional mediation. However, information technologies that students need to use in real-world contexts are also essential for schools to incorporate. These basic information technologies for schools utilize the computer for providing access to the school library collection, as well as to a network of libraries and information systems outside the school. In addition, a selection of indexes and full text databases make a wide range of current sources available online and through CD ROM. The fact that many schools do not have these technologies seriously hampers ability to prepare students for full participation in the information society. Although the availability of technology is important, there is much more to the information-age school than the mere presence of technology. The major objectives are to use technology for learning and to develop skills and knowledge that can be applied to real-life situations. Underlying these objectives is the concept of information literacy, which is literacy for the information age.

The Presidential Committee on Information Literacy of the American Library Association defined an information-age school as one where information literacy is a central, not a peripheral, concern. The final report, published in 1989, describes what the information-age school would look like.

> The school would be more interactive, because students, pursuing questions of personal interest, would be interacting with other students, with teachers, with a vast array of information resources, and the community at large to a far greater degree than they presently do today. One would expect to find every student engaged in at least one open-ended. long-term quest for an answer to a serious social, scientific, aesthetic, or political problem. Students' quests would involve not only searching print, electronic, and video data, but also interviewing people inside and outside of school. As a result, learning would be more self-initiated. There would be more reading of original sources and more extended writing. Both students and teachers would be familiar with the intellectual and emotional demands of asking productive questions, gathering data of all kinds, reducing and synthesizing information, and analyzing, interpreting, and evaluating information in all its forms. In such an environment, teachers would be coaching and guiding students more and lecturing less. (9)

The report goes on to describe the role of the librarian, methods of assessment, and infusion of technology in an information-age school. The key point made is that information literacy is considered the central goal for all students.

The fundamental question facing educators today is, how to prepare children for living full, productive lives in an information society? Underlying the movement to restructure education is the acknowledgment that schools designed to meet the needs of people in an industrial society are inadequate for educating people for the information age. When we consider the nature of the society in which we live and the environment in which learning takes place, it becomes clear that major restructuring is in order. Although restructuring is in progress in schools across the United States, a clear understanding of the nature of the information society is missing from many restructuring efforts. Without an understanding of the demands of the dynamic, information-rich environment in which we live, there can be little recognition, much less a consensus, of the knowledge and skills required to be successful in an information society.

The information-age school is based on a principle of construction of understanding rather than on transmission of facts (Bruner, 1986; Sizer, 1984, 1992). Students are actively engaged in the process of learning from information. Information literacy is learning how to address real problems in an information age. In the information-age school, problem-driven research prompts investigation of a variety of resources using current information technologies. Through problem-driven research students learn to recognize problems in the context of real-life situations, find information about a problem, formulate a focused perspective from information in a variety of sources, and use information to solve problems, and present solutions and new understandings.

Studies on the student's perspective of the process of accessing and using information reveal a complex, constructive process requiring high-level thinking, reflection, and self-awareness (Kuhlthau, 1991). A series of studies of the information search process indicate that the early stages of exploring and formulating are difficult and confusing for most students. Low level of confidence is commonly found in these early stages when thoughts are vague and ill-formed. Confidence often dips in the early exploratory stage, after a project had been initiated, but before basic constructs about the problem or topic have been formed. At this point, sources of information may be inconsistent and incompatible with each other and may not fit with constructs the student already holds. By reading and reflecting as the search progresses, constructs about the general topic develop from which a focused perspective may be formed. Interest in the problem is likely to be higher in the later stages of the search process after a focus perspective is clearer. Confidence also increases as thoughts become clearer and more focused.

The information search process approach guides students through six stages of seeking meaning (Kuhlthau, 1989). The process is initiated by identifying an engaging problem requiring investigation through the use of a variety of sources of information, rather than by the assignment of a research paper. After initiation, the second stage is selection, when the general area or topic to be investigated is chosen. The third stage, exploration, involves exploring general information for a focus or perspective to pursue. In the fourth stage, formulation, a focus is formulated from the information encountered in the exploration stage. During the fifth stage, collection, information related to the focus or perspective is collected, organized, and documented. The sixth stage, presentation, brings the process to a close with a new understanding of the topic, question, or problem under investigation that results in some action or product.

Much of the advice given to children for locating and using information in the past is no longer helpful and may actually obstruct productive progress. For example, advice to take detailed notes early in the process might inhibit the process of integrating new ideas into former constructs. Better advice might be to note interesting ideas, puzzling questions, and concepts that relate previously held notions. A fundamental restructuring of instruction in the information-age school is needed that is built on sensemaking, the process of seeking meaning (Dervin, 1983; Kuhlthau, 1993).

Enabling learning environments need to be created with opportunities for children to begin with what they already know, their intuitive theories (Gardner, 1991), to form new constructs from a variety of sources of information. Enabling learning environments in an information-age school not only provide technology, but provide opportunities for reflecting, exploring, speculating, formulating, documenting, and presenting. The goal is to foster understanding rather than stressing memorization of the right answer. Assessment of understanding is more difficult than testing of memorized facts. Serious attention needs to be paid to what is being called authentic assessment of the process as well as the products of learning (Gardner, 1983).

When the process of information seeking and use is learned the student has transferable skills for lifelong learning. In longitudinal studies of the information search process from the student's perspective, one participant explained how this learning had affected his later information-seeking behavior.

> I learned not to panic if it doesn't all fall in together the first day you walk into the library. I have learned to accept that this is the way it works. I will read this over and some parts will fall into place and some still won't. The mind doesn't take everything and put it into order automatically and that's it. Understanding that is the biggest help. (Kuhlthau, 1988, 282)

In an interview four years later, this same participant was employed in a position requiring extensive reporting using large databases. He explained that he can never have too much information, because he knows how to select the pieces he needs to state his case. Students can learn the skills of managing information overload through experience, coaching, and instruction in the process of seeking meaning in the information-age school.

Instruction should be organized to provide students with guidance and advice, particularly during the early formative stages of the information search process to work through their uncertainty and confusion. An important strategy for learning from information is the skill of forming a focused perspective in the early stages of the process to guide the collection of information in the later stages in preparation for presenting, creating, or predicting. A knowledge of this process and the skills for working through each stage in the process prepares students for managing information. Understanding that information seeking and use is a constructive process enables students to be tolerant of their uncertainty and confusion in the early stages, to seek a focus from general information, and to collect only that which is pertinent to their focus in preparation for resolving their task.

Information-age schools need to prepare children for succeeding in a dynamic environment of vast amounts of information and rapid change of events. Students need to learn how to learn and to develop skills for lifelong learning, problem solving, critical thinking, and creativity. They need to understanding that learning is a constructive process requiring reflection and the skills for going "beyond the information given" (Bruner, 1973; Dewey, 1933).

Information literacy is not a separate subject, but a way of learning within each discipline. Subject experts in each area of the curriculum are addressing the underlying themes and fundamental principles of their disciplines and identifying new approaches to teaching. Many are addressing the need for stressing the process of learning within the discipline as well as developing a knowledge base of facts. Project 2061: Science for all Americans (1989) is an excellent example of restructuring learning for the information age. This Project stresses that students need to learn how to learn within each discipline. They need to understand the underlying principles and process of using information for learning throughout their lives. They need high-level skills that go beyond reading and simple arithmetic to problem solving and creating. Students can become aware of the more important issues and questions that are emerging on the boundaries between disciplines integrated in real-life situations.

The mission of the information-age school is to enable children to develop skills for living full, productive lives in an information-rich environment. Basic skills for lifelong learning are established in the process of information seeking. Without an understanding of the constructive process of information seeking it is easy for people to become lost and overwhelmed in an information society. Literacy in the information age calls for competence in using information to address problems and make decisions that require deep understanding.

References

Bruner, J. (1973). *Beyond the information given*. Edited by J. M. Arglin. New York: Norton.

———. (1986). *Actual minds, possible worlds*. Cambridge, Mass.: Harvard University Press.

Dervin, B. (1983). *An overview of sense-making research: Concepts, methods, and results to date*. Seattle: School of Communication, University of Washington.

Dewey, J. (1933). *How we think*. Lexington, Mass.: Heath.

———. (1944). *Democracy and education*. New York: MacMillan Publishing.

Gardner, H. (1983). *Frames of mind: The theory of multiple intelligences*. New York: Basic Books.

———. (1991). *The unschooled mind: How children think and how schools should teach*. New York: Basic Books.

Goodlad, J. (1983). *A place called school*. New York: McGraw Hill.

Kuhlthau, C. (1988). Longitudinal case studies of the information search process of users in libraries. *Library and Information Science Research 10*(3), 257–304.

———. (1989). Information search process: A summary of research and implications for school library media programs. *School Library Media Quarterly 18*(5), 19–25.

———. (1991). Inside the search process: Information seeking from the user's perspective. *Journal of the American Society of Information Science 42*(5), 361–71.

———. (1993). *Seeking meaning: A process approach to library and information services*. Norwood, N.J.: Ablex.

McLuhan, M. (1964). *Understanding media: The extensions of man*. New York: McGraw Hill.

Naisbitt, J. (1982). *Megatrends: Ten new directions transforming our lives*. New York: Warner Books.

Presidential Committee on Information Literacy: (1989). Final report. Chicago: American Library Association.

Project 2016 Science for all Americans (1989). Summary. Washington, D.C.: American Association for the Advancement of Science.

Sizer, T. (1984). *Horace's compromise: The dilemma of the American high school*. Boston: Houghton Mifflin.

———. (1992). *Horace's school: Redesigning the American high school*. Boston: Houghton Mifflin.

Stotsky, S. (1991). *Connecting civic education and language education: The contemporary challenge*. New York: Teachers College Press.

Zuboff, S. (1988). *The age of the smart machine*. New York: Basic Books.

21

"The Tools Tell the Story": Toward an Analysis of the "Museum Experience"

Tamar Katriel

Drawing on an ethnographic study of some Israeli vernacular museums, this chapter explores the experiential dimensions of museum going as a cultural practice in a way that accommodates the shifting balance and tension between the museum's informational function and knowledge claims and its ritual function of concretizing and enshrining core cultural meanings and values. The ways in which the representational strategies employed in the museum context serve to establish a sense of cultural value and claims to knowledge are delineated both as they relate to the material display and with respect to the tour guides' verbal elaborations. It is argued that a proper understanding of the "structure of experience" museum encounters are designed to promote requires a recognition of the implicit cultural code that regulates curators' and museum guides' collecting, display, and interpretation practices on the one hand, and visitors' expectations on the other.*

Introduction

In writing about the history of ethnological museums and collections in the United States, Bronner discusses the cultural context for the shift from text-based learning to learning anchored in the visual mode, which has marked a shift from descriptive writing to pictures to the use of actual objects in instruction. The latter shift is marked by the emergence and popularity of the phrase "object lessons" in the educational idiom of

* A grant I received from the Basic Research Fund administered by the Israel Academy of Science and Humanities for my project on Israeli settlement museum representation is gratefully acknowledged.

449

the last part of the nineteenth century. Bronner notes: "The concept of education in the early nineteenth century was cerebral, almost spiritual, free from the influence of object and environment. But by the late nineteenth century, increasing numbers of Americans desired a flourishing material life more than a spiritual life. Objects took on more power to educate and strengthen society as a world of exotic trinkets, labor-saving devices, and affordable fashions came to the fore. . . . Reformers, advisers, and educators repeated the phrase [object lessons] often to emphasize the need to make concrete the moral imperatives of the age" (Bronner, 1989, 217–18).

Museums, as pointed out by museum promoter George Brown Goode in 1897, should find a congenial place amid such tendencies, "for it is the most powerful and useful auxiliary of all systems of teaching by means of object lessons" (cited by Bronner, 1989, 223). The dramatic increase in the number and scope of local heritage museums of various kinds in countries around the world in recent years marks a century in which museums have indeed become increasingly important participants in the pedagogical and cultural endeavors of modern societies. This suggests the emergence of shared codes of material display as well as the cultivation of learners' capacities to participate in their decoding. Literacy in the information age, then, must also include a consideration of what it takes to become "literate" in museum contexts, which form part of the "exhibitionary complex" (Bennett, 1988) of our contemporary public cultures.

In this chapter, then, I attend to the ways in which heritage museums construct and inscribe their overall message, that is, the ways in which they make knowledge claims and confer cultural value on the displays they house. In so doing, I will address a number of basic assumptions that ground some of the central presentational strategies employed in heritage museums in Israel, as I believe the issues raised by my observations hold for this type of museum encounter more generally.[1]

In line with phenomenological approaches to ethnographic inquiry (Geertz, 1973), I will try to delineate the "structure of experience" that museum encounters are designed to generate through a combination of visual and verbal means. Indeed, the term *experience* is not only an analytic term here, but a folk term as well: it is pervasive in museum discourse itself, and reflects a fundamental conceptualization of the museum encounter within members' professional lore and the public's expectations. Thus, I was repeatedly told by curators and guides in the museums

I have studied that the museum's goal is to provide an "experience." Learning historical facts, they said, can be done just as well at school, you don't need the museum for that. I am asking, then, how museum curators and guides envision the "experience" they are supposed to manufacture for their audiences, and how their conception of the museum encounter is inscribed in their observed museological practices of collecting, displaying, and interpreting objects of historical-cultural value. Clearly, these practices are grounded in a distinctive presentational code that visitors are expected to decipher. It is to the learning of this code that the curators I have interviewed were referring when they described their pedagogical mission as one that involves not just the goal of "bringing to life" a particular chapter of history, but also that of teaching visitors, especially children, to become "museum goers."

The elucidation of this code must perforce touch upon more general issues of epistemology, pedagogy, and cultural authority. As public institutions, which confer visibility and command attention, museums make both explicit and implicit claims to knowledge and value. These claims come in the form of "object lessons" in and through which visitors assign meaning to the objects on display. As noted by Taborsky (1990), in the museum context objects exist as social, not material, truths. They are, so to speak, "discursive objects." Thus, "an object exists as a sign, which is a meaning defined and existent within a group consciousness" (70–71).

Drawing on C. S. Peirce's trichotomy of signs (1955), Taborsky attempts to characterize the effects museum objects have vis-à-vis their visitor-interpreters. The sign in Peirce's theory exists in a number of meaning formats. The first is the unembodied "qualisign," an experience without reference, that which is experienced without any understanding of the experience. In the context of a heritage museum it is "the sensation of being in a heritage house, of smelling the cooking, feeling the rough floors, feeling the heat from the fire. That is all. A qualisign is an experience but does not move beyond that into an awareness that the smell refers to cooking, that the feel refers to a rough floor, that the heat refers to the fire" (Taborsky, 1990, 71).

The second category of signs is the "sinsign," a term which refers to "an actual existent thing or event which is a sign" (Taborsky, 1990, 72), which involves differentiation. Thus, "our sinsign experience of the heritage house is a distinct awareness of heat, as being warm (as differentiated from being cold), as coming from the woodfire (and not from a gas furnace); that the floors are rough (as differentiated from smooth, and this is because they are wood and not carpeted. It is an understanding of the singular identity and the causal forces of those sensations" (72).

The third category is the "legisign," which is "not a single object but a general type which, it has been agreed, shall be significant. . . . In the heritage house, the legisign experience is an understanding that these objects exist within a social frame of meaning, which by social habit, agreement or 'law,' used fire for cooking and heating, built their homes of wood, made many goods in their home, rather than by the market system and so on. It is the understanding of this 'object,' the heritage house, within a social group in a particular time and space" (Taborsky, 1990, 72). Museum objects as signs thus involve all three sign categories, as defined by Peirce, and their rhetorical efficacy lies in the extent to which their claims to meaningfulness and value are accepted.

Vernacular museums have a distinctive flavor as legitimizing institutions in the public sphere: the objects they house do not enjoy the social aura of High Culture objects, or the temporal aura of Antiquity. They are mainly mundane objects of the recent past, ones that have only recently been disengaged from the flow of everyday experience, often by being salvaged from the status of "rubbish" (Thompson, 1979). The museums' presentational efforts are, therefore, significantly oriented to the goal of conferring cultural value, through a process of "sight sacralization," as Fine and Speer (1985) and MacCannell (1989) have called it. This process of enshrining mundane objects supplements, or at times even replaces, the goal of inducing familiarity with unfamiliar objects, or that of energizing the memory of half-forgotten ones, by providing visual access and cultivating factual knowledge. The balance of these two presentational functions—elevating the familiar and familiarizing the exotically remote—varies, of course, with the type of visitors that participate in every given museum encounter. Visitors range in terms of their "cultural distance" from the museum display: old folk for whom the museum objects have autobiographical significance differ from adults, who have only some direct but a good deal of mediated experience with the topic and object of the display, and both differ from "cultural recruits," such as new immigrants or children, or from cultural outsiders such as tourists. These differences must be taken account of by curators and guides, particularly as they shape the verbal interpretation accompanying the skeletal material display. While they generally discuss this issue in informational terms, as the "amount of information" different audiences require, it is clearly more complex than that. The whole texture of the museum is affected by guides' perceptions of the audience's degree of involvement.

I was initially alerted to the centrality of this factor as I witnessed a tour of old timers led by an old-timer guide transform the museum encounter into a collaborative discursive production, jointly engaged in by the guide and her knowledgeable and involved audience. In this particular type of museum encounter, the informational value of the guide's discourse is practically nullified, and the affective and existential dimensions that attend participation in a context of self-narration are foregrounded. Thus, although museum guides seemed fond of reiterating that "the tolls tell the story," some of the efficacy of the material display in these vernacular museums lies precisely in the evocative power of the partial and fragmented renditions of the stories they potentially anchor. To be rendered both meaningful and valuable, they need to be complemented discursively by written labels, by the guides' strategically constructed tales, and by the spoken or unspoken memories they invoke in some of their audiences. These encounters are, indeed, tenuous junctures of presentational and interpretive activities, involving words and objects, curators and tour guides, communal tales and personal stories, all culturally sanctioned and attractively packaged to provide a "museum experience."

I therefore propose that an expanded framework for the "reading" of museum going as a cultural practice is required, one that can accommodate the shifting balance and tension between what Carey (1988) has termed the "informational" and the "ritual" views of communication. In what follows, I attempt to elaborate a notion of museum going as a form of ritualized activity, embedded in the context of the world of tourism. One dimension of this activity involves the gaining of knowledge in the form of factual information, another involves the signalling of cultural value. These dimensions are not unrelated, but will be distinguished here for analytic purposes. The purposeful accumulation of bits of certified knowledge about an object or topic enhances their cultural value, whereas assertions of value ("this is important") in turn argue for the further accumulation and preservation of factual knowledge about display objects. In the following sections, I attend to each of these dimensions of museum practice separately, pointing out links where appropriate.

Conferring Cultural Value

Museum going today is an integral part of touristic endeavors, whether in the form of school excursions (pedagogical tourism), or family and other group outings (recreational tourism). MacCannell (1989) has cogently argued for a view of tourism as a form of "secular pilgrimage" in which focal sites are culturally constructed through a process of "sight sacralization," which includes strategies of "framing" (setting apart) and "elevation." Adopting this view shifts our analytic focus from museum objects and the stories they "tell" to ritualized cultural practices and the structure of experience they entail. In this view, "reading" the museum display is seen not as an isolated activity that stands on its own, but as part of a larger activity complex. In other words, museum going is thereby envisioned first and foremost as part of a voluntary—actual and imaginary—journey. The framing of the museum as an enclosed space set apart, culturally consolidated and elevated, physically and verbally enshrined, thus marks it both as an expression and as a source of cultural value. I use the term "cultural value" advisedly, seeking to emphasize not only the value-conferring power of the museum display, but also to capture the deliberately designed quality of the museum environment as culturally constructed, as an environment in which culturally elaborated objects are put on display. One is not expected to walk along the museum tour route as one would along a nature trail, admiring the beautiful landscape. Even though aesthetic appreciation is always part of one's response, the "reading" of the display in this context is very different since visitors know that museums, like other man-made enclaves, provide an environment constituted of signifying practices and ask questions of meaning and value—what the objects mean (the story "behind them") and what makes them worthy of inclusion in the museum story.

As in the case of any deliberately designed cultural context, participants in the museum scene—curators, guides, and visitors—must share basic assumptions concerning the meaningfulness of the museum environment both in terms of the selection of items for display and their arrangement in a spatially organized whole. Visitors' keen sense of the constructedness of the museum environment shapes their expectations of the museum encounter as a communicative occasion wherein messages are strategically deployed. The sense of the cultural value that attaches to the basic "museumifying" move of removing objects and stories from their natural life contexts of production and use, and recontextualizing them in the setting of the museum (Kirshenblatt-Gimblett, 1991), is itself a value-conferring yet ambiguous gesture. On the one hand, it makes objects and meanings accessible and salient in the public sphere, yet at the same time the transfer of objects and meanings to a museum signals their removal from, or marginality in, the culture's ongoing life. We may formulate this essential paradox of museum displays by noting that they confer *cultural* value on objects and their meanings even while affirming their *social* irrelevance.

Thus, including an object in a museum display is in itself a gesture of valuation, and this opens up the question of the criteria by which objects are valued and deemed appropriate for inclusion in any such display. The major claims for the cultural value of objects in vernacular museums are made not in reference to their uniqueness, as in the case of the "aura" attached to works of art, but with reference to their representativeness on the one hand and authenticity on the other. The objects' claim to authenticity suggests that objects are valued for their fidelity to a time and place of origin, which constitute the spatio-temporal focus of the museum display. It is as traces of another time and/or another place that heritage museum objects mediate the world displayed for museum visitors, inviting them to bridge spatial and/or temporal distances through their "authentic messenger" value. Tour guide interpretations support and amplify this "bridging" function by engaging in discourse that constantly moves between past and present, here and elsewhere. It is a discourse that shifts between a nostalgic attitude toward the past, to the point of disparaging the present, and a celebration of continuity through the creation of links between past endeavors and present accomplishments.

The value of representativeness suggests that museum objects are assembled and arranged in such a way as to fit a pre-existing master narrative that grounds the museum display, whether it is more or less explicitly articulated in its interpretive practices. In the case of the museums I have studied, the master narrative is the story of the Socialist-Zionist revolution in Jewish life, that is, the story of the return of Jews to the land of Israel both in the geographical sense and in the sense of undertaking agricultural work as a central, ideologically driven occupation. Kibbutz museums add to this story a narrative emphasis on the communal way of life in collective pioneering settlements. Display objects thus represent various interlocking junctures in the larger narratives and visual imagery they concretize, and may be specifically sought out to complete some part of it that is felt to be "missing." Thus, when a museum curator said to me, "I am looking for more items to construct a schoolroom," he was indicating that he was out to "complete" a scenario whose contours were clearly delineated in his mind so as to better represent an image of the past with whose verbal and visual traces, such as circulating stories and old photographs, he (and some of his visitors) was familiar.

There is a certain tension that is inherent in museum presentations of this kind. Alongside claims to authenticity and verisimilitude, they also highlight the constructed nature of the display, particularly through the use of what I call "frame narratives," which are stories about collecting activities, elaborations of the dilemmas concerning the arrangement of the display, and so on. Authenticity rests with the objects and is communicated not only through their appearance (which many visitors are not equipped to judge), but also through labelings and stories relating to their provenance. Obviously stylized display strategies (such as hanging agricultural implements on the wall in a picturelike arrangement), as well as "frame narratives" recounting how the objects got into the museum, or how they were reconstructed, have the effect of denaturalizing the museum's version of the past and foregrounding the curatorial activity through which it is constructed. On the one hand, this two-pronged narrative move—telling the museum story via the story of how the museum is made—serves to enhance visitor involvement by inviting to identify directly with curator-guides, who personify the museological efforts they tell about. On the other hand, this strategy highlights the constructed, fictional dimensions of the enterprise as a whole even while the authenticity of particular display objects is underscored. Therefore, a double-layered "reading" and "hearing" is required of museum visitors, one that would allow them to accommodate simultaneously the narratives and meta-narratives that populate museum discourses.

In sum, the visit to a heritage museum gains its experiential distinctiveness as a cultural practice through its embeddedness within a pilgrimagelike cultural agenda, through the web of significations that constitutes the museum environment, and through the value-conferring power of the museum as a cultural institution. Curators, tour guides, and visitors share—or come to share—a "reading" of the museum encounter that incorporates these experiential and societal dimensions. At the same time, museum going also incorporates claims to the cultivation of knowledge, as will be discussed in the next section.

Cultivating Knowledge

The dictum that "the tools tell the story" encapsulates central features of the museum's claims to knowledge and knowledge cultivation. Museum objects speak in what we might call "a rhetoric of presence," communicating through their sheer materiality. They function as powerful synecdoches which visually concretize, invoke, and thereby make accessible specialized bits of knowledge. The overall move is one of familiarization organized in terms of three broad presentational principles: classification, mimesis, and discursive elaboration.[2] Just as museum visitors entertain a set of assumptions about museum going as a cultural practice, they must also have a prior understanding of the claims put forth in and through the use of these representational strategies and their manner of articulating the museum's master-narrative.

Classification is a major representational strategy in museum displays, one that echoes scientific taxonomies through spatial arrangements, and thus speaks to the museum's claim to specialized systematic knowledge. The parameters according to which display items are classified and arranged are, of course, content dependent. In the museums I am studying, tools tend to be classified in accordance with functional principles—tools for ploughing in one corner, harvesting tools and machinery in another, various craftman's tools in a third. Within each such category, there tends to be an internal logic of display—linear spatial arrangement represents temporal progression, which in this case implies a movement of technological progress and modernization from the more "primitive" tool to the more "advanced" one. The unspoken implications of this type of spatial-taxonomical representation are grounded in patterns of classification that are, in principle, familiar to visitors, so that they can provide new knowledge in terms of "received" ways of knowing.

Mimetic reconstruction is another major representational strategy. Reconstructed "typical" settings and scenes from the past, such as the interiority of a room, or a street scene, whether they make use of "authentic" objects or not, work within a well-defined mimetic tradition whose basic rhetorical efficacy is associated with claims to verisimilitude, with the iconic dimension of representation. At times, these claims are reinforced by the inclusion of photographic images, which are used to support the reconstruction's claim to mimetic fidelity.

Heritage museums tend to combine classificatory and mimetic forms of display, which introduce variability along the museum route. The sense of variation and enhanced interest this combined presentational form induces relates to the different ways in which classificatory and mimetic displays work to inform visitors' variable readings and experience of the museum encounter. Mimetic displays allow for a more holistic experience of the depicted museum scene, particularly when visitors are invited to become part of the setting, as they often are in the heritage museums I am studying (e.g. entering a reconstructed scene such as a pioneers' tent or shower, or sitting around the tables in the reconstructed dining hall). Classificatory displays support a more removed, analytic stance, which involves a knowledgeable discernment of differences within a larger category of objects (e.g., ploughs of different kinds).

Notably, both the classificatory and the mimetic forms of the display tend to be discursively complemented through the labeling they are given, as well as through the guides' oral interpretations. These discursive elaborations involve naming practices, specification of contexts of production, explanatory comments concerning forms of use, and a variety of narrative practices. It is precisely because these museums are about cultural meanings and not about aesthetic appreciation that the verbal interpretations that accompany the display are an essential component of it.

Museum goers are expected to emerge from the "museum experience" knowing something they did not know before. This new knowledge combines "propositional" knowledge ("knowing that something is so and so") with the experiential kind of knowledge based on direct exposure of the senses that can be discussed under the heading of "knowledge of." Museum curators and guides design and occasion differently inflected museum encounters that variously cater to this knowledge-enhancing role through the representational strategies they employ. Heritage museums are thus both "houses of knowledge" and "houses of memory." They are purveyors of a culturally cherished body of knowledge transmitted through the material traces of another time and/or place. Reframing mundane objects as museum objects, and thereby putting them up for contemplation, those museums that display the everyday practices and objects of local heritage serve as powerful catalyzers of memory, rearticulating, rearranging, and reframing the familiar, everyday experience of everyday reality. When visitors can mobilize their own personal experience of the world depicted in the museum display, the museum is no longer an authoritative source of privileged knowledge, but becomes an evocative arena for reminiscing about half-forgotten times. Museum going in such cases is less about the acquisition of new knowledge and more about a reflexively created sense of self, less about bridging over the visitor's distance from a displayed Other, and more about an intensified experience of Self as a distanced Other. The "museum experience" in this context is therefore shaped by a double expectation, which involves the cultivation of culturally privileged information through a set of representational strategies that productively blur the line between factual and experiential knowledge. Visitors, in turn, must be attuned to the implications of these strategic choices to properly interpret the displays. In other words, they must become "literate" in the museum idiom.

Concluding Remarks

In the foregoing analysis I have tried to trace ways in which the representational strategies employed in a heritage museum context serve to establish a sense of cultural value and claims to knowledge through the medium of objects and the stories they anchor. In so doing, I foregrounded the shared assumptions concerning the forms and functions of museum displays that visitors must bring with them for the museum to communicate its overall message effectively. These assumptions, as I have argued, go far beyond the substantive details which make up the content of the museum display. They relate to the cultural value and authority of the museum as a legitimizing institution, so that the fact of an item being in a museum is far more significant than the particular meanings it may have.

The pilgrimagelike quality of museum going encompasses and affirms the museum's claim to cultural value. It is within the context of representational practices, which both claim and enhance cultural value, that the museum's claims to knowledge must be "read." The materially asserted "facticity" of museum-generated knowledge becomes another move in the game of cultural affirmation. Factuality is made meaningful within a more encompassing construction of cultural value. At the same time, the cultural value attached in Western societies to the mode of facticity, with its "scientific" and "objective" reverberations, contributes an added aura to these historically oriented objects-as-signs.

I therefore propose that museum going and museum learning can make full sense only if viewed as institutionally endorsed ritualized practices, in which the cultivation of factual knowledge and the reaffirmation of core cultural values are intimately intertwined. While different museums will invoke different stories and sets of values for cultural affirmation, all of them share assumptions concerning the distinctive representational authority and rhetorical efficacy of museum displays. As I have tried to argue in this essay, these assumptions are fundamental to the "museum experience," which curators and tour guides—those "ritual experts" of the museum world—strive to invoke. When visitors share in them as well, the museum encounter can be successful to the point that the tools, rather than the people who have collected, arranged, and interpreted them, are credited with the telling of the museum story.

In some ways, museums function like other legitimizing institutions or cultural forms of communication which inscribe their meanings through processes of selection and framing of a similar order. Like encyclopedias and anthologies, they showcase and valorize particular bits of knowledge and social meanings to which they ascribe a sense of permanence. Like film and television, they highlight and valorize visual images, yet eschew the ephemeral quality that attends mass media viewing. Defying the museum-as-text metaphor, I would argue that the distinctive quality of the heritage museum experience lies in the particular structures of ritualized participation they define, and in the "object lessons" they provide, lessons that give voice to the sensuality, materiality, and concreteness of the multilayered sign-objects on display—qualisigns, sinsigns, and legisigns—which find their home in an environment so heavily populated by fleeting images and verbal constructions, a world otherwise known as the Information Age.

Notes

1. For more details related to the ethnographic project this "think piece" grows out of, see Katriel (1993a, 1993b, and 1994).
2. Another, increasingly popular representational strategy, which is central to "living history" contexts worldwide, involves the incorporation of theatrical re-enactments of historical scenes. It is only beginning to make its way into the museums I am studying. For a full-fledged account of ethnohistorical role playing in Plymouth Plantation, see Snow (1993).

References

Bennett, T. (1988). The exhibitionary complex. *New Formations*, *4*, 73–102.

Bronner, S. J. (1989). Object lessons: The work of ethnological museums and collections. In S. Bronner (Ed.), *Consuming visions: Accumulation and display of goods in America, 1880-1920* (217–54). New York: W.W. Norton.

Carey, J. W. (1988). *Communication as culture: Essays on media and society*. Boston: Unwin Hyman.

Fine, E., & Speer, J. (1985). Tour guide performances as sight sacralization. *Annals of Tourism Research*, *12*, 73–95.

Geertz, C. (1973). *The interpretation of cultures*. New York: Basic Books.

Katriel, T. (1993a). Re-making place: Cultural production in an Israeli settlement museum. *History & Memory*, *5*, 104–35.

———. (1993b). Studying heritage museums as ideological and performative arenas. *Communication Monographs*, *60*(1), 69–75.

———. (1994). Sites of memory: Discourses of the past in Israeli pioneering settlement museums. *The quarterly Journal of Speech*, *80*, 1–20.

Kirshenblatt-Gimblett, B. (1991). Objects of ethnography. In I. Karp & S. D. Lavine (Eds.), *Exhibiting cultures: The poetics and politics of museum display* (386–443). Washington, D.C.: Smithonian Institution Press.

MacCannell, D. (1989). *The tourist: A new theory of the leisure class*. New York: Schocken Books.

Peirce, C. S. (1955) *Philosophical writings of Peirce*. J. Buchler (Ed.). New York: Dover.

Snow, S. E. (1993) *Performing the pilgrims: A study of ethnohistorical role-playing at Plymouth plantation*. Jackson: University Press of Mississippi.

Taborsky, E. (1990). The discursive object. In S. Pearce (Ed.), *Objects of knowledge* (50–77). London: The Athlone Press.

Thompson, M. (1979). *Rubbish theory*. Oxford: Oxford University Press.

Contributors

PATRICIA AUFDERHEIDE is an Associate Professor in the School of Communication at The American University, teaching media studies. She is an award-winning journalist and author, and has frequently written on cultural politics and communication policy. She is the editor of *Beyond PC: Toward a Politics of Understanding,* on the political correctness controversies on campus, and an associate editor of *In These Times* newspaper, *Black Film Review,* and the *Journal of Communication.*

CARY BAZALGETTE taught English and film-making in London secondary schools before she became an Education Officer at the British Film Institute in 1979. She has edited a key text on media education: *Primary Media Education: A Curriculum Statement.* In 1990 she was co-director of the international conference "New Directions in Media Education" organized by the BFI, CLEMI and UNESCO in Toulouse, France. She has lectured widely on media education in Britain and in other countries including the USA and Canada, France, Germany, Spain, Finland, Chile and Peru. She is the co-editor with David Buckingham of *In Front of the Children: Children's Audio-Visual Culture.*

DAVID BUCKINGHAM is a Lecturer in Media Education at the Institute of Education, University of London. He is currently directing research projects on children and TV (funded by the British Standards Council) and on practical work in media education (funded by the Gulbenkian Foundation). His books include *Public Secrets, Watching Media Learning, Children Talking Television, Reading Audiences, In Front of the Children,* and *Cultural Studies Goes to School* (with Julian Sefton-Green).

DAVID CONSIDINE is an Australian, with some twenty years of experience teaching and promoting media literacy in both the U.S. and his homeland. A professor of Media Studies/Instructional Technology, he teaches in the College of Education at Appalachian State University in North Carolina. He is the author of *The Cinema of Adolescence,* and the co-author of *Visual Messages: Integrating Imagery Into Instruction,* and *Imagine That: Developing Critical*

Viewing and Critical Thinking Skills Through Children's Books. He has served on the board of directors of The International Visual Literacy Association and is currently on the board of The National Telemedia Council.

COSTAS CRITICOS is a Senior Lecturer in Educational Technology at the University of Natal in Durban, South Africa. He is also Director of the Media Resource Center, a nongovernmental organization that is committed to address the unequal provision of education resources that has resulted from Apartheid policies. He has published widely in the field of education media and critical pedagogy. In the field of media this includes an edited book on *Media Education in South Africa,* and a chapter on media selection in the forthcoming *International Encyclopedia of Education, 2nd Edition, 1994.*

MAIRE MESSENGER DAVIES is Director of Studies for the Media Studies degree program at the London Institute, London. Before becoming a teacher, she worked as a journalist for many years. She is the author of *Television is Good for Your Kids* and co-author of *Baby Language.* She was an Annenberg Scholar at the Annenberg School for Communication, at the University of Pennsylvania, in 1993, where she investigated media literacy in elementary school children. She is editor of *The Journal of Educational Television.*

ROGER DESMOND is Professor of Communication at University of Hartford. This chapter was developed while he was a fellow at the Annenberg School for Communication at the University of Pennsylvania. Desmond's published research is in the areas of media and cognition, and parental mediation of television for young children. He wishes to thank Kathleen Hall Jamieson and Elihu Katz for their support and encouragement of this project.

MICHELINE FRENETTE holds a doctoral degree from Harvard University and is currently Associate Professor in the Department of Communication at the Université de Montréal in Quebec. She is affiliated with the Center for Youth and Media Studies and the Research Laboratory on New Technologies in that department. Her research interests and publications focus on the educational potential of television and interactive technologies for young people and adult learners. She recently co-authored a book on adolescents and television.

W. LAMBERT GARDINER has published three textbooks in psychology—*Psychology: A Story of a Search, An Invitation to Cognitive Psychology,* and *The Psychology of Teaching.* Currently an Associate Professor in the Department of Communication Studies at Concordia University in Montreal, his focus is indicated in the subtitle of his book, *The Ubiquitous Chip: The Human Impact of Electronic Technology.*

LUC GIROUX is a cognitive Psychologist and Professor in the Department of Communication Studies, Université de Montréal. His fields of interest include cognitive aspects of human-computer interaction, television audiences, and quantitative research methods. He has published numerous articles in journals, such as: *Behavior and Information Technology, Communication,* and *The International Journal of Man-machine Studies.* He is currently director of the Joint Ph.D. Program in Communication at Université de Montréal, Universite du Quebec a Montreal and Concordia University.

PETER GREENAWAY is an Australian media educator. He began his career as an art teacher and since 1973 has been involved in media teacher education at Deakin University and on the executive committee of the Australian Teachers of Media. His recent book *Teaching The Visual Media* promotes a media education theory.

ANDREW HART teaches Media Studies in the School of Education at the University of Southampton, England. He has published widely on media education and works closely with teachers through the Southampton Media Education Group. He wrote (with Gordon Cooper) the BBC Radio 4 series *Understanding the Media,* and a book of the same title based on the series. He is currently working on a book for secondary English teachers on Media Education.

RENEE HOBBS is Associate Professor of Communication at Babson College and Director of the Institute on Media Education at Harvard Graduate School of Education. She is the co-author of *TV Eye: A Curriculum for the Media Arts,* supported by the National Endowment for the Arts, a media literacy curriculum for grades seven through twelve. Dr. Hobbs also explores the cognitive and perceptual skills involved in the comprehension of film and television and co-edits the Media Education series with Robert Kubey, for Lawrence Erlbaum Associates.

TAMAR KATRIEL is on the faculty of the School of Education at the University of Haifa, Israel. She works in the areas of the ethnography of communication, discourse studies and cultural anthropology. She has published extensively in scholarly journals in these fields, and is author of *Talking Straight: "Dugri" Speech in Israeli Sabra Culture,* and *Communal Webs: Communication and Culture in Contemporary Israel.*

ROBERT KUBEY is Associate Professor of Communication at Rutgers University in New Brunswick, New Jersey, and Research Director of the Media Education Laboratory at Rutgers, Newark. Dr. Kubey has been an Annenberg Scholar in Media Literacy at the University of Pennsylvania, a National Institute of Mental Health postdoctoral research fellow at the University of California at Irvine, and a fellow of the Center for the Critical Analysis of Contemporary Culture at Rutgers. Professor Kubey has also been a Visiting Associate Professor at Stanford University and has taught in the Institute on Media Education at Harvard University. Dr. Kubey is co-author of *Television and the Quality of Life,* and is completing *Creating Television: Then and Now,* a book about the creative decision making process in Hollywood. With Renee Hobbs, Professor Kubey co-edits the Media Education Series for Lawrence Erlbaum Associates.

CAROL C. KUHLTHAU is Associate Professor and Director of the Educational Media Services Program in the Department of Library and Information Studies, Rutgers University. Her books include: *Seeking Meaning: A Process Approach to Library and Information Services, Teaching the Library Research Process, Information Skills for an Information Society,* and *School Librarian's Grade by Grade Activities Program.*

DAFNA LEMISH is Director of Communication in Education, The New School of Media Studies, College of Management, Tel-Aviv. She has served as an adviser and curricula developer for the Ministry of Education in Israel in the area of media literacy and is the author of several textbooks that have been approved for use in the Israeli school system. Her areas of research include children and television, and gender portrayals in the media. As an Annenberg Scholar she completed a study on the development of television literacy among kindergarten children.

PETER LEMISH is Head of the Division of Education at the School of Art, Beit Berl College, Israel. His primary areas of interest are in education and social change, the role of education in deeply conflicted societies, curriculum studies and in the use of action research, and formative evaluation in the development of educational and social interventions.

TAMAR LIEBES is a Senior Lecturer in the Hebrew University of Jerusalem. She co-authored *The Export of Meaning: Cross Cultural Readings of Dallas* (1993, with Elihu Katz), and has written numerous articles about the media and public space, communication as popular culture, and viewers' decoding and involvement in television narratives.

LEN MASTERMAN is Senior Research Fellow in Media at the University of Liverpool. He is the author of *Teaching About Television* (1980), *Teaching the Media* (1985), and *Television Mythologies* (1985). He is a consultant on media education to UNESCO and The Council of Europe.

CHARLES R. MCCLURE is Professor at the School of Information Studies, Syracuse University, Syracuse, N.Y. He teaches courses in U.S. government information management and policies, information resource management, library/information center management, and planning/evaluation of information services. He is the editor of *Internet Research,* a quarterly journal, and has written extensively on topics related to U.S. government information, information resources management (IRM), and information policy. His most recent book is *Libraries and the Internet/NREN: Issues, Perspectives, and Opportunities.*

BARRIE MCMAHON is the Manager of Curriculum Development, Ministry of Education, Western Australia. He has been a teacher, a consultant, an administrator, and a writer. With Robyn Quin, McMahon has published widely in the field of media literacy over the last decade. Their published texts for students include *Exploring Images, Real Images, Stories and Stereotypes, Meet the Media,* and *Understanding Soaps.*

PAUL MESSARIS is an Associate Professor at the Annenberg School for Communication, University of Pennsylvania. He teaches and does research in the area of visual communication. He is the author of *Visual "Literacy": Image, Mind, and Reality.* His current work deals with persuasive uses of visual media, especially in social advocacy campaigns.

JACQUES PIETTE is Professor in the Department of Literature and Communications at l'Universite de Sherbrooke. His field of interest and research concern the theoretical dimensions of media education. Over the years he has worked as a consultant for organizations aimed at promoting media education and helped to establish the Association for Media Education in Quebec (AMEQ). He recently undertook a study for the association of teachers of Quebec (Centrale d'enseignement du Quebec) on the place of media education in the school system for the year 2,000.

ROBYN QUIN is Head of the School of Languages, Literature and Media Studies at Edith Cowan University in Western Australia. She has been a secondary school media studies teacher, an educational consultant and a researcher in media education. She is currently working in audience research and studying the reception of adolescent girls to such teen soap operas as *Beverly Hills*

90210 and *Melrose Place*. In 1995, she co-organized a world meeting of media educators from twenty-seven countries in La Coruña, Spain. She has written numerous books with Barrie McMahon (see his entry).

JULIAN SEFTON-GREEN is a lecturer in Media Education at the Central School of Speech and Drama in London. His publications include *The Music Business* and *Cultural Studies Goes to School* (with David Buckingham, 1994). He is currently engaged in research on practical work in media education.

Author Index

Subject Index